SACRAMENT AS GIFT
A PNEUMATOLOGICAL AND PHENOMENOLOGICAL APPROACH

TEXTES ET ÉTUDES LITURGIQUES
STUDIES IN LITURGY
XXV

SACRAMENT AS GIFT
A PNEUMATOLOGICAL AND PHENOMENOLOGICAL APPROACH

by

Sebastian Madathummuriyil

ABDIJ KEIZERSBERG
FACULTEIT THEOLOGIE
EN RELIGIEWETENSCHAPPEN

PEETERS
LEUVEN
2012

A catalogue record for this book is available from the Library of Congress.

ISBN 978-90-429-2596-0

D/2012/0602/16

FOREWORD

This book is the fruit of doctoral research at the Faculty of Theology at the Catholic University of Louvain in the field of sacramental theology and liturgy within the contours of a scientific project concerning sacramental presence in the postmodern context. The author has developed in 2008 a dissertation on the efficacy of the sacraments from the specific approach in pneumatology and phenomenology, resulting in a hermeneutics of givenness. The interest for the specific pneumatological dimension in sacramentology and for the phenomenology of the pure gift led him to a fundamental re-interpretation of the relation between God and the human beings as it is lived out in sacramental behaviour. The main and central concept is that of givenness: not as a simple gift, but as a kenotic self-communication of God to the human being in the divine love of the Holy Trinity as an ongoing gift from the Holy Spirit.

The point of departure lays in the observation of the *Geistvergessenheit* in traditional sacramentology. Therefore the author designed a full theology of the Holy Spirit in the Trinity, creation and redemption, Church and sacraments. The philosophical context, more specifically, the phenomenology of givenness is described, necessary for a right understanding of the sacramental efficacy. With Jean-Luc Marion, Louis Marie Chauvet and David Noël Power as guides, the central categories of the contrast between idol and icon, and of saturated phenomenon in excess, are analysed and brought to the realm of the sacraments. The hermeneutical elaboration comes to its climax with a profound synthesis in an attempt to conceive of the sacraments outside the metaphysical scheme as the language of God's giving, iconic-symbolic representations of Christ's redemption in the power of the Holy Spirit, where the divine gives itself in the icon in maximum phenomenality as 'saturation of saturation'. The pneumatological and symbolic dimensions are explained in relation to the liturgy of the Word and the Eucharist.

This book represents a very rich treatise on postmodern sacramentology with an in depth inquiry into the pneumatological and phenomenological approach with regard to the sacramental life. It offers a systematic and consistent study of the topic of givenness as central category and sufficient explanation of the sacramental efficacy without reference to the metaphysical/aristotelian notions of cause and effect. The sacraments are described in the iconographic language, respecting the laws of an apophatic theology where the existential participation in the divine life is conceived with a profound sensitivity for the unconceivable mystery of God. Being in excess as saturated phenomenon, the symbolic mediation of the sacraments is a mystical process as a progressive participation in the life of Christ, the *eikoon* of the invisible Father, through the fulfilling mission of the Holy Spirit, the 'mediated immediacy' of the divine. This book offers a systematic exploration of the anthropological, philosophical and theological concepts that underpin this mysterious participation and explain the sacramental efficacy.

Not only is this book innovative with regard to the correction of a unilateral christomonic approach by a large pneumatological description that integrates also the Christological dimension, but it has also been proven that the contemporary context of a sacramentology in the postmodern time was not neglected. The author is aware of the most recent evolutions in western sacramentology and has taken up the terms of the debate in our Louvain project of postmodern sacramento-theology. The categories of idol and icon, elaborated in their mutual relationship and their distance by Jean-Luc Marion and Louis-Marie Chauvet, as well as the categories of excess and saturated phenomenon, are in this book discussed with their application to the sacramental experience. Theologizing on sacraments in terms of the language of God's Giving, typical for the approach by David Noël Power, is integrated here in a hermeneutics of the pure gift. The role of the Holy Spirit comes clearly out not only as the gift of Pentecost, but also as the divine and personal Giver of life and salvation. Finally, the theme of *kenosis*, typical for a postmodern sacramentology in the consideration of the absence, the withdrawal and distance of God, has received also a decisive place in this book.

I may conclude by stating again that the author has achieved a remarkable study in elaborating the two main perspectives, that of pneumatology and that of the phenomenology of givenness, and bringing those two together in a perfect synthesis that clarifies the sacramental life, as fruitful and pertinent in the postmodern context. The reflections that are made in this book witness of the intellectual abilities, flexibility and excellence of the author. Besides the heuristic capacities, he has shown a firm determination in his exploration and interpretation of the sacramental theology for our days. He is a religious, member of the Missionary Congregation of the Blessed Sacrament, belonging to the Zion province, Kerala, India. He has explored to the last limits and final depths the Holy Mystery of the Blessed Sacrament, the Eucharist.

5 March 2011, Emeritus Professor Lambert Jan Leijssen
Faculty of Theology, Catholic University Louvain, Belgium

PREFACE

"Look Sebastian. See, that is Jesus." When I was young, my mom would whisper those words to me as the priest elevated the Host during the consecration of the Eucharist. I may not have understood what they meant, but as I watched her pray – her hands joined together, eyes closed, and head bowed down – I was filled with a great feeling of peace, and I realized that something holy was happening. As I grew older, the question of how Christ is present in the Mass and especially in the Eucharist stayed with me, through my teenage and young adult years and even when I became ordained a priest. My faith in the presence of Christ in the Eucharist remained unshaken, but I still did not know how to answer that question. So, in the tradition of Anselm's "faith seeking understanding," I sought to make sense of what I believed and practiced. My liturgical upbringing in the East Syrian liturgical tradition taught me that the Holy Spirit plays an active role during the liturgy. I knew this must be true since human action would not be capable of bringing about something divine, even though the Mass naturally needs symbols and words derived from human experience and language. I eventually reached a hypothetical conclusion that the sacraments might be the site where the divine and human intersected. The present book is the result of my exploration to interpret the conjunction of the divine-human domains in the sacred events of the Church called sacraments.

Each page of the book investigates the pertinent question of sacramental presence, or in scholastic terminology, sacramental efficacy. The historical-critical survey which is undertaken in the first chapter takes the reader to identify two shortcomings in sacramental theology, i.e., a 'Pneumatological deficit' and an overemphasis on the efficacy of language and symbols. This presents a dual task of exploring the role of the Holy Spirit in the sacramental event as well as the importance of the linguistic and symbolic aspects of the sacraments. The second and third chapters achieve these dual goals. The second chapter establishes the definitive role of the Holy Spirit considering the role of the Spirit within the Trinitarian scheme of God's self-communication. The third chapter integrates the linguistic and symbolic dimensions with Pneumatology in a balanced way by developing a theology of gift by employing the phenomenological insights provided by Jean-Luc Marion and current insights from the theology of the Holy Spirit. The theological status which Marion ascribes to icon as being realized in the revelation of Christ is applied to the New Testament revelation of the Spirit. Interlacing Pneumatology with the notion of the icon provides us with the key to interpret sacramental symbols as iconic, which in turn, helps us to understand the efficacy of the language and symbols without overshadowing the definitive role of the Holy Spirit in the sacramental event. The fourth chapter proposes a plausible theology of sacraments as the iconic-symbols of God's gift in which the divine enters the human domain mediated by the Holy Spirit, whose role in the sacramental event is explained as 'mediated immediacy'. This is achieved with particular reference to the sacrament of the Eucharist as embodied in the liturgical dynamics unfolded in the liturgy of the Word and the Liturgy of the Eucharist in the Roman rite.

This book is the revised form of my doctoral dissertation. In a project such as this a debt of gratitude is owed to many. First, I must thank Prof. Emeritus Lambert Leijssen for his scholarly guidance, critical remarks and constructive corrections coupled with his warmth of encouragement helped me to accomplish this daunting task. He also blessed me with an erudite foreword for the book. I also thank most sincerely George S. Worgul, Jr., Stijn van den Bossche and Joris Geldhof for their meticulous reading, scholarly appreciation and insightful remarks of this book in its dissertation form. My indebtedness goes to Jean-Luc Marion for his correspondence and discussion with me which shed light into complex notions of his phenomenology. Thanks also to the Dean Lieven Boeve and the staff (faculty) of the Theology Faculty of K.U. Leuven. The Holy Spirit College and its staff created a homely atmosphere to make my life in Leuven interesting. I am also deeply indebted to the *Kirche in Not* for offering a scholarship to support my research. My gratitude is due to Sr. Michele Ransil, Barry Swan, Eric Dart and Benjamin Champa for revising the language at various stages of my work.

I would like to thank Frs. George Karintholil, the former Superior General and George Kizhakkemury, the present Superior General of the Missionary Congregation of the Blessed Sacrament (M.C.B.S.), for always being supportive to my academic endeavors. A special thanks to Frs. Augustine Paikkatt, the former provincial and Jose Mulangattil, the present provincial for their encouragement and friendship. My research and writing would have been tedious without the warm friendship of my friends in Leuven and my confrères and well-wishers in the U.S.A., Germany, Italy and Switzerland. The affection and concern of my family back home has meant very much to me in completing this project. Moreover, the academic collegiality, friendship and support I enjoyed at the Department of Theology, Duquesne University, U.S.A. during the time of its revision was remarkable.

I thank Joris Geldhof, the head of the Liturgical Studies Institute, Leuven and its board members for accepting this work in *Textes et études liturgiques* /Studies in Liturgy series and to Peeters Publishers, Leuven.

TABLE OF CONTENTS

Chapter One

RE-IMAGINING SACRAMENTAL EFFICACY   7-70

Chapter Two

A PNEUMATOLOGICAL THEOLOGY OF SACRAMENTAL EFFICACY

Chapter Three

THE PHENOMENON OF GOD'S SELF-COMMUNICATION 152-235

Chapter Four

THE SACRAMENTAL GIFT   236-308

309-19

$1 - 6$

At the center of all Christian theology is the relationship between humanity and God. From this relationship emerges the question of the nature of God – 'what kind of God' or 'who is God' for example – which then influences the dynamic of this God-human relationship. Furthermore, this central question of the nature of God unfolds and develops throughout all theological disciplines: hermeneutics, ecclesiology, sacramental theology, ethics and so on. This question is particularly important for the sacraments since these 'sacred acts' are the physical celebrations of this divine-human relationship and a better understanding of the concept of God should lead to a stronger sacramental relationship with this God.

During the Scholastic Period, sacramental theology developed in accordance with the metaphysical culture and climate within which the reflection on God and other theological concepts were developed.[1] Christian theology, which was patterned along metaphysical lines, came under attack when the legitimacy of its claims was challenged by the modernity. As a result, Christian theology adopted a way of confronting modernity through the support of reason and developed categories and concepts for affirming the claims of revelation. This triumph of rationality in Christian theology expresses itself in the advent of an autonomous subject who is in possession of the knowledge of God. The so-called onto-theological God of metaphysics is a product of a constituting and self-asserting subject which thinks everything is under the grip of its own mastery. The critique of modern subject calls into question the affirmations of the truth claims based on revelation by setting limit to what rationality can grasp or explain. For this reason, the notion of the Christian God which is onto-theologically constructed lost its ground in much of Christian theology.

Since Heidegger's critique of onto-theology Western philosophy has attempted to decentralize subjectivity (constituting subject), or to limit the

---

1. The present work uses the terms 'metaphysics', 'metaphysics of presence', onto-theology, etc. interchangeably. In general, they refer to the theology which is based on classical metaphysics.

power of an autonomous subject. This de-centering of subjectivity has brought to light the falsity of subjugating the object to the representation of the subject's power to know and represent. This has opened the way for philosophers and theologians to see objects as they are, rather than reducing them to the subjective representation of the constituting subject. This 're-versed' thinking has deconstructed the traditional speculative/conceptual construct of God – i.e., the metaphysical God of onto-theology that governed the theological thinking for centuries – and has enabled humanity to relate to God in a more independent manner by not relegating God to merely being understood in relation to the subject.

Postmodern theology is in favor of such a God. Many postmodern philosophers and theologians attempt to give a sense of 'being' to God through reversing subject-object thinking; through disallowing the constituting subject and power to define this subject-object relationship. The so-called death of the metaphysical God that Nietzsche proclaimed assumes full shape in the attempt of postmodern thinkers to open room for God to appear as himself.

The question "What kind of God is meaningful after the 'death of God'?" pushes postmodern thinkers not into the direction of rejecting rational thinking and the role of philosophy in explaining religious truths, but rather, toward the re-discovering of the relationship between them. Through this line of reasoning, a notable trend has arisen amongst postmodern thinkers to 'turn toward religion;' this is especially true in the so-called "theological turn" of French phenomenology.[2]

This appreciation of a God finds expression in Jean-Luc Marion's concept of God "without being," which he explains through the contrasting pictures of the idol and the icon.[3] For Marion, the idol represents the self-created image of God, which is the creation of the constituting subject. Accordingly, God is reduced to our capacity of knowing and experiencing God and to finite conditions of appearance. The icon, on the other hand, opens the possibility of revealing God without being confined to human experience and conditions. Marion develops a 'reversed' understanding of God, through a phenomenology of givenness. Marion does this by accounting for a phenomenon which gives itself, from itself, without the interference of subjectivity.

2. Dominique Janicaud, et al., *Phenomenology and the "Theological Turn:" The French Debate*, ed. John D. Caputo, Perspectives in Continental Philosophy (New York: Fordham University Press, 2000). The translation of Dominique Janicaud, *Le tournant théologique de la phénoménologie française* (Paris: Éditions de l'Éclat, 1990).
3. Jean-Luc Marion, *God Without Being*, trans. Thomas A. Carlson (Chicago, IL/London: The University of Chicago Press, 1991).

Thus, God is spoken of in terms of "givenness" before "being." To receive the phenomena as given in the maximum phenomenality, the desire and intention of the subject is reversed or subordinated to the givenness of the phenomena. This is a reversal of the conceptual idols of God, allowing God to appear as he is, as true love. The thrust is to transfer the concept of God, conformed to a human conceptual image, to a God who is revealed in Jesus Christ as love. Placing givenness anterior to the representation of the perceiving subject means, for Marion, ascribing supremacy to revelation over reason. Marion's phenomenological project opens the way to think about God as revealed in Christ. Within the phenomenology of givenness, God has the freedom to reveal himself.

The postmodern critique of the 'metaphysics of presence' challenges a sacramental theology founded in classical metaphysics to find its own basis for interpreting sacramental presence. In this connection, Marion's phenomenology of givenness seems to offer a revelation-based approach to sacramental thinking. Contemporary sacramental theology has appropriated the insights provided by the phenomenology of language and symbols in order to explain and explore sacramental presence, efficacy and grace. Marion, David N. Power and Louis-Marie Chauvet (among others) try to develop sacramental theology in terms of givenness with various emphases. Thus, contemporary sacramental theology exhibits an understanding of sacramental efficacy, informed by phenomenology of language and symbols. Postmodern theologians are in favor of explaining sacramental efficacy and presence in terms of "symbolic efficacy," "exchange," "mediation," "givenness," "gift," etc.

Parallel to this, in systematic theology, there has been a renewed interest in the theology of the Holy Spirit, especially since Vatican II. The so-called "forgetfulness of the Holy Spirit" (*Geistvergessenheit* – Lothar Lies) in Western theology has been overcome to a great extent. This is evidenced by the subsequent recognition of Pneumatology in the West. However, it seems insufficient attention has been given to integrating both Pneumatology and phenomenology into sacramental thinking. The insights gained from these respective movements are seldom understood in relation to one another, and in fact, Pneumatological insights into sacramental theology have been overshadowed by phenomenology. Even though postmodern theology does not attribute sacramental presence solely to the efficacy of the symbols and language, the question regarding the role of the Holy Spirit in the sacramental event needs to be made clearer. It can be claimed that postmodern theologians have not seriously reflected on the import of Pneumatology in explaining sacramental presence, although there is agreement that it is the Holy Spirit who is at work within the sacraments.

For this reason, we will argue in this book that the phenomenological and linguistic approach to sacramental presence has to be completed by incorporating the role of the Holy Spirit. The presence of Christ is to be understood, not only as a symbolic mediation, but also a mediation made possible by the Holy Spirit, who is the interior principle of the Church which makes the Church the body of Christ. The corporeality of the Church is the basic symbol in which the corporality of the sacramental body becomes a "real-symbolic" mediation of the presence of Christ. As Hans Urs von Balthasar argues, the activity of God is to be given ascendancy over the corporeal and cultural elements and human longing and actions.[4] This is possible only through a non-metaphysical way of reflecting upon God as Trinity – based on God's self-revelation in the person of Christ and the Spirit – and its implications in the understanding of the sacraments.

Therefore, we may hold that contemporary notions of symbolic efficacy and sacramental grace need to possess a Pneumatological foundation and to acknowledge the definitive role of the Holy Spirit. This requires us to elucidate what is precisely the role of the Spirit in the sacramental event, while subscribing to symbolic efficacy. Only then, will postmodern sacramental theology be free from the charge of a serious lack of Pneumatological insight. Therefore, our study will be directed towards a hermeneutical theology of sacramental efficacy, integrating the insights of Pneumatology and the function of sacramental symbols from a phenomenological perspective. This task will be undertaken within the framework of God's self-communication and the phenomenology of givenness proposed by Marion.

We will examine whether the sacraments can be explained, both from phenomenological and Pneumatological perspectives, in spite of their belonging to different domains. Can these perspectives be considered mutually enriching? If such a correlation is possible, can it be done while avoiding the overarching meta-narratives which once propped up onto-theological claims or without falling into onto-theological pitfalls ourselves. Is it possible to use phenomenology in process of God-talk? We intend to discuss these and other related questions in our study, bringing into focus the question of symbolic efficacy and the role of the Holy Spirit. This project's challenge consists not only in interpreting sacramental symbols, but also in interpreting the Church

---

4. Hans Urs von Balthasar, *The Glory of the Lord: A Theological Aesthetics*, trans. Erasmo Leiva-Merikakis, vol. 1 (San Francisco, CA: Ignatius Press, [2]1982), 575.

in a systematic manner as the basic symbol in relation to God's outreach to us in the Word and the Spirit. Thus, our study aims at developing a systematically built theology of the sacraments, explaining the function of sacramental symbols in relation to the work of the Holy Spirit in effecting sacramental reality.

This study consists of four chapters. The first chapter undertakes a cursory survey of the understanding of sacramental efficacy, beginning from the early Christian and patristic periods to postmodernity, highlighting the Pneumatological shortfall and the significance of phenomenology of language and symbols in sacramental thinking. Thus, we place the theme of our study in its historico-theological context.

The second chapter explores the relevance of Pneumatology in the understanding of the sacraments. The study will center around the Trinitarian concept of God as revealed and explained through the Bible. It will attempt to move beyond an abstract concept of God by grounding its arguments in historical revelation, which culminated in the Mission of the Word and the Spirit. This will be done by reconstructing the intra-Trinitarian relationship so as to accommodate a Pneumatologically dependent Christology from a biblical-theological background. Thus the distinctive roles of Christ and the Spirit will be explained as constitutive to God's self-communication with humanity. We achieve this by taking into account the Rahnerian theology of God's self-communication as our structural framework. This chapter helps us to base our approach to the sacraments developed in this project on a well-grounded Pneumatological theology.

In the third chapter, we explore whether this specifically Christian way of speaking about God can be done phenomenologically in terms of the gift. First, we discuss the sociological and anthropological notions of the gift, and then, the phenomenology of givenness and the possibility of revelation within the phenomenology of givenness. Second, after having created a phenomenological platform to think about revelation, we move on to consider God's self-communication in Christ and the Spirit as a saturated phenomenon of God's excess of givenness. We do this by employing the phenomenological notions of the icon and the idol and the notion of saturated phenomenon. Finally, in the light of these discussions we try to develop a plausible theology of the gift, in view of reflecting on God's gift in the sacraments, the gift of presence, sacramental grace etc.

The fourth chapter aims at a sacramental hermeneutics in the light of the discussions pursued in the second and the third chapters. First, we explore how sacramental presence and grace can be understood in a way different from the metaphysics of presence, i.e., in terms of the gift. Second, we will explore how the role of the Spirit can be explained within the dynamics of the liturgical rites and symbols. The primary question to be considered will be whether sacramental efficacy can be solely placed on the efficacy of symbols in itself. Third, we integrate both the Pneumatological and the symbolic dimensions, in order to have a better explanation of the sacraments. Finally, we also identify some related theological and practical aspects that are likely to occur in the understanding of sacramental presence, liturgical celebration and sacramental praxis.

CHAPTER ONE

RE-IMAGINING SACRAMENTAL EFFICACY

The question concerning the efficacy of the sacraments may appear, to us who live in the present century, entirely a medieval concern. It no longer preoccupies the theological agenda of postmodernity, as it once did in the scholastic and the reformation eras. Nevertheless, an interest exploring the reality that is present in the sacraments beyond sacramental signs and symbols was accentuated by ongoing developments in philosophy, anthropology, and other human sciences.[1] An enquiry into the history and development of sacramental theology up to the present century sheds light on the modes in which theologians have tried to explain the mysterious realities that sacraments make present. One can discover that these attempts have taken different courses in the past, giving rise to certain controversies. Moreover, diverse approaches to the sacraments that developed in the past point to their unfathomable richness and profundity of meaning which encourages further study and explanations with a view to a better understanding, meaningful celebration, and enhanced Christian living. However, furthering the understanding of the sacraments should take its lead from an objective and comprehensive analysis of the existing theories and their implications for formulating our own approach to the sacraments, in a way that serves Christians of our time. Therefore, in this chapter, our attempt is to make a cursory survey of the important shifts in sacramental theology, particularly, how the notion of the realisation of the sacraments has been understood from the early Christian

1. For a brief historical survey of the developments in sacramental theology and the influences of various branches of sciences, see Joseph Martos, "The Copernican Revolution in Sacramental Theology," in *The Church in the Nineties: Its Legacy, Its Future*, ed. Pierre M. Hegy (Collegeville, MN: The Liturgical Press, 1993), 104-116. See also Joseph Martos, "Sacraments and the Human Sciences," in *The Dictionary of Sacramental Worship*, ed. Peter E. Fink (Dublin: Gill and Macmillian, 1990), 576-586. For a more recent review of the literature (up to 1994) on sacramental theology, highlighting the shifts in sacramental theology, see David N. Power, Regis A. Duffy, and Kevin W. Irwin, "Sacramental Theology: A Review of Literature," *Theological Studies* 55 (1994): 657-705.

period to the present. We make this analysis, bearing in mind the central issue of our examination, i.e., the contemporary notion of symbolic efficacy and the renewed understanding of the role of the Holy Spirit.[2]

The present chapter consists of five main sections which focus on the important phases in the history of sacramental theology. First, we make a cursory survey of the early Christian and patristic sources in order to see how the notion of sacramental efficacy was understood in the primitive Church. Second, considerable space has been devoted to discussing the scholastic synthesis of sacramental theology, highlighting the idea of the efficacy of the sacraments. Third, we discuss the anthropological and symbolic dimensions of sacramental efficacy, which were introduced by Karl Rahner, giving prominence to the concept of *Realsymbol*. Fourth, the postmodern approach to sacramental theology is examined, taking Louis-Marie Chauvet and Jean-Luc Marion as representatives, situating them within the postmodern critique of metaphysics as onto-theology. Fifth, in the light of different shifts and currents of thinking in sacramental theology, we highlight the insufficient treatment of Pneumatology in postmodern sacramental theology, and propose a sacramental theology with its point of departure in Pneumatology.

1. Early Christian and Patristic Understanding

Any serious discussion on the sacraments in general, especially regarding the realisation or the efficacy of the sacraments in particular, will call our attention back to the manuals of the scholastic period.[3] However, it is equally important to recognize the early Christian and patristic period where no systematic explanation and formulaic definitions of the sacraments were given. The early Christian and patristic sources can illuminate our insight into the sacraments because of their proximity to the sacramental tradition of the early Church. Therefore, before entering into the discussion on the scholastic view of sacramental efficacy, we will enquire how the notion of sacramental efficacy was understood in the early Christian and patristic periods.

---

2. In this study we use at random 'he', 'she, 'his', 'her', 'himself', 'herself, 'one', etc. (not 'he or she', 'himself or herself', etc.) in order to be inclusive, while referring to human persons. Quotes are retained in their original form in spite of their exclusivist tone.

3. The terms "realisation" and "efficacy" have scholastic overtones when used in the discussion of the sacraments. We retain these terms in our discussion, although our stance in this study would be against the scholastic understanding of sacramental efficacy, which is minimalist, legalistic and mechanical, as we will explain.

1.1. New Testament Evidence

The sources that shed light into early sacramental practices are scriptural evidences that are in themselves scanty, and, to a great extent, abstract. In the early centuries, there existed neither a systematically developed theology of the sacraments, nor the forms as we have them today. As it becomes clear from scripture, especially the Pauline letters, early Christians had performed some ritual actions which can be considered to be the embryonic form of the sacraments. Baptism (Acts 2:37-41; 8:34-39), the laying on of hands, (Acts 19:4-6; 8:14-17) and the Lord's Supper (1 Cor 11:23-26; 10:16-17) were the ritual actions that occupied great significance in the early Christian community. Through these ritual actions, they experienced something that was beyond their ordinary human experience. When they shared the bread and wine in memory of Jesus, they experienced their oneness with the Lord (1 Cor 10:16) and with each other (1 Cor 10:17). The ritual washing, that often followed their preaching, symbolised the change they underwent in their hearts (Acts 2:37-41; 8:34-39). Moreover, it expressed the acceptance of the Christian message and their unity with the death and resurrection of Christ through whom they died to sin and were born anew (Acts 8:12-13; 16:32-34). The laying on of hands and the prayer over the newly baptised symbolised the outpouring of the Spirit on them (Acts 19:4-6; 8:14-17). They had, then, the experience of being filled with the Spirit. In this way, various ritual actions that existed in the early Christian community symbolised realities beyond those actions, invisible and mysterious. Therefore, they were sacramental actions.

The scriptural evidences that show that the Christian sacraments had a pre-established theology and a clear view of sacramental efficacy are meagre and obscure. Sacramental actions were not explained systematically. However, rather than taking the form of an explanation, sacramental efficacy was based on the experience of faith supported by the interpretation of the scripture and practices transmitted by tradition.

1.2. Testimony of the Fathers

A precise terminology and systematic theology of the sacraments was developed relatively late. In the early Christian and patristic periods, the question regarding the efficacy of the sacraments was not of primary concern, because in the first five centuries, the sacraments were considered as "'mysteries', or

⁴
ᵛ religious rites to be celebrated rather than truths to be formulated."⁴ Sacramental celebrations needed interpretation, by way of polemics and apologet-
ics, when those practices and experiences of the community came under attack in the wake of heresies. In this situation, the Fathers of the Church
turned to the scripture and the experience of the community in order to provide an authentic explanation of the ritual practices. Thus, both in the East
and the West, the theological understanding of Christian sacraments came to
be gradually developed, mainly based on scripture and the experience of
sacramental rituals and the understanding of tradition.

Based on the scripture, sacramental efficacy was ascribed to the power of
the word. Just as God's word was effective in creation, so also the word of
God is at work in the sacraments, effecting what each sacramental ritual signifies. Therefore, if the scripture said that baptism forgives sins, they believed that it really happened. If Jesus said, "this is my body," the bread and
wine must be the body and blood of Jesus; if the Spirit was conferred by the
imposition of the hands of the Apostles, it would happen when their succes-
sors did the same. So they believed that Christian rites were effective through
the power of the word of God. John Chrysostom says that we should give
preference to the word, more than any reasoning, when we approach the reality of the sacraments. He also indicates that there is a reality beyond the visible elements of the sacrament signified by them, and is understandable only
by faith and a proper comprehension of the word of God. As he puts it,

> [l]et us then in everything believe God, and gainsay Him in nothing, though
> what is said seems to be contrary to our thoughts and senses, but let His word
> be of higher authority than both reasonings and sight. Thus let us do in the
> mysteries also, not looking at the things set before us, but keeping in mind
> His sayings.
>
> For his word cannot deceive, but our senses are easily beguiled. That has nev-
> er failed, but this in most things goes wrong. Since then the word says, "[t]his
> is my body," let us both be persuaded and believe, and look at it with the eyes
> of the mind.⁵

5
ᵛ Apart from the scripture, the individual sacramental experience of the Fathers
and the experience of other fellow Christians enriched their understanding of

---

4. Paul F. Palmer, *Sacraments and Worship: Liturgy and Doctrinal Development of Baptism Confirmation and the Eucharist*, ed. Paul F. Palmer, Sources of Christian Theology, vol.
1 (Westminster, MD: Newman Press, 1957), 72.

5. John Chrysostom, "Homilies on the Gospel of Saint Matthew," in *Nicene and Post-
Nicene Fathers*, vol. 10, ed. Philip Schaff (Grand Rapids, MI: Eerdmans, 1978), 82:4.

sacramental efficacy. The overwhelming experience they had in the celebration of Christian sacraments was powerful enough to shape their understanding of the sacraments. In the letter to Donatus, Cyprian of Carthage attests to his inner experience with baptism as follows:

> [A]fter that [baptism], by the help of the water of new birth, the stain of former years had been washed away, and a light from above, serene and pure, had been infused into my reconciled heart, – after that, by the agency of the Spirit breathed from heaven, a second birth had restored me to a new man; – then, in wondrous manner, doubtful things at once began to assure themselves to me, hidden things to be revealed, dark things to be enlightened, what before had seemed difficult began to suggest a means of accomplishment, what had been thought impossible, to be capable of being achieved.[6]

Cyprian's statement also makes clear that what the scripture says about baptism (Jn 3:3,5; 1Cor 6:11) was realised in his own experience.

Moreover, the Fathers made use of popular beliefs, concepts and philosophies to illustrate the reality represented in and through the celebration of the sacraments. For instance, it was an ancient belief that material bodies can become the 'vehicle' of the Spirit and can sanctify the spirit of human beings.[7] Relying on this principle, Irenaeus of Lyons (c.177) explained the sacramental principle of the Eucharist against the Gnostics. Accordingly, through the invocation of God, the material objects of bread and wine can be converted into the spiritual entities by which human beings are brought into contact with the heavenly body of Christ so that human beings are made immortal. As he puts it,

> [just] as the bread, which is produced from the earth, when it receives the invocation of God, is no longer common bread, but the Eucharist, consisting of two realities, earthly and a heavenly; so also our bodies, when they receive the Eucharist, are no longer corruptible, having hope of resurrection to eternity.[8]

---

6. Cyprian of Carthage, "Epistles of Cyprian," in *Ante-Nicene Fathers*, vol. 5, ed. James Donaldson (Grand Rapids, MI: Eerdmans, 1978), 1: 4.

7. According to this principle, matter is good. Therefore, all material things, such as water, oil, bread and wine are susceptible to God's action and are capable of becoming the medium of sanctification. This principle is based on the principle of the incarnation, whereby 'Word made flesh', the visible instrument of God for the sanctification of humanity. This sacramental principle is clearly found in the sacrament of the Eucharist, wherein the flesh of Christ becomes the medium whereby Christians are brought into the most intimate contact with the Holy Spirit, the Spirit of Christ. Palmer, *Sacraments and Worship*, 72.

8. Irenaeus, "Against Heresies," in *The Ante-Nicene Fathers*, vol. 1, ed. Alexander Roberts and James Donaldson (Edinburgh: T & T Clark, 1996), 4:18,5. Similarly, when explaining the

Thus, the function of the material elements in the sanctification of human beings finds highest expression in the transformation of the bread and wine in the Eucharist. Similarly, in Christian initiation, the material elements of water and oil assume a unique function when sanctified by the invocation of the Spirit. Cyril of Jerusalem (c.350) articulates the same when he says:

> [B]eware of supposing that this to be plain ointment. For as the Bread of the Eucharist, after the invocation of the Holy Ghost, is mere bread no longer, but the body of Christ, so also this holy ointment is no more simple ointment, nor (so to say) common, after the invocation, but the gift of Christ; and by the presence of His Godhead, it causes in us the Holy Ghost. It is symbolically applied to thy forehead and thy other senses; and while thy body is anointed with visible ointment, thy soul is sanctified by the Holy and life-giving Spirit.[9]

Thus the Fathers were quite clear about the divine activity operative in and through sacramental actions. They believed that through the ministry of men [*sic*], but beyond all human factors, it is Christ who acts in and through the sacraments. Thus they believed that it is Christ who "baptizes," "forgives sins," and "feeds us in the Eucharist."[10] As John Chrysostom writes, "neither angel nor archangel can do anything with regard to what is given from God; but the Father, the Son, and the Holy Ghost, dispenses all, while the priest lends his time and affords his hands."[11] An obvious and inseparable relationship between the ritual celebration and the reality signified is brought about as follows:

> Believe, therefore, that even now it is that supper at which he himself sat down. For this is in no way different from that other one; but both this and that are his own work. When therefore you see the priest delivering it unto you, reckon not that it is the priest that does this, but that it is Christ's hand that is stretched out.[12]

The above-mentioned passages make clear that the Fathers attempted to establish a correlation between the sacramental rituals and the reality signified

---

sacrament of baptism Tertullian also makes use of the same principle in opposition to the dualistic pessimism of people like Marcion, who held that matter was evil. See Bernard Leeming, *Principles of Sacramental Theology* (London, New York, Toronto: Lonngmans, Green, 1955), 43.

9. Cyril of Jerusalem, "On the Mysteries," in *Nicene and Post-Nicene Fathers*, 2nd Series, vol. 7, ed. Philip Schaff (Edinburgh: T & T Clark, 1996), 3:3.

10. John P. Schanz, *Introduction to the Sacraments* (New York: Pueblo, 1983), 105.

11. John Chrysostom, "Homilies on the Gospel of St. John," in *Nicene and Post-Nicene Fathers*, 1st Series, vol. 14, ed. Philip Schaff (Edinburgh : T & T Clark, 1996), 86:4.

12. *Ibid.*, 5:18.

by them, based on their understanding of the scriptures, popular beliefs, and their own individual experiences. Accordingly, the Fathers have acknowledged the reality of the sacraments present, invisibly beyond their visible elements and ritual actions.

1.3. Sign and Signification

The Patristic period also witnessed the development of the sacraments into a collection of symbolic rituals. Sacramental theology was developed by philosophical reflection on those rituals, which gave rise to the understanding of the sacraments in terms of signs. Accordingly, the sacraments were understood to be the signs and symbols of something sacred.

The Patristic notion of sacraments as signs can be understood in the light of the terms, *sacramentum* and μυστήριον and the implications of their context. The Greek word μυστήριον was originally derived from pagan mystery religions.[13] In pagan religious contexts, μυστήριον meant "something hidden" or "sacred." Ritual actions were considered to have some hidden performative meaning, which was inaccessible to the ordinary persons. Therefore, outsiders were not allowed to partake in them. The Greek Fathers made use of this term μυστήριον, that originally had non-Christian implications, to explain the sacraments, especially baptism.[14] Accordingly, sacramental actions came to be understood as representing "something invisible" or "myste-

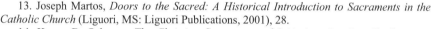

13. Joseph Martos, *Doors to the Sacred: A Historical Introduction to Sacraments in the Catholic Church* (Liguori, MS: Liguori Publications, 2001), 28.

14. Kenan B. Osborne, *The Christian Sacraments of Initiation: Baptism Confirmation Eucharist* (New York, Mahwah, NJ: Paulist Press, 1987), 57. It was a common practice to prevent non-Christians from taking part in the last stage of Christian initiation, i.e., the celebration of the Eucharist. For Christian writers of the second century, it was convenient to explain this practice in conjunction with the religious secrecy of pagan cults, which was familiar to them. Therefore, Clement of Alexandria, who knew pagan and Christian rites, speaks about Christian rites as representations of sacred realities, which only those initiated could understand. See Martos, *Doors to the Sacred*, 28. St. Paul uses the term μυστήριον to refer to the mystery of Christ, which was hidden, but made known through the Spirit (Eph 3:3-36). In the Latin translation of the Bible μυστήριον was sometimes rendered as *sacramentum*. Due to the influence of Tertullian on other writers, *sacramentum* became a common expression to denote Christian rites of initiation. Gradually μυστήριον came to denote any of the seven rites known as sacraments. The term μυστήριον is also found in the scripture, but it has been used in a broader sense than seven rites of the sacraments. See Kevin W. Irwin, "Sacrament," in *The New Dictionary of Theology*, ed. Joseph A. Komonchak, Mary Collins, and Dermot A. Lane (Dublin: Gill and Macmillan, 1987), 910-911.

rious." By the third century, Greek Christian writers began to apply the term μυστήριον to Christian rituals, as well as to the mysteries of faith.[15]

Originally, the term *sacramentum* was used in Rome to denote the ceremonies by which a person is initiated into the army. These ceremonies signified the beginning of a new way of life.[16] Among the Latin Christians, the term *sacramentum* began to be used to refer to sacraments through the influence of Tertullian. He used the term *sacramentum* as an equivalent for μυστήριον while he addressed his Latin speaking audience (c.210).[17] Tertullian took this meaning and applied it to the sacraments of initiation. Consequently, other Christian writers began to employ the term *sacramentum* in reference to the sacrament of initiation. In a broad sense, it was also applied to Christian rituals and objects, such as oil, water, etc. *Sacramentum* was now referring to Christian rituals, particularly to the sacraments. Because of the similarity between the Latin word *mysterium* and the Greek word μυστήριον, the term *sacramentum* was preferred by Latin authors for Christian rituals, whereas the term *mysterium* for the invisible mysteries of faith.[18] Thus, *sacramenta* (sacraments) were considered to be the signs of *mysteria*.

The application of the categories of reality and sign can be traced back to Augustine's (354-430) division of Christian doctrine into reality (*res*) and signs (*signa*).[19] According to Augustine, signs are the words of scripture, and reality is the triune God. Peter Lombard (1095-1160) followed the Augustinian distinction of reality and sign. Reality, for Lombard, as for Augustine, is the triune God, whereas signs become the sacraments. This Augustinian differentiation of reality and sign was passed through Peter Lombard to the understanding of the efficacy of the sacraments.[20]

As it becomes clear from the *Sentences* of Lombard and Bonaventure, the philosophical concept of causality was employed already in the twelfth century. For instance, Peter Lombard employed the notion of causality in order to illustrate the realisation of the sacraments.[21] For Lombard, the reflection

15. Martos, *Doors to the Sacred*, 29.

16. *Ibid.*

17. Osborne, *Sacraments of Initiation*, 11, 57.

18. Martos, *Doors to the Sacred*, 29.

19. Augustine, "Christian Doctrine," in *Nicene and Post-Nicene Fathers*, vol. 2, ed. Philip Schaff (Grand Rapids, MI: Eerdmans, 1979), 1:2-3.

20. Francis Schüssler Fiorenza, "Systematic Theology: Tasks and Methods," in *Systematic Theology: Roman Catholic Perspectives*, ed. Francis Schüssler Fiorenza and John P. Galvin (Dublin: Gill and Macmillan, 1992), 16-17.

21. Before Aquinas, Peter Lombard explained the sacraments as signs of grace indicating their causal efficacy. He says, "'Sacrament' is said properly of what is so much a sign of the

on causality is subordinated to the discussion on signification. This is because the treatment of the sacraments forms only a part of the discussion on "teaching about signs" (*doctrina signorum*). Bonaventure also presents a lengthy review on the efficacy of the sacraments, although he remains inconclusive regarding the efficacy of the sacraments. As he puts it,

> [I] do not know which [opinion] is truer, since when we speak of things that are miracles, we ought not to adhere much to reason. We thus concede that the sacraments of the New Law are causes, that they produce effects and that they dispose things, according to the loose sense of 'cause' … and it is safe to say this. Whether they have something more, I wish neither to affirm nor to deny.[22]

In the second and third centuries, the term *sacramentum* had only a universal sense in that it was used to designate any ritual that represented something symbolically. For instance, Hilary of Poitiers applied this term in a broad sense to everything in the Jewish scriptures that prefigured the Christian mysteries. In the same way, Ambrose of Milan broadened the meaning of *sacramenta*, to designate feasts such as Easter and Pentecost.[23] However, with the time of Augustine, the idea of the sacraments as effective signs was rather nonflexible.[24] Augustine, relying on Neo-Platonic philosophy, con-

grace of God and so much the form of invisible grace, that it produces the image of it and stands forth as a cause" (*ipsius imaginem great et causa exsistat*). See Peter Lombard, *Sentences: On the Doctrine of Signs* (accessed September 2, 2008); available from http://www.franciscan-archive.org/lombardus/opera/ls4-01.html. Authors like Guido of Orchelle, William of Auxerre, Bonaventure and many of Aquinas' Dominican predecessors employed the language of causality inherited from Lombard. But the unique contribution of Aquinas is that he gave a prominence to the causal efficacy of the sacraments. Norman Kretzmann and Eleonore Stump, eds., *The Cambridge Companion to Aquinas* (Cambridge, New York: Cambridge University Press, 1993), 242; Schanz, *Introduction to the Sacraments*, 107. In contrast to Augustine, Aquinas was mainly interested in affirming the sacraments as true causes.

22. Bonaventura, *Sentences* (accessed August 12, 2008); available from http://www.franciscan-archive.org/bonaventura/opera/bon04019.html. Albert the Great was also not in a position to explain how the sacraments effected or contained grace. He was wary of describing sacramental causality in terms of material dispositions and in rejecting the understanding of the sacraments in the ordinary sense of saving grace that is in some way tied to the sacraments. See Kretzmann and Stump, eds., *Aquinas*, 242.

23. Martos, *Doors to the Sacred*, 30.

24. When the fathers speak of the sign, it means that there are two aspects, namely, the external and visible and the other invisible, which contains the power of the Holy Spirit that produces grace. The Greeks referred to that which is external by μυστήριον, whereas for the Latin Fathers its equivalents are *signum, figura* or *sacramentum*. For example, in baptism, the grace is that of baptismal regeneration and in the Eucharist it is the grace of the body and

ceived sacraments as signs pointing to a spiritual reality, which is sacramental grace.[25] According to him, the sacraments signify the grace that is bestowed on the faithful when they participate in the sacrament.[26]

The survey we have undertaken reveals that the early Christian and patristic periods do not present a full-fledged theology of sacramental efficacy. However, our survey shows that it was commonly believed in the early Christian and patristic periods that the visible rituals and symbols of the sacraments contained some sacred and mysterious realities beyond their physical appearances. These realities could be understood by faith alone and perceived by personal religious experience. The sacramental experience of the early Christians direct us to assume that they had a relatively clear understanding of an inseparable relationship between the signs and the reality symbolised by them. Sacramental efficacy was understood to be this indispensable relationship between the rituals and the reality symbolised by them. Some of the texts make a clear and objective connection between the rites and the grace manifest in the mysterious realities that they represent. The efficacy was not considered a magical efficacy caused by the inherent potency of the material elements of the sacraments, but as something brought about by the intervention of God. They understood the sacraments as representing something spiritual or sacred whose reality can be ultimately attributed to God. Apart from crediting sacramental efficacy to the activity of God, no systematic theological exposition was made to clarify the dynamics between the sacramental signs and the signified reality, as in the scholastic period. For Christians of the early Church, the sacrament was something to be celebrated and experienced. Nonetheless, a certain understanding of this relationship and the symbolism of the rituals was essential in order to experience the mysterious realities represented by them. In the wake of heresies, the Fathers had to reflect on the reality that was invisibly present in the visible rituals and actions of the sacraments. Catechetical homilies and exhortations of the Fathers were intended to make the relationship between the ritual actions and their meaning clear and to prepare the audience for a real sacra-

blood of Christ. See Thomas Aquinas, *Summa Theologiae*, trans. David Bourke, vol. 56 (London, New York: Blackfriars, 1975), xv.

25. Edward J. Kilmartin, *The Eucharist in the West: History and Theology*, ed. Robert J. Daly (Collegeville, MN: Liturgical Press, 1998), 28-30.

26. The grace that is bestowed upon the faithful is understood differently in the Latin patristic tradition. For Augustine, grace means the Spirit of Christ. Grace was referred to as corporate grace that is obtained through the Eucharist, which makes those who partake, one with the body and blood of Christ and one with the Church. See Kilmartin, *Eucharist in the West*, 6.

mental experience.[27] As Joseph Martos observes, there exists a dialectical relationship between the sacramental experience of Christian communities and sacramental theologies. According to him, sacramental theology developed through a reflection on the sacramental experience of early Christian communities, which in turn contributed to the sacramental religious experience of the celebrating community. The dictum *lex orandi* and *lex credendi* underscores this dialectical relationship between the liturgical practices, as evidenced by texts and the faith of the community. In the light of our investigation, we may suggest that, even at the time of the Fathers, the notion of the sacraments as effective symbols that really caused what they signified was present at least in a germinal form, although their understanding was often diverse and flexible. Nevertheless, they were aware of the fact that it was God who caused those effects and not any intervention of human beings.

2. The Synthesis of Aquinas

The rudimentary notion of the sacraments as efficacious signs that already existed in patristic theology was given a systematic exposition in scholastic theology. The distinctive contribution of Aquinas was that he gave a systematic exposition to the idea of sacraments as causes, employing the philosophical notion of causality that he developed from an attentive reading of Aristotle. In succeeding pages, we will analyse the scholastic notion of sacramental efficacy developed by Aquinas in terms of symbolic causality.[28]

2.1. Instrumental Causality

The debate concerning the efficacy of the sacraments was a crucial issue that captured the attention of theologians for centuries, especially in the Middle Ages.[29] As a result, attempts were made to clarify what precisely is the effect

---

27. Martos, *Doors to the Sacred*, xv.

28. Although Aquinas' notion of sacramental efficacy is characterised as symbolic causality, as will be seen, the notion of symbolic reality was dormant in Aquinas' theology of the sacraments. That is why Karl Rahner considers Aquinas' theology of the Eucharist and the sacraments as the "*locus classicus* of symbolism in Catholic theology." See Stephen M. Fields, *Being as Symbol: On the Origins and Development of Karl Rahner's Metaphysics* (Washington, DC: Georgetown University Press, 2000), 38.

29. The discussion on the efficacy of the sacraments cannot be considered only as a medieval concern. For instance, the *Catechism of the Catholic Church* still speaks about the notion of efficacy as attached to the sacrament (nos. 1127-1129). As our historical survey makes clear, the notion of sacramental efficacy occupies a place in theological discussions,

of the sacraments, and how the effect is produced. Credit goes to Aquinas for having treated this problem in a systematic manner in terms of the theory of causation. The basic notion underlying his treatment is that sacraments *cause* something to happen.

A prominent idea that existed in scholasticism regarding the efficacy of the sacrament was the theory of "concomitance" or "occasion."[30] This theory holds that "as signs, sacraments cause only as signs cause, by conveying knowledge."[31] According to this view, God bestows grace on the recipient concurrently upon the administration of the sacraments. The 'giving' of the sacraments only reminds the recipient of the grace that is being received from God, who acts simultaneously with the sign. Therefore, the sacraments become effective, in the sense that they constitute the condition in which God acts unfailingly.[32] On the contrary, in *Summa Theologiae*, Aquinas makes a shift in the understanding of sacramental causality by incorporating the Aristotelian notion of instrumental causality or physical causality.[33]

Aquinas defines sacrament as "a sign of a sacred reality, inasmuch as it has the property of sanctifying" human beings.[34] There are three elements in this definition: sacramental sign, sacramental reality, and effect. As he understands it, "a sign is something through which a person arrives at knowledge of some further thing beyond itself."[35] When he calls sacraments "signs," it refers to a mutual relationship between the signs and the signified reality. Therefore, according to his understanding, sacraments are intrinsic symbols of the reality signified.

---

although the understanding of the efficacy has taken different turns in modern and postmodern theology.

30. David Bourke, "Introduction," in *Summa Theologiae*, vol. 56, p. xvii. This theory finds its origin in Peter Lombard, and was taken over to scholasticism and nominalism. See Fields, *Being as Symbol*, 40.

31. Thomas Aquinas, "Commentary on the Sentences of Peter Lombard," in *Opera Omnia*, ed. E. Frette *et al.* (Paris: Vivès, 1878), 4:3,4. Cited in Fields, *Being as Symbol*, 40.

32. Fields, *Being as Symbol*, 40.

33. Aquinas, *Summa Theologiae*, 3a.64,1-3. Physical causality is distinguished from moral causality and juridical causality. Physical causality regards grace as inherent in the sacramental rites themselves or disposes the recipient to receive the grace (*res et sacramentum*) that God offers freely and really. Moral causality implies that sacramental actions are more like propitiatory acts which contain a moral or persuasive effect to induce God to bestow grace (as in the theory of concomitance or occasion). Juridical causality means that the recipient is authorised or entitled to receive grace from God through the performance of sacramental actions. See Leeming, *Principles of Sacramental Theology*, 287-290.

34. Aquinas, *Summa Theologiae*, 3a.60,2.

35. *Ibid.*, 3a.60,4.

Thus, for Aquinas, sacramental actions are not mere extrinsic occasions of grace, but the intrinsic media of it.[36] What Aquinas understands by instrumental causality is a common finality brought about by the effects of both the instrumental and the principal agents. For example, in the case of a carpenter, in producing a desired object by sawing, this process comes into play. The saw is the instrumental cause by which the principal cause, the carpenter, produces a designed object. In producing the effect, the instrument exercises two powers, namely, "the power of the instrument," which is innate in the instrument, by which it performs its own proper activity and "the instrumental power," the power that emerges from the activity of the principal agent.[37] The effect by which the desired object is produced, results from the proper form of the instrumental cause and the power of the principal cause. The instrumental cause possesses power only when the instrument is moved by the power effected by the principal agent. Therefore, in producing the designed effect, the exemplary cause of the agent's activity functions as the formal cause of the act, and incorporates the instrumental causality to result in the desired effect. In this scheme of causality, the principal agent does not become the instrumental cause, but only moves the innate power of the instrument in such a way that the instrumental cause may achieve a final cause, which it could not achieve through its own innate power by acting itself. The instrumental cause achieves the final cause because the principal agent contains some power that it transfers to the instrumental cause.[38] The principal agent acts through an instrumental cause; thus, both the principal agent and the instrumental cause are acting as a single cause to produce the effect. The final cause here is the activity of producing the desired object, which is actualised by moving the instrumental cause so that the effect is produced according to the design of the principal agent. To put it another way, the saw, together with the carpenter and his design, participates in the design, and joins hand in hand with the agent in translating the design into reality. What is basic to the theory of instrumental causality is that the power contained in

36. Bourke says that this notion was found originally in Origen and in the Alexandrian tradition from which Aquinas might have borrowed. See Bourke, "Introduction," xv.

37. James S. Albertson, "Instrumental Causality in St. Thomas," *New Scholasticism* 28 (1954): 412.

38. Thomas Aquinas, "Commentary on the Sentences of Peter Lombard," 4:19,1,2,1. Cited in Fields, *Being as Symbol*, 40.

the instrument is capable of producing the effects, which surpasses the capacity of the instrument in itself.[39]

2.2. Symbolic Reality

Aquinas applies this scheme of instrumental causality to explain the sacraments. Christ, the Incarnate Word, is the exemplar cause of the divine grace that is conferred through the sacraments. Sacramental actions become effective so as to sanctify the person by signifying the source of sanctification, the passion of Christ.[40] Thus, the sacraments operate by virtue of the passion of Christ, which is the cause of the sanctification.[41] The passion of Christ has an instrumental or a causal function, because it effects sanctification. The sacraments contain natural signs, which act as instrumental causes. Christ, as the principal agent, confers on these natural signs an "instrumental power" through the words of the ordained minister to sanctify by means of "the power of the instrument" that is innate in the signs.[42] Since the instrumental cause and the power of the instrument are identical, the exemplary cause can realise the effect of sanctification in the recipient by infusing the innate power of the instrumental (sacramental) signs. In this sense, Aquinas speaks of the instrumental cause as "the sign of a hidden effect because it is not only a cause but in some way an effect, inasmuch as it is moved by the principal agent."[43] According to Aquinas, grace is caused by signification. In effecting grace, God acts as the principal agent, while the humanity of Christ acts as a conjoined instrument, of which the sacraments are a separate instrument joined

---

39. Mark D. Jordan, "Theology and Philosophy," in *The Cambridge Companion to Aquinas*, ed. Norman Kretzmann and Eleonore Stump (Cambridge, New York: Cambridge University Press, 1993), 245.

40. Aquinas, *Summa Theologiae*, 3a.60:3.

41. *Ibid.*, 3a.61:1,3.

42. There are several instruments or agents involved in the sacraments. Christ is the chief agent who works through his sacred humanity as a conjoined instrument. The Son of God, who is acting as a conjoined instrument, acts through a series of separate instruments, namely, the priest of the Church, the elements and words of the sacraments of matter and form which eventually produce grace. Aquinas, *Summa Theologiae*, 3a.62:5. Christ's work is expressed as a "conjoined instrument" because the human nature of Christ was united to the Second Person of the Trinity. Even though Aquinas speaks of the minister of the Church, what he emphasises is a direct movement from the action of Christ to the sacraments without emphasising the role of the Church. The scheme of operation is Christ – Priest – Sacramental Act. This is because there was not a highly developed ecclesiology when Aquinas wrote his treatise on the sacraments.

43. Aquinas, *Summa Theologiae*, 3a.62:1,1.

to it. Therefore, it is necessary that the grace of salvation, which comes from the divinity of Christ, reaches the sacraments through the humanity of Christ.[44] The sacramental theology of Aquinas is a prolongation of his Christology, particularly, the hypostatic union.[45] In the celebration of the sacraments, sanctification of the participants is realised, or the finality is achieved, because the principal agent incorporates the sacramental signs into his exemplary causality. Explaining how the sacraments become efficacious, Aquinas says, "the very fact that the term 'sacrament' signifies the reality which sanctifies means that it should signify the effect produced. For the notion of this is implicitly contained in the very concept of the sanctifying cause precisely as sanctifying cause."[46] Sacraments effect what they signify and signify what they effect. In this way, he establishes an essential link between sign and cause. Hence, there exists a close relationship between the ritual celebration and the effect of the sacrament. It becomes evident that Aquinas' definition of the sacraments implies that the sacraments are intrinsic and efficacious signs of the effects produced. For example, in baptism, the instrumental power, the grace of sanctification is conferred in and through the innate power of the act of physical washing. Therefore, the efficacy of the sacrament is based on the instrumental power and the power of the instrument acting as one cause. Therefore, the sacramental signs are vested with a symbolic efficacy, because the innate power of the signs is decisive in achieving finality.[47]

Augustine already had the understanding of the sacraments as intrinsic and efficacious signs, which is supposed to have been inherited by Isidore of Seville (c.560-636).[48] Augustine shared the view that the material elements of the sacraments, more than being conventional signs, should, by their very

44. *Ibid.*, 3a.60:6.

45. Louis-Marie Chauvet, *Symbol and Sacrament: A Sacramental Reinterpretation of Christian Existence*, trans. Patrick Medigan and Madeleine Beaumont (Collegeville, MN: Liturgical Press, 1995), 453.

46. Aquinas, *Summa Theologiae*, 3a.60:3.

47. Aquinas extends the notion of causality, saying that the sacraments effect a change in the moral condition of the individual, because the sacraments enable them to perform virtuous actions, such as worship of God, which brings them to the end, the beatific vision of God, which is an individual's supreme and profoundest desire. Thus Aquinas insists that the sacramental instruments contain a causal power, some of which are permanent, and effect morally significant change in the soul. Aquinas even goes to the extent of using the term "cause" saying that the richest kind of causality is that which makes creatures to participate in the divine life. See Jordan, "Theology and Philosophy," 247.

48. Fields, *Being as Symbol*, 39. According to Augustine, sign is that which leads to the knowledge of something once the sign is known. Piet F. Fransen, "Sacraments, Signs of Faith," *Worship* 37 (1962-63): 424.

nature, resemble the spiritual reality that is signified by them.[49] For example, baptismal water naturally symbolises spiritual cleansing and regeneration. What is innovative in the thought of Aquinas is the accent he lays on the intrinsic relation between the material element of the sacrament and the spiritual reality represented by it. Augustine and Isidore subscribed only to an extrinsic conception of the sacraments in the sense that the elements of the sacraments constitute symbols of God's grace that he bestows every time the sacrament is enacted.[50] The idea of an intrinsic relationship between the elements and the signified reality is absent in their thought. Aquinas explained sacramental efficacy in terms of the intrinsic relationship between the physical elements and the signified reality.[51]

Furthermore, concerning efficacy, Aquinas held the view that the sacraments effected *ex opere operato* if specific conditions of validity are fulfilled. The words and actions in the sacraments are made God's instruments to produce desired effects. These effects are not dependent on the merits of the minister and the recipient, but on the divine power itself.[52] In other words, the efficacy is not dependent on human agents, but on divine institution and power.

In conjunction with efficacy, there arises the question of the specific effects of the sacrament. Hence, scholastic theology distinguishes a twofold effect; namely, the *res et sacramentum* and the *res tantum*. The *res et sacramentum* is the first effect which is automatically produced by the valid ad-

49. Bourke, "Introduction," in *Summa Theologiae*," vol. 56, p. xvi.

50. Peter B. Garland, *The Definition of Sacrament According to St. Thomas* (Ottawa: University of Ottawa Press, 1959), 46, 85.

51. In developing this intrinsic understanding of efficaciousness, he makes a contrast between the Old and New Laws. According to him the Old Law had sacraments, but they were not efficacious. On the contrary, the sacraments of the New Law became efficacious by the redemptive work of Christ and because they were instituted by Christ. He considers the Old Law cults as sacraments inasmuch as they prefigured the sacraments of the New Law, but they could not make present the saving work of Christ because they had no intrinsic relation to it. See Aquinas, *Summa Theologiae*, 3a.60:1,2; Garland, *The Definition of Sacrament*, 24-25; Fields, *Being as Symbol*, 39. Aquinas also sees a common source that unites both the sacraments of the Old and the New Laws, which he calls the immanence of the divine creature that overshadows the created world. As the creator of the world, God bestows his presence upon nature and enables nature to function as the efficacious medium of his grace. The sacraments of the New Law become properly efficacious, because the Incarnate Word, who became God's definitive word in history itself has established specific natural signs as sacred symbols and instituted the ministry of the priesthood to consecrate the natural sign in order to perpetuate the work of the divine Word in history. See Bourke, "Introduction," xx, xiii-xix.; Aquinas, *Summa Theologiae*, 3a.60:5,6.

52. Leeming, *Principles of Sacramental Theology*, 5.

ministration of the sacrament. It is the intermediary between the external rite and the grace produced.[53] There is an objective consecration of the natural signs in each sacrament, which generates a sanctifying effect, the "symbolic reality" (*res et sacramentum*).[54] Consequently, the symbolic reality consti-tutes the medium that effects the sanctification of the person who receives the sacrament.[55] In other words, the *res et sacramentum* is the concurrent grace which is caused by the signifying power of the sacraments. The sym-bolic reality confers the grace of the sacrament on the participants when an ordained minister administers the sacrament.[56] The *res et sacramentum* also came to be called "sacramental character," given that the sacrament imprints an indelible mark on the soul.[57] The sacraments that are not repeated, namely, baptism, confirmation and orders are of this nature.[58] These sacraments are of great significance, because in addition to their sacramental character, they also enable the recipients to participate in Christian worship.[59] They confer

---

53. *Ibid.*, 322.

54. Stephen Fields, "The Metaphysics of Symbol in Thomism: *Aeterni Patris* to Rahner," *International Philosophical Quarterly* 37 (1997): 279.

55. Leeming, *Principles of Sacramental Theology*, 279.

56. The concept of symbolic reality was originally implicitly contained in Augustine, and was explicitly developed by Berengar of Tours (1000-1088). Berengar applied this only to the Eucharist. Aquinas extended this idea to the seven sacraments. Accordingly, each sacrament confers a specific grace corresponding to each sacrament. For example, in the Eucharist, the effect is the real presence of Christ's body and blood under the species of bread and wine; in reconciliation, it is the penitents sorrow and amendment. Baptism, confirmation and orders imprint an indelible mark, which effects an ontological change and bestows certain powers permanently in such a way that they need not be repeated.

57. Disputes on the baptism in Schismatic Churches arose as early as the time of Cyprian of Carthage. There had also been a decision before Augustine by the Church against Cyprian of Carthage, who argued for the rebaptism of the Novatians when they rejoined the Church. However it became a crucial issue in the fourth century with the Donatist schism. Augustine, refuting the Donatists, had held the view that the baptism of those who sought reconciliation coming from Donatist communion was valid because it caused a kind of permanent mark in the soul. See David N. Power, *Sacrament: The Language of God's Giving* (New York: Cross-road, 1999), 214-215. The permanent character of baptism was attributed to the character that is left in the soul. This understanding became the basis for the medieval development of the *res et tantum*.

58. Unrepeatable sacraments, namely, baptism and priestly ordination, not only produce grace, but also effect a permanent "character" in the soul of the recipient. Aquinas, *Summa Theologiae*, 3a.63.

59. *Ibid.*, 3a.63:3. Bestowal of the permanent "character" means that it is a spiritual power that enables the recipients to participate in the worship of God (63:2; 63:4,2). The power itself is instrumental because it creates "ministers" for the service of God. The recipients of these sacraments are not given some external attributes, but there is something that is put in their

the competence to participate in the priestly worship of Christ to the Father in varying degrees. The reality of the sacrament can be distinguished in each individual sacrament. For instance, in the Eucharist the symbolic reality is the "real presence" of the body and blood of Christ under the "species" of bread and wine, which takes place by transubstantiation.[60] The real presence confers sanctification of the recipient when the sacrament is received under the species of bread and wine.[61]

Res tantum, as compared to *res et sacramentum*, is the ultimate effect, which is specific to each sacrament that is generally understood in relation to

souls that place them in a relationship signified in the service of God (63:2,3). This relationship is an intrinsic attribute that is of permanent "character," in the sense that it participates in the permanency of its divine cause (63:5), i.e., in the universal priesthood of Christ (63:3).

60. The term "transubstantiation" was commonly used by 1150, but it appears first in the *Sentences* (c.1140) or Roland Bandinelli, and later Alexander III (pontificate 1159-1181). Joseph M. Powers, *Eucharistic Theology* (London: Burns & Oates, Herder & Herder, 1968), 30. The theory of transubstantiation is different from the "annihilation" theory which holds that Christ's body and blood expels the bread and wine that lapse into nothingness.

61. Louis Billot (1846-1931), in his book, *De Ecclesiae Sacramentis*, 1st ed., 2 vols. (Rome: Gregorian University, 1893) discusses the notion of symbolism latent in Aquinas' Eucharistic theology. Fields makes a summary presentation of the entire discussion of Billot and argues that Billot's understanding of the relationship between the visible medium of the sacrament and the symbolic reality helped Rahner's metaphysics to explain the identity and difference that exists between the symbol and the signified reality. Fields, " Metaphysics of Symbol," 279-280. Billot has tried to understand the nature of the identity that exists between the consecrated elements and the real presence or between the symbolic reality and the visible elements. In transubstantiation the elements of bread and wine obtain a potentiality that is immanent in them to be transformed into the body and blood of Christ, by the divine power or divine presence which pre-exists the change and into which the elements are transformed. Billot also observes that the change of bread and wine into new substantiality does not cause the annihilation of being. The bread and wine preserve their material mode of being, however, their material substances are re-oriented into divine reality, into the reality of the Eucharist, which is the real presence of Christ. The reality of the Eucharist, or the real presence, intrinsically unites the sacrament's visible media, namely, the bread and wine, the Eucharistic species. Billot interprets the Eucharistic conversion that causes the symbolic reality, which is immanent in Aquinas' understanding of transubstantiation in terms of an "intrinsic" notion of symbolism. Accordingly, the symbolic reality requires a visible media to be communicated or to make the reality present. So, as far as the Eucharist is concerned, bread and wine are the visible and necessary medium in which the symbolic reality is conveyed. In other words, bread and wine become intrinsic symbols whereby the symbolic reality is being manifested or made present. The relationship between the media and the symbolic reality are intrinsic to the extent that the media is identical with the reality that is being signified. Therefore, in the Eucharist, after consecration, bread and wine do not co-exist with the real presence, but has been substantially changed into the body and blood of Christ. See also Fields, *Being as Symbol*, 43-46.

the disposition of the recipient, since it presupposes a state of grace.[62] More- over, *res tantum* is essentially associated with the *res et sacramentum*, be- cause it produces the ultimate efficacy of the sacrament, if the recipients are properly disposed, i.e., if they are in a state of grace and are free of any hin- drance on the way.[63]

In order to explain how the symbolic reality causes grace, there are two prevalent theories: the "perfective" theory and the "dispositive" theory.[64] Perfective theory holds that the grace of the sacrament is given concomitant- ly with the symbolic reality independently, by divine activity in the celebra- tion of the sacramental rituals. On the other hand, dispositive theory holds that the infusion of the sanctifying grace effected by divine activity is in, and through, the symbolic reality. Accordingly, symbolic activity is the instru- mental cause of grace, as distinct from the perfective theory. For instance, in baptism, sanctifying grace is bestowed in the soul by divine activity, in and through the sacramental character that is imprinted on the soul. In other words, the sacramental character imprinted on the soul disposes the soul to receive the sanctifying grace of the sacraments. Aquinas distinguishes the Eucharist from other sacraments. As he explains, in the Eucharist, the sym- bolic reality, i.e., the presence of Christ is first extrinsic to the recipient, whe- reas in all other sacraments, the symbolic reality cannot exist apart from the persons who receive them.[65]

---

62. Schanz, *Introduction to the Sacraments*, 55. In Biblical Greek the term χάρις (grace) refers to the source of the gift in the giver and the effect of that gift in the receiver. Grace as a gift has its beginning in God's favor and benevolence. Jahweh's grace is manifested in the gift of his Son (Jn 1:17). Grace is freely bestowed. The work of grace is manifested in recipients in a variety of manners as charisms (1 Cor 12).

63. Having defined the number of sacraments at the Council of Lateran IV (1215), and re- asserted by the Council of Trent (1545-1563), concern was focused on specifying the special graces that follow each sacrament. For a detailed discussion of the specific graces conferred by each sacrament, see Schanz, *Introduction to the Sacraments*, 112.

64. Scholars and commentators are divided as to which of these theories was held by Aquinas. His early view appears to favour the dispositive theory as expressed in *Summa The- ologiae*. Leeming, *Principles of Sacramental Theology*, 264, 288. Aquinas, while speaking about baptism, claims that the words of the ordained minister is the instrumental power, which consecrates the natural sign of water by which a transcendental instrumental power is effected, which ultimately effects the symbolic reality to sanctify the soul. The symbolic reality also acts as a form, which confers an effect proper, a grace proper to that form. See Aquinas, *Summa Theologiae*, 3a.69:10.

65. Thomas Aquinas, *Summa Theologiae*, 3a.73:1,3; Leeming, *Principles of Sacramental Theology*, 327.

In sum, Aquinas' perception of the sacraments contains three elements: the natural sign, the symbolic reality, and the effect in the recipient. These elements participate in the sacrament's signified reality, which is sanctification. According to Aquinas, these elements of the sacrament participate in the reality that is signified "appropriately by means of formal or final causality."[66] The efficaciousness of the sacrament rests on the fact that the signified reality and the effects become the same. Therefore, in the sacraments, through instrumental causality, the saving work of Christ becomes present in the participant. All elements of the sacraments participate in their final cause, i.e., sanctification, by effecting as an ontological unity.[67] Aquinas distinguishes the Eucharist from the other sacraments, because the other sacraments signify Christ, whereas he is present in the Eucharist, "not only as sign … but according to the mode proper to this sacrament."[68] By "proper mode" he means that, in the Eucharist, the signs do not produce instrumentally the symbolic reality, as in other sacraments, but rather, the signs themselves become the symbolic reality that causes the sanctification of the recipient.

2.3. Critique of Aquinas

In the light of our investigation of the scholastic theology of the sacraments, we cannot but laud the efforts and achievements of scholastic theologians, especially that of Aquinas in treating the sacraments within the parameters of a single system. At the same time, the diminution of sacramental thinking within a single scheme of Aristotelian metaphysics caused stagnation in the sacramental thinking of the successive period, until Vatican II called for new theoretical paradigms within Catholic thinking. It was the case that the scholastic paradigm was viewed, in itself, as self-contained and perfect; therefore, other systems were considered incomplete and defective. While there was neither a single theology of the sacraments, nor a single form of liturgical celebration in the patristic period, diversity and tolerance were the principal features of the period.[69]

The point of departure of scholastic theologians, based on a physical and metaphysical definition of the sacraments, is methodologically challenged. By introducing the notion of physical and metaphysical change, the sacraments were made "epiphenomenal to human life and human environment,"

66. Aquinas, *Summa Theologiae*, 3a.60:1,1.
67. Fields, *Being as Symbol*, 46.
68. Aquinas, *Summa Theologiae*, 3a.75:1,3.
69. Martos, "Revolution in Sacramental Theology," 105.

transferring them from the natural order to the metaphysical or supernatural order.[70] The doctrinal and deductive approach, beginning from doctrinal statements about the nature and the number of sacraments and applying the method of reasoning to their effects, detached scholastic sacramental theology from experiential and existential concerns. The deductive and doctrinal approach of understanding sacramental efficacy *ex opere operato* was often misunderstood, especially in such spiritual matters as the remission of sins, or infusions of grace with no visible effect. Hence, under the deductive and doctrinal approach, sacramental efficacy was thought of as entirely automatic and magical.

According to the scholastic paradigm, sacraments are *products*. To some extent, this is due to the overemphasis on the *res et sacramentum,* which pertains to the question of *what* is conferred through the performance of the rites and received by the individual. This way of understanding the efficacy of the sacraments is minimalist, and mechanical. Although we see the development of the scholastic theology of the sacraments in *Sententiae* and *Summae* as being part of dogmatics and systematics, the nineteenth and early twentieth century manuals dealt with the sacraments as part of canon law, because of the extraordinary emphasis on proper administration and reception of the sacraments, rather than on understanding and meaningful celebration.[71] This approach to the sacraments gradually led to a mechanistic, pragmatic and utilitarian dimension, which limited the efficacy of the sacraments on an exclusive criterion: "what does this sacrament give that others don't give?"[72]

The Thomistic understanding of instrumental causality has been charged as being too mechanical and productionist. It fails to take into account the dynamic exchange that takes place in the sacrament, the descending and ascending aspect represented by the symbolic activity.[73] The scholastic paradigm of the sacraments as metaphysical entities to be administered and received doesn't exist in the contemporary sacramental vocabulary. Sacraments are understood as neither given, nor received, but celebrated. They are not things, but corporative symbolic activities of the religious community, the

---

70. Kenan B. Osborne, *Christian Sacraments in a Postmodern World: A Theology for the Third Millennium* (New York, Mahwah, NJ: Paulist Press, 1999), 44.

71. Martos, "Revolution in Sacramental Theology," 107.

72. Piet F. Fransen, "Sacraments as Celebrations," *Irish Theological Quarterly* 43 (1976): 443.

73. Fransen, "Sacraments, Signs of Faith," 428.

Church.[74] As Chauvet develops it, there is a symbolic exchange that takes place in the sacrament. Sacraments viewed as symbolic actions are not "some-thing," but we encounter "some-one" who is God, and we encounter God as persons and community.

One of Aquinas' unique contributions is the understanding of the sacraments as actions of Christ. However, his sacramental theology seems to be an appendage to Christology, solely determined by the hypostatic union. This Christology failed to consider the mystery of Christ's resurrection, exaltation and the sending of the Spirit at Pentecost.[75] Thus, the approach of scholastic theology diminishes the historical unfolding of the economy as present in the life of Jesus and the Church, which is unfolding up to our time through the Spirit in the sacraments.[76]

In spite of some references to the action of the Holy Spirit and in contrast to the importance that Aquinas ascribes to Christology, his theology of the sacraments is pneumatologically weak.[77] He is satisfied with the Pneumatological understanding of his time, without any attempt to develop it further. His reflection on Pneumatology is too minimalist and overpowered by Christology to claim that his sacramental theology duly accommodates Pneumatology.

When Aquinas emphasizes the notion of action in *persona Christi*, he also lays emphasis on the intention to do what the Church does. As he puts it, *facere quod facit Christus et Ecclesia* (to do what Christ and the Church does).[78] He understands the sacraments as the actions of Christ in the Church, so much so, that he calls them sometimes *sacramenta Ecclesiae*.[79] However, he does not explain the efficacy of the sacraments in relation to the Church.

74. *Ibid.*, 425.
75. Chauvet, *Symbol and Sacrament*, 456.
76. *Ibid.*
77. However, this doesn't imply that a rich Pneumatology is absent in Aquinas. He considers that the grace of the sacraments is principally caused by the Spirit's power. Thomas Aquinas, *Summa Theologiae*, trans. Cornelius Ernst, vol. 30 (London, New York: Blackfriars, 1972), 2a-2a.112:1,3. Although Aquinas ascribes the efficacy of baptism to the passion of Christ, he also admits the role of the Spirit as principal cause. Aquinas, *Summa Theologiae*, 3a.66:11-12. Similarly regarding the transformation of the bread and wine, he ascribes an instrumental power to the Spirit as the principal agent, although he does not hold the Eastern view that the conversion is through the power of the Holy Spirit. Aquinas, *Summa Theologiae*, 3a.78:4.
78. *Ibid.*, 3a.64:8,1.
79. Chauvet, *Symbol and Sacrament*, 465.

Therefore, the scholastic theology of the sacraments remains truncated from ecclesiology.

The topic of efficacy, or how the sacraments work, preoccupied the theology of Aquinas, especially in terms of the conditions for the validity of the sacrament and for the lawful or fruitful reception of the sacraments. The efficacy of the sacraments was considered as a kind of magical or mechanical efficacy. The scholastic understanding of efficacy became more mechanical and juridical by the Tridentine explanation of the scholastic notion of *opus operatum*, which further minimized the role of the recipient as causing no obstruction from receiving grace.[80] Consequently, the attention paid to causality overshadowed the revelatory and celebrative functions of the sacraments. This impoverishment in sacramental theology, which began to be more evident in the Post-tridentine period, prevailed up to the early and middle part of the twentieth century, when eminent theologians such as Odo Casel, Gottlieb Söhngen, Otto Semmelroth, Edward Schillebeeckx and Karl Rahner (among others) began to re-interpret the efficacy of the sacraments. These theologians employed different models, such as anthropological and phenomenological perspectives; they were also inspired by developments in biblical, patristic studies, and systematic theology. Of these models, Rahner's concept of *Realsymbol* has been very influential in the understanding of sacramental efficacy.

3. The Anthropological and Phenomenological Turn

The early and mid-twentieth century witnessed a shift beyond scholasticism and neo-scholasticism to the patristic period, explaining sacramentality in terms of an intrinsic connection to the incarnation itself and to the Church. Rahner, Schillebeeckx and Semmelroth were the chief proponents of this anthropological and phenomenological move. Although their writings marked a point of departure for many Catholic theologians, and still remain influential, our discussion will be restricted to Rahner as a representative of this movement in twentieth century sacramental theology.

---

80. It has been generally agreed that the Council of Trent's insistence on *opus operatum* at the expense of *opus operantis* was intended to establish a difference between Protestant and Catholic positions and to condemn the Protestant position, rather than giving a theological explanation of the sacraments. Fransen, "Sacraments as Celebrations," 441.

3.1. Rahnerian Synthesis

Rahner's innovative contribution to sacramental theology consists in explaining the causality of the sacraments in terms of the symbol. His point of departure is a critique of Aquinas' notion of instrumental causality. Rahner levels two main charges against Aquinas. First, he argues that Aquinas' concept of instrumental causality diminishes the efficacy of the sacraments to a transient form of efficient causality. He points out that Aquinas fails to adequately explain how natural signs intrinsically cause the sanctification which they signify.[81] Second, he charges that the relationship between the efficaciousness of the sacraments and the Church remains accidental, rather than being essential.[82] He opines there was a failure to assert the role of the Church, as far as the sanctification of the individuals is concerned. According to him, Aquinas' way of understanding the efficacy of the sacraments gives the impression that God directly gives sanctification to the individuals without the mediation of the Church. Rahner attempts to overcome the limitations of instrumental causality with the notion of symbolic causality. Therefore, a study of Rahner's theology of symbols is required to understand his theology of the sacraments.[83]

3.1.1. The Realsymbol

Rahner studies symbol from an ontological point of view. He is mainly concerned with the task of investigating the "highest and primordial manner" in which "one reality renders another present," or the "representation which allows the other 'to be there'."[84] For this reason, he formulates the notion of

---

81. Karl Rahner, "Introductory Observations," in *Theological Investigations*, vol. 14 (London: Darton, Longman & Todd, 1976), 150-151; Karl Rahner, *The Church and the Sacraments*, trans. W.J. O'Hara (New York: Herder and Herder, 1963), 35-37. Fields observes that Rahner's criticism is overstated and argues that Aquinas has sufficiently tried to establish the link between sacramental signs and their causal relationship as far as their efficacy is concerned. See also, Fields, *Being as Symbol*, 40-42, 46.

82. Rahner, "Introductory Observations," 151-153, 158-159; Rahner, *The Church and the Sacraments*, 9-10. Here, in the introductory part itself, Rahner calls into question the average Catholic understanding of a superficial and external relationship between the Church and the sacraments.

83. Rahner first introduced his theology of symbol in an article published in 1959 as "Zur Theologie des Symbols," *Schriften zur Theologie*, 16 vols. (Einsiedeln: Benziger, 1954-1984). Later it was translated as "The Theology of the Symbol," in *Theological Investigations*, vol. 4 (London: Darton, Longman and Todd, 1966). Hereafter, all references are from the English translation.

84. Rahner, "The Theology of the Symbol," 225.

Realsymbol is fundamental to his metaphysics.[85] According to the theory of
Realsymbol, all beings are essentially symbolic, because they express themselves in order to constitute the very nature of their being, or they mediate
themselves.[86] So the function of the symbol is twofold; symbol stands out as
the medium by which the form is externally manifested, thereby giving the
form a way of actualising itself. His assumption is based on his categoriza-
tion of symbolism as "intrinsic" and "extrinsic." In intrinsic symbolism, the
reality that the symbol represents, requires a symbol to mediate or to realize
itself, whereas, in extrinsic symbolism, the relation between the signified
reality and the symbol that the reality represents is arbitrary or accidental.[87]
Therefore, in intrinsic symbolism, medium is a constitutive element of the
structure of the reality itself, whereas, in extrinsic symbolism, it is accidental.

Rahner distinguishes between really genuine symbols (symbolic reality)
and arbitrary signs, signals, and codes (symbolic representations), which may
have some symbolic function of representing a reality to a certain extent.[88]
The difference is that the arbitrary sign does not constitute the reality that it
signifies, whereas, the *Realsymbol* expresses intrinsically the reality signified

85. The concept of *Realsymbol* has its origin in philosophical theories of symbol. From
Heidegger, he borrows the term "origin" and uses it to refer to the source, from which something springs forth, specifically as it reveals its nature or essence. According to Rahner, the
method that explains the origins of *Realsymbol* consists of three aspects. The first aspect is
constitutive of four predicates, which structure the inner nature of the *Realsymbol* that traces
their origin in Rahner's interpretation of Thomism by tradition from Kant to Heidegger. Accordingly, the first predicate implies that *Realsymbol* is "analogous," which insists that Being
is a continuum that contains both finite and infinite modes. The second predicate asserts that
Realsymbol is sacramental, which means that Being is efficacious: it causes what it signifies.
For example, in the human person, Being is brought to conscious self-presence through
knowledge. The third predicate affirms that the *Realsymbol* is "self-perfecting," because the
unity of being is maintained by an immanent dialectic. The fourth predicate suggests that the
Realsymbol is "embodied thought," which considers the self-presence of being as manifested
by way of knowledge in signs, sounds, characters and other empirical symbols of language.
These predicates are extracted from Rahner's seminal work, "The Theology of the Symbol,"
221-311. Stephen M. Fields gives an extensive treatment of the topic in his book, *Being as
Symbol* tracing back the origin of these predicates in Rahner's reflection on Thomism by way
of the tradition from Kant to Heidegger. Our treatment of the subject will be limited to the
sacramental aspect of the *Realsymbol*.

86. Rahner, "The Theology of the Symbol," 224.

87. *Ibid.*, 221-251, esp. 225.

88. *Ibid.*, 225. We can also notice that he uses the term "sign" and "symbol" interchangeably.

by it.[89] Symbol makes a reality present. Being is and comes into being by giving itself in a way that is other than itself. In other words, being comes into existence by being symbolized. Thus, the symbolic nature of being is that the being gives itself into the "other" so as to manifest or make it really present. Therefore, the fact of giving, and the realizing of being, implies that being expresses and possesses itself simultaneously.

Symbol belongs to the very essence of being, because the self-realization of beings is attained through a medium by which the being manifests itself. Therefore, all finite beings, through their accidental qualities, constitute the medium by which they express their identity and realize themselves as unique substances.[90] On the one hand, symbol signifies a finite being's self-expression and, on the other hand, functions as a means of self-realization. When equating symbol with self-expression, Rahner underscores that primary meaning of symbol in a being's self-expression and self-realization, because symbol is a necessary element as the medium of self-expression to accomplish the self-realisation of the being. Thus, the essence of every being is specifically knowing and being known. In this sense, all finite substances are "real-symbolic."[91] He uses the term *Realsymbol* to understand beings as "dynamically self-mediating realities."[92]

Rahner also distinguishes between the form and its external manifestation: the symbolized and the symbol. He draws out a second principle of his theory of symbol, which implies that symbol is the self-realization of being itself, constituting the very essence of being. Rahner sums up this as follows: "The symbol, strictly speaking (symbolic reality), is the self-realization of a

89. Annice C. Callahan, "Karl Rahner's Theology of Symbol: Basis for His Theology of the Church and the Sacraments," *Irish Theological Quarterly* 49 (1982): 196.

90. Rahner, "The Theology of the Symbol," 231-232.

91. The primary meaning of the symbol is not based on a kind of agreement between two realities that point to one another, which inherently contain a differentiation between the two. But *Realsymbols* are distinct from symbolic representations such as arbitrary signs, signals or codes in that they imply a differentiation and function as the symbol of another. See Maria Elizabeth Motzko, "Karl Rahner's Theology: A Theology of the Symbol" (Unpublished doctoral dissertation, Department of Theology, Fordham University, New York, 1976), 4.

92. Fields, *Being as Symbol*, 2. The idea of *Realsymbol* lies at the centre of Rahner's thought. Studies have been made on Rahner's understanding of *Realsymbol*, tracing it back to its roots. See for example, Joseph H.P. Wong, *Logos-Symbol in the Christology of Karl Rahner* (Rome: Las, 1984) which was originally a doctoral dissertation written between 1978 and 1981 at the Gregorian University in Rome. See also Callahan, "Karl Rahner's Theology of Symbol," 195-205.

being in the other, which is constitutive of its essence."[93] Now we shall explain how beings realize their own being through symbolization.

3.1.1.1. Being and Reality

We have seen that by *Realsymbol*, Rahner means that all beings express
themselves so as to constitute their nature or essence. According to him, being can be symbol through an immanent dialectic of emanation and return,
which he calls "self-consummation" (*Selbstvollzug*), by which being constitutes its own unity.[94] The notion of self-consummation is that the being mediates itself, or signifies its own reality, by its self-constituted medium (immediate mediation).[95] According to this notion, being is the signified reality
and the medium of signification at the same time.[96] There is a double movement of "emanation" and "return" that structures self-expression, which is
constitutive of being.[97] In the movement of emanation, the being moves or
emanates from itself to its own "other," and constitutes itself as a concrete
reality by signifying as its own other, rendering itself as a mediating sign.[98]
In the movement of return, the being returns to itself its self-signifying other.
It is this return that realizes the being, and brings the being to perfection and
the consummation of its essence.[99] This "other," that being emanates from
itself, signifies the being that it possesses, because it intrinsically belongs to
the unity of being. Therefore, in Rahner's ontology of symbol, there exists a
unity and distinction between the signified reality (symbolic reality) and its

93. Rahner, "The Theology of the Symbol," 234.
94. Rahner's metaphysics of symbol on which he bases his systematic theology, especially
sacramental theology, has been derived from the basic insight that "phenomena derive from
noumenon which they manifest." This ontological dialectic was basically originated in Neo-
Thomism and was developed by Joseph Maréchal and Maurice Blondel. Rahner extends to it
his understanding of Being as "real-symbolic" constituted by the dialectic of emanation and
return. For an extensive reading of this influence, see Fields, "Metaphysics of Symbol," 283-
287; Stephen Fields, "Blondel's L'action (1893) and Neo-Thomism's Metaphysics of Symbol," *Philosophy & Theology* 8 (1993): 25-31.
95. Fields, *Being as Symbol*, 288; L. Silos, "A Note on the Notion of 'Selbstvollzug' in
Karl Rahner," *Philippine Studies* 13 (1965): 467.
96. Fields, "Blondel's L'action (1893)," 32.
97. Rahner, "The Theology of the Symbol," 229, 233.
98. Karl Rahner, *Foundations of Christian Faith: An Introduction to the Idea of Christianity*, trans. William V. Dych (New York: Crossroad, 1978), 120-122.
99. Rahner, "The Theology of the Symbol," 234.

medium. However, the identity is more original than difference, because the symbol is constitutive of the reality by manifesting itself.[100]

The emanation and return that concerns being is a dynamic, intrinsic and reciprocal causality, true to finite substances and infinite being.[101] It is called "dynamic," because it emanates its own other and returns to it. It is intrinsic, because it causes its own unity by rendering present its own other. It is reciprocal, because it constitutes itself by way of returning through its self-caused other. The dynamic, intrinsic and reciprocal causality of emanation and return suggests that all beings consist of three aspects, namely, "original unity," a medium or an "other," and a "perfect unity."[102]

Furthermore, every being is constituted as substance through this ontological dialectic of identity and difference. The being renders itself substantially present through the unity that exists between the accidents, the medium by which the original unity of the substance is being manifested, a unity that the accidents symbolize and cause.[103] There exists unity and plurality in a substance, but ontologically it is the unity as such, that is emerged into plurality as the media that expresses its original unity.[104] Therefore, Rahner argues that accidents constitute the essential medium by which the inner reality of a substance is being manifested. In this sense, Rahner's metaphysics of symbol implies that substance's accidents are intrinsic symbols for rendering its ontological form really present. Therefore, the accidents as visible medium are indispensable in communicating the reality that they signify. Similarly, in the sacrament, the real presence is communicated to the recipient through the indispensable mediation of the sacramental species.

3.1.2. *Sacrament as* Realsymbol

Rahner's original contribution to sacramental theology consists in interpreting sacrament as *Realsymbol*. He accomplishes this by replacing instrumental causality with symbolic causality, applying causality to the Church. However, this new understanding of the sacraments is based on his application of symbolism to the theology of the Logos and the Church.

100. *Ibid.*, 252.
101. Fields, *Being as Symbol*, 6.
102. *Ibid.*, 229.
103. Fields, " Metaphysics of Symbol," 289.
104. Rahner, "The Theology of the Symbol," 228, 232, 252.

3.1.2.1. Realsymbol *and the Theology of the Logos*

Rahner considers the theology of the Logos as the theology of symbol. He applies the notion of *Realsymbol* to explain the theology of the Logos. For him, the Christian God is an intrinsically symbolic being, because, as Trinity, God's oneness is constituted of plurality. Thus, the Trinity constitutes its own nature, its ontological unity, by expressing itself in the Incarnate Logos. God is a unity because the Father is perfectly manifested in the Son, who is His only begotten image.[105] Logos, as the word of the Father, expresses the Fa- ther in his human nature as the Incarnate Word. As he puts it, "the Logos is the 'word' of the Father, his perfect 'image', his 'imprint', his 'radiance', his self-expression."[106] Therefore, the Incarnate Logos is the "absolute symbol of God in the world," the "expressive presence" of his free, irreversible and unsurpassable grace to the world.[107] Rahner develops his theology of the Church and the sacraments on this basic concept of the Logos as the self-expression of God's offer of grace to the world.

3.1.3. Symbolic Function of the Church

Rahner's theology of the sacraments in general springs from his understanding of the Church as the fundamental or primal sacrament of the saving presence of Christ's grace. The Church, as the body of Christ, is the unique and visible sign in history exhibiting God's free offer of salvation in Christ. The Church continues the symbolic function in the world as the persisting presence of Christ in space and time, containing and manifesting the presence of God in the world as the sacrament of God. Thus, the very existence of the Church is made sacramental. However, this sacramental dimension of the Church is based on Christ, the Incarnate Word, the "primal sacrament of the word of God" (*Ursacrament*), in whom, God's irrevocable mercy was revealed.[108] The Church, as the persisting presence of the Incarnate Word in

---

105. *Ibid.*, 235-237.

106. *Ibid.*, 236. In seeing the Logos as the symbol of the Father, Rahner sees no incongruity with St. Augustine's psychological or mutual love theory of the Trinity.

107. *Ibid.*, 237.

108. Rahner, *The Church and the Sacraments*, 18. Along the line of Rahner, Schillebeeckx also understood the humanity of Jesus as the sacrament of God, but with a Trinitarian focus. He states, "The man Jesus, as the personal visible realisation of the divine grace of redemption, is *the* sacrament, the primordial sacrament, because this man, the Son of God himself, is intended by the Father to be in his humanity the only way to the actuality of redemption." Edward Schillebeeckx, *Christ the Sacrament of the Encounter with God*, trans. P. Barret and N.D. Smith (London: Sheed and Ward, 1963), 15.

space and time, continues the symbolic function in the world. In Christ, God's free offer of salvation embraces humankind, of which the Church is the unique and visible sign as his mystical body, present in history. The Church, as the enduring presence of Christ in the world, is truly the fundamental sacrament (*Grundsakrament*), the well-spring of the sacraments.[109] It is "the universal sacrament of salvation."[110] Through the mediation of the Church, particular sacraments make present the salvation offered in Christ until the end of time.

According to Rahner, the efficaciousness of the sacraments cannot be understood as an efficacy as a matter of course, in terms of a philosophical concept of a transient efficient cause. The nexus between the sign and grace cannot be explained in terms of causality. He does not reject the importance of signs: "God wills the grace as dependent on the sign, but does not will this grace because of that sign ... Sign is the cause of grace, not of God's decision physically to confer grace." Therefore, he claims that a better explanation can be given through the concept of *Realsymbol*. As he asserts, when one says that sacraments as signs cause grace, it implies that signs are of causation by symbols, which means that the signs, by their very nature, are a symbol or, in other words, "natural symbols" or "intrinsically real symbols."[111] Sacramental signs, as real symbols, are both tangible and invisible, which possess the capacity to manifest or make something present. There is an intrinsic relationship between the actual manifestation and that which is bodying forth this manifestation even though they are really distinct. To put it differently, a symbol can really be distinct from what it symbolises and, at the same time, be an intrinsic or essential part of it. Thus, symbols manifest something other than what they are, at the same time, manifesting themselves, presenting their own existence and identity.[112] As Rahner says,

109. Rahner, *The Church and the Sacraments*, 18.

110. *Lumen Gentium*, no. 48. A few parallel expressions are, "a living instrument of salvation" (no. 8), "the visible sacrament of this saving unity" (no. 9), "the tremendous sacrament" (*Sacrosacntum Concilium*, no. 5.) and "the sacrament of unity" (no. 26). We see this concept already in the vocabulary of the Church. The *Missale Romanum* of Pius V refers to the Church as the "*sacramentum* of salvation for the world" as we see in the *Oratio* after the fifth reading of the Liturgy of Holy Saturday.

111. Rahner, *The Church and the Sacraments*, 37.

112. *Ibid.*, 38. Rahner's notion of real-symbolism marks a development in the notion of symbolic reality that is dominant in the Eucharistic doctrine of Aquinas. Rahner retrieves the seminal notion of intrinsic symbolism in Thomism (empirical media can constitute an essentially supra-sensuous reality) and interprets it in the light of his metaphysics of symbol. Rahner also admits that Aquinas understood the Eucharist to be intrinsically symbolic. According

Reality and its appearance in the flesh are forever one in Christianity, incon-fused [*sic*] and inseparable. The reality of the divine self-communication creates for itself its immediacy by constituting itself present in the symbol, which does not divide as it mediates but unites immediately, because the true symbol is united with the thing symbolized, since the latter constitutes the former as its own self-realization.[113]

Rahner employs this concept of *Realsymbol* so as to illustrate the nature of the sacramental causality in their ecclesiological origin. The Church, in her historical and visible form, is a symbol of God's grace that she makes present in space and time.[114] Therefore, it is in the Church that sacraments, in and through the natural signs, can confer infallibly the divine life of grace. Sa-cramental signs can be truly *opus operatum*, and assure and guarantee grace only when they are conferred as the signs of the Church as such.[115] As Rah-ner puts it,

> … this symbol of the grace of God (Church) really contains what it signifies; that is, the primary sacrament of the grace of God, which does not merely de-signate, but really possesses what was brought definitively into the world by Christ: the irrevocable, eschatological grace of God which conquers trium-phantly the guilt of man. The Church as indefectible, as [the] Church of infal-lible truth and as [the] Church of the sacraments, as *opus operatum* and as in-destructibly holy as a whole, even in the subjective grace of men – by which it is not merely object, but even [a] motive of faith – really constitutes the full symbol of the fact that Christ has remained there as triumphant mercy.[116]

This efficacy is that of the intrinsic symbol; Christ acts through the Church in the life of the individual through the sacramental signs realizing the gift of

to him the theory of symbol that he develops is perfectly Thomistic, because in Aquinas' Eucharistic theory the bread and wine that remains even after transubstantiation constitute the outward sign through which the reality of the sacrament is being manifested. See Rahner, "The Theology of the Symbol," 233-234. Fields argues that Rahner might have been familiar with Billot's theory of transubstantiation as conversion, since Billot's idea was dominant in theo-logical textbooks until Vatican II. Therefore, Fields opines that Billot's theory influenced Rahner's metaphysical explanation of the relationship between the species and the real pres-ence although Rahner himself does not give any indication of this assumption. However, Rahner's contribution is also distinct from the analysis of Billot, because he tried to interpret the above-mentioned Thomistic notion of the relation between the empirical and the supra-sensuous in transubstantiation and *res et sacramentum*. See Fields, " Metaphysics of Symbol," 289-290.

    113. Rahner, "The Theology of the Symbol," 252.
    114. Rahner, *The Church and the Sacraments*, 39.
    115. *Ibid.*, 32.
    116. Rahner, "The Theology of the Symbol," 241.

grace in the sacrament.[117] Through the mediation of the Church, particular sacraments make present the salvation offered in Christ till the end of time.

Moreover, the sacraments, being the real presence of God's grace, make concrete and actual for the individual the symbolic reality of the Church as the primary sacrament.[118] This presence of grace is nothing other than the actuality of the Church as the irrevocable and visible manifestation of God's grace.[119] The relationship between the Church as the sign of grace in space and time, and the grace itself, is extended in relationship between the signs and the grace conferred. Sacramental signs cause grace by making sacraments that signify the sanctification that is brought forth.[120] The Church realizes her essence as the presence of grace by the manifestation of grace in the sacraments that effect sanctification. The Church is the fundamental sacrament, because she effects what she signifies. Rahner distinguishes himself from Aquinas, placing the efficaciousness of the sacraments on the salvific presence of God in history, which the Church signifies, not on natural signs. Rahner's approach of shifting the efficacy of the sacraments from instrumental causality to symbolic causality, ascribing causality to the Church, and thereby establishing an essential link between the sacramental symbols and the reality of the sacraments, seems to correct the double flaws attributed by him to Aquinas.

3.1.4. Beyond Rahner

As we have already seen, Rahner's main achievement consists in making a shift in the understanding of sacraments in general, specifically, that of the efficacy of the sacraments from the mechanical and productionist scheme of causality to symbolic causality. His point of departure was the understanding of Jesus, in his humanity, as the primordial sacrament and the Church as the foundational sacrament. The innovativeness of the approach is considered to be the understanding of sacramentality as intrinsic to the Church with an incarnational base, and locating the individual sacraments with a foundational base in the Church, in contrast to an institutional base in Jesus based on the

---

117. Rahner, *The Church and the Sacraments*, 39.

118. Rahner, "The Theology of the Symbol," 241.

119. It is in this sense that the sacraments can be described as "sacred signs of God's grace." Therefore, the axiom remains valid for Rahner, *Sacramenta efficiunt quod significant et significant quod efficiunt*. See Rahner, *The Church and the Sacraments*, 39.

120. *Ibid.*, 40.

New Testament.[121] The Rahnerian approach is significant in the sense that it
established an essential link between the Church and the sacraments, which
is missing in the scholastic theology of the sacraments. By assigning a primordial basis to the incarnation and a foundational basis to the Church in the
understanding of the sacraments, Rahner gave impetus to the sacramental
thinking of the late twentieth and early twenty-first centuries. Nevertheless,
Rahner's approach to sacramental efficacy has its own shortcomings, as we
will see now.

Modern Catholic theology, particularly of the eighteenth and nineteenth
centuries, is characterised by an attempt to attend to the challenges of modern
philosophy initiated by René Descartes and Immanuel Kant. The result has
generally been called "the turn to the subject," which may be understood as a
"focus on human subjectivity and its role within human knowledge and religious belief."[122] The turn to the subject was an important movement in addressing the challenges of modernity by taking human subjectivity more seriously. This approach raised serious challenges to the so-called "objectivity"
of scholastic theology. Rahner also attempted to incorporate the subjective
approach in his theology.[123] He develops this approach based on the analysis
of human experience of knowledge and freedom as an experience of an "absolute and limitless transcendentality."[124] However, his approach remains
basically qualified as transcendental Thomism. Although Rahner lays so
much emphasis on the incarnation, he is basically Thomistic. Thus, Osborne
observes, some of the charges that can be levelled against Aquinas can also
be raised against Rahner.[125] According to Osborne, even when we relate sacramentality to the incarnation and the individual sacraments to the sacramentality of the Church, it is equally important to observe the language we
employ in order to speak of incarnation and the Church. There is a danger of
presenting the incarnation and the Church in an epiphenomenal or onto-
theological way. Therefore, Osborne says that we must do more than just

121. Osborne, *Sacraments in a Postmodern World*, 47.

122. Fiorenza, "Systematic Theology," 35.

123. In spite of being attentive to the thought of modernity, Rahner was also open to the
developments of late modernity. For instance, Karl Rahner's understanding of sacrament and
symbol was strongly influenced by Heidegger.

124. Karl Rahner, "Reflections on Methodology in Theology," in *Theological Investigations* (New York: Crossroad, 1974), 11: 94. For a detailed explanation of Rahner's method,
see Rahner, *Foundations*, 208-212. For a concise presentation, see Fiorenza, "Systematic
Theology," 39-40.

125. Osborne, *Sacraments in a Postmodern World*, 48.

relate the sacraments to the Church as the foundational sacrament and Jesus as the primordial sacrament.

The "Pneumatological weakness" which has been levelled against scholastic sacramental theology can also be raised against Rahner's sacramental thinking. Even though Rahner pays sufficient attention to highlighting the sacramentality of the Church in order to situate the sacraments on an ecclesiological basis, the sole basis of his argument is Christology, predominantly, a Logos Christology. He develops the sacramentality of the Church from the notion of Jesus as the primordial sacrament. We should keep in mind that it is the pervading presence of the Spirit, which is at the kernel of the mystery of the incarnation and the entire life and ministry of Jesus that makes Jesus the primordial sacrament. In the same way, it is the Spirit of Jesus that is bestowed on the Church that makes the Church the basic sacrament. Therefore, there is a Pneumatological thread that is missing in Rahner's sacramental approach, both in his consideration of Jesus' humanity as the primordial sacrament, and the Church as the basic sacrament.

Besides, Rahner's fidelity to Thomism and his transcendental approach as its corollary can be seen as making his thought, to a great extent, epiphenomenal or onto-theological. Although Rahner considers grace as a basic phenomenon of human experience and, as such, takes on an anthropological character, his view of human existence as supernatural existential seems to be ontologically and metaphysically formulated. Therefore, it has been argued that the anthropological approach, in particular as it is developed by Rahner, reduces religious truth to anthropological perspectives which does less justice to other perspectives.[126]

The "Copernican revolution" in sacramental theology, which was brought about by Rahner, can in no way be underestimated. His anthropological approach to theology and the understanding of the sacraments gave a new direction for succeeding generations to think about the efficacy of the sacraments in the light of anthropology, particularly in terms of subjectivity and language. Thus, in a way, contemporary theological approaches go beyond the transcendental approach, emphasising the linguistic formation of the subject. Accordingly, the human subject exists and is being formed within a world of language, tradition and a culture of meaning. It is to this aspect we turn our attention now.

---

126. Fiorenza, "Systematic Theology," 42.

4. The Symbolic Turn   4?-6?

The classical treatise of the sacraments according to the categories of "sign" and "cause" is subject to criticism today. A recent and general trend in sacramental theology is a growing appreciation for rituals and symbols. It is evidenced by numerous conferences, books, and articles dedicated to the themes of ritual and symbols ranging from the mid-nineties.[127] Efforts have been made to investigate the importance of symbols for theology in general and sacramental theology in particular. More recently, charges have been levelled against the scholastic theology of the sacraments, especially the concept of presence and sacramental efficacy informed by classical metaphysics. Consequently, attempts have been made to appropriate the insights of postmodernism into the understanding of the sacraments. We will consider this new development in contemporary sacramental theology taking Louis-Marie Chauvet and Jean-Luc Marion as representatives. But first we will glance at the postmodern critique of classical metaphysics that frames their thinking of the sacraments.

4.1. The Postmodern Critique of Metaphysical Theology

The "triumph of reason" that is so characteristic of modernity, poses great challenges against religious claims and leave little space for understanding the question of transcendence. The philosophical rationale, which tried to capture everything within the confines of reason, gave no hope for affirming or thinking about the reality of presence. However, with the advent of the

---

127. Sacramental theology during and after the time of Rahner shows different turns influenced by the developments in philosophical world. The efforts to explore the implications of symbols in the field of religion, particularly in the understanding of the sacraments may go back a half century. Notable works in this field are: David N. Power, *Unsearchable Riches: The Symbolic Nature of Liturgy* (New York: Pueblo, 1984); Rahner, "The Theology of the Symbol;" Paul Tillich, "The Meaning and Justification of Religious Symbols," in *Religious Experience and Truth: A Symposium*, ed. Sydney Hook (New York: New York University Press, 1961); David Tracy, *The Analogical Imagination* (New York: Crossroad, 1989). A considerable amount of literature has come out in the light of French reflection on symbol influenced by thinkers like Claude Lévi-Strauss, Edmond Ortigues, Immanuel Levinas, Julia Kristeva, Jaques Derrida, Jacques Lacan, Paul Ricœur and the French reception of Martin Heidegger. The influence of French thought on contemporary sacramental theology is evident in the works of Louis-Marie Chauvet, David N. Power, etc. Similarly, Jean-Luc Marion, a philosopher theologian, develops and applies phenomenology to sacramental theology. For a basic understanding of their approaches, see Chauvet, *Symbol and Sacrament*; Jean-Luc Marion, *God without Being*, trans. Thomas A. Carlson (Chicago, IL, London: 1991); Power, *Sacrament*.

postmodern age,[128] characterized by a loss of faith in reason, sacramental theology is confronted with new challenges to re-interpret/construct the understanding of the presence of transcendence, which is congenial to Christian theology. The postmodern deconstructionist tendency of faith in reason has been viewed by many as promising to re-think sacramental presence in a way different from the traditional fashion.[129]

The point of departure, for those who take this path in their understanding of sacramental presence, is the deconstruction of the metaphysics of presence which has its beginning in Heidegger's critique of metaphysics as onto-

128. The terms "postmodernity" and "postmodernism/postmodern" are frequently used interchangeably. However, there seems to be a distinction between them. "Postmodernity" is often understood as a philosophical approach that is critical of modernism. Graham Ward, "Introduction," in *The Postmodern God*, ed. Graham Ward (Oxford: Blackwell, 1997), xv-xlvii, xxiv. On the contrary, "postmodernism" refers to "certain cultural conditions pertaining to developed countries in the 1970s and 1980s," especially the movements in French philosophy known as post structuralism, which is a critical reaction not only to the modern, but also to the entire age-old metaphysical system. Robyn Horner, *Jean-Luc Marion: A Theological Introduction* (Aldershot, UK, Burlington, VT: Ashgate Publishing Company, 2005), 15; Ward, "Introduction," xv-xlvii, xxiv. See also Osborne, *Sacraments in a Postmodern World*, 2. In this sense "postmodernity" is understood as a period that follows "modernity," but "postmodernism" can have a reference to "modernism" in a historical sense as well. Therefore, a distinction in the strict sense seems to be simplistic. "Postmodernism" is also considered as a response to modernist movements in art, literature, and architecture. Lawrence Cahoone, "Introduction," in *From Modernism to Postmodernism: An Anthology* (Malden, MA: Blackwell, 1996), 1-23, 3. He would also understand postmodern as referring to the aesthetic responses as well as to the developments in philosophising. So, in general, he understands the period of "postmodernity" as a kind of culmination of "postmodern sensibilities." Horner, *Jean-Luc Marion: A Theological Introduction*, 15. Some authors like Marion identify a radical discontinuity between the "modernity" and "postmodernity." Marion, *God without Being*, xx. On the contrary Jean François Lyotard considers "postmodenism" as not being opposed to "modernism," but the former inhabits the latter in spite of their radical difference. For him "postmodernity" and "postmodern" are without any reference to a historical period, but "postmodernism" denotes a progress in linear fashion in history. Jean François Lyotard, *The Postmodern Explained*, trans. Don Barry *et al.* (Minneapolis, MN: University of Minnesota Press, 1993), 227. See also Horner, *Jean-Luc Marion: A Theological Introduction*, 16. So it becomes clear that there is no uncontroversial way of understanding these three terms, because of an apparent continuity and discontinuity that exists between the sensibilities of modern and postmodern. In our consideration, however, we understand postmodern, postmodernity and postmodernism in a general sense as a collection of philosophical concerns, especially as discussed in the context of poststructuralism.

129. Osborne prefers to qualify the changes that are taking place in the beginning of the third millennium as a "revolution" rather than "renewal" considering the multitude of aspects that dominate contemporary sacramental theology. Osborne, *Sacraments in a Postmodern World*, 40.

theology.[130] According to Heidegger, metaphysic's search for a unifying principle that grounds beings, fails to consider "what is present in its presence," and only "represents it in terms of its ground as something grounded."[131] In other words, metaphysics is charged with the approach of explaining phenomena in terms of causality. As Mitchell Nathan observes, phenomena are perceived as given, but not as produced by a causal "being." Therefore, it follows that the proper nature of being is "givenness," not of "being."[132] However, a metaphysical approach ignores the "phenomenality of beings" and the "mode of presencing of beings" as "givenness."[133] If phenomena are given, there must be a "Given" and the "Giver" that saturate intuition and shatter all our preconceived ideas of Giver.[134] Thus, there arises the dualistic understanding of reality as "ground/grounded, source of presence/what is present," that, in turn, fails to recognize what Heidegger calls the "ontological difference," which simultaneously connects Being and beings and holds them apart.[135]

According to Heidegger, the God of onto-theology, who is *causa sui*, is incompatible with the God of the Bible. He is different from the God of Ab-

---

130. The critique of metaphysics as onto-theology is ascribed to Martin Heidegger. Reiner Schürmann, *Heidegger on Being and Acting: From Principles to Anarchy* (Bloomington, IN: Indiana University Press, 1987), Introduction; Heidegger's critique of onto-theology is a landmark in the postmodern attempt to overcome metaphysics. See Anthony J. Godzieba, "Ontotheology to Excess: Imagining God without Being," *Theological Studies* 56 (1995): 5. However, the Thomistic articulation of the relationship between Being in itself and the being of finite beings is subject to questioning since Cartesian scepticism and the Kantian critique of the primacy of reason. Since Husserl, the attempt to liberate God from Being was transferred from reason to phenomenology, which assumes its present manifestation in the postmodern attempts to overcome onto-theology. A few important works that mark these shifts are: Martin Heidegger, *Identity and Difference*, trans. Joan Stambaugh (Chicago, IL: Chicago University Press, 2002); Martin Heidegger, *Being and Time*, trans. John Macquarrie and Edward Robinson (Oxford: Blackwell, 2004); Edmund Husserl, *Phenomenology and the Crisis of Philosophy* (New York: Harper Torch Books, 1965); Immanuel Kant, *Critique of Pure Reason* (London: Macmillian, 1933). *Being and Time* is a translation of *Sein und Zeit* which was originally published in 1927 in the *Yearbook for Philosophy and Phenomenological Research* (vol. 8). The standard German edition is published by Max Niemeyer: Martin Heidegger, S*ein Und Zeit* (Tübingen: Niemeyer, 1986).

131. Martin Heidegger, "The End of Philosophy and the Task of Thinking," in *On Time and Being* (New York: Harper and Row, 1972), 56.

132. Nathan D. Mitchell, "Mystery and Manners: Eucharist in Post-Modern Theology," *Worship* 79 (2005): 135.

133. Godzieba, "Ontotheology to Excess," 7.

134. Mitchell, " Mystery and Manners," 135.

135. Godzieba, "Ontotheology to Excess," 7.

raham, Isaac and Jacob, who entered the scene, saying, "I have observed the misery of my people who are in Egypt; I have heard the cry on account of their taskmasters. Indeed, I know their sufferings, and I have come down to deliver them" (Ex 3:7-8). The metaphysical language of *causa sui*, with its *how*, turned the *what* of the Judeo-Christian God of the Bible into the God of philosophy.[136] Onto-theology concerns the *how* rather than the *what* of speaking of God. According to Heidegger, we "can neither pray nor sacrifice to this god" of philosophy.[137] Onto-theology consists, not merely in affirming God as creator, the Highest Being, or as the ultimate reference of all beings. Therefore, Heidegger's critique is not against the God of the Bible or the Koran or any theistic discourse, but the entire metaphysical project that renders the whole of reality intelligible to human understanding and refuses to respect the limit of knowledge. In other words, what is subject to Heidegger's critique is a philosophy (metaphysics) that is onto-theologically constituted, a philosophical tradition that renders the whole of reality intelligible to reason and that conceives of God as the highest being to this end.[138] Consequently, one even tends to assume that metaphysics, constituted as onto-theology, implies that God exists only in so far as the principle of reason grasps Him. This calculative and representational way of thinking runs the risk of subjecting God to our disposal.

Heidegger distinguishes theology as an ontic science and philosophy as an ontological science. Faith and thought constitute themselves independent of each other and exclude each other, so much so, that there is no passage between them.[139] He considers faith as the Alpha and Omega of theology, and therefore, theology can find its own motivation only through faith.[140] Thus Heidegger's critique is an invitation and challenge to let theology stand by itself, freeing God from the Hellenistic language of speaking about Him. What Heidegger attempts is a deconstruction of the tendencies of philosophy and theology which fall into onto-theological discourse. Instead he recommends phenomenology as a new way of doing theology. In the theologies of Paul, Augustine and Luther, Heidegger observes a positive trend toward remaining faithful to biblical tradition. They challenge the philosophical tradition which attempted to flee from factical life, which is the concrete field of

136. Merold Westphal, *Overcoming Onto-theology: Toward a Postmodern Christian Faith* (New York: Fordham University Press, 2001), 13.

137. Heidegger, *Identity and Difference*, 2.

138. Westphal, *Overcoming Onto-theology*, 30.

139. Chauvet, *Symbol and Sacrament*, 63.

140. Westphal, *Overcoming Onto-theology*, 30-31.

pure theology. Therefore, phenomenology, "a-theistic philosophy" enables theology to remain faithful to the biblical tradition, by freeing itself from the clutches of metaphysical theology.[141]

Heidegger's acceptance in the Western world resulted in an abandoning of the 'onto' aspect of metaphysics and an acceptance of postmodern thinking. Metaphysical theology had to establish itself, having lost its own grounds. As Osborne expresses it,

> this "onto-" aspect of the correlation has been seriously questioned, and indeed a new paradigm has been established in the West so that Westerners find themselves at this threshold to the third millennium wondering if the "onto-" aspect of their onto-theology has any currency left.[142]

Postmodern theologians have undertaken the challenge of freeing theology from the clutches of metaphysics. According to postmodern theologians the crucial problem of metaphysics is that, generally, it guarantees finality, but yields itself to limitation.[143] The metaphysical way of speaking about God, as *causa sui*, itself is challenged by postmodernists. They challenge the claim of metaphysics that the notion of God, as *causa principalis* or *causa sui*, is intelligible through *effects*.[144] The new paradigm that they propose is to think of God as devoid of the parameters of a metaphysical Being as Marion has done in his *God Without Being*.[145] Thus postmodern theology tries to explain transcendence, absoluteness, presence, and so on, by dissociating God from Being, as was advocated by Heidegger.[146] A substantial change in the pattern

---

141. *Ibid.*, 46.

142. Osborne, *Sacraments in a Postmodern World*, 49.

143. Mitchell, " Mystery and Manners," 135.

144. *Ibid.*

145. In the Catholic tradition, Walter Kasper has taken a similar position. See Walter Kasper, *The God of Jesus Christ*, trans. Matthew J. O'Connell (New York: Crossroad, 1986). Recently, some have taken a position close to that of Marion and Kasper, but remain faithful to the metaphysical tradition. See, for example, W. Noris Clarke, *The Philosophical Approach to God: A Neo-Thomist Perspective*, ed. William E. Ray (Winston-Salem: Wake Forest University, 1979); William J. Hill, *Search for the Absent God: Tradition and Modernity in Religious Understanding*, ed. Mary Catherine Hilkert (New York: Crossroad, 1992); Ghislain Lafont, *God, Time, and Being*, trans. Leonard Maluf (Petersham, MA: Saint Bede, 1992); Johannes B. Lotz, *Martin Heidegger und Thomas von Aquin: Mensch-Zeit-Sein* (Pfullingen: Günther Neske, 1975); Johannes B. Lotz, *Vom Sein zum Heiligen: Metaphysisches Denken nach Heidegger* (Frankfurt am Main: Joseph Knecht, 1990).

146. Heidegger believed that transcendence and absoluteness can be better explained dissociating God from Being. John Martis, "Thomistic *Esse* – Idol or Icon? Jean-Luc Marion's God Without Being," *Pacifica* (1996): 55.

of thought as such, has come with the advent of postmodern thinking. This can be easily misinterpreted or misunderstood as the rejection of the idea of transcendence, or an aversion of everything that is designated as religious, rather it is a reversal in our approach to reality, transcendence, and God-thought. In other words, it is employing a new language, suitable to contemporary culture and climate that characterizes postmodernity.

In the twenty-first century, we find ourselves in a culture and social scenario which the world is seen as no longer religious. The contemporary phenomenon that characterises postmodernity has been qualified by Max Weber as the "disenchantment of the world." By this he means the 'high-tech' society's peculiar way of being in the world, having no self-evident religious reference.[147] In this century, Christianity finds itself in an increasingly difficult situation to prove the meaning and credibility of its confessions and practices for the majority of the society. As Christians, we cannot understand ourselves as immune from this corrosion of theistic meanings which are deeply embodied in contemporary society or culture. However, Christianity continues to be the frame of reference which gives meaning and orientation to their life and practices. There is an erosion of credibility of any religious 'grand narrative'. Apart from convinced believers, there are also many others who attend church out of their sense of obligation or a habit. There are also others who make religion a point of reference in the wake of catastrophe or important phases of life like marriage, funerals, etc. Nevertheless, there are those who continue to be communities of people who gather on Sundays with the expectation that religious meaning can help them to shape the meaning of the week's life lying before them. In spite of falling numbers, aging membership, and receding budgets, Churches continue to exist, giving meaning to a minority. There are also many who once may have attended worship as they were young and who now say to themselves that such practices are meaningless. Theologians are challenged with the fact of addressing these people of multiple backgrounds to explain the meaning of the religious practices. The question pertaining to our purview is how we might 'make sense' or 'draw sense' from the sacraments and ritual enactments of faith in Christian worship.

147. Max Weber, "Religious Rejections of the World and Their Directions," in *From Max Weber: Essays in Sociology*, ed. H.H. Gerth and C.W. Mills (London: Routledge and Kegan Paul, 1974), 139, 155, 350-351, 357; Max Weber, *Economy and Society: An Outline of Interpretative Sociology* (Berkeley, CA: University of California Press, 1978), 506. See also Marcel Gauchet, *The Disenchantment of the World: A Political History of Religion*, trans. Oscar Burge (Princeton, NJ: Princeton University Press, 1999).

As Osborne observes, a sacramental theology presented in an onto-theological form, reminiscent of the scholastic period, will be meaningless to contemporary generations.[148] It is in this background that the demand of re- flecting on the sacraments, in a way other than through the categories of metaphysics, assumes relevance. Accordingly, postmodern sacramental theology seems to have made progress in benefiting from phenomenology as a way of thinking about sacramental presence, and remaining faithful to the biblical tradition and revelation without falling into the clutches of metaphysics.

4.2. *Postmodernism and Sacramental Theology*

With regard to sacramental theology, the influence of postmodernism does not find expression in the disavowal of sacramental thinking as such, as though there is no more relevance for reflecting on the sacramental and liturgical celebrations of the Church. Apart from that, postmodern sacramental theology is characterized by a totally different perspective, a reversed look at the sacraments in view of exploring ways of talking or interpreting, avoiding grand narratives. It detaches itself from the classical, metaphysical approach of defining, conceptualising, systematizing, and classifying, as if everything concerning sacramental presence or grace is within the reach of the perceiving subject. Thus, there is radical change in the way of talking, which expresses itself in the use of vocabulary different from classical sacramental theology, like, "exchange," "mediation," "givenness," "gift," "excess," "presence," "absence," etc. As such, the attempt is to deconstruct the metaphysical concept of presence, which confines God within the limits of categories informed by classical metaphysics, freeing God from naming as essence, because God is beyond all names.[149] Postmodern theologians argue that the starting point for sacramental theology should be located at the core of the Christian message, the mystery of Christ, as manifested by revelation itself, rather than being based on the notion of the metaphysics of presence and causality.[150] Now, we may briefly consider the sacramental theologies of Chauvet and Marion, with respect to the developments in systematic theology, particularly thinking of sacraments within the framework of a sound Tri-

---

148. Osborne, *Sacraments in a Postmodern World*, 49.

149. Jean-Luc Marion, *In Excesss: Studies of Saturated Phenomena*, trans. Robyn Horner and Vincent Berraud (New York: Fordham University Press, 2002), 156.

150. Mitchell, " Mystery and Manners," 140.

nitarian theology, duly accommodating the role of Christ and the Holy Spi-rit.[151]

4.2.1. Sacramental Re-interpretation of Louis-Marie Chauvet

Chauvet tries to develop a new understanding of the sacraments, by bringing in the notion of symbolic mediation.[152] He develops the notion of symbolic mediation through an extensive study of the function of language and symbols from phenomenological, linguistic and anthropological perspectives.

Chauvet begins by questioning the scholastic presupposition of the existence of an independent subject who is in possession of a direct access to reality, and the instrumental concept of language as the expression of thought. In this approach, what is at stake, is the precedence of language and the linguistic formation of consciousness.[153] This way of approaching reality fails to take into account the world in which we find ourselves, and of which we are a part, and results in the reduction of reality within the categories of thought.[154] In contrast to the instrumental understanding of language, Chauvet develops a non-instrumental view, whereby language is understood as having the function of bringing something into presence, rather than being the expression or representation of that which is already there.[155] In this way, language is not an instrument, but mediation, as it mediates the subject's coming into presence and constitutes human experience by preceding it. Therefore, the understanding of a preexisting subject and the claim toward an objective reality becomes subject to criticism.

Along these lines, Chauvet also develops a non-instrumental understanding of the body. This understanding rejects the notion of the body as the seat

---

151. The Trinitarian grounding of the sacraments has been emphasised in the works of Theodor Schneider, Lothar Lies and Edward J. Kilmartin. See Edward J. Kilmartin, *Christian Liturgy: Theology and Practice* (Kansas City, MO: Sheed & Ward, 1988); Lothar Lies, *Sakramententheologie: Eine Personale Sicht* (Graz: Styria, 1990); Theodor Schneider, *Zeichen der Nähe Gottes: Grundriss der Sakramententheologie* (Mainz: Matthias-Grünewald, 1987).

152. The spectrum of Chauvet's sacramental theology is not limited to the question of the efficacy of the sacraments or the "how" of the sacraments as something objective. Rather, as he claims at the outset, he develops a "fundamental theology of sacramentality" that embraces the whole of Christian existence and living. See Chauvet, *Symbol and Sacrament*, 1. However, our treatment of Chauvet will be limited to understanding how he interprets the efficacy of the sacraments in a way different from the scholastics.

153. *Ibid.*, 29-36; Vincent J. Miller, "An Abyss at the Heart of Mediation: Louis-Marie Chauvet's Fundamental Theology of Sacramentality," *Horizons* 24 (1997): 232.

154. *Ibid.*, 232.

155. Chauvet, *Symbol and Sacrament*, 55-56.

of the soul that makes use of the body to speak. Contrary to this view, Chauvet understands corporeality as the basis of human existence. As he puts it, "humans do not ex-sist except as *corporality* whose concrete place is always their *own bodies*. Corporality is the body's very speech."[156] Thus, he considers corporeality as constitutive of, and intrinsic to, existence. It is through corporeality that subjects become present to each other. Individual bodies differ from each other by the fact that they are socially and culturally constituted, and therefore, they carry unique histories of tradition, which determine their identity.[157] Following Heidegger, Chauvet argues that the selfhood of subjects, as corporeality, is formed by the subject's "*being-in-the world*" (*in der Welt sein*), the "being-with" (*Mit-sein*), and "historicity."[158] For Heidegger, "*being-in-the world*" is essentially "*being-in-the-world-with*."[159] This primordial mode of being, "*being-in-the world*," places being "outside itself" and, at the same time, "next to each other."[160] This primordial mode of beings as corporeal, in proximity to one another, forms the foundation upon which Chauvet develops the understanding of the body as the "arch-symbol" in the order of symbols.[161] It is through the mediation of the body that a subject becomes present to other subjects, a presence which is also coincided by an absence.[162]

Chauvet applies the symbolic function of language and body to develop an understanding of the sacraments as "effective symbolic expressions." Accordingly, he tries to understand grace from the perspective of the symbolic efficacy of ritual language acts. He attempts to free the understanding of grace, which in fact, is 'non-value' and 'immeasurable', from the constraints of onto-theology, especially from the scholastic category of instrumental cause.[163] In order to enunciate the reality of sacramental grace, Chauvet ad-

---

156. *Ibid.*, 146.

157. *Ibid.*, 150.

158. *Ibid.*, 150; Martin Heidegger, *Being and Time*, 85.

159. *Ibid.*, 150-151.

160. *Ibid.*, 85.

161. Chauvet, *Symbol and Sacrament*, 111, 151. Hans Urs von Balthasar, understands the patristic and Johannine notion of the institution of the sacraments with reference to the symbol of water and blood from the side of Christ as the bodily aspect of the Spirit that realises a relationship between Christ and the Church in the manner of Intra-Trinitarian relationship. See Balthasar, *Glory of the Lord*, 241.

162. Miller, "An Abyss at the Heart of Mediation," 233.

163. Chauvet criticizes the scholastic use of the "productionist scheme" in explaining sacramental grace, which is "no-thing," or "non-value," reducing grace to object or value. See Chauvet, *Symbol and Sacrament*, 7. He illustrates grace as "non-value" and "no-thing" using the imagery of manna (Ex 16:9-21). See *ibid.*, 44-45.

vocates the modality of symbolic exchange, rather than that of causality. He
conceives the process of symbolic exchange that existed in traditional societies as telling in understanding the "marvelous exchange" that takes place
between God and humankind in the sacraments, which is generally referred
to as "grace." He opines that, in traditional religions, the performance of
certain rites was believed to have produced an empirical efficacy, through the
mediation of symbolic efficacy, by placing the members in a network of relationship with one another and their socio-cultural world. According to the
scheme of symbolic exchange, the gift that is exchanged between two persons is something beyond monetary or material value. The gift is more than
what is given, because what is given is actually a part of the giver. According
to Chauvet, this mode of exchange, which is outside the order of values or
business exchange, brings the subject into being in relation to other subjects.[164] Thus, in symbolic exchange, the gift symbolises the presence of one
to the other, and at the same time, their absence to each other. In the symbolic order things are more than they are in themselves. Hence, what is actually
exchanged are the subjects themselves. Through the exchange of the gift, the
subject enters into a relationship of alliance, or renews its relationships, and
reveals their identity, placing themselves, as well as others, in their proper
place.[165] Christian rites of the sacraments, which are in the order of non-value
as effective symbols, place the believers in a new relationship, a horizontal
and vertical one, which is designated by the term "grace."[166] According to the
symbolic order, grace is understood as being "mediated" and not "produced,"
as in the instrumental mode of causality in the sacraments. Sacraments understood in the symbolic order are non-instrumental, in the sense that they
are inseparable from what is revealed in the sacraments.[167]

   According to Chauvet, sacramental efficacy, which has been traditionally
designated as "grace," cannot be explained according to the metaphysical
scheme of cause and effect. Instead, he explains the efficacy of the sacrament
according to the "symbolic scheme of communication," through language
and symbols. He explains the sacraments as "expressive" mediations of the
Church and the believer.[168] He bases his arguments on the efficacy of lan-

---

164. *Ibid.*, 100.
165. *Ibid.*, 106-107.
166. *Ibid.*, 425.
167. *Ibid.*, 431.
168. Chauvet develops his position by carefully examining the defects of three dominant
sacramental models present in post-Reformation sacramental theology. He identifies them as
objectivist model, with its accent on the production of grace and objective efficacy of sacra-

guage and symbols through which the subjects come into being in a network of relations within a common "world" of meaning.[169] He considers sacramental efficacy as "symbolic efficacy." In this regard, it is important to examine to what extent Chauvet incorporates Pneumatology in his understanding of sacramental efficacy.

4.2.1.1. Sacramental Efficacy and the Role of the Holy Spirit

As we have pointed out, postmodern sacramental theology attempts to free the sacraments from the confines of classical sacramental theology. Understanding sacramental presence, through the category of language and symbols, helps to overcome the problems of a productionist and instrumentalist way of understanding sacramental efficacy and grace. However, an approach to the sacramental efficacy, solely based on the efficacy of language and symbols, seems to be minimalist and simplistic. The divine realities that sacraments make present are not something that human beings, in their capacity can actualise, even though they are represented by rituals and symbols. Therefore, it is important to understand the action of God, particularly, the activity of the Holy Spirit in realizing the sacraments, something which postmodern theologians are well aware of.

4.2.1.2. Pneumatology and Chauvet

Chauvet is aware of the weakness of the scholastic theology of the sacraments that has its point of departure in Christology, particularly with regard to the hypostatic union, which in turn marginalizes the role of the Holy Spirit. He is convinced of the importance of Pneumatology in developing a foundational theology of the sacraments, and believes that the starting point must be the *Pasch of Christ.* rather than the hypostatic union. According to Chauvet, the understanding of

> ... sacraments should take its starting point, not from the hypostatic union as the Scholastic tradition proceeded, but from the *Pasch of Christ* taken in its

---

mental signs *ex opere operato*; the subjectivist model, in part as a reaction to the objectivist model, which considers sacraments as the "instrument of transmission" of grace, already received by the faithful; and the middle way of the Vatican II model, as a corrective to the objective model, which considers sacraments as operative expression (means or cause) of sanctification, placing God as the operating subject. Louis-Marie Chauvet, *The Sacraments: The Word of God at the Mercy of the Body* (Collegeville, MN: Liturgical Press, 2001), xiii-xxv; Chauvet, *Symbol and Sacrament*, 410-424.

   169. *Ibid.*, 140.

full scope, that is, from his death (and thus also from his concrete life, without which his death cannot be understood theologically as "death for us") and re-surrection, which includes the gift of the Spirit at Pentecost from which the visible Church was born, and the parousia.[170]

This implies, for Chauvet, that after Easter, any thinking about God must begin from the paschal mystery of Christ, in which the resurrection plays a central role, together with the work of the Holy Spirit. As he understands it, Easter faith is the faith and recognition of the crucified and resurrected One. In contrast to the hypostatic union, Chauvet's point of departure for a founda-tional theology of sacraments is based on the paschal mystery of Christ, which finds its summit in the resurrection, ascension, and Pentecost. There is an all-encompassing presence of the Holy Spirit who is at work in all these events. As he expresses it,

> it is the Spirit who makes it possible, in Jesus, for God to efface God's very self "inside" humanity; it is the Spirit – at work in cross, resurrection, Ascen-sion, and Pentecost – who makes it possible for God to take on an "eschato-logical body" in humanity and so to be present (*gift*) among us forever.[171]

According to Chauvet, the centrality of the Pasch is attested to, by the litur-gical tradition of the nascent Church. As he points out, the Church's liturgic-al tradition from the early centuries suggests that the starting point for the theology of the sacraments must locate itself in the Pasch of Christ in its to-tality, rather than centering on the hypostatic union. The Church's liturgical tradition leads us back to the central event of Christianity: The resurrection of Jesus, the Crucified. The origin of the liturgical tradition and the earliest redaction (*kerygma*) starts in this core event of the passion and proceeds from faith in the resurrection (Acts 3:13-15). According to Chauvet, in the manner of the gospels, interpreting the incarnation, starting from the resurrection, duly takes into account the historical "*for*" of the paschal mystery. As he says, "his [Jesus'] dying-for cannot be understood except as the expression of his living-for..."[172] During the first three centuries, the paschal mystery of Christ was celebrated as a single reality.[173] The paschal mystery of Christ – the death, resurrection, glorification, giving of the Spirit and the parousia – in its totality, was first celebrated on each Sunday. The unity of the mystery was

170. *Ibid.*, 450.
171. *Ibid.*, 536; Mitchell, " Mystery and Manners," 146.
172. Chauvet, *Symbol and Sacrament*, 488.
173. *Ibid.*, 484.

fragmented only after the fourth century through the liturgical year. For Chauvet, to start from the Pasch means,

> ... to locate the sacraments within the dynamic of a history, that of a Church born, in its historic visibility, from the gift of the Spirit at Pentecost and always in the process of becoming the body of Christ all through history. To start from the Pasch is consequently to be obliged to build sacramental theology not only on *Christological* but also on the *pneumatological* principle.[174]

Chauvet seems to be convinced that the Holy Spirit has a definitive role as far as the efficacy of the sacrament is concerned. This is obvious from how he integrates the Christological and Pneumatological dimensions in his elucidation of the Eucharist. Accordingly, the Christological dimension of the sacraments has to be balanced by the Pneumatological aspect. The Church's celebration of the memorial of Jesus becomes sacramental memory, solely by the involvement of Christ in the historical "today" of the believers, which is made possible by the Holy Spirit.[175] The Spirit brings into historical presence the past relating it to the future. "In order for the past of what is commemorated in the narrative of the institution (of the Eucharist) to be sacramentally given [to] us in the present and to open a future for us, the Spirit must bring it to the memory of the Church."[176] Theologians such as von Balthasar, Kilmartin and so on held the same notion of Pneumatology when speaking about the efficacy of the sacrament. Referring to the Eucharist, Kilmartin writes, "at the time of the Eucharist, the Spirit gives to the Church the grace to recall, to render herself present to the Christ of history, passing from the world to the Father."[177] As von Balthasar understands it, "every Eucharistic meal is a memorial of the passion and death of Christ in contemporaneity with the past

---

174. *Ibid.*, 487.

175. *Ibid.*, 510. Odo Casel (1886-1948) was the pioneer who introduced the idea of an active presence of the saving deeds of Christ in the Eucharist. This was a breach from the scholastic notion of sacramental presence, which confined sacramental presence and efficacy to grace and the presence of the body and blood of Christ. Odo Casel, *The Mystery of Christian Worship*, ed. Burkhard Neunheuser, trans. Darton, Longman, and Todd, Milestones in Catholic Theology (New York: Crossroad, 1962). Casel published his work *Das Christliche Kultmysterium* in 1932. *The Mystery of Christian Worship* is a translation of the fourth edition, published by Friedrich Pustet in 1960. For a concise presentation of the *Mysteriumgegenwart*, see George S. Worgul, *From Magic to Metaphor* (New York, Ramsey, NJ: Paulist Press, 1980), 205-209.

176. Chauvet, *Symbol and Sacrament*, 510.

177. Kilmartin, *Christian Liturgy*, 193.

event and the very presence of the risen Lord here and now. It also looks into the future as 'an eschatological meal, only sacramentally veiled'."[178]

According to Chauvet, the Spirit is present in establishing a filial relationship between the believers and God, which is being realized in and through the sacraments.[179] It is the Spirit who brings the event commemorated to its ultimate relational possibility, establishing an inseparable connection between the historical event and the celebration of the community. For this reason, Chauvet regards epiclesis as an integral part of the narrative of the memorial event. He makes this connection quite obvious in his presentation of the narrative analysis of the Eucharistic prayer, placing epiclesis in the narrative movement of the whole Eucharistic prayer.[180]

It is important to note that Chauvet understands the sacraments as the memorials in the Holy Spirit, situating the Pneumatological and Christological poles as parallels and feeding each other within the framework of a Trinitarian Christology. It is true that Chauvet tries to ascribe a rightful position to Pneumatology in his theology of the sacraments. Without undermining the Pneumatological accent that Chauvet is giving, it has to be argued that what Chauvet does is shift the emphasis from the hypostatic union to the Pasch of Christ. Therefore, Chauvet's sacramental thinking revolves around Christology, rather than Pneumatology. In spite of his attempt to correlate sacramental theology with Trinitarian Christology in part four of *Symbol and Sacrament*, this part seems to be detached from the dynamics of language and symbol which comes into play in the celebration of the sacraments, although he claims the unity in his work.[181] In this regard, we purport to say that developing a Pneumatological Christology within a Trinitarian framework will take us beyond what Chauvet has achieved in ascribing the role of the Holy Spirit as far as the efficacy of the sacraments is concerned. Moreover, an attempt has to be made to explain how the dynamics of language and symbols and the work of the Holy Spirit are mutually related in effecting the sacraments.

178. Mark Miller, "The Sacramental Theology of Hans urs von Balthasar," *Worship* 64 (1990): 56. See also Balthasar, *Glory of the Lord*, 572.

179. Chauvet, *Symbol and Sacrament*, 510.

180. *Ibid.*, 268-272. Considering the Eucharistic prayer as a single unit will help us to understand the account of institution and epiclesis as mutually complementary. As Kilmartin says, the integration of the liturgical account of institution into the literary-theological movement consists of showing how the narrative institution and anamnesis-offering prayer form a unit and how the unit of epiclesis-intercessions is linked to the former unit. Kilmartin, *Eucharist in the West*, 354.

181. Chauvet, *Symbol and Sacrament*, 451.

4.2.2. Sacramental Hermeneutics of Marion

As has been pointed out, as with Chauvet, the point of departure for Marion is the critique of metaphysics as onto-theology. Marion's reputed work, *God Without Being* calls into question the metaphysical determination of God as Being, and emphasises the need for freeing God from metaphysical calculations and giving back to God her own proper name "charity."[182] In doing so, Marion posits himself against Aquinas' concept of God as *ipsum esse* (existing itself), and tries to detach the discourse of God from Being. He does this by using his own 'category' of *distance*, naming God as "love," which is not a category as such, but a "non-categorical 'category'" as David B. Burrel puts it.[183] According to Marion, interpreting God in a metaphysical concept of Being, as *ipsum esse*, misrepresents the God, revealed in Jesus Christ, under the name of *agape*.[184] Marion borrows from Heidegger's "ontological difference" (*Sein/seiende*), Levinas' concept of the "Other" and Derrida's "différence."[185] In naming God Love (*agape*) as being manifested in the self-emptying of Jesus on the cross, Marion goes beyond the "ontological difference" or the "question of being."[186] Marion's theology is shaped by such an understanding of God as love.

Marion has not developed a systematic theology of the sacraments. Nevertheless, he is frequently discussed in contemporary sacramental theology. Marion's relevance for sacramental theology consists, not as a "sacramental theologian," but being "intensely sacramental in his thinking, which is promising for developing a contemporary understanding of the sacraments.[187] His basic theological motifs of distance, the icon, love and the gift have been recognised as promising formulations for a theology of the sacraments, different from the metaphysical approach of scholastic theology.[188] Marion's

182. Thomas A. Carlson, "Postmetaphysical Theology," in *The Cambridge Companion to Postmodern Theology*, ed. Kevin J. Vanhoozer (Cambridge, UK: Cambridge University Press, 2003), 58; Godzieba, "Ontotheology to Excess," *Theological Studies* 56 (1995): 5; Marion, *God Without Being*, xx-xxi; Mitchell, "Mystery and Manners," 135.

183. David B. Burrel, "Reflections on 'Negative Theology' in the Light of a Recent Venture to Speak of 'God Without Being'," in *Postmodernism and Christian Philosophy* (Mishawaka, IN: The American Maritain Association, 1997), 64.

184. Marion, *God Without Being*, 123.

185. Burrel, "Reflections on 'Negative Theology'," 59.

186. Marion, *God Without Being*, 73, 46-47.

187. Charles Lock, "Against Being: An Introduction to the Thought of Jean-Luc Marion," *St. Vladimir's Theological Quarterly* 37 (1993): 371.

188. Horner makes a concise presentation of the theological motifs of Marion. See Horner, *Jean-Luc Marion: A Theological Introduction*, 51-74. We do not intend to present an elaborate

attempt to transgress Being, which is foundational to his thinking, helps us to consider the efficacy of the sacraments and sacramental presence from a phenomenological perspective in a way different from the language of sacramental causality.[189] However, the question of whether postmodern sacramental theology takes into account the role of the Spirit in the understanding of sacramental efficacy, is also significant with regard to the sacramental thinking of Marion.

According to Marion, Easter becomes the innovative site for developing the real presence, without yielding to the metaphysical concept of being and causality. As Marion understands, it is Easter that "innovates," and the innovation of Easter motivates us to think of the "real presence" without confining it to an "empirical place."[190] Easter becomes the vantage point for the reinterpretation of the understanding of sacramental presence. However, to achieve this, we have to overcome the empirical or localised notion of presence. He says that Christ is neither present in the visible, empirical and passing flesh, nor in the conceptual memory of the community. The understanding of presence supercedes our ordinary mode of presence (touch, sight), because Christ is neither present in the body, nor absent, but present in spirit and memory in the Eucharistic bread that is shared daily.[191] But paradoxically, the presence of the body and the spirit is maintained and radicalised in absence, rather than in a spiritualised presence. As he says, the new concept of presence, that Easter innovates, consists "not in a reduction of presence to the spirit, but in a reinforcement of the presence of the body and the spirit as such."[192] Marion develops this innovative aspect of the concept of presence illustrating the biblical account of the resurrection and ascension of Christ as witnessed by the evangelists. He establishes a link between *blessing* and *presence, recognition,* and *gift,* in his theological exegesis of the Emmaus story (Lk 24:13-35) and the story of ascension in the gospel of Luke (24:50-53).

treatment of these categories at this point as they will be discussed highlighting their theological motifs and implications for sacramental theology in the third chapter.

189. Chauvet and Power are two important theologians who, among others make use of Marion in their sacramental theologies. Chauvet, *Symbol and Sacrament;* Power, *Sacrament.* Osborne also advocates a postmodern approach and basically agrees with the approach Marion has taken. See Osborne, *Sacraments in a Postmodern World.*

190. Jean-Luc Marion, *Prolegomena to Charity* (New York: Fordham University Press, 2002), 124.

191. *Ibid.,* 142.

192. *Ibid.,* 127.

4.2.2.1. Marion's Interpretation of Lk 24:50-53

Marion interprets Christ's paschal entry into Jerusalem as an entry of glorification of the Father by Christ and the glorification of Christ by the Father
which culminates in his arrest, trial and death, in order to explain his concept
of presence.[193] He understands Jesus' withdrawal from the Temple (Mt 24:1;
Lk 21:37; Mk 13:1) as the result of the people's failure to recognise and bless
him as the one sent by the Father. "Presence depends directly on blessing: ...
where men do not bless the Father, the Father cannot make himself present
... there is no presence of God among men, if men do not bless him and the
one he has sent."[194] This does not mean that the blessing by men [and wom-
en] constitutes the condition for God's presence, but consists of God's presence being recognised by them [us], because God's (Christ's) presence is
disclosed as gift, which can be recognized only by blessing God as Christ
did, and as the disciples at the Temple (Lk 24:53), welcoming and acknowledging "the gift of presence of God in and as his Christ."[195] Marion's interpretation of presence in terms of gift differentiates itself from the metaphysical understanding of presence. This is brought to light further in his interpretation of the Emmaus story.

4.2.2.2. Marion's Interpretation of Lk 24:13-35

Marion's interpretation of the Emmaus event is based on what he believes to
be a popular understanding of faith. Faith is a compensation for the lack of
concepts in understanding the overwhelming intuition given by revelation.
Faith fills this lack of intuition, adequately completing our concepts about
God. In this sense, faith is considered as a derivative, which comes after the
revelation has occurred.[196] He also introduces the notion of the "saturated
phenomenon," the excess of intuition, which consists of an intuition which is
inherently excessive, rather than what is normally required to fill a particular
concept.[197] Revelation, as a phenomenon, saturated with intuition, stands in

---

193. *Ibid.*, 128.
194. *Ibid.*, 129.
195. *Ibid.*, 129-130.
196. This is contrary to the notion of faith as the precondition for the phenomena to be received as revelatory and as the existential commitment, which makes revelation possible.
Shane Mackinlay, "Eyes Wide Shut: A Response to Jean-Luc Marion's Account of the Journey to Emmaus," *Modern Theology* 20 (2004): 448.
197. Marion, *God Without Being*, 227. The notion of the "saturated phenomenon" and its
implications for theology will be explained in the last two chapters of this work.

need of faith to fill the lack of our conceptual capability.[198] Faith broadens our limited conceptual capacity to receive the excess of intuition given in revelation. Thus presence is received as given, rather than 'produced', as exemplified in his hermeneutics of the Emmaus event.

Marion sees the obtuseness of the disciples as significant. They were sufficiently informed about the events that took place in Jerusalem, because they had been with Jesus during his ministry. Being disciples, they experienced the excess of intuition, because their concepts were inadequate to contain the overwhelming intuition given to them and to understand its meaning.[199] That is why they did not recognize Jesus who walked along with them. Their problem was not that they lacked visibility, but that they lacked the capacity to understand what they saw; in other words, their conceptual capacity was limited. The referent himself interprets the text referring to himself (Lk 24:15, 25-27).[200] By interpreting the scriptures, Jesus gave them new concepts, adequate to the intuition they received. Finally, Jesus breaks the bread and they recognize him. Marion says that the interpretation of the scripture and the breaking of the bread gave meaning to their intuitions, which remained scattered and incomprehensible.[201] Marion understands the interpretation of the scripture and the breaking of the bread as significations by which Jesus makes visible his own phenomenon. Once Jesus became visible to them, he (the interpreter or the hermeneut himself) disappears from them.[202]

There exists a close connection between hermeneutics and the Eucharist. Interpretation is completed in the Eucharist. According to him, "the hermeneutic lesson appears truncated, even absent, only if one takes it to be different from the Eucharistic celebration where recognition takes place; for immediately after the breaking of the bread, not only did the disciples 'recognize' and at last 'their eyes were opened' (Lk 24:31)."[203] By receiving these "significations and concepts," the disciples were able "to constitute the intuitions ... into a complete phenomenon" and they see Jesus.[204] Because of faith, their concepts were equated with the intuition which otherwise exceeded them, and the Jesus who was invisible became visible to them; they

---

198. Jean-Luc Marion, "They Recognised Him; and He Became Invisible to Them," *Modern Theology* 18 (2002): 146.

199. *Ibid.*, 146.

200. Peter-Ben Smit, "The Bishop and His/Her Eucharistic Community: A Critique of Jean-Luc Marion's Eucharistic Hermeneutic," *Modern Theology* 19 (2003): 31.

201. Marion, "They Recognised Him," 150.

202. Smit, "Marion's Eucharistic Hermeneutic," 32.

203. Marion, *God Without Being*, 150.

204. Marion, "They Recognised Him," 151.

recognize Jesus. But as soon as they recognize Jesus, he disappears. The reason he gives for the disappearance is that the disciples should not only *see* him, but also make him *seen*. Disappearance also pertains to the nature of such "saturated phenomenon par excellence" that it can neither be touched (Jn 20:17), nor even contemplated in the world.[205] Marion considers the Eucharist as the context in which the hermeneutic is completed and becomes meaningful. Any hermeneutic which is not completed in the context of divine self-revelation and self-giving, and any hermeneutic that resounds the unspeakable speech of the Son, is incomplete and ceases to be hermeneutic at all.[206] Thus, Marion's interpretation of the Emmaus event helps us to understand sacramental presence as "given" and to overcome the metaphysical temptation for confining presence to speculation and conceptual clarification. Furthermore, the depth of Marion's sacramental thinking finds expression in the re-interpretation of the "real presence" as "given" while subscribing to the theory of transubstantiation. In his opinion, transubstantiation cannot be rejected as though it has no validity and meaning. What must be resisted, however, is not transubstantiation, but the temptation to misconstrue presence to a mute thing, to the species alone.[207] Marion's attempt to re-imagine presence, remaining faithful to Catholic tradition has to be welcomed. Nevertheless, it must be observed that he has not developed a systematic discourse on the sacraments explaining the "how" of the "given." It is more or less self-evident that Marion's interpretation of the Eucharistic and the real presence are Christological in character. It is all the more important to see the amount to which his sacramental thinking is Pneumatological.

4.2.2.3. Pneumatology and Marion

As has been noted above, Marion's importance to sacramental theology consists, not in providing a systematic theology of the sacraments, but providing categories which helps us to develop a sacramental theology conducive to postmodern sensitivity. He never asks how the sacraments are being effected; rather, he is concerned with the phenomenality of sacrament. He lets the Eu-

---

205. *Ibid.*, 151.

206. Smit, "Marion's Eucharistic Hermeneutic," 32-33. As we will see in the fourth chapter, Marion's understanding of the Eucharistic hermeneutics elucidates not only the inseparable relationship between the hermeneutics and the Eucharist, but also shed light into the understanding of the liturgical role of the priest who acts in *persona Christi*.

207. Marion's charge is against his adversaries who undermine the theory of transubstantiation. Marion, *God Without Being*, 163-164. In this connection he refers particularly to L. Charlo and R. Besret . See *ibid.*, p. 166, n. 12.

charist speak itself, as it is, without being determined by human conceptuality. In other words, Marion tries to let the Eucharist determine its own conditions to present its own reality and understands the Eucharist as the superabundance of gift that is overflowing.[208] He never deals with the *how* of sacramental presence, although he admits the role of the Holy Spirit in making the presence real. Marion is of the view that it is the Holy Spirit who acts in the Church, the Eucharist, and in the glorified body of Christ, who gives himself to us as a gift or present.[209] He acknowledges the activity of the Holy Spirit in bringing Christ into presence by connecting the Spirit to praise. He argues, "the highest presence of Christ lies in the Spirit's action of making us, with him and in him, *bless* the Father."[210] The hermeneutics of the Word that takes place in the incarnation leads us to argue that hermeneutics cannot be reduced to Christological dimension alone; it is Pneumatological as well. Strictly speaking, the Eucharistic hermeneutics cannot be separated from the hermeneutic that took place in the incarnation. Therefore, Marion's understanding of hermeneutics is Pneumatologically unsound. In brief, like Chauvet, Marion's sacramental thinking suffers from a serious lack of Pneumatology.

4.3. Critique of Postmodern Sacramental Theology

The appropriation of postmodern thinking into sacramental theology liberates sacramental theology from a mechanical and productionist scheme of sacramental theology and directs us to think about presence in an illocutionary and non-empirical manner. However, this non-empirical or illocutionary presence is mediated through the body. Both Chauvet and Marion employ the story of Emmaus to explain this notion of presence. Easter gives presence a body and makes the presence present.[211] As we have examined, the unique act of blessings and the ascension, and the blessing and disappearance of Jesus after the blessing and the breaking of the bread in the story of Emmaus are interpretative keys for explaining sacramental presence after Easter. The Emmaus incident fills the disciples, who sought intimate knowledge of the empirical body, its proximity and certainty, with the *presence of absence*.[212] Believing in the Eucharistic presence after Easter means, "we must consent to an ab-

---

208. Lieven Boeve and John C. Ries, eds., *The Presence of Transcendence* (Leuven, Paris, Sterling, VA: Peeters, 2001), 10.

209. Marion, *God Without Being*, 141.

210. *Ibid.*, 144.

211. Mitchell, " Mystery and Manners," 142.

212. *Ibid.*, 143.

sence in order to experience the presence…, the paradigmatic figure of the presence-of-the-absence of God."[213]

The postmodern disavowal of absolutism, regarding any particular claim itself, creates a conducive atmosphere for questions and clarifications. The postmodern view of sacramental presence is not free from limitations. It seems to us that, although the steps taken by postmodern theologians are progressive and rewarding, certain problems are likely to arise.

It may be asked, can sacramental theology be complete in a theology of presence by "absence"? Chauvet himself has responded to this, saying, "theology's critical thrust" lies, not "in a prolongation of the negative onto-theology stressing the unknowability of God, but rather, in the direction of the believing subjects themselves."[214] He tried to face this challenge, locating the subjects at the centre of the scheme of symbolic exchange, overcoming the subject-object dichotomy of the metaphysical scheme of sacramental economy. Hence, the postmodern sacramental theology must refrain from being a negative theology of presence.

The postmodern perspective of sacramental presence (efficacy) has to be perfected by Pneumatology. The influence of postmodern philosophy has assisted sacramental theology to detach itself from metaphysical roots and to take a phenomenological and linguistic direction. Philosophical studies of language and symbols have highlighted their importance in constructing meaning and effecting presence. Postmodern sacramental theologians have tried to think about sacramental presence from the standpoint of these human sciences. Thus, in general, we perceive in postmodern sacramental theology an attempt to establish itself, transposing its roots from the metaphysical to the symbolic. The postmodern antipathy towards rationalization, mastery, and meta-narratives about God persuaded sacramental theologians to think of sacramental presence mainly relying on phenomenology of language and symbols. There seems to be a wide positive reception of this approach, especially among those who were dissatisfied with the scholastic-tridentine synthesis of the sacraments. What is positive about the postmodern approach is that it liberated sacramental thinking from the conceptual framework of metaphysical theology. Conversely, the postmodern approach seems not to have paid sufficient attention to integrating into sacramental thinking the insights of the progress that have been prominent in various branches of theology, particularly in Trinitarian theology, Christology, Pneumatology, and ecclesi-

---

213. Chauvet, *Symbol and Sacrament*, 405.
214. *Ibid.*, 41.

ology. The Heideggerian critique of philosophical theology has compelled postmodern theologians to base sacramental theology in the Bible and revelation. Sacramental theology has not profited adequately from an increased awareness of Pneumatology in the postmodern idea of sacramental presence. Admittedly, Chauvet is an exception, having advanced much in this direction by appropriating the results of the developments in systematic theology, specifically, Trinitarian theology, Christology, and Pneumatology. Nevertheless, as was pointed out, Chauvet's theology is not sufficiently Pneumatological. Besides, Chauvet's understanding of sacramental presence through the notion of symbolic mediation is not free from criticism, as we will see in the third chapter.

With regard to the sacramental understanding of Marion, it can be argued that, although he lays emphasis on the work of the Holy Spirit in effecting presence, his theology is basically Christologically textured. It is important to notice that, although Marion prepares the basis for reflecting on the revelation of Christ within a phenomenological framework, he is almost silent about the possibility of developing the revelation of the Spirit in this manner. We purport to argue that reflecting on the revelation of the Spirit from a phenomenological perspective is as important as the revelation of Christ in developing a sacramental theology which is Pneumatological and phenomenological in character. Such an approach will enable us to explain systematically the role of the Spirit in the sacramental event, while subscribing to the efficacy of language and symbols.

To sum up, what is lacking in the postmodern understanding of sacramental presence is the correlation between the aspects of symbolic efficacy (mediation) and the economy of the Trinity as it is unfolded in the history of salvation. This correlation can be made only by explaining God's engagement in history in the person of Jesus and God's sacramental encounter in the historical today of believing subjects from a phenomenological perspective. Such an approach will be possible only by placing Pneumatology at the center of the sacramental encounter, as it is unfolded in Christian revelation. Pneumatology can be accommodated without diminishing Christology if sacramental theology is done within the parameters of a Pneumatological Christology, which is different from the way Chauvet has dealt with it within the framework of a Trinitarian Christology. Therefore, the future of postmodern sacramental theology consists in appropriating the import of Pneumatology within the Trinitarian mode of revelation, which is substantial to Christian revelation.

5. Sacramental Efficacy and the Holy Spirit

The question concerning the efficacy of the sacraments preoccupied the Christians of all times, although in various degrees and in manifold directions. The early Christian and patristic period considered the sacraments as something to be believed and celebrated, rather than as a matter of intellectual comprehension. They attributed the efficacy to the action of the divinity, rather than to the inherent potency of the rituals and symbols used in the sacraments. There was no single theology of the sacraments or an accepted synthesis under a closed system, but the understanding of the efficacy was rather flexible, and there existed no particular theology that was commonly accepted.

Scholastic theology synthesised the sacraments systematically into a single and self-contained system, employing the category of causality. The Rahnerian synthesis tried to rescue the scholastic theology of instrumental causality, by introducing the notion of *Realsymbol* and highlighting the instrumentality of the Church. Although the Rahnerian approach introduced a new twist by incorporating anthropological and phenomenological aspects in sacramental thinking, Rahner's fundamental faithfulness to Thomism and the transcendental approach became subject to criticism. Admittedly, Rahner's innovative approach provided a new incentive for the reflection on the sacraments in the Rahnerian and post-Rahnerian period.

The point of departure of postmodern sacramental theology is the radical breach with onto-theology. Doing sacramental theology, without addressing postmodern concerns, would be unsatisfactory, as well as defective. The phenomenological and linguistic approach in interpreting sacramental presence has to be taken seriously. Even though postmodern theology does not attribute sacramental presence solely to the efficacy of symbols and language, the question regarding the role of the Holy Spirit in the sacramental event seems to be relevant. To our knowledge, postmodern theologians have not made a serious reflection on the import of Pneumatology in explaining sacramental presence, even though they agree that it is the Holy Spirit who realizes the sacraments. For this reason, we propose that the phenomenological and linguistic approach to sacramental presence has to be complemented with the role of the Holy Spirit. The relevant questions in this regard would be: Can such a synthesis be made; are the aspects of symbolic efficacy and the notion of the efficacy by the Holy Spirit entirely of different domains and therefore mutually exclusive, or complementing each other? If such a synthesis might be possible, could it be done, avoiding meta-narratives and without falling into metaphysical temptation? Is a Spirit-talk or God-talk (informed by phenomenology) possible? We intend to discuss these and other related questions in our study bringing into focus the question of symbolic efficacy and the role of the Holy Spirit.

5.1. A Pneumatological Contour for Sacramental Theology

Osborne discusses what could be the point of departure for sacramental theology in a postmodern context.[215] Having analysed different approaches to the sacraments from a historico-theological perspective, he suggests that the point of departure for a sacramental theology should readdress the notion of Jesus' humanity as the primordial sacrament and the Church as the foundational sacrament. Moreover, he argues that doing sacramental theology in the third millennium should take into account the postmodern approach of overcoming onto-theology, and apply sacramentality to the totality of the Church (including churches other than the Roman Catholic Church) and to the world at large. Agreeing with Osborne, and even furthering our scope, we may argue that the point of departure for a third millennium sacramental theology must first and foremost take its lead from Pneumatology. Indeed, the notion of Jesus' humanity as the primordial sacrament and the Church as the foundational sacrament can only be fully understood and appreciated by acknowledging the presence and the work of the Holy Spirit as the Spirit of Jesus, and the Holy Spirit as the Spirit of Jesus in the Church. In other words, the primordial sacramentality of Jesus and the foundational sacramentality of the Church are grounded on the third person of the Trinity. Moreover, without yielding to a metaphysical paradigm, the basis for sacramentality of the totality of the Church and of the world has to be well thought-out in the light of the all-encompassing presence of the Spirit who "swept over the face of the waters" (Gen 1:2). Thus, we identify a few implications of a Pneumatological point of departure in sacramental theology.

5.1.1. The Geistvergessenheit in the West

Most recent monographs and articles on Pneumatology generally begin with a remark on the marginal importance devoted to the theology of the Holy Spirit. A trivial consideration of Pneumatology typifies both Catholic and Protestant theologies of the last few decades. It has to be admitted that the charges against the so-called "forgetfulness of the Holy Spirit" or "poverty in

---

215. Osborne, *Sacraments in a Postmodern World*, 41-53.

the reflection on the role of the Holy Spirit" are reasonable.²¹⁶ Quite often, Western Catholic theology is accused of assigning to Pneumatology an ornamental or subordinate position, as compared to the position assigned to Christology. As McDonnell observes,

> in the West, we think essentially in Christological categories, with the Holy Spirit as an extra, an addendum, a "false" window to give symmetry and balance to theological design. We build up our large theological constructs in constitutive Christological categories, and then, in a second, non-constitutive moment, we decorate the already constructed system with Pneumatological baubles, a little Spirit tinsel.²¹⁷

216. Otto Dilschneider speaks about this as *Geistvergessenheit* of theology. See Otto Dilschneider, "Geistvergessenheit der Theologie," *Theologische Literaturzeitung* 86 (1961). The shortfall in the theology of the Holy Spirit of the twentieth century theology has been variously expressed by authors. Pope Leo XIII observes that there has been a "heavy darkness" that surrounded the theology of the Holy Spirit. See Leo XIII, *"Divinum Illud Munus," Acta Apostolica Sedis* 29 (1896/1897). Congar refers to this period as the "years of famine" while Rahner refers to it as the "fear of the Spirit." Yves Congar, *Tradition and Traditions: A Historical and Theological Essay*, trans. Michael Naseby and Thomas Rainsborough (London: Burns and Oates, 1966), 397; Karl Rahner, "Fear of the Spirit, Thoughts for Pentecost," in *Opportunities for Faith. Elements of a Modern Spirituality* (New York: Seabury, 1970), 40-45. Rowan Williams observes that a minimalist treatment of the doctrine of the Holy Spirit is applicable to both Catholic and Protestant theologians. For example, on the Protestant side, even Barth's doctrine of the Holy Spirit is not a sufficiently developed system. Also his disciple, Eberhard Jüngel, is of no exception. On the Catholic camp, Karl Rahner, Hans Küng and Edward Schillebeeckx in their respective works, namely, Hans Küng, *On Being a Christian* (London: Collins, 1977); Rahner, *Foundations*; Edward Schillebeeckx, *Jesus: An Experiment in Christology* (London: Collins, 1978), did not attempt a separate treatise on Pneumatology. However, he admits the Pneumatological emphasis of Jürgen Moltmann and Hans Urs von Balthasar. For instance, Hans Urs von Balthasar, *On Prayer* (London: SPCK, 1973); Jüngen Moltmann, *The Church in the Power of the Spirit* (London: SCM Press, 1977). See Rowan Williams, *On Christian Theology* (Oxford: Blackwell, 2000), 107. Paul Tillich in the third volume of *Systematic Theology* developed a rather sound Pneumatology treated in a separate section, but not as a part of ecclesiology or grace as Schleiermacher considered. See Kilian McDonnell, "The Determinative Doctrine of the Holy Spirit," *Theology Today* 39 (1982): 155-157. Orthodox theologians like Vladimir Lossky have criticised the West based on the *filioque* for confining the Holy Spirit to the margins of ecclesiology, liturgy and so on. See David Coffey, "Spirit Christology and the Trinity," in *Advents of the Spirit: An Introduction to the Current Study of Pneumatology*, ed. Bradford E. Hinze and D. Lyle Dabney (Milwaukee, WI: Marquette University Press, 2001), 8-9.

217. McDonnell, "Doctrine of the Holy Spirit," 142. It is true that Western theology is commonly charged for its neglect of the Holy Spirit. One has to admit that there is much truth in such charges. However, it would be improper to level charges indiscriminately. For the Holy Spirit was not completely neglected; rather, the emphasis was laid on the indwelling of

These and similar charges amply testify to the failure of Western Catholic theology in developing a Trinitarian theology incorporating the Pneumatological and Christological elements in a consistent manner. The imbalanced treatment of the Third Person of the Trinity causes even Trinitarian theology to be shaped like a kind of "binitarianism,"[218] or "a dyad of either Father and Word, or a dyad of transcendent God and immanent Spirit."[219]

This forgetfulness of the Holy Spirit of Western theology was transferred to the scholastic synthesis of the sacraments minimising the role of the Holy Spirit over and against the action of Christ. Therefore, the contemporary discussion on sacramental efficacy has to take the question of the role of Christ and the Holy Spirit seriously. Given this fact, we may say that the advantage of a Pneumatological start in sacramental thinking would mean attending to the charges of the *Geistvergessenheit*.

5.1.2. The Vatican and Post-Vatican Eras

There has been an unprecedented interest in Pneumatology among modern theologians, notably during the Vatican and post-Vatican era. The amount of scholarly articles and monographs on the doctrine of the Holy Spirit published during this period attests to this Pneumatological renaissance in the Church. The renewed interest in Pneumatology is also characterised by an interrelation with other branches of theology, such as ecumenism, liturgical theology, eco-theology, liberation theology, etc.[220] Today, theologians are

the Holy Spirit and the theology of appropriations. Elizabeth Teresa Groppe, *Yves Congar's Theology of the Holy Spirit* (New York: Oxford University Press, 2004), 4.

218. Bernd Jochen Hilberath, "Identity through Self-Transcendence: The Holy Spirit and the Fellowship of Free Persons," in *Advents of the Spirit: An Introduction to the Current Study of Pneumatology*, ed. Bradford E. Hinze and D. Lyle Dabney (Milwaukee, WI: Marquette University Press, 2001), 265. Hilberath says that it is not correct to speak about the "forgetfulness of the Spirit" as seen in almost every introduction to the writings about the Holy Spirit. On the contrary, it is better to speak of a Pneumatological "deficit" in the sense that the Holy Spirit was attributed only a subordinate role.

219. Williams, *Christian Theology*, n. 12, p. 109.

220. See D. Lyle Danbey, "Why Should the Last Be First? The Priority of Pneumatology in Recent Theological Discussion," in *Advents of the Spirit: An Introduction to the Current Study of Pneumatology*, ed. Bradford E. Hinze and D. Lyle Danbey (Milwaukee, WI: Marquette University Press, 2001), 240; Veli-Matti Kärkkäinen, *Pneumatology: The Holy Spirit in Ecumenical, International and Contextual Perspective* (Grand Rapids, MI: Baker Academic, 2002), 11-13; Veli-Matti Kärkkäinen, *Towards a Pneumatological Theology: Pentecostal and Ecumenical Perspectives on Ecclesiology, Soteriology, and Theology of Mission*, ed. Amos Yong (Lanham, MD: University Press of America, 2002).

more convinced of the importance of treating Pneumatology in relation to other branches of theology, rather than in isolation. For "after Pentecost, one cannot do theology as though Pentecost has no theological meaning. Cross and resurrection are way-stations on the way to the presence of the Spirit, who proclaims the Christ."[221] The significance of Pneumatology for theology means going beyond the functional understanding of the doctrine of the Holy Spirit, namely, what the Spirit effects and does in individual lives. In sacramental theology, this would demand a renewed understanding of the sacraments from a Pneumatological perspective. Vatican II has moved in this direction, admitting the role of the Holy Spirit in its liturgical reform, introducing an epiclesis, although split in order to retain the focus of the words of Christ. Much has to be done along these lines. The scope of Pneumatology in systematic theology and its import for sacramental theology remains to be further explored. Therefore, the Pneumatological approach to sacramental theology that we advocate is in line with the renewed Pneumatological awareness of the West and in accordance with the liturgical and sacramental renewal of the Council.

5.1.3. The Ecumenical Significance

Today, Western theologians in general appreciate the Pneumatological thinking of the East and attempt to retrieve the Pneumatological aspect, which deteriorated considerably in the scholastic-tridentine synthesis of the sacraments. Any reflection on sacramental efficacy ought to take into consideration the Pneumatological controversy of the fourteenth century, which resulted in the inclusion of the *Filioque* without prejudice and objectivity. The main problem of the dispute between the Greeks and Latins was about the procession of the Holy Spirit, which also had implications for the understanding of the sacraments and ecclesiology. Indeed, the doctrinal formulations of the Church councils have juridical weight and binding force to order the faith and life of the community. However, "they do not, and never did, constitute the entire teaching on a point, but they were a point of reference to assess teachings, where clarity and accuracy were required."[222] Without diminishing or rejecting their value, the context in which those propositional statements were formulated has to be revisited, considering the present milieu in which

---

221. McDonnell, "Doctrine of the Holy Spirit," 146.
222. Power, *Sacrament*, 210.

the Church finds herself. This may also provide us with insights, which may
be helpful in explaining the efficacy of the sacraments in a better way.

In contrast to the Western position, Pneumatology was central to the East,
both in their understanding of the sacraments and the Church. The understanding of the procession of the Spirit "from the Father alone" helped them
to understand the role of the Spirit as being equal to that of the Son. Thus the
operation of Christ in the Church and in the sacraments was understood to be
through the action of the Holy Spirit. Nicholas Cabasilas took a reconcilia-
tory position, contending that consecration of the Eucharistic elements was
by the joint action of the Word and the Spirit through the recitation of the
words of Christ and the invocation of the Holy Spirit.[223] Eastern perspectives
on the procession of the Spirit also served in understanding the sanctification
of the assembly with and through the sanctification of the gifts, whereas the
West understood both as two separate actions. The invocation of the Spirit is
also significant for a Eucharistic and community centered ecclesiology,
where the Spirit acts as the agent who transforms the gift into the body and
blood of Christ and acts as the principle of the unity of the community as the
ecclesial body of Christ.[224] This is quite different from the understanding of
communion in the West, which is primarily juridical in nature. The West still
holds that sanctification of the gifts and sanctification of the community are
separate entities. Sanctification of the gifts is attributed to the ecclesiological
understanding of a direct relationship of the minister to Christ, and the Spirit
is subordinated to priestly power as a gift given through the exercise of an
ecclesial authority through the recitation of the words of Christ.[225] As Power
observes, a strong retrieval of Eastern ecclesiology will account for a better
understanding of the mission of the Word and the Spirit in their complementariness.[226] Therefore, sacramental theology launched from Pneumatology
will, therefore, be ecumenical in character.

5.1.4. The Trinitarian Structure of Pneumatology

In starting from Pneumatology, we signify that the theology of the sacraments must be based on a Trinitarian theology, balancing the role of Christ
and the Holy Spirit in the economy of salvation. For Pneumatology, as a

223. Nicholas Cabasilas, *A Commentary on the Divine Liturgy*, trans. J.M. Hussey and
P.A. McNulty (London: SPCK, 1966), 220.
224. Power, *Sacrament*, 220-221.
225. *Ibid.*, 222.
226. *Ibid.*

discipline of theology, in general, and in relation to the sacramental theology in particular, cannot be viewed in isolation from Trinitarian theology. Trinitarian theology is "the necessary framework for a theology of the Holy Spirit,"[227] and Pneumatology is "inseparable from the triunity of God himself."[228] Therefore, it becomes clear that any attempt to discover the role of the Holy Spirit in the reflection on sacramental efficacy has to take into account the Trinitarian schema of salvation in its integrity. This invites us to revisit the Intra-Trinitarian relationship of the three divine persons in the immanent Trinity and the economic Trinity. The Trinitarian theology we propose to develop should delineate the role of the Holy Spirit in relation to the second person of the Trinity. It may be suggested that approaching Pneumatology within the framework of the doctrine of the triune God will help us to comprehend the role of the Son and the Holy Spirit in the liturgical celebration of the Church. Indeed, it will also provide certain valuable insights which may enable us to harmonise the incongruities surrounding the Pneumatological and Christological polarities in the understanding of the sacraments. Consequently, what we propose is not a Trinitarian Christology, as Chauvet proposes, but a Pneumatological Christology without subordinating one to the other in the immanent Trinity and the economic Trinity. Accordingly, we purport to argue that a Pneumatological Christology within a Trinitarian framework seems to be more appropriate for explaining the role of the Holy Spirit in the sacraments than a Trinitarian Christology.

5.1.5. Postmodern Sensibility

A Pneumatological point of departure in sacramental theology ought to take into account postmodern concerns. For this reason, our project of retrieving the Holy Spirit in the sacraments ought to face the challenge of avoiding an onto-theological approach. We are bound to stay away from any kind of meta-narrative in reflecting on the Holy Spirit and the Trinity. Consequently, the daunting task is to consider the Spirit from a phenomenological perspective, bearing in mind the Spirit as the basic phenomenon in the immanent and economic Trinity. In conjunction with this, the role of the Holy Spirit in the per-

227. Groppe, *Congar's Theology of the Holy Spirit*, 51.

228. Yves Congar, *I Believe in the Holy Spirit*, trans. David Smith, Milestones in Catholic Theology (New York: Crossroad, 2006), 3:xv. In our work all the citations are from the reprint of Congar's three-volume work in the "Milestones in Catholic Theology," which was originally published in 1983 by Geoffrey Chapman, London, from the French original *Je crois en l'Esprit Saint* (Paris: Les Éditions du Cerf, 1970-1980).

son of Christ and in the Church, in making Christ the primordial sacrament and the Church the fundamental sacrament, need to be explained without falling into metaphysical temptation. Moreover, the role of the Spirit in sacramental celebration, as well as in the sacramental life of the participants, should be discussed in the light of the phenomenology of language and symbols.

6. Conclusion

Our study of the idea of sacramental efficacy from a historical and theological perspective brings into focus the Pneumatological shortfall that permeates the Catholic theology of the sacraments since the scholastic period. Although patristic sources give no conclusive evidence to articulate that the efficacy of the sacraments was considered to be by the activity of the Holy Spirit, an intrinsic connection between the signified reality and the sacramental elements/symbols was emphasised by the Fathers. Patristic evidences seem to suggest that the understanding of the efficacy was rather flexible. The efficacy was understood diversely as being by the "power of the word of God," "invocation of God," "invocation of the Holy Spirit," "Christ's hand," and so on. However, there was no developed theology of the Holy Spirit in the patristic period. The Holy Spirit was often identified as the power of the Logos. For instance, some expressions like the "power of the word of God" is ambiguous as to determine whether it denotes the "word of Christ," or is referring to the Holy Spirit understood as the power of the Logos. Nevertheless, Fathers such as Irenaeus of Lyons, Cyril of Jerusalem, and John Chrystostom are clearer about the role of the Holy Spirit in effecting sacramental change. Although the witness of the Fathers is not supportive enough to assert the role of the Holy Spirit, it is indicative of admitting the role of the Holy Spirit as something important in our understanding of sacramental efficacy. In scholastic theology, we see a move contrary to this overemphasising the Christological dimension and overlooking Pneumatology. The impact of scholastic theology was radical in Western sacramental theology, so much so, that the traces of the *Geistvergessenheit* continue to prevail in some way in postmodern sacramental theology. Therefore, while acknowledging the linguistic and symbolic shift at its face value, concerted efforts have to be made to interpret sacramental presence, taking Pneumatology seriously. Our next chapter will try to formulate a theological synthesis, which is predominantly Pneumatological, delineating its significance for a contemporary understanding of sacramental efficacy.

CHAPTER TWO

A PNEUMATOLOGICAL THEOLOGY OF SACRAMENTAL EFFICACY

The Pneumatological deficit that spreads through Western sacramental theology is the outcome of the one-sided emphasis on Christology which has gained precedence since the scholastic period. The purpose of the present chapter is to re-discover the role of the Holy Spirit alongside the role of Christ in the economy of salvation within the broader context of the Trinitarian schema of salvation. The crux of the issue consists in explaining the economic mission of Christ and the Holy Spirit as constitutive of a single reality of God's self-communication to what is other than himself. The scope of our study consists in developing a Pneumatological theology on the bedrock of the doctrine of the triune God duly accommodating both Christology and Pneumatology without eclipsing or marginalizing either of them. Thus, having defined the role of the Son and the Holy Spirit as complementary, we make an effort to show the significance of Pneumatology in the understanding of the sacraments of the Church. A few introductory observations are to be made in order to initiate our discussion.

1. Theology of the Holy Spirit

In his monograph on Pneumatology, Jürgen Moltmann remarks, "[f]rom the very beginning, the personhood of the Holy Spirit was an unresolved problem, and the problem is as difficult as it is fascinating."[1] The difficulty and problems involved in the study of the Holy Spirit were also underscored by Yves Congar, a theologian of the Holy Spirit, as he confessed that it is more important to live in the Spirit as adopted sons, than to explain the mystery of

---

1. Jürgen Moltmann, *The Spirit of Life: A Universal Affirmation*, trans. Margaret Kohl (Minneapolis, MN: Fortress Press, 1992), 10. Ralph Del Colle begins his article with the same citation from Moltmann. Ralph Del Colle, "The Holy Spirit: Presence, Power, Person," *Theological Studies* 62 (2001): 322.

the Spirit.[2] Nonetheless, he appreciates the inevitability and significance of a systematic theological reflection on the Holy Spirit.[3] Therefore, the task we undertake in this chapter will be challenging, as well as significant, for the study of the sacraments.

1.1. 'Spirit'/'Holy Spirit': Etymology

The Greek term *pneuma* derives from the verb *pneo* (to blow), which denotes "wind," "breeze," or "breath." *Pneuma* is a common name coined from the natural phenomena of wind and breath.[4] In classical Greek, *pneuma* denotes "wind," "breath," "life," and, metaphorically, to the phenomenon which are perceptible by their effects, although they are invisible.[5] According to the Oxford English Dictionary, the term "spirit" is mainly derived from *spiritus* in the Vulgate, which is used to translate the Greek *pneuma* and Hebrew *ruah*. The spirit is generally defined as "the active essence or essential power of the Deity, conceived as a creative, animating, or inspiring influence."[6] The suffix *ma*, lays emphasis on the dynamic force or power that results when the air is set in motion.[7] Moreover, the term *pneuma* has a rich variety of meanings which are often symbolic, metaphorical, spiritual, etc. The Old Testa-

---

2. Congar, *I Believe in the Holy Spirit*, 2:92. See also Elizabeth Teresa Groppe, "The Contribution of Yves Congar's Theology of the Holy Spirit," *Theological Studies* 62 (2001): 451-452; Groppe, *Congar's Theology of the Holy Spirit*, 3.

3. Yves Congar, *The Word and the Spirit*, trans. David Smith (San Francisco, CA: Harper & Row Publishers, 1986), 5.

4. Jacques Guillet, "The Spirit of God," in *Dictionary of Biblical Theology*, ed. Xavier Léon-Dufour (London: Cassel Publishers, 1988), 571. *Neshamah* is also used as an equivalent of *ruah* in the OT (Job 27:3; Gen 2:17; cf also, Job 33:4; 34:4; Isa 57:16) which can be translated as spirit. This word is used in the second creation story (Gen 2:5-7) as the 'breath of life'. See George T. Montague, *The Holy Spirit: Growth of a Biblical Tradition* (New York, Paramus, NJ, Toronto: Paulist Press, 1976), 6.

5. Friedrich Wilhelm Horn, "Holy Spirit," in *The Anchor Bible Dictionary*, ed. David Noel Freedman (New York: Doubleday, 1992), 262. For a rather clear understanding of the diverse meanings in which the term spirit in the Hebrew Bible, in the LXX, New Testament, see Petro B.T. Bilaniuk, *Theology and Economy of the Holy Spirit* (Bangalore: Dharmaram Publications, 1980), 8-23.

6. *The Oxford English Dictionary [Cd-Rom]*, 2 ed., version 3.0 (New York: Oxford University Press, 2002), 617.

7. James D.G. Dunn, "Spirit, Holy Spirit," in *The New International Dictionary of New Testament Theology*, ed. Colin Brown (Exeter, UK: The Paternoster Press, 1978), 689.

ment equivalent *ruah* also denotes "wind," "respiration," "the spirit of man," and "the spirit in man."[8]

1.2. The Old Testament Use

The Biblical notion of the Spirit has to be inferred from a reflection on the images of the Spirit which collectively exhibit a coherent development of thought, beginning from "life-breath," "wind," "fire," "water," "cloud," "the dove," and to "the Paraclete."[9] In the Old Testament, the term *ruah* occurs 389 times, of which 378 are found in the Hebrew texts, whereas 11 are found, in Aramaic passages.[10] All these expressions basically mean "wind/moving air" and "breath."[11] In an anthropological sense, the spirit is the breath of Jahweh (*ruah Jahweh*) that enlivens human beings.[12] In the *Yahwist* and *Elohist* traditions, "spirit" was understood anthropologically as the life-breath received from God, the gift and the source of life. Moreover, the Spirit was understood as a divine impulse of wisdom, knowledge, and prophecy.[13] Apart from the physical meaning, this term was used to designate the qualities of human beings and God, including animals and supernatural spirits.[14] It was reasonable to apply this term to God due to his immateriality and obvious power. In the Old Testament, the Spirit of God was understood

8. Dunn, "Spirit, Holy Spirit," 690; Jacques Guillet, "The Spirit of God," 570.

9. George T. Montague, "The Fire in the Word: The Holy Spirit in Scripture," in *Advents of the Spirit*, ed. Bradford E. Hinze and D. Lyle Dabney (Milwaukee, WI: Marquette University Press, 2001), 36-45. Here, Montague makes a concise presentation of the images of the Holy Spirit that encompass the material, animal, and personal worlds showing how they contribute to the biblical notion of the mystery of the Spirit.

10. Congar, *I Believe in the Holy Spirit*, 2:3; Horn, "Holy Spirit," 262.

11. *Ibid.*, 262. Congar classifies roughly the use of the term *ruah* in three groups according to their meaning. Congar, *I Believe in the Holy Spirit*, 2:3. Admittedly, there is no sustained exegetical treatment in what follows, but we depend on secondary and tertiary literature to set the stage for our discussion.

12. Hans Schwarz, "Reflections on the Work of the Spirit Outside the Church," *Neue Zeitschrift für Systematische Theologie und Religionsphilosophie* 23 (1981): 197. Genesis 2:7 is one of the earliest traditions of the notion of the Spirit, whereby God is said to breath into the nostrils of man and the man becomes a living being. The Hebrew term employed here is *neshamah* instead *ruah* which is found elsewhere (e.g., Job 27:3) referring to the breath, the spirit of God (*ruah eloah*). See Montague, "The Fire in the Word," 36.

13. Montague, *The Holy Spirit*, 3-16.

14. Horn, "Holy Spirit," 262.

as the transforming power of God that strengthens human beings (judges, kings, prophets, etc.) for exceptional deeds.[15]

The expression "Holy Spirit" (*pneuma hagion*) derives from the combined use of the terms *pneuma* and *hagios*, in Hebrew, *quodes* and *ruah*.[16] The terms "holy" and "spirit" do not appear jointly in the Greek texts, although we can find at least two instances in the Old Testament (Is 63:10,11; Ps 51:13). *Pneuma hagion* (meaning "the holy spirit") occurs more often in the New Testament, even though these instances are negligible compared to the sole use of the term *pneuma* in the whole New Testament literature.

1.3. Pneumatology in the New Testament

God reveals himself as Trinity. The doctrine of the Trinity has been developed in response to the gospel story, whereby God is named as Father, Son and Holy Spirit, in attempting to explain the plurality and unity implied in that naming.[17] The doctrine of the Trinity is a response to the question of explaining the unity and the difference in the Godhead. Therefore, in order to explore the distinctiveness of the Holy Spirit in relation to the other divine persons, it is important to see what the New Testament says about the Third Person of the Trinity.

1.3.1. The Synoptics and the Acts

The personal identity of the Holy Spirit in relation to the Father and the Son is quite ambiguous in the scriptures. Etymologically, the New Testament term *pneuma* has the same meaning as *ruah*.[18] However, there is no clear teaching about the personhood of the Holy Spirit in the New Testament. This combination of *pneuma* and *hagion* became a technical expression in Christian usage through Luke and rabbinic literature.[19] Of the three hundred and seventy one occurrences of substantive *pneuma*, only ninety-two are absolutely understood as *pneuma hagion*, the "Holy Spirit."[20] Other references to

---

15. John Breck, "The Lord Is the Spirit," *The Ecumenical Review* 42 (1990): 116; Guillet, "The Spirit of God," 571.

16. Horn, "Holy Spirit," 261.

17. John E. Colwell, *Promise and Presence: An Exploration of Sacramental Theology* (Waynesboro, UK: Paternoster, 2005), 20.

18. Kärkkäinen, *Pneumatology*, 28.

19. Horn, "Holy Spirit," 261.

20. *Ibid.*, 265.

pneuma can be understood as "spirit of God," "spirit of holiness," "spirit of the Father," "spirit of his Son," "spirit of Jesus," etc. Only three references (Jn 3:8; Heb 1:7; and 2 Thess 2:8) are used in the original meaning, "wind" or "breath," The predominant tendency is of speaking about God (Trinity) in a binitarian way, referring only to the Father and the Son. There are several verses that speak about the Spirit in "power categories," as in Luke 4:14. The Spirit is often identified as the power of God, or Christ (Lk 1:17; 24:49; Acts 6:5,6; 10:38; see also 1 Cor 2:4; 1 Thess 1:5; Eph 3:16). In fact, the distinction between the activity of Christ and the Spirit is not very clear in the New Testament. Sometimes the activity of the Spirit is also more or less identified with angelic activities.[21] For example, in Acts 8:26, 39; 23:9, the same activity is attributed both to the angels and to the Spirit, and the sending of the angel is expressed in the same language as sending the Spirit (Lk 24:49; Acts 12:11; Gal 4:6).

Among the synoptists, only Luke gives prominence to the Spirit; Mark and Matthew have little to say clearly about the Spirit. Compared to Matthew and Mark, Luke is more generous in mentioning the Holy Spirit. In his gospel, there are seventeen, possibly eighteen, references to the Spirit, while fifty-seven references occur in the Acts.[22] There are various interpretations regarding the event of Pentecost, about which Luke enthusiastically reports.[23]

21. Similarly, in the Old Testament revelations made to the prophets, it is often impossible to identify whether the agent of revelation is "the angel" or "the Lord" himself. See Isa 63:10-14; Gen 21:17-19; 16:7-16; 22:11-18; 31:11-13; Ex 3:2-14; Judg 6:11-24).

22. Joseph Fitzmyer, *The Gospel According to Luke I–IX* (Garden City, NY: Doubleday, 1981), 227.

23. Scholars arrive at two main conclusions about the event of Pentecost; first, it is a theological construction of Luke which has a historical nucleus; second, it is an explicit narration of a series of experiences of the Spirit in the community. Ernst Haenchen discusses various positions of scholars and contends that Luke's depiction of Pentecost is completely a theological construction. See Ernst Haenchen, *The Acts of the Apostles: A Commentary* (Philadelphia, PA: Westminster: 1971), 172-175. According to Richard F. Zehnle the improbability of any spectacular intervention on the day of Pentecost is attested by the lack of any positive evidence in other early Christian literature. Richard F. Zehnle, *Peter's Pentecost Discourse* (Nashville, TN: Abingdon: 1971), 112. Dunn is reluctant to make a conclusive statement as to whether or not the Pentecost was a historical event. He briefs, "In short, it is by no means certain, but not at all unlikely, that the historical events underlying Acts 2:1-13 took place on the first Pentecost after Jesus' death." James D.G. Dunn, *Jesus and the Spirit: A Study of the Religious and Charismatic Experience of Jesus and the First Christians as Reflected in the New Testament* (London: SCM Press, 1975), 136-146, esp. 142; Luke Timothy Johnson, *The Acts of the Apostles* (Collegeville, MN: Liturgical Press, 1992), 45-47. Johnson concludes his discussion on the topic with the note that the incongruities surrounding the Pentecost must not

Although Luke speaks about the Holy Spirit more than the other evangelists, it is not clear whether the Holy Spirit is referred to as a person, or as an impersonal power.[24] Nevertheless, what becomes evident is that there is a clear Pneumatological link in the Lucan writings that runs through the whole ministry of Jesus and extends to the period of the Church. Both the ministry of Jesus and the period of the Church are presented as being under the power and guidance of the Spirit. The Spirit is present and active at his conception, baptism, the events in Nazareth, and in the period of the Church (Acts 2:5).[25] Luke connects the period of Jesus to the period of the Church by presenting the outpouring of the Spirit (Acts 1:4) as the fulfillment of the "promise of the Father" (Luke 24:49).[26]

Mark mentions the Spirit six times (Mark 1:18, 10, 12; 3:29; 12:36; 13:11), while Matthew does so twelve times (Mt 1:18, 20; 3:11, 16; 4:1; 10:20; 12:18, 28, 31, 32; 22:43; 28:19).[27] Even though the references to the Spirit in Mark and Matthew are scant, they are significant, considering the context of the gospel story. Both Matthew and Mark have significantly placed such references at the beginning of their gospels (Mt 1:18, 20; Mk 1:10). In the retro-development of the gospel story, which begins with the resurrection, the Spirit is playing a definitive role in defining the identity of Jesus.[28] The backward reflection, which begins with the resurrection, moves through Jesus' public ministry (Luke 4:14-22) and baptism (Mt 3:16, 17), and finally reaches back to the conception (Matt 1:18, 20). In all of these stages, the identity of Jesus is associated with the Spirit. The Spirit is constitutive of the identity of Christ. There is an integral relation between Christology and Pneumatology. According to McDonnell, by descending on Jesus at baptism, the Spirit functions in identifying who Jesus is, and what constitutes

---

make us fail to notice the precision and clarity with which Luke reports that event of Pentecost. See Johnson, *The Acts of the Apostles*, 45-47.

24. Kilian McDonnell, *The Other Hand of God: The Holy Spirit as the Universal Touch and Goal* (Collegeville, MN: Liturgical Press, 2003), 13.

25. The role of the Spirit as constitutive of the identity of Christ and the Church will be further expatiated with its importance for a Spirit Christology, this being the basis of developing Pneumatological theology.

26. Fitzmyer, *The Gospel According to Luke I–IX*, 227-228.

27. *Ibid.*, 227.

28. Raymond E. Brown asserts that in the pre-gospel period resurrection was the pivotal event in the proclamation of the identity of Jesus, and the starting point of the backward reflection (Rom 1:4). Raymond E. Brown, *The Birth of the Messiah* (London: Chapman, 1977), 29-32.

his mission.[29] Moreover, at the beginning of the Church, there is the creative and prophetic power of the Spirit as the very presence of Christ among his people (Acts 2). In the Acts, there takes place a series of Spirit events (Acts 6:2-6; 8:5-13; 19:1-6; 9:17-18) followed by the outpouring of the Spirit (Acts 2:1-4). Thus, we clearly see how the Spirit guides the Christian community in the period of the Church. The Acts shows how the Spirit, that constituted Jesus in his conception and commissioned him at the baptism, constitutes the Church through the outpouring of the Spirit and empowers the proclamation of the disciples.

1.3.2. John and Paul

John devotes more room for the Holy Spirit in his gospel, but he approaches the Holy Spirit in a different manner than the synoptic gospels. The Spirit is given after Jesus is lifted up (Jn 16:7; 19:30; 20:22). According to John, it is the risen and glorified Lord who communicates the Spirit (Jn 20:22). In the period between the "already" and the "not yet," Christ's presence is realized for the community through the Spirit. C.K. Barrett says that, according to Johannine theology, the Spirit is "the means by which the historical past and the historical future (in two 'Comings' of Jesus) are brought to bear upon the present in such a way as to determine the immediate spiritual presence of Jesus."[30]

Different again from the account of Luke in the Acts, John gives an account which is known as the "Johannine Pentecost" (Jn 20:19-23). According to this account, the risen Christ imparts the Spirit by breathing on the disciples (Jn 20:22) as the fulfillment of the promise of giving the Spirit (Jn 7:39), or the Paraclete (Jn 14:26). In contrast to Mark and Matthew, Luke centralizes the resurrection events in Jerusalem. Similarly in contrast to John, for Luke the outpouring of the Spirit is centralized in Jerusalem. According to McDonnell, regardless of the disparities that exist between the settings of the outpouring of the Spirit, the significance and the message of Luke and John are one and the same: the bestowing of the gift of the Holy Spirit by the Risen and Ascended Lord on the Church, thereby empowering the mission of the community. Both John and Luke affirm, that after the Jesus' period, dur-

---

29. Kilian McDonnell, *The Baptism of Jesus in the Jordan: The Trinitarian and Cosmic Order of Salvation* (Collegeville, MN: The Liturgical Press, 1996), 1-14.

30. Charles Kingsley Barrett, "The Place of Eschatology in the Fourth Gospel," *The Expository Times* 59 (1947-1948): 304.

ing the period of the Church, his work is continued by the Spirit. Thus, the gift of the Spirit bestowed on the Church "belongs constitutively to the church's deepest identity."[31]

Paul speaks extensively about the Holy Spirit, but he presents no unified view regarding the identity of the Holy Spirit. Paul's statement, "Now the Lord is the Spirit" (2 Cor 3:17) is sometimes interpreted as blurring the identity of the Spirit.[32] Joseph Fitzmyer opines that according to Paul, the Spirit is the end result of Christ's death and resurrection. Paul ascribes resurrection to the work of the Father (Rom 4:24; 6:4; 8:11; 10:9; 1 Thess 1:10; Gal 1:1; 1 Cor 6:14; 15:15; 2 Cor 4:14). It is important to notice that Paul also attributes the resurrection of Jesus not only to the Father, but also to the Spirit. For instance, Paul writes, "... the gospel concerning his Son, who was descended from David according to the flesh and was declared to be Son of God with power according to the spirit of holiness by resurrection from the dead, Jesus Christ our Lord..." (Rom 1:3-4). However, he sees the expression "spirit of holiness" as denoting the fact that, although the resurrection was an act of the Father, the Spirit was intrinsic to it.[33] Paul refers to the pre-

---

31. McDonnell, *The Other Hand of God*, 59.

32. *Ibid.*, 64.

33. Through the resurrection Jesus was enthroned as the Son of God in the power of the Spirit of Holiness. "[T]he spirit of holiness" is interpreted in different ways. See Otto Kuss, *Der Römerbrief*, vol. 2 (Regensburg: Friedrich Pustet, 1959), 6-7. Ernst Käsemann associates the expression "the spirit of holiness" to the power by which Jesus was appointed Son of God in line with the tradition that relates Jesus' messianic appointment by the Holy Spirit at baptism. Ernst Käsemann, *Commentary on Romans* (Grand Rapids, MI: Eerdmans, 1980), 12-13. Joseph Fitzmyer opines that the "spirit of holiness" is not to be interpreted as the Holy Spirit, the Third person of the Trinity. Instead, it is more in line with the Old Testament understanding of the Spirit as the Holy Spirit. Paul understands *pneuma*, not in a Hellenistic sense, but rather as in the Old Testament "the Spirit of God," the presence of God to his people; the animating and creative Spirit (Gen 1:2; Num 24:2; 1 Sam 19:20,23; 2 Chr 15:1; 24:20; Ps 51:12; 139:7; Isa 11:2; 61:1; Ezek 2:2l; 11:5). Joseph Fitzmyer, *Romans: A New Translation with Introduction and Commentary*, The Anchor Bible, 33 (New York: Doubleday, 1993), 125. See also *ibid.*, 236. On pp. 394 and 398 he acknowledges that Rom 1:4 refers "indirectly to the holy Spirit." Dunn justifies the Pneumatological significance of Rom 1:4 in explaining the spirit as resurrection-power interpreted within the context of Rom 6:4; 8:11; 2 Cor 13:4 and 1 Cor 15:44, 46, although Paul is hesitant to present explicitly the exalted Christ as the Lord of the Spirit and Jesus' risen life as the creation of the Spirit. James D.G. Dunn, *Christology in the Making: A New Testament Inquiry into the Origins of the Doctrine of the Incarnation* (Philadelphia, PA: Westminster Press, 1980), 144.

sence of God among Christians as "God's Spirit," "Christ's Spirit," "Christ," and "the Spirit of him who raised Jesus from the dead" interchangeably.[34]

A fleeting look at the New Testament literature does not lead us to conclude that it contains a developed theology of the Holy Spirit. However, our brief survey shows that there is a solid and uninterrupted Pneumatological link throughout the New Testament. The ambiguity and reticence that encompasses the account of the Trinitarian persons in scripture, as well as in the tradition of the Church, made the study complex and difficult.[35] Nevertheless, attempts were made in the patristic period to explain the unity and plurality that is present in the gospel portrayal of God's revelation. Hence, the theology of the Holy Spirit developed in the patristic period alongside the reflection on the Trinity.

2. The Doctrinal Development of Pneumatology

Christian faith in the Trinity implies that God is Trinity: Father, Son, and Holy Spirit. They are three distinct persons. As the Trinitarian theology developed, "Holy Spirit" came to prevail in theological vocabulary and in the use of the Church as the "third One" distinct from the Father and the Son. However, personhood was attributed to the Spirit much later, and with caution, because of the ambiguity and reticence in the New Testament. In the following, we will identify specific stages in the development of the theology of the Holy Spirit in the patristic period, and the theological controversies which led to the diverse understanding of the Spirit in the Christian East and West.

2.1. The Patristic Period

Due to the lack of unified evidence and obscurity about the Holy Spirit in the New Testament, the early Church had the difficult task of distinguishing the identity of the Holy Spirit in the Trinity. However, in the light of the scanty evidence and information, there developed in the early Church confessions of

---

34. Fitzmyer, *Romans*, 124-125.

35. Albert Outler, "Veni, Creator Spiritus: The Doctrine of the Holy Spirit," *New Theology*, no. 4 (1967): 195-196. McDonnell also makes mention of the ambiguous and unreflective nature of the biblical witness of the Spirit and the consequent difficulty in the understanding of the Spirit in the postapostolic period. Kilian McDonnell, "A Trinitarian Theology of the Holy Spirit?," *Theological Studies* 46 (1985): 194-204.

faith which were different in forms and content.[36] Among them, the most difficult one was the confession of the Holy Spirit.[37] Nevertheless, Pneumatology developed in the post-biblical period based on the triadic formulations where the Father, Son, and Holy Spirit are mentioned or implicated.[38] In the early Church, Pneumatology developed hand in hand with Christology, based on the Christological texts that relate the Spirit with Christ.[39] Because of the ambiguity about the identity of the Holy Spirit in the scriptures, patristic theology developed in a more Christological fashion. In the early patristic period, including the early part of the fourth century, Trinity was explained in a "binitarian Father and Son language."[40] The discussion about God prior to the fourth century was in a binitarian manner, although Trinity was implied in their discussions. Fathers like Origen and Tertullian, in spite of their Trinitarian intent, were struggling to explain the unity of the Trinity in a consistent manner.[41] Therefore, they speak about the distinction and unity of the Trinity only in terms of the Father and the Son.[42] The Holy Spirit was often identified with the Logos. Thus, for Justin, the Spirit of Luke 1:35 is the power of the Logos.[43] This implies that the Logos effects His own incarnation. This thought was also applied to the understanding of the sacraments, especially the Eucharist. In this sense, Justin seems to hold that the Logos effects the historical incarnation and the Eucharistic incarnation.[44] The change of the Eucharistic elements is seen as Eucharistic incarnation effected by the Logos. C.W. Dugmore says that there is a common feature which runs throughout the writings of the early Fathers that the consecration is made

36. For a study of the New Testament confessions of faith, see J.N.D. Kelley, *Early Christian Creeds* (London: Longman, 1950), 13-23.

37. Harry Austryn Wolfson, *The Philosophy of the Church Fathers* (Cambridge, MA: Harvard University Press, 1964), 141.

38. Walter Kasper observes that although there was no explicit reference to the Trinity, the threeness was implied in the triadic formulations from the beginning. See Walter Kasper, *Jesus the Christ* (New York: Paulist Press, 1976), 249.

39. McDonnell, *The Other Hand of God*, 69.

40. *Ibid.*, 16.

41. For a concise presentation of the unity and difference of God in Tertullian, see Basil Studer, *Trinity and Incarnation: The Faith of the Early Church*, ed. Andrew Louth, trans. Matthias Westerhoff (Edinburgh: T & T Clark, 1993), 70-75, 83-87.

42. Wolfson, *The Philosophy of the Church Fathers*, 317.

43. Johannes Betz, *Die Eucharistie in der Zeit der Griechischen Väter: Die Aktualpräsenz der Person und des Heilswerkes Jesu im Abendmahl nach der Vorephesinisschen Griechishen Patristik*, vol. 1/1 (Freiburg: Herder, 1955), 33.

44. Edward J. Kilmartin, "Sacrificium Laudis: Content and Function of Early Eucharistic Prayers," *Theological Studies* 35 (1974): 277.

through the word of prayer, which is from Him.[45] Pneumatology remained undeveloped and detached from sacramental thinking. The gradual development of the binitarian manner of speaking about God assumed a Trinitarian fashion with the distinction of the Holy Spirit from other Divine Persons which was made at the Council of Nicea (325).

2.1.1. The Nicene Church

The main concern of the Christian writers of the pre-Nicene period was to attend to the challenges levelled against the identity of Jesus Christ, the Incarnate Logos. The Council of Nicea was convened in 325 in order to settle the dispute concerning the divinity of the Son in relation to the Father, which was fuelled by the Arian controversy. The Council, after debating the problem, issued a creedal statement declaring that "the Son is coeternal and equal in substance with the Father." Thus the Council of Nicea settled the dispute about the divinity of Christ, by affirming that Jesus Christ is truly divine just as is God the Father. The Council did not take up the issue of the Holy Spirit, but just included in the creed a sentence, "And [we believe] in the Holy Ghost."[46]

The Council of Nicea was silent about the divinity of the Holy Spirit. The Council did nothing more with the Holy Spirit save for affirming the faith in the Holy Spirit, because the Spirit was not an issue at that stage. The inclusion of the statement about the Holy Spirit, together with Christian experience, liturgical practices, and the necessity of responding to those who rejected the divinity of the Holy Spirit, contributed to a clarification of the identity of the Spirit in relation to the other divine persons. There was hardly any interest in the Holy Spirit in the early part of the fourth century, and even in the thirty-five years after Nicea. Only around 355 did the Spirit emerge as a theological issue.[47] In the post-Nicene period, it became necessary to go

45. C.W. Dugmore, "Sacrament and Sacrifice in the Early Fathers," *The Journal of Ecclesiastical History* 2 (1951): 25.

46. Stanley M. Burgess, *The Holy Spirit: Ancient Christian Traditions* (Peabody, MA: Hendrickson, 1984), 94; Hugo Meynell, "Two Directions of Pneumatology," *Irish Theological Quarterly* (1982): 173; "The Nicene Creed," in *Nicene and Post-Nicene Fathers,* 2nd Series, ed. Philip Schaff and Henry Wace (Edinburgh: T & T Clark, 1991), 14:3-7. The Council of Nicea was content in simply stating, "[We believe] in the Holy Spirit," because in 325 the divinity of the Holy Spirit was not an issue. The Council was also keeping in line with the general tradition of not going beyond what was stated in the scripture. See McDonnell, *The Other Hand of God*, 71-72.

47. *Ibid.,* 125.

beyond Nicea in defending the divinity of the Holy Spirit. Amphilochius, who presided over the Synod of Iconium in 376, wrote, "what was sufficient for Nicea is not sufficient for us. Nicea committed us to a Trinitarian doctrine, but no Trinitarian doctrine is possible if the Spirit is not recognised as Trinitarian, and therefore divine."[48] Thomas Smail relates, the attention of the Council was concentrated largely on the binitarian question of the relationship between the Father and the Son, at the expense of the question of the Spirit's relatedness to the Father and the Son. Thus, the Council neglected the pre-and post-Pentecostal activities of the Holy Spirit as witnessed by the New Testament.[49] The doctrine of the Holy Spirit, especially the way he is related to the Father and the Son and his personhood, remained to a great extent untouched and undeveloped in the pre-Nicean period, although the Holy Spirit was mentioned, along with the Father and the Son in the early creeds and doxologies, and in the writings of Tertullian and Origen.[50] The divinity of the Holy Spirit became a major topic of discussion only around the time of the Council of Constantinople (381).

2.1.2. The Post-Nicene Church

After the Council of Nicea, the focus of attention became centred on the "mysterious third being" who is mentioned in the gospels, along with the Father and the Son, as distinctive, yet related to them, and who is active in the Church, inspiring and guiding the community as witnessed by the Apostles.[51] Although there was some reflection on the Holy Spirit in the post-biblical period, in spite of the common reticence to go beyond what is stated

---

48. "Amphilochi Episcopi Iconii Epistola Synodica," in *Patrologia Graeca*, ed. J.P. Migne (Paris: Seu Petit-Montrouge, 1858), 93-98.

49. Thomas A. Smail, "The Holy Spirit in the Holy Trinity," in *Nicene Christianity: The Future for a New Ecumenism*, ed. Christopher R. Seitz (Grand Rapids, MI: Brazos Press, 2001), 149. By affirming this, however, the Council was relating the spirit integrally to the Trinity. *Ibid.*, 77.

50. Burgess, *The Holy Spirit: Ancient Traditions*, 12. Trinitarian theology was developing since the third century due to the influence of Origen and Tertullian, respectively, in the Greek-speaking East and in the Latin-speaking West. See Gerald Bray, "The *Filioque* Clause in History and Theology," *Tyndale Bulletin* 34 (1983): 104.

51. The early Church was confronted with the problem of identifying the person of the Holy Spirit as different from the other two divine persons. The early Church seems to have ascribed great importance to the person and function of the Spirit, as evidenced by the innumerable references, especially in the gospel of John as well as in the Acts of the Apostles and in the letters of St. Paul. Cf. Gal 4:4-6; 1 Cor 12:4-6; 2 Cor 13:13; Rom 15:16; Eph 2:18; 4:3-6; Jn 14:16-17; 16:13-15; Acts 2:4; 4:8; 8:29; 10:19; 11:12; 13:2; 15:28; 20:28.

in the scriptures, an impetus to further the development of the theology of the Holy Spirit was provided by the *Pneumatomachi* who denied the divinity of the Holy Spirit.[52] Once the consubstantiality of the Son with the Father was clarified, discussions were mainly about the identity of the Holy Spirit in relation to the Father and the Son. Thus, following the Council of Nicea, the divinity of the Holy Spirit was clearly affirmed at the Council of Constantinople. The Council added to the creedal definition of the Council of Nicea, "And [we believe] in the Holy Ghost," the formula "the Lord and the Giver-of-Life, who proceedeth from the Father, who with the Father and the Son together is worshipped and glorified, who spoke by the prophets."[53] Thus the creed of Constantinople clearly affirms the divinity of the Holy Spirit, and requires for Him, worship and glory with the other persons of the Trinity. The creed also declares the procession of the Spirit from the Father; however, the mode of relation to the Trinity and to the Son is not explained. In other words, the Council did not consider the way in which the Holy Spirit is a person in the life of God. The question as to how the "three" and "one" could be understood was left to the theological speculation of successive centuries. So, from the fourth century, the question about the relation of the Spirit to the Trinity and to the Son became an important issue both in the East and the West.[54] So after the Council of Constantinople, the focus of attention was shifted to the relationship of the Holy Spirit to the other divine persons. The discussion was mainly pivoted on the processional relationship of the Holy Spirit to the other persons.

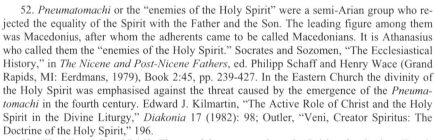

52. *Pneumatomachi* or the "enemies of the Holy Spirit" were a semi-Arian group who rejected the equality of the Spirit with the Father and the Son. The leading figure among them was Macedonius, after whom the adherents came to be called Macedonians. It is Athanasius who called them the "enemies of the Holy Spirit." Socrates and Sozomen, "The Ecclesiastical History," in *The Nicene and Post-Nicene Fathers*, ed. Philipp Schaff and Henry Wace (Grand Rapids, MI: Eerdmans, 1979), Book 2:45, pp. 239-427. In the Eastern Church the divinity of the Holy Spirit was emphasised against the threat caused by the emergence of the *Pneumatomachi* in the fourth century. Edward J. Kilmartin, "The Active Role of Christ and the Holy Spirit in the Divine Liturgy," *Diakonia* 17 (1982): 98; Outler, "Veni, Creator Spiritus: The Doctrine of the Holy Spirit," 196.

53. "The Nicene Creed," 163. The creedal statement about the Spirit refers back to Tertullian's famous formula *una substantia – tres persona* which asserts the personhood of the Holy Spirit and places the Spirit in equal position with the other two divine persons requiring worship and glorification. See Moltmann, *The Spirit of Life*, 11.

54. The variant readings in the gospel of John that the Holy Spirit proceeds from the Father (Jn 14:16; 15:26), sent by the Son (Jn 15:26), receives from the Son (Jn 16:14) gave rise to the different views regarding the procession of the Holy Spirit in relation to the Father alone or as from the Father and the Son.

2.1.3. The Filioque *Question*

The reflection on the processional relationship of the Spirit to the other divine persons took different courses in the East and the West, with necessary implications for the understanding of the person and mission of the Holy Spirit. In the East, the Capadocian Fathers brought the doctrine of the Holy Spirit to a new stage of development by clarifying the "unity" and "three-ness" of the Godhead, employing the terms, *hypostasis* and *ousia*. They applied the term *ousia* to denote the essence that is shared by all persons of the Godhead, whereas the term *hypostasis* was used to designate that in which the Godhead is three. Accordingly, in the Trinity, there is the presence of three *hypostases* in one *ousia* that exist in mutual indwelling and reciprocal relationship to the other two, which they clarified by the notion of *perichoresis*.[55] The foundation of God's Trinitarian existence as Father, Son, and Holy Spirit is this "eternal perichoretic *koinonia*."[56] The use of the term *hypostasis* indicates, not simply something about the being of God, i.e., the being of God is of the same substance, but rather, ontologically, the being of God as "being-in-relation." As Gregory of Nazianzus explains, the name of the Father is actually the name of the Father in relation to the Son; the Father is distinguished from the Son through "unbegottenness," the Son through "be-

---

55. Tertullian was the first theologian who introduced into Christian language the concept of the Trinity and persons, differentiating the person and work of the Spirit from the Father and the Son. Burgess, *The Holy Spirit: Ancient Traditions*, 63. He used the term "person" (*persona*) for the first time in response to the erroneous teaching of Sabellianism which held the view that the Father, Son and the Holy Spirit are merely temporary models of God in relation to creation. Colwell, *Promise and Presence*, 31-32. Tertullian writes, "I testify that the Father, and the Son, and the Spirit are inseparable from each other … and that They are distinct from Each Other … the Father is the entire substance, but the Son is a derivation and portion of the whole … even as we say that the Son is also distinct from the Father, so that He showed a third degree in the Paraclete, as we believe the second degree is in the Son … Besides, does not the very fact that they have the distinct names of *Father* and *Son* amount to a declaration that they are distinct in personality?" Tertullian, "Against Praxeas," in *The Ante-Nicene Fathers*, 1st Series, ed. Alexander Roberts and James Donaldson (Grand Rapids, MI: Eerdmans, 1993), 3:603-604. Here, using the analogy of a tree he also illustrates the otherness and the inseparability of the three divine persons (he also uses the other analogies of "the spring and the river" and "the sun and the ray"). As he says, the shoot is produced from the root, yet being distinct from the root, so also the Son was produced from the Father, but both remain united, yet remain to be two as the root and shoot are two. The Holy Spirit is the third one in the Trinity as the fruit is the third from the tree.

56. Trevor Hart, "Person & Prerogative in Perichoretic Perspective: An Ongoing Dispute in Trinitarian Theology Observed," *Irish Theological Quarterly* 58 (1992): 54.

gottenness" and the Spirit through "procession."[57] Regarding the manner of procession, the Greeks held the notion of a twofold procession of the Spirit "from the Father through the Son" which was widely accepted throughout the East by the fourth century.[58]

The Western Church developed a theology relatively independent from the theological thinking of the East. Concerning the procession of the Spirit, the Western Church held the view that the Holy Spirit proceeds from the Father and the Son (*Filioque*).[59] Augustine adopted the *Filioque* and explained it from the unity of divine substance.[60] In reaction to Arianism, he

---

57. Gregory of Nyssa, "Oration on the Son," in *The Nicene and Post-Nicene Fathers*, ed. Philip Schaff and Henry Wace (Grand Rapids, MI: Eerdmans, 1996), 29:2, p. 301.

58. Stanley M. Burgess, *The Holy Spirit: Eastern Christian Traditions* (Peabody, MA: Hendrickson, 1989), 2. According to the twofold procession, the Spirit is understood as proceeding from the Father through the Son; the Son is not the originator of the Spirit, but it is the Spirit that the Son actually receives from the Father. In the light of Jn 15:26 and 16:12-14 Epiphanius held the view that the Holy Spirit proceeds from the Father (παρὰ ... ἐκπορεύεται) and receives from the Son (ἐκ ... λήψεται). See Oliver Kösters, *Die Trinitäts-lehre des Epiphanius von Salamis: Ein Kommentar zum „Ancoratus"*, Forschungen zur Kirchen und Dogmengeschichte, 86 (Göttingen: Vandenhoeck & Ruprecht, 2003), 271. This cannot be equated with the *Filioque* position of the West, but their concern was to be attentive to the Johannine notion of the Spirit as from the Father (Jn 14:16) and receives from the Son (Jn 15:26).

59. For a detailed treatment of the *Filioque* controversy, see Donald L. Berry, *"Filioque* and the Church," *Journal of Ecumenical Studies* 5 (1968): 535-554; Hieromonk Boniface, "The Filioque Question," *Ecumenical Trends* 13 (1984): 68-72; Emmanuel Clapsis, "The Filioque Question," *Patristic and Byzantine Review* 1 (1982): 127-136; Terrence R. O'Connor, "Homoousios and Filioque: An Ecumenical Analogy," *Downside Review* 83 (1965): 1-19; Lukas Vischer, ed., *Spirit of God, Spirit of Christ: Ecumenical Reflections on the Filioque Controversy*, Faith and Order Paper, 103 (London: SPCK, 1981).

60. It has been generally admitted that the Western theology of the Trinity begins with the unity of essence and proceeds to the notion of the threefoldness of persons. On the contrary the Greek starts from the persons and moves to an explanation of their consubstantiality. Augustine follows this traditional Western pattern in developing his Trinitarian theology. Paul Henry argues that in many respects Marius Victorinus' *Adversus Arium* prepared the way for Augustine's *De Trinitate*. Paul Henry, "The *Adversus Arium* of Marius Victorinus, the First Systematic Exposition of the Doctrine of the Trinity," *Journal of Theological Studies* 1 (1950): 52-55. Victorinus' refutation of Arianism manifests his adherence to Platonism as transmitted by Numenius, which also influenced his interpretation of the Trinity in a triadic manner. Hermigild Dressler and others, eds., *Marius Victorinus: Theological Treatises on the Trinity*, The Fathers of the Church, 69 (Washington, DC: The Catholic University of America Press, 1981), 12-16. Burgess opines that Augustine's emphasis on the unity rather than on the difference of persons might have been a response to Marius Victorinus, who presents God as a "triple being." Burgess, *The Holy Spirit: Ancient Traditions*, 167.

tried to stress the divinity of the Son, equating the Son with the Father, and
saying that the Son is of the same substance with the Father.[61] Therefore, for
him, it was reasonable to argue that originating the Spirit as a divine prerogative is not only of the Father alone, but also of the Son. Thus, Augustine
claimed that the Spirit proceeds from the Father and the Son. By ascribing a
role to the Son in the procession of the Spirit, Augustine was trying to defend
the divinity of the Son with the Father. In *De Trinitate* (416), he says that the
Father and the Son spirate the Spirit acting as a single principle.[62] But what is
at stake is that the affirmation of the unity of divine operation is located on
the unity of divine essence, rather than in the persons as such. There was the
need to illustrate the unity of divine operation and the distinctiveness of the
divine persons. Thus, the Spirit is distinguished from the Son by the fact that
the Spirit proceeds from the Father and the Son (*Filioque*) who act as one
principle, whereas the Son alone is generated from the Father.[63] The distinctions between the Son and the Spirit are retained through the distinctions
within the modalities of their personhood. Accordingly, the Spirit's *hypostasis* differs from that of the Son in the fact that the Son is "generated," and the
Spirit is "breathed forth, or spirated."[64]

According to the traditional Western pattern of Trinitarian thinking, there
is a clear and logical inner connection between the Son and the Spirit. In the
West, the *Filioque* clause explains the connection between the immanent
Trinity and the economic Trinity. The economic sending of the Spirit by the
Son is understood in correspondence with the sending of the Spirit by the
Son in the immanent Trinity.[65] So, there is a necessary correspondence between the inner procession of the Spirit and the economic mission of the
Spirit. The movement is from the Trinity in itself, to the Trinity in the economy. According to Karl Barth, the missions of the Word and the Spirit correspond to a prior ordering of inner-Trinitarian processions. He calls this
inner ordering an *economia* of three "modes of existence" of the Trinity,
existing coeternally in a logical priority, although not in temporal succes-

61. Augustine, "*De Trinitate*," in *The Nicene and Post-Nicene Fathers*, 1st Series, ed. Philip Schaff (Grand Rapids, MI: Eerdmans, 1978), Book 1: no. 9, pp. 21-22.

62. *Ibid.*, 15, 26, 46.

63. Edward J. Kilmartin, "The Active Role of Christ and the Holy Spirit in the Sanctification of the Eucharistic Elements," *Theological Studies* 45 (1984): 245.

64. Del Colle, "The Holy Spirit," 335.

65. Duncan Reid, *Energies of the Spirit: Trinitarian Models in Eastern Orthodox and
Western Theology* (Atlanta, GA: Scholars Press, 1997), 3.

sion.[66] Rahner's idea of God's self-communication follows the same pattern, while favoring an ordering of the Trinitarian "modes of subsistence." According to Reid, Rahner's *Grundaxiom* implies an implicit inner-Trinitarian *Filioque* that explains the logical relationship of the origin of the Son and the Spirit as in Barth, although it gives room for the procession of the Word and the Spirit to condition each other.[67]

The divergent ways in which both the East and the West explained the mystery of the Trinity, and the mutual relationship of Trinitarian persons, characterised their diverse theologies. It is important to note that the distinctive ways in which the East and the West understand the manner of procession of the Spirit has radical consequences in their understanding of the personhood and the role of the Spirit.[68] Thus, it can be claimed that the Eastern way of understanding the procession articulates the person and the role of the Spirit better than it does by the *Filioque*. Western theology also recognises the definitive role of the Holy Spirit in the person and work of Christ in the economy of salvation. However, the difference lies in the fact that, traditionally, the East ascribes to the Spirit a personal and proper mission, whereas in the West, the Spirit is attributed a mission by "appropriation."[69] In the West, the role of the Holy Spirit has often been limited to an instrumental role of extending the salvation accomplished by Christ to humankind.[70] This limited role does not do justice to the person and active role of the Holy Spirit in the

66. Karl Barth, *Church Dogmatics*, trans. G.T. Thomson, vol. 1/1 (Edinburgh: T & T Clark, 1963), 424-425.

67. Reid, *Energies of the Spirit*, 60.

68. The question about the personhood of the Holy Spirit pertains not to the experience of the Spirit in outward efficacies, but rather, on the relationship of the Trinitarian persons and how they constitute the being of the Spirit. So, the study about the personhood of the Holy Spirit must be located within the Trinity. Moltmann, *The Spirit of Life*, 11.

69. Kilmartin, "Sanctification of the Eucharistic Elements," 233.

70. Burgess, *The Holy Spirit: Ancient Traditions*, 5. Some authors call into question the personhood of the Holy Spirit, although they accentuate the functional role of the Holy Spirit. Geoffrey Lampe raises strong criticism against the traditional doctrine of the Trinity and argues that the Spirit should not be considered as a divine being distinct from the Father and the Son, but rather, as the "outreach" of God towards humankind who serves the purpose of bringing human beings to their destiny. See Geoffrey Lampe, *God as Spirit* (Oxford: Clarendon, 1977), 33. For a brief and critical study of Lampe's understanding of the Spirit, see Meynell, "Pneumatology," 178-182. Similarly, Karl Barth who gives paramount importance to the Holy Spirit depersonalises the Holy Spirit, representing the Spirit as the "mode of existence" of the one divine Subject or the Lord. The Spirit is not a third "person" in the modern sense of the term, but rather a "common factor" or "communion" of the Father and the Son. Barth, *Church Dogmatics*, 1/1, 573; Hart, "Trinitarian Theology," 47-51.

economy of salvation, as is witnessed in the New Testament. Doing justice to the biblical witness of the Spirit is far from merely acknowledging the work of the Holy Spirit, but rather, consists in acknowledging the personhood of the Holy Spirit. It is not simply recognising the gifts of the Spirit, but rather, the giver himself; it is not just considering the Spirit as an indeterminate power or transforming presence, but as the person who mediates presence. Therefore, we propose to reconsider the inter-relationship of the Trinitarian persons in their immanent and economic manifestations. We hold that this will move us towards acknowledging the full role of the Spirit, as revealed in the economy of salvation, and in so doing, see its implications for the understanding of the sacraments as well. In what follows, we propose a Pneumatological theology in this direction, and examine how it can serve the purpose of acknowledging the person and role of the Holy Spirit in the sacraments.

3. Pneumatological Theology

The scope of Pneumatological theology consists of constructing a systematic and comprehensive theology of the Spirit, which has its point of departure in God's engagement in the history that culminates in the person of Christ. This involves highlighting the activity of the Spirit in creation, incarnation, and in the whole process of the destiny of human beings and of the world at large. It is a daunting task because of the extensiveness of its scope and varied range of disciplines with which we have to engage. Added to this, is the necessity of refraining from idolizing or extracting the Spirit from the Trinity as such, and more importantly, not to conflict with, or undermine, the person and mission of the Word. A comprehensive treatment of the Holy Spirit within the Trinitarian framework of revelation in this way seems to avoid such potential pitfalls, and serves as the foundation of constructing a Pneumatological theology.

3.1. Pneumatological Format of Theology

Pneumatology is generally understood as a branch of systematic theology like other disciplines, such as Christology, ecclesiology, and so on. The expression "Pneumatological theology" seems to have shown up very recently in theology.[71] Pneumatological theology consists, not only in identifying

---

71. Recently, two books that specifically deal with "Pneumatological theology" were published. As their titles indicate, basically they approach certain areas of theology from the

itself simply as a branch of theology, but also in treating theology as such, in a Pneumatological way. This is far from merely assigning a place to Pneumatology, along with other branches of theology, but rather, it is a Pneumatological approach to theology as such, or a Pneumatological way of doing theology. Karl Barth had already envisioned the possibility of such a theology which is entirely Pneumatological in character. According to him there is:

> [T]he possibility of a theology of the third article, a theology where the Holy Spirit would dominate and be decisive. Everything that one believes, reflects, and says about God the Father and God the Son in understanding the first and second articles would be demonstrated and clarified basically through God the Holy Spirit, the *vinculum pacis* between the Father and the Son. The work of God on behalf of creatures for, in, and with humanity would be made clear in a teleology which excludes all chance. I give only indications of what I occasionally dream of regarding the future of theology.[72]

A theology of the third article, as envisaged by Barth, encourages us, not only to consider Pneumatology as an appendix to God-thought, but as decisive component for the understanding of God. As a result, Pneumatological theology patterns the entire theology. In this sense, a Pneumatological theology of the sacraments is the way of doing sacramental theology along the lines of a systematically constructed Pneumatology.

3.2. Pneumatology and Trinitarian Theology

The mystery of the Trinity has always been of theological interest, because the doctrine of the Trinity is considered to be the grammar of speaking adequately about God as revealed in the gospels.[73] Besides, it is upon the know-

perspective of Pneumatology. Kärkkäinen, *Towards a Pneumatological Theology*; Amos Yong, *Beyond the Impasse: Toward a Pneumatological Theology of Religions* (Grand Rapids, MI: Baker Academic, 2003).

72. Karl Barth, *Schleiermacher-Auswahl mit einem Nachwort von Karl Barth*, ed. Heinz Bolli (Munich: Siebenstern-Taschenbuch, 1968), 311. As cited in McDonnell, "A Trinitarian Theology of the Holy Spirit," 193.

73. Some authors who advocate a similar approach to Trinitarian theology are: Robert W. Jenson, *The Triune God*, Systematic Theology, 1 (New York: Oxford University Press, 1997); Thomas F. Torrance, *The Ground and Grammar of Theology* (Charlottesville, VA: University Press of Virginia, 1980); Williams, *On Christian Theology*. Jenson insists that the norm for theological truth must always be the reflection on the Triune God himself, based on the gospel story, rather than each one's particular tradition. A number of essays in William's book manifest a Trinitarian perception of God, more evidently the essay entitled "the Grammar of God," wherein he also introduces Raimundo Panikkar. Torrance's concern is mainly in overcoming

ledge of God as Trinity – Father, Son, and Holy Spirit, that Christian faith
and worship are anchored and take different directions. The divinity and personhood of the Holy Spirit can be better understood in terms of his relation to
the Father and the Son. Thus, the doctrine of the Trinity is the theological
field wherein the theology of the Holy Spirit can be formulated.

The Pneumatological way of doing theology, that we propose, is not disengaged from Christology or Trinitarian theology. Pneumatological theology
implies re-discovering the role of the Holy Spirit in relation to the Father and
the Son. Therefore, Trinitarian theology is "the necessary framework for a
theology of the Holy Spirit."[74] In other words, Pneumatology is "inseparable
from the tri-unity of God himself."[75] Therefore, Trinitarian theology will be
the structural framework for formulating a systematically constructed Pneumatology. As Amos Yong says, Pneumatological theology is nothing, but "a
robustly Trinitarian theology."[76] According to him, Pneumatology completes
and fills out the Christian understanding of the Trinity. Pneumatological theology pertains to the recent awakening in the theology of the Holy Spirit and
a Trinitarian approach to theology.[77] In this connection, we hold that doing
theology in a Pneumatological way will have crucial significance in re-
discovering the identity and role of the Holy Spirit, and thereby influencing
other disciplines of theology, especially ecclesiology, sacramental theology,
etc.

---

the bifurcation between the treatises, *De Deo Uno* and *De Deo Trino*, and showing how the
doctrine of the Trinity encompasses creation, Christology, Christian life, worship, etc.

74. Groppe, *Congar's Theology of the Holy Spirit*, 51.

75. Congar, *I Believe in the Holy Spirit*, 3:xv.

76. Yong, *Beyond the Impasse*, 20.

77. Traditional Western theology which was formalised by Aquinas detached the doctrine
of God from the doctrine of the Trinity, as though the doctrine of one God could be explained
within the framework of reason without reference to God as Trinity. Theologians like Karl
Rahner and Karl Barth tried to reverse this rupture by setting the doctrine of God within the
framework of God's revelation and his saving acts in history. See Torrance, *The Ground and
Grammar of Theology*, 147; Thomas F. Torrance, *Trinitarian Perspectives: Toward Doctrinal
Agreement* (Edinburgh: T & T Clark, 1994), 3-4. There has also been a revival in the study of
the Trinity with special emphasis on bridging the gap between the theology of the Trinity and
Christian life and praxis. A few remarkable attempts in this connection are: Leonardo Boff,
Trinity and Society (Maryknoll, NY: Orbis, 1988); Catherine Mowry LaCugna, *God for Us:
The Trinity and Christian Life* (San Francisco, CA: Harper, 1991); Jürgen Moltmann, *The
Trinity and the Kingdom of God: The Doctrine of God*, trans. Margaret Kohl (London: SCM
Press, 1981); Karl Rahner, *The Trinity*, trans. Joseph Donceel (New York: Crossroad, 1997).

3.3. The Trinitarian Structure of God's Self-communication

The God of Christianity is the 'God of revelation'. The characteristic feature of Christian revelation is that God has been revealed as Trinity: Father, Son, and the Holy Spirit. The triuneness of God belongs to the very structure of revelation, the mode of God's self-communication to what is other than himself.

3.3.1. Revelation: A Constitutive Phenomenon of God's Self-communication

In revealing himself, God was not rendering himself as an intelligible object. God is not like any other possible object of knowledge to be known by a human subject. God's revelation is neither a mere communication of certain principles or ideas, nor the expression of emotions. As Karl Barth says, God's revelation is not something that God *gives* to humankind, but God *himself*, because God is not other than the revelation given. Accordingly, God is "Revealer, Revelation and Revealedness."[78] In revealing himself, God not only manifested, but also communicated himself. As Vatican II clearly states, "[it] has pleased God, in his goodness and wisdom, to reveal himself and to make known the secret purpose of his will." What we see in the Trinitarian pattern of God's self-communication is nothing other than this complete outreach of God to human beings. The Council further explains that "by thus revealing himself, God, who is invisible, in his great love, speaks to humankind as friends, and enters into their life, so as to invite and receive them into relationship with himself."[79] In this sense, the radical meaning of God's self-communication implies a complete and unreserved giving of himself in love. It is important to notice that revelation implies God's self-communication of himself to humankind. God "invite[s] and receive[s] them [human beings] into relationship with himself." Thus God's communication in its entirety is not simply an "information-communication," but God's own very self, God's self-communication *per se*. It is not mono-logical, but rather, a dialogical process which engages two parties that consists of an offer that evokes a reception and a response, namely, God's invitation and human being's acceptance in freedom. This communication of God in love has its eternal origin in God himself which was made manifest in time, through creation, and became visible, audible, and tangible in the person of Jesus Christ

---

78. Barth, *Church Dogmatics*, 1/1, 219.
79. "*Dei Verbum*," no. 2.

(cf. Heb 1:1). Thus, the incarnation is the peak point of the revelation of God who is essentially revealing.

The Revelation of God, as self-communication, is constitutive of God, because there is a communication in love that takes place in the Triune God. According to the traditional Western understanding, the Father gives himself completely to his Son, the Son receives the Father completely into himself, so as to be of one divine substance, and the Holy Spirit is the love between the Father and the Son: the gift, or the result of the mutual giving of the Father and the Son. God, as triune, is communication in himself. According to John Zizioulas, "Love as God's mode of existence 'hypostasizes' God, constitutes His being."[80] This divine love is dynamic. As W.J. Hill puts it, "divine love is not a sterile symbiosis of lovers, but an *élan* of perfect life, wherein the love itself becomes a reality over and against the lovers, with all the density of ontological personhood."[81] Briefly speaking, revelation becomes a constitutive phenomenon of God, while "Revealer, Revelation, and Revealedness" of God is interior to God. We have access to this knowledge of the interior life of God through God's revelation in history.

3.3.2. History of Revelation

The history of revelation is the history of God's self-communication. Human history and the salvation history are co-existing, although they are not identical; the affinity between them is a differentiated unity.[82] When we reflect upon God's engagement in history, we have to admit, not only the fact that God enters history, but also that we ought to see that history is in God.[83] The totality of human life is a history of the presence of God; it is the history of God's presence within the history of human life. In fact, the entirety of history is permeated by divine presence. Moreover, the history of humanity, with all its racial differences and diverse expressions of religion and culture,

---

80. John D. Zizioulas, *Being as Communion: Studies in Personhood and the Church*, vol. 30 (London: Darton, Longman & Todd, 1985), 46.

81. W.J. Hill, *The Three-Personed God* (Washington, DC: Catholic University of America Press, 1988), 75. As cited by Laszlo Lukacs, "Communication – Symbols – Sacraments," *Questions Liturgiques/Studies in Liturgy* 81 (2000): 202.

82. Anne D. Carr, "Starting with the Human," in *A World of Grace: An Introduction to the Themes and Foundations of Karl Rahner's Theology*, ed. Leo J. O'Donovan (Washington, DC: Georgetown University Press, 1995), 27-28.

83. Thomas F. O'Meara, "A History of Grace," in *A World of Grace: An Introduction to the Themes and Foundations of Karl Rahner's Theology*, 79.

forms a single human history, a common history of God.[84] Thus, the history of salvation is the history of grace present in the whole history.

God's self-communication enters a new phase in the history of Israel. In the experience of Israel, we see the intensification of the history of salvation leading to its climax in Jesus Christ. Medieval theologians sufficiently understood God's sacramental encounter in the Old Testament, so much so that they call them the "sacraments of the Old Testament." Even though the entirety of human history can be understood, in general, as a history of salvation, this revelation and presence of God, in a particular religious history, becomes vital, and comes into sharp focus in the history of Israel which has its zenith in Jesus of Nazareth.[85] In other words, in Jesus Christ, God's self-communicating presence meets us and in Jesus, we encounter the One who himself strives to make his love tangible, visible and audible, as the culmination of human religious aspirations. Indeed, the history of God's self-communicating presence is the history of the evolution of grace which has its culmination in Christ. The history of salvation reaches its climax in the death and resurrection of Jesus. But this is not the final stage, or the end of the history of salvation, but the triumph of God's grace. With the Christ event, God's plan of salvation enters into a more intense and final phase with the Kingdom of God and the intense experience of the Spirit.[86] Thus, in Judeo-Christian revelation, this action of God became more tangible and experiential; perceptibly we see therein the concrete presence of God with his people. Nevertheless, as we will see, revelation in history is mediated through symbols.

3.3.3. Symbolic Mediation and Revelation

In recent years, there has been a growing consensus about the connection between symbol and revelation. The concept of "revelation as symbolic disclosure" has gained wide acceptance in theological discussions, although with various nuances and emphases.[87] The symbolic approach to revelation

---

84. O'Meara, "A History of Grace," 81.

85. *Ibid.*, 85.

86. *Ibid.*, 89.

87. Avery Dulles, "The Symbolic Structure of Revelation," *Theological Studies* 41 (1980): 55. In his article Avery Dulles discusses different approaches to revelation. For an elaborate study of the same, see Avery Dulles, *Models of Revelation* (Maryknoll, NY: Orbis Books, 1992), esp. 131-154.

holds that revelation is mediated through symbols. Such symbols are revelatory symbols, because they express and mediate God's self-communication.

Noticeably, there is a mediatory aspect in the whole schema of God's self-communication. God's engagement in human history takes place by God's coming to the worldliness and historicity of human beings. According to Rahner, God's personal self-communication "can only enter explicitly, reflectively, and thematically as an object into human consciousness by virtue of an historical mediation. One *needs the symbolic mediation* of an external event, or an objective and specifying medium."[88] "Revelation comes to us in the midst of peoples' histories and it emerges out of lives lived in world history, but it comes to us with particular intensity through men and women conscious of being set apart as bearers of revelation."[89] In this sense, Christian revelation, as it is unfolded in the Bible, has a symbolic structure and revelation is mediated through symbols.[90] In the Old Testament, God's self-communication, his presence, was mediated through symbols as found in the "burning bush," the miracles of Exodus, the theophanies of Mount Sinai, the "still small voice" heard by Elijah, etc. As Colwell points out, a particular event, or a material object, becomes the medium of God's presence only by the Spirit and the word of God. The burning bush is distinct from all other bushes in that it mediates God's presence by the Spirit.[91] In the Old Testament, God spoke to the Patriarchs his words and actions in history. God manifested his presence through the mediation of the word; he has spoken through the prophets, and it is the Spirit who helped them to understand and speak the word of God. God's presence was manifested through the Word and the Spirit.[92] Also, certain events and objects become the symbols of God's presence through his promise, i.e., through his word.[93] Avery Dulles points out that even the gospels unfold the life and message of Jesus through

88. Rahner, *Foundations of Christian Faith*, 51-55. See also Roger Haight, *Jesus Symbol of God* (Maryknoll, NY: Orbis Books, 1999), 13.

89. O'Meara, "A History of Grace," 88. According to Dulles, one of the major approaches, namely historical, implies that revelation is given objectively in historical events. Dulles, "The Symbolic Structure of Revelation," 53. Without denying the validity of this approach, it can be asserted that historical events are the vehicles of revelation through their mediatory and symbolic dimension.

90. Here we use the term 'symbol' in an inclusive sense, applying it to both visible and invisible objects, events and to language pregnant with more meaning than explicitly stated.

91. Colwell, *Promise and Presence*, 56-57.

92. Rahner, *The Trinity*, 41-42.

93. Colwell, *Promise and Presence*, 57.

symbolic events, words, and deeds. The events surrounding the birth of Jesus, the coming of the Holy Spirit at baptism in the form of a dove, the transfigurations, the healing of the sick, and even his death on the cross have a symbolic aspect. The climaxing events of his death and resurrection and the sending of the Holy Spirit are symbolic events that disclose a major point in the history of salvation.[94] All these translate the message of salvation audibly, visibly, and tangibly. However, the revelatory symbols in the Bible have also revealing and concealing aspects. "In being revealed, [the transcendent] does not cease to remain concealed, since its secrecy pertains to its very essence, and when, therefore, it is revealed it is so precisely as that which is hidden."[95] In revelation there is the dialectics of "presence" and "absence," which is fundamental to the concept of sacramentality. In this connection, it is important to notice that, evidently, the presence-absence dialectic of God's manifestation is primarily experienced in creation and its evolution to an ultimate destiny. It is to this discussion that we turn now.

3.3.4. Sacramentality of Creation

The whole universe can be seen as God's sacrament in a broad sense.[96] The first phase of God's self-communication is his self-communication in creation. As we have pointed out, a systematic and comprehensive theology of the Spirit has its point of departure in the Spirit's activity in creation. A Pneumatological approach to the sacraments should take into account the presence of God that embraces the created order itself, which is mediated in and through the Spirit, the fundamental principle of divine presence and activity.

God's relation to the world, his abiding presence and activity in the universe, is asserted invariably by the three monotheistic religions, namely, Judaism, Christianity, and Islam. Christian theology basically affirms the

---

94. Dulles, "The Symbolic Structure of Revelation," 58. According to Dulles, Christ is the revelatory symbol. The cross and the resurrection of Christ are the two central symbols of Christ who is the summit of revelation. *Ibid.*, 156.

95. Dulles, *Models of Revelation*, 138.

96. From the very beginning Christian tradition viewed the world as sacrament. Mathai Kadavil presents an excellent study on the subject from the perspectives of the Latin, Greek and Syriac traditions, taking Leonard Boff, Alexandeer Schmemann and Saint Ephrem as representatives. Mathai Kadavil, *The World as Sacrament: Sacramentality of Creation from the Perspectives of Leonardo Boff, Alexander Schmemann and Saint Ephrem* (Leuven: Peeters, 2005).

presence of the Spirit as the life-giving one, the *ek-stasis* of God that encompasses creation, incarnation, and sanctification. Accordingly, the world was called into existence by God and it neither existed eternally, nor did it come into existence out of some pre-existent substance, or by chance.[97] Christian tradition ascribes a creative and conservative role to the Spirit. The early Christian tradition identifies Gen 1:2 with the "Spirit of God," and interprets the "hovering over the waters" in reference to the activity of God at creation.[98] The Spirit who hovers over the waters can be understood to be the power of God being active in what is other than God. The patristic doctrine of *creatio ex nihilo* originally means, not only that God created everything from nothing, but also that it is the divine creative presence in the Spirit that holds everything in being.[99] This doctrine relates, not only to the creative action of God, but also to the sustaining energies of God to the existence of creation. In this sense, the world does not have a "self-evident existence," but it was "created *post nihilum*," which means the existence of the world depends on "God's will and energy."[100] As Zizioulas interprets it from his Orthodox theological background, *creatio ex nihilo* means that it is "no thing," but "someone" (God) who creates.[101]

Aquinas gave a systematic exposition to the notion of divine omnipresence that is fundamental to the existence of creatures, using Aristotelian categories and the concept of being as *esse*. Accordingly, it is the divine interior presence that brings everything into being and conserves them in exis-

---

97. John Moorhead, "The Spirit and the World," *The Greek Orthodox Theological Review* 26 (1981): 113.

98. Colin E. Gunton, *Father, Son & Holy Spirit: Toward a Fully Trinitarian Theology* (London, New York: T & T Clark, 2003), 108; Emmanuel Kaniyamparampil, *The Spirit of Life: A Study of the Holy Spirit in the Early Syriac Tradition* (Kottayam, India: Oriental Institute of Religious Studies India, 2003), 44. Basil, "Homily on the Hexaemeron," in *The Nicene and Post-Necene Fathers*, ed. Philip Schaff and Henry Wace (Edinburgh: T & T Clark, 1996), 2: 6; Origen, "De Principiis," in *The Ante-Nicene Fathers*, ed. A. Cleveland Coxe (Edinburgh: T & T Clark, 1994), 1: 3,3.

99. Denis Edwards, "Ecology and the Holy Spirit: The 'Already' and the 'Not yet' of the Spirit in Creation," *Pacifica* 13 (2000): 146.

100. Christos S. Voulgaris, "The Holy Trinity in Creation and Incarnation," *The Greek Orthodox Theological Review* 42 (1997): 246. Eastern Trinitarian theology makes a distinction between the essence and energies of God, whereas, the Western Trinitarian thinking principally identifies our experience of God in the economy with God in God's self.

101. Jaroslav Z. Skira, "The Ecological Bishop: John Zizioulas' Theology of Creation," *Toronto Journal of Theology* 19 (2003): 203.

tence.[102] According to Rahner, we have to go beyond Aquinas' understanding of God not only as the cause of the existence of creation, but also as the dynamic ground of their becoming. He argues that, beyond divine conservation and "*concursus*," we need to think of God's act of ongoing creation, which enables the creation for a process of "active self-transcendence" in which all beings realize their own nature and brings forth what is "new."[103] It is God who enables this becoming, empowering the creatures from within. According to the theology of Athanasius and Basil, this ongoing creation can be understood as being realized by the activity of the Spirit who is the life-giver, present in all things who makes this evolution and unfolding possible from within.[104] This is also similar to the Syriac tradition which gives more importance to the Spirit. The Spirit's activity is not terminated at creation, but continues throughout the history of salvation.[105] Thus, the Christian tradition, in general, helps us to reflect on creation in terms of the activity of the Spirit. Nonetheless, the Christian tradition interprets the overwhelming activity of the Spirit in relation to the Trinity in such a way that creation and its unfolding can be understood as the work of the whole Trinity.

3.3.5. Trinity in Creation and Incarnation

The theology of creation is fundamentally the question of God's relation to the world. Creation can be understood as the first sacrament in the sense that

---

102. Edwards, "Ecology and the Holy Spirit," 146-147. According to Aquinas, God is not only the cause of the existence of creatures, but also maintains the creatures in existence as the sun keeps the atmosphere lit up remaining itself lit up. According to him, things exist only as long as God enables them "to be" (*esse*). So, there is a continuing relationship between the creature and the Creator which is the fundamental principle of its very being. Thomas Aquinas, *Summa Theologiae*, trans. Timothy McDermott, vol. 2 (London, New York: Blackfriars, 1964), 1a.8,1.

103. Karl Rahner, "Evolution," in *Sacramentum Mundi*, ed. Karl Rahner, et al. (New York: Herder and Herder, 1968), 292.

104. Edwards, "Ecology and the Holy Spirit," 147.

105. Kaniyamparampil, *The Spirit of Life*, 44. For a detailed study of the Holy Spirit in the East Syriac tradition, see Jan N. Bremmer, ed., *The Apochryphal Acts of Thomas*, Studies in Early Christian Apocrypha, 6 (Leuven: Peeters, 2001); James H. Charlesworth, ed., *The Odes of Solomon* (Oxford: Clarendon, 1973); "Ephraim Syrus, Aphrahat," in *The Nicene and Post-Nicene Fathers* (Edinburgh: T & T Clark); Kathleen McVey, *Ephrem the Syrian* (Mahwah, NJ: Paulist Press, 1989); Aphrahat the Persian Sage, "Demonstrations," in *The Nicene and Post-Nicene Fathers*, ed. John Gwynn (Grand Rapids, MI: Eerdmans, 1979); Ephraim the Syrian, "Hymns and Homilies," in *The Nicene and Post-Nicene Fathers*, ed. John Gwynn (Edinburgh: T & T Clark, 1979).

it is through creation that God communicates and facilitates the divine-human relation.[106] In the gift of creation, the Creator/God was giving himself to us as our Father, bestowing upon us the possibility of receiving him as Creator/Father.[107] In God's self-communication through creation, God is encountered as Trinity. Some of the Eastern Fathers tried to view creation as such solely as the work of the Trinity. For instance, Basil attributes the work of the Trinity *ad extra* as the work of the three divine persons: "the original cause of all things that are made, the Father; the creative cause, the Son; the perfecting cause, the Spirit."[108] Gregory of Nyssa says, "Therefore, then, the Holy Trinity works every activity according to the manner stated, not divided according to the number of hypostases, but one certain motion and disposition of good will occurs, proceeding from the Father through the Son to the Spirit."[109] Therefore, the role of the Spirit in creation should be viewed in relation to the Father and the Son, in order to keep a distance from an anthropocentric approach of considering the Spirit as an independent agent of creation.[110]

God's self-communication in creation cannot be regarded in isolation from the incarnation, because God's relation to the world reaches its fullness in the incarnation. C. K. Barrett points out that there is a clear link between the activity of the Spirit in the birth of Jesus, and the understanding of creation. The Spirit of God, who was at the foundation of the world, was also presupposed in its renewal leading to its fulfillment. The same Creator Spirit of the Book of Genesis was legitimately thought to be present in the incarnation as the fulfillment of God's promised redemption in a new act of creation.[111] According to Athanasius, the Spirit who is involved in the incarna-

---

106. Theodore Runyon, "The World as the Original Sacrament," *Worship* 54 (1980): 500.
107. *Ibid.*, 501.
108. Basil, "De Spiritu Sancto," in *The Nicene and Post-Nicene Fathers*, 2nd Series, ed. Philip Schaff and Henry Wace (Edinburgh: T & T Clark, 1996), xvi, 38.
109. Gunton, *Toward a Fully Trinitarian Theology*, 114.
110. *Ibid.*, 114.
111. Charles Kingsley Barrett, *The Holy Spirit and the Gospel Tradition* (London: SPCK., 1966), 23-24. Christos S. Voulgaris makes a distinction between the Fatherhood and creatorship of God based on God's relationship to Christ in the incarnation and to the creation, respectively. He opines that God's Fatherhood has to be differentiated from God as creator, because "God is not the cause of creation in the same way as he is the cause of his Son ... on the contrary, he is Creator because he is Father, and he cannot be Creator unless he is the Father of his eternal Son." Begetting of his Son is internal and timeless, whereas creating is external to his essence and bound to time. In other words, God has always been Father, whereas he has not always been Creator; creation does not concur with his existence, but has a

tional process and salvation is also active in creation.[112] In this sense, the incarnation, which is mediated by the activity of the Holy Spirit, marks the beginning of a New Age and a new act of creation. God's self-communication in the person of Jesus Christ becomes the culmination of God's self-communication in creation.

3.3.5.1. Spirit in Creation and Its Evolution

Classical theology developed the understanding that God is present in creation through his creative power, and set things in motion towards perfection. The Spirit was understood as the divine presence in all things. "God in the Spirit is ultimately interior to each creature [more] than they are to themselves."[113] The Spirit of God is present and active in creation, as well as in evolution, enabling them to emerge into new things. As Pannenberg puts it, "the Spirit of God is the life-giving principle, to which all creatures owe life, movement and activity."[114] So, the Spirit is the innermost reality of every being as the life-giving Spirit who enables the unfolding of the universe. Since the Spirit is the innermost reality of beings, they have a distinctive relation to God as the source of life in the Spirit and to other creatures as fellow beings, each with its own integrity.[115] According to Moltmann, the Spirit not only creates all things, but also brings all creatures into a fellowship with all creatures. As he writes, "*the community of creation*, in which all created things exist with one another, for one another, and in one another, is also *the fellowship of the Holy Spirit*."[116]

---

beginning and is not eternal. The knowledge of God as the Father precedes the knowledge as creator, because the Son's timeless birth from the Father precedes his creative activity. Voulgaris, "Trinity in Creation and Incarnation," 247-248.

112. "The Father creates all things through the Word in the Spirit; for where the Word is, there is the Spirit also, and the things which are created have their vital strength out of the Spirit from the Word." Athanasius, "Letter to Serapion," in *The Letters of Saint Athanasius Concerning the Holy Spirit*, ed. C.R.B. Shapland (London: Epworth Press, 1951), 3:5, p. 174. About the incarnation he writes, "When the Word visited the Holy Virgin Mary, the Spirit came to her with him, and the Word in the Spirit moulded the body and conformed it to himself; desiring to join and present all creation to the Father through himself." *Ibid.*, 1:31, p. 45ff.

113. Edwards, "Ecology and the Holy Spirit," 148.

114. Wolfhart Pannenberg, *Systematic Theology*, vol. 2 (Grand Rapids: MI: Eerdmans, 1994), 76.

115. Rosemary Radford Ruether, *Gaia and God: An Ecofeminist Theology of Earth Healing* (San Francisco, CA: Harper San Francisco, 1992), 277-278.

116. Moltmann, *The Spirit of Life*, 10.

The understanding of the role of the Spirit in creation, and its evolution, developed in early Christian thinking along biblical lines. Apart from Genesis 1:3, there are other passages that attribute creation and evolution of the world to the activity of the Spirit. For instance, the Psalmist seems to place in parallel columns the role of the Word and the Spirit: "By the word of the Lord were the heavens made, their starry host by the breath of his mouth" (Ps 33:6). The Spirit is also understood, not only as the creator, but also the preserver and maintainer of life: "When you take away their spirit, they die and return to the dust. When you send your spirit, they are created, and you renew the face of the earth" (Ps 104:29b-30). Here, the creedal affirmation of the Spirit as the Lord and giver of life is reflected. The Spirit is referred to as the breath of the Lord which gives life. As we read in Gen 2:7, "the Lord God formed the man from the dust of the ground and breathed into his nostrils the breath of life, and the man became a living being." So the Spirit can be identified as the principle of life in creation. However, even though the idea of the mediation of the Spirit in creation, its preservation and evolution is widespread in the scriptures, they do not clearly refer to the Holy Spirit. As Congar says, the "immortal breath" of Wisdom 12:1 and other similar verses (Ps 104:28-30; Job 34:14-15) are not strictly identical with the Holy Spirit, because the Holy Spirit was not fully revealed at that time.[117] Nevertheless, it is important to notice how the biblical tradition emphasises the creative and sustaining power of God that is present in the whole universe.

Jürgen Moltmann seems right in critiquing that the cosmic role of the Spirit as creator has not been developed in Catholic theology.[118] That resulted in a minimalist understanding of sacramentality which disengaged sacramentality from creation and the eschaton. In fact, redemption cannot be understood exclusively as human redemption, but rather, as the recapitulation or restoration of the whole of creation to its eschatological destiny. The Spirit, who dwells in the whole of creation, is understood as the one who brings the whole of creation into eschatological newness and perfection. As Paul speaks, the whole of creation is groaning for redemption (cf. Rom 8:19-23). According to him, the resurrection experience of the Spirit is the guarantee for an eschatological transformation of creation. Thus, the redemption of

---

117. Congar, *The Word and the Spirit*, 125.
118. Jürgen Moltmann, "Heiliger Geist in der Geschichte," *Orientierung* 47 (1983): 128-130. Taking Moltmann's criticism at its face value, Congar attempts to develop a theological understanding of the Spirit in the cosmos. See Congar, *The Word and the Spirit*, 122-129.

humanity is connected to the restoration of creation.[119] Retrieving the cosmic
role of the Spirit would help us to understand sacramental presence in a
broader perspective, which would eventually lead us to overcome the tendency of truncating sacramentality from creation and the eschaton.[120] We argue
that a comprehensive theology of the sacraments also should take into account the presence and activity of the Spirit in creation as its point of departure, because, "… the universe as such, is the primary religious reality, the
primary sacred community, the primary revelation of the divine, the primary
subject of incarnation, the primary unity of redemption, the primary referent
in any discussion of reality or of value."[121]

3.3.5.2. Sacramentality of Creation and Sacramental Presence

A sacramental theology that begins with the notion of the sacramentality of
creation will help us to understand sacramental presence in a broader perspective. Regrettably, the overemphasis on Christology has truncated our understanding of sacramentality, and reduces our ability to consider the cosmos
as the primary sacrament. It was only in the second millennium that the concept of sacramentality became rigid and confined, due to differing, albeit
legitimate reasons. Thus came the numbering of the sacraments as "seven,"
and only seven, at Trent. But this may be better understood as the broadening
or the expansion of the concept of sacramentality against the Reformist's
confinement of the sacraments according to the notion of divine institution
based on a literal reading of the scriptures.[122] At present, there is a growing
consensus among theologians regarding the importance of a theology of creation in explaining sacramental presence. According to Martien E. Brinkman,
there is a necessary relation between the sacraments and the doctrine of creation. As he puts it, "the salvation proclaimed in the sacraments would be-

---

119. Edwards, "Ecology and the Holy Spirit," 152.
120. It seems that orthodox tradition, to a great extent, ascribes more importance to the
cosmic role of the Spirit in relation to creation and eschaton. However, it is not totally extinct
in Catholic tradition. Congar opines that a cosmic role can be accorded to the Holy Spirit in
the light of the writings of the Fathers, documents of the Vatican Council, and other theological literature. See also Congar, *I Believe in the Holy Spirit*, 3:271-272.
121. Anne Lonergan and Carolyn Richards, *Thomas Berry and the New Cosmology* (Mystic, CT: Twenty-third Publications, 1991), 37-38. Cited in Dorothy McDougall, "The Cosmos
as Primary Sacrament: An Ecological Perspective for Sacramental Theology," *Questions
Liturgiques* 81 (2000): 294.
122. Kevin W. Irwin, "Sacramentality and the Theology of Creation: A Recovered Paradigm for Sacramental Theology," *Louvain Studies* 23 (1998): 163.

come docetic, lose all contact with the day-to-day concrete world, and the doctrine of creation would become cynically fatalistic, if there were no prospect of salvation."[123] Kevin W. Irwin follows Brinkman, in re-investigating how the sacramentality of creation can be a paradigm for thinking about sacramentality and sacramental presence. He advocates a retrieval of the patristic notion of the sacramentality of creation as a prior step in reflecting on the sacraments.[124] Similarly, McDougall argues that a broad understanding of sacramental theology should extend the salvific process to the entirety of the cosmos, rather than confining it to the anthropocentric perspective.[125] In fact, the world is the object of God's redeeming and transforming activity. Therefore, Christology, Church, and sacraments must all be seen within the context of an overarching purpose.[126]

While agreeing with the position of those who situate the theology of creation at the beginning of sacramental thinking, our approach to sacramental theology is predisposed to bring to light the activity of the Spirit as the core of every sacramental presence and experience. Thus, we argue that any consideration of the sacramentality of creation should be explained in terms of the activity of the Spirit, because sacramentality is the phenomenon of the experience of the Spirit, which can only be understood in terms of God's self-communication, whereby God reaches out in the Word and the Spirit. As Rahner says,

> [t]o put [it] in biblical terms: if God as he is in himself has already communicated himself in his Holy Spirit always and everywhere and to every person as the innermost center of his existence, whether he accepts it or not, and if the whole history of creation is already borne by God's self-communication in this very creation, then there does not seem to be anything else which can take place on God's part.[127]

Briefly speaking, the history of creation is the history of God's self-communication in the Spirit. The presence of the Spirit in the life-breath of every human being as *imago Dei* and in the whole of creation is the basis of

123. Martien E. Brinkman, *Sacraments of Freedom: Ecumenical Essays on Creation and Sacrament: Justification and Freedom* (Zoetermeer: Meinema/IIMO Research Publications, 1999), 70.

124. Irwin, "Sacramentality and the Theology of Creation," 165.

125. McDougall, "The Cosmos as Primary Sacrament," 297. The main thrust of her article is to present the cosmos as the primary sacrament as a resource for constructing an ecological sacramental theology.

126. Runyon, "The World as the Original Sacrament," 498.

127. Rahner, *Foundations*, 139.

sacramentality. The understanding of the Spirit does not subsist only on the ontological level, but the experience of the Spirit is intrinsic to human existence as our innermost reality.

However, the experience of the Spirit cannot be divorced from the experience of God as Trinity which the human beings experience fundamentally in creation. In the words of Dennis Edwards, the underlying relation between the creation and redemption of the universe is the "*self-expression of the Trinitarian God.*"[128] That is why the understanding of creation was developed in the Christian tradition along Trinitarian lines. God's communication of himself is a Trinitarian act which is of the three consubstantial persons that come in the order of procession from the Father. "The divine persons are made present by means of the gifts of grace, the effects of the invisible movements of the Word and the Spirit, as partners in spiritual communion."[129] "The triune God is present, in the Spirit, to each creature here and now, loving it into existence and promising its future."[130] The Trinitarian self-communication of God in creation has its zenith in God's self-communication in the Word and the Spirit in the economy of salvation. Sacraments are to be located in the trajectory of God's self-communication in the Word and the Spirit.

3.4. God's Self-communication in Christ and the Holy Spirit

The New Testament attests to the mission and the sending of both the Son and the Holy Spirit. The divine missions of the Son and the Spirit have been understood as the two aspects of the whole economy. Thus, the economy viewed as the work of the Trinity, the mission of the Son, and the Spirit, shed light on two aspects of the mystery of the Trinity, namely, the idea of the mission and the procession of the Persons in the Trinity. A reflection on the mission of the Son and the Spirit can be approached in two ways, either beginning from the immanent Trinity, as God in God's own self prior to his relation to history, or from the historical and salvific experience of the Son and the Spirit to the eternal processions interior to God's life. Both of these approaches are valid and tenable. However, we have no immediate access to the knowledge of God's self, other than what is given in the economic ma-

---

128. Denis Edwards, *Jesus the Wisdom of God: An Ecological Theology* (Maryknoll, NY: Orbis Books, 1995), 122.

129. Congar, *I Believe in the Holy Spirit*, 3:151.

130. Edwards, "Ecology and the Holy Spirit," 154.

nifestation. For this reason, we begin to examine the temporal missions of the Son and the Spirit in the economy of salvation and trace them back to the interior life of God. Our conceptual framework enabling us to think along these lines is the Rahnerian category of God's self-communication. Karl Rahner's theology of the Trinity, in terms of God's self-communication, gave incentive to reassess the mission of the Word and the Spirit in a Trinitarian framework. The foundational basis of exploring Pneumatology is the structural framework of God's engagement in the history of humankind. As McDonnell expresses it, "the key to Pneumatology, if there be any, is salvation history."[131] For the entire salvation history is God's self-communication to humanity in tangible ways. Developing the doctrine of the Holy Spirit amounts to exploring the role of the Holy Spirit in the Trinitarian scheme of salvation. At the same time, exploring the role of the Holy Spirit is not an attempt to define the Holy Spirit as an independent reality. On the contrary, our concern must be to reaffirm the distinctive role of the Holy Spirit in relation to the Father and the Son. Irenaeus' imagery of the Word and the Spirit as "two hands" of God with which he touches human history must contradict every stance taken to the detriment of any of the Persons of the Trinity.[132] There can never be a balanced doctrine of Christ without the recognition that Pneumatology is the point of entry into Christology and, ultimately, into the Trinity. A true Christo-centric approach is without validity unless it is thought out in relation to the Spirit.[133] Losing the Trinitarian grounding runs the risk of limiting the role of the Holy Spirit to the periphery of God's involvement in human history. Therefore, the Trinitarian mystery serves as the structural framework within which the Christological and Pneumatological dimensions are shaped.

3.4.1. Economic Trinity and Immanent Trinity

As was mentioned, traditional Western theology, which was formalised by Aquinas, detached the doctrine of God from the doctrine of the Trinity, as though the doctrine of one God could be explained within the framework of reason without reference to God as Trinity. Aquinas treated God under two treatises, namely, "On the One God" and "On the Triune God." Trinitarian theology was developed with an inner logic of its own, independent of salva-

---

131. McDonnell, "Doctrine of the Holy Spirit," 143.
132. Congar, *I Believe in the Holy Spirit*, 2:9. See also pp. 116-117.
133. McDonnell, "Doctrine of the Holy Spirit," 152.

tion history, even though Augustine tries to tie it to salvation history.[134] The neo-scholastics tried to follow faithfully the order of treatment, beginning with the treatise "On the One God," and following through to the treatise "On the Triune God." The Trinity was touched upon only after discussing God's being, attributes, knowability, etc.[135] The Thomistic approach, which was transmitted through neo-scholasticism, shaped the pattern of Christian theology, beginning the debate concerning the Trinity from the unity of divine essence and attributes, rather than from the distinctiveness of the divine persons. Thus, the traditional Western way of treating the mystery of the Trinity, beginning with the unity of divine essence, minimised the diversity of the divine persons as manifested in the biblical revelation of salvation history and in the Christian experience of God through Christ and the Spirit.[136] This way of looking at the mystery of the Trinity and salvation history disjointed the eternal procession and the economic missions of the Word and the Spirit. In contrast, the Greek emphasis on the diversity of divine persons in the economy of salvation seems to adhere more to the biblical, creedal, and liturgical confessions of the Church, and also better explains the doctrine of the Trinity and God's economy. The pre-Augustinian, Greek approach to God, that considers the Father as the source of the divinity of the Son and the Spirit, explains the economy as the work of the Trinity, in contrast to those undertaken by the scholastics.

In this context, the Rahnerian approach to the Trinity creates a linkage between the economic and immanent Trinity.[137] Rahner's distinct contribution

134. Reid, *Energies of the Spirit*, 13. According to Reid the Western way of treating the economic Trinity and immanent Trinity might have been influenced by the patristic distinction of *theologia* and *economia*. See *ibid.*, 21.

135. Fred Sanders, *The Image of the Immanent Trinity*, ed. Paul D. Molnar, Issues in Systematic Theology (New York: Peter Lang, 2005), 57.

136. The Western refusal to accept the distinctive missions of the Trinitarian persons, which is characteristic of Western theology, may be traced back to the Augustinian rule that "the outward acts of the Trinity are divided" (*opera trinitatis ad extra sunt indivisa*). The distinctiveness of the Trinitarian persons was eclipsed by "the God of an abstract, non-trinitarian monotheism." Sanders, *The Image of the Immanent Trinity*, 60.

137. The terms "economic" and "immanent" which became common in Trinitarian discussions originally comes from Greek patristic theology. In Greek patristic theology, *oikonomia* refers to the "administration of God's plan of salvation." In a broad sense, *oikonomia* means "God's unfolding purpose in the world." By the time of Ignatius of Antioch and Irenaeus, *oikonomia* assumed a Christological sense to designate Christ's fulfilment of God's plan of salvation. Later fathers employed *theologia* to distinguish the triune God *in se*, without reference to creation and incarnation from God *pro nobis* in the economy of salvation (*oikonomia*). Accordingly, immanent Trinity is Trinity *ad intra*, the life and action of God in Godself,

to theology is the idea of conceiving revelation as God's self-communication, and sketching the inner and outer dimensions of the triune God in parallel strokes. Rahner, in his *Trinity*, develops a Trinitarian theology which has close bearing to the Christian faith, practice, and spirituality. He begins with a critique of the dichotomy in traditional Western theology that separated the treatise on the one God from the treatise on the Trinity, which, consequently, bore no relation to salvation history.[138] Its concern was totally centered "on the one divinity." Rahner, on the contrary, affirms that the mystery of salvation has a Trinitarian structure. According to him, God's self-communication (*selbst-Mitteilen*) is necessarily triune, which is actualized by Christ and the Spirit. For Rahner, the theology of the Trinity is actually God's self-communication in the mystery of salvation. In the light of this statement, Rahner intends to convey that God's economic relation to the world has a Trinitarian structure: In communicating himself, the threefoldness of God has only "one" relation to the world, but a relationship which is threefold, in the sense that each person relates with the world in the way proper to him.[139] Each of the divine persons communicates to the human being gratuitously in each one's particularity and diversity in their mutual relations, as the Father, Son, and Holy Spirit: The threefold manner of their relationship to each other. This self-communication is not simply saying something about the Trinity, but is the communication of the Trinity as such, the triune God. Thus, he tries to establish a connection between the doctrine of salvation and the doctrine of the triune God, and explains the unity and threeness (tri-unity) as two aspects of the mystery of the triune God.

In fact, what Rahner does is to reflect upon God as he is experienced in relation to creation. Therefore, he claims that our knowledge of the Trinity is based on God's self-communication in the Son and the Spirit. The Father communicates his divine being to the creatures through the mission of the

---

whereas economic Trinity is God in relation to the world in the Son and the Spirit. See Sanders, *The Image of the Immanent Trinity*, 3-5. Reid also observes that the Western way of treating the economic Trinity and immanent Trinity might have been influenced by the patristic distinction of *theologia* and *economia*. Reid, *Energies of the Spirit*, 21.

138. Rahner, *The Trinity*, 15-21. Like Rahner, another prominent figure among the theologians who tried to reverse this rupture by setting the doctrine of God within the framework of God's revelation and his saving acts in history is Karl Barth. See Torrance, *The Ground and Grammar of Theology*, 147; Torrance, *Trinitarian Perspectives*, 3-4. In contrast to Rahner, Barth speaks about God's movement to the world as "self-revelation of God" instead of "God's self-communication."

139. Rahner, *The Trinity*, 28.

Son and the Holy Spirit, the two modalities of the self-communication of the Father.[140] God's self-communication takes place within a relational structure of the Father, Son, and Holy Spirit. The history of salvation is the history of the Self-communication of the triune God. Therefore, the mystery of salvation has to be viewed in the light of the relational structure of the Trinitarian life. Thus, it becomes clear that, in Trinitarian theology, when we speak of God, we speak about him whom the scriptures and Jesus speaks of as the Father, who sends the Son, and gives himself in the Spirit. Rahner discovers a correspondence between the relational structure of the economy of salvation and the relational structure of the immanent Trinity. He attempts to establish a connection between the treatise on one God and the treatise on the Trinity with his axiomatic statement: *"The 'economic' Trinity is the 'immanent' Trinity and the 'immanent' Trinity is the 'economic' Trinity."*[141] The

140. Coffey, "Spirit Christology and the Trinity," 14; Jerome M. Hall, *We Have the Mind of Christ: The Holy Spirit and Liturgical Memory in the Thought of Edward J. Kilmartin* (Collegeville, MN: Liturgical Press, 2001), 79; Kilmartin, *Christian Liturgy*, 101; Congar, *The Word and the Spirit*, 104.

141. Rahner, *The Trinity*, 22. Rahner's axiom might originally have existed in theological circles before Rahner in some form. Rahner acknowledges this: "We are starting out from the proposition that the economic Trinity is the immanent Trinity and *vice versa*. I do not know exactly when and by whom this theological axiom was formulated for the first time." Karl Rahner, "Some Implications of the Scholastic Concept of Uncreated Grace," in *Theological Investigations* (London: Darton, Longman & Todd, 1974), 114. The respondents to the Rahnerian axiom can be placed in two camps; first, those who favour a radical application of the axiom; second, those in favour of a restrictive interpretation and application. Prominent among the radicalisers are: Robert W. Jenson, Piet Schoonenberg, Hans Küng, Jürgen Moltmann, Wolfhart Pannenberg and Catherine Mowry LaCugna. In the restrictive camp are: Walter Kasper, Yves Congar, Hans Urs von Balthasar, Thomas F. Torrance, and Paul D. Molnar. They reject a complete equation of the Trinity *ad extra* with Trinity *ad intra*. Fred Sanders calls the first group of theologians "radicalisers" and the second group "restricters." He dedicates two chapters (4 and 5) for the discussion of these authors. Sanders, *The Image of the Immanent Trinity*, 83-158. Congar expresses Rahner's view in somewhat similar terms that there is an identity between the "Trinity of the economy" and the "Trinity of the eternal mystery." We have no other way of knowing God apart from that which is revealed in the economy. Congar, *The Word and the Spirit*, 104. He makes a critical study of the interrelationship between the "economic" Trinity and "immanent" Trinity, in which he proposes a restrictive application of the axiom. Congar holds that God revealed in history cannot exhaust the reality of God in God's self. See Congar, *I Believe in the Holy Spirit*, 3:11-18, esp. 13ff. According to P. Schoonenberg the immanent Trinity is a Trinity of persons only because the Trinity is an economic Trinity. See Michael O'Carroll, *Trinitas: A Theological Encyclopedia of the Holy Trinity* (Wilmington, DE: Michael Glazier, 1987), 94. Rahner's methodology of Trinitarian theology stems from this perception of the mystery of the Trinity. He starts from the self-revelation of God as given in the salvation history as mediated by the Word and the Spirit. See

fundamental thesis of this equation is to show that there is a real connection between the two treatises, and that the Trinity is nothing other than the mystery of salvation.[142]

According to Rahner, economy means the plan of God in creation and the redemption of human beings, or covenant grace. The economic Trinity and the immanent Trinity are identical, because God's communication to the world in the Son and the Spirit will not be a real self-communication if the God for us in the Son and the Spirit are not essential to God himself. The Rahnerian axiom reflects the twofold dimensions of God's givenness, first "economically," as "three concrete ways of being given," or "givenness" and then, "immanently" as the "three relative ways of existing as the one and same God."[143] The "givenness" in the immanent Trinity can be understood only in terms of the "givenness" in the economic Trinity, because the Son and the Spirit, as the self-expression of the Father, is, in fact, the "manners of the givenness of the Father."[144] The entire effort of Rahner is to help us understand how the two ways of God's self-communication through the Son and the Spirit are two essential and integral moments, internally related to each other, and constituting one self-communication of God.[145] These two moments refer to one another and distinguish each other, constituting one salvation history. Thus, to be incarnate is the proper mission of the Son, while to be sent is the proper mission of the Spirit.[146] In other words, the question is how can we "conceptualize" incarnation and the descent of the

Patrick Burke, *Reinterpreting Rahner: A Critical Study of His Major Themes* (New York: Fordham University Press, 2002), 78. Eastern theology also makes a distinction between the inner being (*ousia*) and the activities (*energeia*) of the triune God. Nevertheless, God in the economy is no less divine than God in himself. See Reid, *Energies of the Spirit*, 1.

142. Sanders, *The Image of the Immanent Trinity*, 58.

143. Rahner, *The Trinity*, 74. Karl Barth prefers to explain this inner divine-order of the Trinity, as three "ways" or "modes of being." Barth, *Church Dogmatics*, 1/1, 407. In contrast to Rahnarian and Barthian understanding, the doctrine of divine energies of the orthodox theology emphasises that God reveals God's eternal glory, but not Godself. However, God's glory is understood as Godself, but not God's essence. This is based on the distinction they make between God's essence and energies. Reid, *Energies of the Spirit*, 56.

144. Rahner, *The Trinity*, 74.

145. *Ibid.*, 84-87. This understanding of the Trinity is not very much different from Barth's understanding. For Barth, economic Trinity is the inner Trinity. It is because God reveals Godself in the economy, and we know about the Trinitarian God through revelation in the economy. See Barth, *Church Dogmatics*, 1/1, 340. He treats elaborately on the revelation of God as the Father, Son and Holy Spirit, respectively. See pp. 441ff., 457ff., 513ff.

146. Karl Rahner, "Remarks on the Dogmatic Treatise 'De Trinitate'," in *Theological Investigations* (London: Darton, Longman & Todd, 1966), 77-102.

Holy Spirit as two moments of the "*one* self-communication of God" and, therefore, form "*one* economic Trinity," rather than as "two functions" of two divine persons.[147]

God communicates himself as a person. God's self-communication brings into being creatures as recipients. God's self-communication presupposes human beings as "addressee," or "recipient," and God's outward activity of creation is the precondition for constituting the addressee.[148] "The self-communication of the free personal God who gives himself as a person ... presupposes a personal recipient."[149] Therefore, already implied in God's self-communication, we find, coextensively with that self-communication, an "offer" from God, on the one hand, and an "acceptance," on the side of the human being. God's self-donation is accepted by the human person in freedom. According to the schema of God's self-communication, human beings stand as the recipients of God's free self-giving. This divine self-communication takes on a Trinitarian way, i.e., in the uttering of the Word by the Father in the incarnation and the sending of the Spirit which makes the recipients receptive and responsive to this self-gift through grace. As Rahner puts it, "God's self-communication consists precisely in the fact that God really arrives at man, really enters into man's situation, assumes it himself, and *thus* is what he is." According to Rahner, the twofold communications of the Word and the Spirit in their distinctiveness of persons "must belong to God 'in himself'"[150] in order to become this self-communication, truly God's self-communication. According to this Trinitarian scheme of God's self-communication, the Father communicates the divine essence by addressing the Son in the incarnation, and the sending of the Spirit evokes a response through grace. A study of the theology of the Logos and the Spirit further makes clear the relationship between the immanent and economic Trinity, and the double sending of the mission of the Son and the Spirit in their economic and inner Trinitarian dimensions.

3.4.1.1. The Incarnate and the Immanent Logos

Rahner's attempt to establish the identity between the economic Trinity and the immanent Trinity is, in fact, meant to show that there exists a clear link

147. Rahner, *The Trinity*, 87.
148. *Ibid.*, 88-90.
149. *Ibid.*, 89.
150. *Ibid.*, 100.

between the Incarnate Logos and the immanent Logos. Rahner argues that, if
the outward acts of the Trinity are undivided as Augustine understands, then
the distinctive missions of the Trinitarian persons in salvation history are
dubious. In order to overcome this impasse, Rahner categorically argues for
the distinctive missions of the Trinitarian persons, utilising the categories
based on Christology and the doctrine of grace or Pneumatology.[151] Refuting
the traditional ascription of incarnation to any of the Trinitarian persons,[152]
Rahner argues, that to be incarnated is the proper mission of the Second Person of the Trinity. Based on classical Christology, he claims that there is a
correspondence between the immanent and economic Trinity, because "Jesus
is not simply God in general, but the Son ... Hence there is at least *one* 'mission', *one* presence in the world, *one* reality of salvation history which is not
merely appropriated to some divine person, but which is proper to him."[153]
According to him, only the Second Person of the Trinity could appear in the
history of salvation, because the mission of the Logos in history is hypostati-
cally proper only to that person of the Trinity. He accentuates that, in the
incarnation, it is one of the divine persons acting out *ad extra*, towards the
world as a person of the Trinity. This is an economic relation of the second
person of the Trinity which is proper to him that "entails the possibility of a
real communication, in salvation history, of the whole Trinity as such, to the
world, therefore, the identity of the economic and immanent Trinity."[154]
Rahner says that "we cling to the truth that the Logos is really as he appears
in revelation..."[155] Thus he identifies the Logos of revelation as the immanent Logos. Hence, it logically follows that the temporal mission of the Son
should necessarily correspond to, and manifests itself from, an immanent
procession from the Father. Therefore, the economic missions and processions are integrally related. As such, the eternal begetting of the Son is the
ground of the sending of the Son in the incarnation, and the eternal proces-

151. Rahner's two-fold argument appears in "the two fold presupposition" in Karl Rahner,
"The Concept of Mystery in Catholic Theology," in *Theological Investigations* (New York:
Crossroad, 1966), 71. He develops this argument in, Rahner, *The Trinity*, 120.
152. Rahner questions the willingness to ascribe the possibility of incarnation to any other
person than to Christ, which prevailed in Christian tradition in the thought of Lombard and
Augustine. Rahner, *The Trinity*, 28-30. For a summary presentation of the discussion see, Karl
Rahner, "Dogmatic Questions on Easter," in *Theological Investigations* (London: Darton,
Longman & Todd, 1966), 125; Sanders, *The Image of the Immanent Trinity*, 62-67.
153. Rahner, *The Trinity*, 23.
154. *Ibid.*, 27.
155. *Ibid.*, 30.

sion of the Spirit is the ground of the sending of the Spirit in the economy. The validity of showing this correspondence or identity between the economic and immanent Logos is attested by his basic thesis of the identity between the economic and immanent Trinity.

Rahner's symbolic ontology (the *Realsymbol*) also comes into play in the theology of the Logos in establishing this correspondence between the immanent and economic Logos. Accordingly, the human nature which Christ takes on in the incarnation is something integral to the Logos, because God expresses himself in the Incarnate Logos.[156] In other words, according to him, incarnation is the Realsymbolic expression of the Logos. In the incarnation, the Son becomes the self-expression of the Father. As Sanders opines, "if we rephrased Rahner's Rule as 'the economic Trinity is the *Realsymbol* of the immanent Trinity', we would have ample justification from Rahner's work, although Rahner himself does not seem to have stated it this way explicitly."[157] Thus, the identity of the immanent and economic Trinity fit well into the whole theological system of Rahner. Having argued the identity of the Logos in the economic and immanent dimensions, he goes on to show how the mission of the Spirit entertains a similar connection to the economic and immanent dimensions, according to his basic thesis defended by the *Grundaxiom*.

3.4.1.2. The Economic Mission and the Immanent Procession of the Holy Spirit

Rahner's argument based on Christology leads to the argument based on Pneumatology, or the doctrine of uncreated grace. Along the line of the arguments of Christology, he claims that the Spirit's capability of a corresponding mission towards the world is proper to the Third Person of the Trinity. The Spirit is present in a direct and proper Pneumatological mission towards the world. The Christological and Pneumatological missions constitute the content of the theology of Rahner. As he puts it, "as is evident from our basic axiom, Christology and the doctrine of grace are, strictly speaking, the doctrine of the Trinity."[158]

---

156. Karl Rahner, "On the Theology of Incarnation," in *Theological Investigations* (London: Darton, Longman & Todd, 1966), 225; Rahner, *Foundations*, 116.

157. Sanders, *The Image of the Immanent Trinity*, 78.

158. Rahner, *The Trinity*, 120.

Rahner does not develop a systematically constructed Pneumatology. For him, Pneumatology is the theology of grace.[159] He questions the traditional separation between nature and grace and rejects the notion of "pure nature" as an independent reality which is to be "graced."[160] As Sanders explains, for Rahner, the starting point is the reflection on grace as the primary element. Accordingly, "grace is, first of all, God's own self-communication to us, God's gift of himself, or the life of the Trinity opened up to us by God's presence in the modality of the Holy Spirit."[161] So, according to the scheme of God's self-communication, the true life of the Trinity is communicated to us through the modalities of the Son and the Spirit.

In our study, we do not intend to identify either with the radicalist camp or the restrictors, although we do principally adopt the axiom accepting the relationship and distinction between the immanent and economic Trinity. Our concern is confined to finding a structural framework in which the mission of the Word and the Spirit can be understood. We accept the position taken by Fred Sanders who rejects a *vice versa* that considers the immanent Trinity as the image of the economic Trinity, while upholding the intrinsic relationship between the immanent and economic Trinity in such a way that it evades any tendency to consider them as two "Trinities." In fact, the relationship between the immanent and economic Trinity consists in showing that what we see in the economic Trinity is our best image of the immanent Trinity.[162]

As LaCugna observes, although Rahner's axiom is valid, it should be interpreted epistemologically, and not ontologically, in order to avoid any separation between them, because, "if the distinction is ontological, then *theologia* is separated from *oikonomia*. If the distinction is epistemological, then *oikonomia* is our means of access to *theologia*, and it is truly *theologia* that is given in *oikonomia*."[163] She understands the distinction and unity between the economic and immanent Trinity in the epistemological manner, and prefers to make it in terms of *oikonomia* and *theologia*. Accordingly, she tries to re-interpret Rahner's axiom as follows: "*theologia* is fully revealed and bes-

159. Rahner makes a systematic treatment of the doctrine of grace. Karl Rahner, "Nature and Grace," in *Theological Investigations* (London: Darton, Longman & Todd, 1966), 165-188.

160. He rejects the post-Tridentine treatment of grace as extrinsic to nature. Accordingly, the idea of "pure nature" without reference to grace is untenable.

161. Sanders, *The Image of the Immanent Trinity*, 72.

162. *Ibid.*, 8.

163. LaCugna, *God for Us*, 217.

towed in *oikonomia*, and *oikonomia* truly expresses the ineffable mystery of *theologia*." In this sense, economic and immanent Trinity are not two distinct Trinities, but rather, *oikonomia* is the realization of *theologia*. As she puts it, "there is neither an economic nor an immanent Trinity; there is only the *oikonomia* that is the concrete realization of the mystery of *theologia* in time, space, history, and personality."[164]

Briefly speaking, Rahner's approach to Trinity shows an acceptance of the Greek patristic theology of the procession of the Son and the Spirit and applies it to the unfolding of the history of salvation. He understands God's self-communication as being unfolded, both eternally and temporarily, in the modalities of the Word and the Spirit. In connecting these two modalities of divine self-communication to the salvation history, he overcomes the dichotomy that was prevalent in the Augustinian and Thomistic traditions of the theology of the Trinity. Rahner prefers to be influenced by the Greek patristic theology, which is primarily based on the Bible and the liturgical celebration. While continuing with the tradition of Augustine and Aquinas,[165] Rahner applies the two processions of the Word and the Spirit, the dual aspects of God's self-communication to the entire salvation history. In doing so he tries to integrate the thought patterns of the West and the East in his Trinitarian theology. Karl Rahner's approach to Trinitarian mystery in its economic and immanent dimensions seems to illuminate our understanding of retrieving the person and role of the Holy Spirit. Consequently, it helps us to interpret the personhood and the role of the Holy Spirit as equal to the mission of the Word.

Rahner's theology of God's self-communication bridges the gap between immanent and economic dimensions of the triune God and sets the Pneuma-

---

164. *Ibid.*, 223. In this connection, we may notice that Vladimir Lossky was criticised for considering the economy of the Spirit in isolation from that of the Son. He postulates a distinct "economy of the Holy Spirit" and treats each "economy" separately in two chapters. See Vladimir Lossky, *The Mystical Theology of the Eastern Church* (London: James Clarke., 1957), 156-173. McDonnell rejects this distinction between the mission of the Son and the Spirit. He says, "there is one economy from the Father constituted by the missions of the Son and the Spirit, each of the missions being present and active at the interior of the other." McDonnell, *The Other Hand of God*, 198. John Breck has also drawn attention to the danger of the tendency of speaking of a "double economy," disjointing the economy of the Son and the Spirit. Breck agrees with McDonnell in showing that such a tendency is prevalent in Lossky. See Breck, "The Lord Is the Spirit," 115.

165. Remaining in the Thomistic tradition, Rahner engaged in dialogue with modern philosophy and tried to re-vitalize and explore the riches of Catholic tradition. Sanders, *The Image of the Immanent Trinity*, 52.

tological and Christological missions on an equal footing. Thus, it seems to provide us with a feasible framework in which a composite theology of Christ and the Spirit can be formulated which will have necessary implications for the understanding of the Church and the sacraments. The rise of Christology at the expense of Pneumatology in the West, and the ascendance of Pneumatology over Christology in the East were largely characterised by their respective ways of explaining the processional relationship of the Spirit with the other divine persons. Therefore, it is required to portray the inner Trinitarian relationship so as to represent the mission of the Son and the Spirit in a consistent manner. Such an attempt must based on the biblical revelation of the Son and the Spirit whereby the two missions interface as constitutive of a single economy. We argue that a Pneumatological Christology will explain this convergence whilst retaining their identity.

4. Pneumatological Christology

Pneumatology developed alongside Christological reflection is firmly grounded within the scriptures. Therefore, our key to Pneumatological theology is Christology. In Christological reflection itself, we can identify two approaches which have different implications for Pneumatology. In the following section, we engage in Christological reflection from a Pneumatological perspective. The purpose of this study consists essentially of perceiving the presence and activity of the Spirit in the life and mission of Christ. Thus, the basis of constructing a Pneumatological theology lies in examining the work of the Holy Spirit as constitutive of the person and mission of Christ.

4.1. Diverse Approaches to Pneumatology

The scriptures testify to a mutual relationship that exists between the eternal procession and the temporal missions of the Son and the Spirit. However, biblical evidences are not completely obscure as to determine whether the Spirit's mission depends on Christ, or Christ's mission depends on the Spirit. In line with biblical revelation, two distinctive but related ways can be identified in the approach to Pneumatology: First, Christologically-conditioned Pneumatology; second, Pneumatologically-conditioned Christology. According to the first approach, Christ sends the Spirit, and the Spirit constitutes the Church as the body of Christ and leads the Church. The Spirit moves the already existing Church. The starting point of this type of Pneumatological reflection is the historical manifestation of the Spirit at Pentecost. The Spirit's role is confined to the mission and expansion of the Church. The Spirit, is in a way, given by Christ and acts as an agent of Christ in carrying out the mission of Christ by animating the Church and leading it to the end. In this sense, it is Christologically-conditioned Pneumatology.

Conversely, Pneumatologically-conditioned Christology goes back to identify the role of the Spirit in the life of Christ, beginning at conception through to the resurrection. According to this approach, the Spirit's presence and activity is traced back, even to the conception, as constitutive of the identity of Christ. Moreover, the Spirit is not understood simply as the "animator," or the "vivifier" of the already existing Church, but rather, the very origin of the Church is understood through the activity of the Spirit. The New Testament supports and attests to both types of Pneumatology. We argue that Pneumatologically-conditioned Christology helps to overcome the tendency of depersonalising and subordinating the Spirit to the Son, without reducing the person and mission of Christ. Therefore, we recommend a Pneumatological approach to Christology as an adequate method of developing a Pneumatological theology. Now, we shall discuss how both these approaches are sustainable according to the evidences in the scriptures.

4.1.1. The Spirit and the Identity of Christ

As we have pointed out, in the light of the Christological awareness that developed after the resurrection, the flow of reflection was from resurrection to public ministry, baptism, and finally to conception and the infancy narrative. As the story develops in the synoptic gospels, Jesus' identity becomes more and more revealed. Admittedly, it is a Pneumatologically-determined Christology (e.g., Mt 3:13-17; Mk 1:9-11; Lk 3:21-22; see also Rom 1:4 & Acts 13:33). The breathing of the Spirit by the risen Lord on the disciples, as well as the sending of the Spirit to the Church at Pentecost, obtain meaning and connection in the light of the role of the Spirit in Jesus' life in constituting his identity as the Son of God and the Lord. Thus, looking through a Pneumatological lens, the Spirit is seen as congenital to the identity of Jesus and constitutive of the actuality of the Church (Acts 1:5; 2:1-13; 1Cor 12:1-13).

The synoptic gospels, especially the gospel of Luke, stand out as a reliable source of Spirit Christology.[166] It is the coming and action of the Spirit

---

166. A concise presentation of the neo-scholastic developments of Spirit Christology is given by Ralph Del Colle, in *Christ and the Spirit: Spirit Christology in Trinitarian Perspec-*

that unites the fruit of Mary's womb to the unity of the Son of God (Lk 1:35).[167] We see how the Spirit is ontologically united to the Word so that the hypostatic union may be realised. Moreover, according to Luke, the subsequent life of Jesus was overwhelmed by the activity of the Holy Spirit. The childhood of Jesus was the visible evidence of the hallowing of the Spirit, culminating in the anointing of Jesus with the Spirit at baptism (Luke 3:21-22; Mt 3:13-17; Mk 1:9-11), making Jesus the anointed one: the Christ (ὁ χριστός).[168] Jesus' baptism and the descent of the Holy Spirit are related to his messianic conception which is mediated by the Spirit. As Barrett puts it, "here [at baptism], as in the birth narratives, the Spirit is the creative activity of God which calls into being the conditions of the Messianic era." Barrett interprets this event as the inauguration of the Messianic office of Jesus.[169] According to the synoptics, the whole event of baptism is about the identity of Jesus. The question "who he is" is answered explicitly by Mark: "the Son of God, endowed with the Spirit."[170] Christ was constituted as the Messiah by the anointing of the Spirit. According to Lukan Pneumatology, the descent of the Holy Spirit upon Jesus at baptism is interpreted as a visible

tive (New York: Oxford University Press, 1994), 34-63; Kilmartin, *Christian Liturgy*, 163-165; Groppe, *Congar's Theology of the Spirit*, 56-59.

167. Matthew 1:18,20 also asserts that Mary's pregnancy was inaugurated by the Holy Spirit. Having studied the differences between the birth narratives in Matthew and Luke C.K. Barrett contends that the variations that exist between them neither confirms nor contradicts the statement that ascribes the birth of Jesus to the Holy Spirit. See Barrett, *The Holy Spirit and the Gospel Tradition*, 5-6.

168. Congar credited Heribert Mühlen with raising the awareness that "Christ" is not simply a proper name as the scholastics understood. On the contrary, the term "Christ" means the "anointed One" or "the Messiah." Congar, *I Believe in the Holy Spirit*, 1:23; Jesus' point of departure, according to Congar, is the baptism in the Jordan. McDonnell says that "For Congar, the baptism is constitutive (not just declarative) of the Messia-Saviour-Lord, but he would add the resurrectio-exaltation as a successive stage in the history of salvation, a second new actuation of the power of the Spirit, also constitutive, and not just declarative. See McDonnell, "Doctrine of the Holy Spirit," 156. Badcock writes, "Congar, by contrast, suggests that if [the] anointing of Christ is to be understood consistently as [a] truly Trinitarian event, the *Filioque* must be either abandoned, or at the very least, modified, and complemented by a parallel "spiritque" Christological doctrine." Gary D. Badcock, "The Anointing of Christ and the Filioque Doctrine," *Irish Theological Quarterly* 60 (1994): 243.

169. Barrett, *The Holy Spirit and the Gospel Tradition*, 45. It is important to notice that, according to the gospel of Mark, the beginning of the ministry of Jesus commences with baptism. Matthew and Luke extend the messianic identity of Jesus back to the incarnation, which is also a Spirit event.

170; McDonnell, *The Baptism of Jesus*, 10.

manifestation of the unseen mystery that took place in Jesus' conception.[171] Thus, strictly speaking, it is the descent of the Spirit that constitutes Jesus as the Son of God and the Messiah. In Acts 10:38, Luke further affirms that Jesus of Nazareth was anointed by God with the Holy Spirit and power which prepare him for his mission. In fact, the baptismal event becomes the theophany of the Trinity, accompanied by the "voice from heaven." Then, he is led by the Spirit into the wilderness and is initiated to begin his messianic ministry (Luke 4:1,14,18; Mt 12:28). During Jesus' first proclamation at Nazareth and throughout the entire ministry, we see the presence and activity of the Spirit. The Spirit's relationship to Christ can also be upheld in the light of the Johannine gospel, even though the evangelist does not present a baptismal account as in the synoptic gospels. Instead, John's allusion to the baptismal tradition (Jn 1:29-34), expresses the Spirit's relationship to the Son rather clearly.[172]

Congar says that there were two "actuating" moments which are Pneumatologically significant in constituting Jesus as the Messiah and the Lord. As he puts it,

> … there were two moments when the *virtus* or effectiveness of the Spirit in Jesus was actuated in a new way. The first was at his baptism, when he was constituted (and not simply proclaimed as) Messiah and Servant by God. The second moment was at the time of his resurrection and exaltation, when he was made the Lord.[173]

The climaxing event of the Spirit in the life of Jesus was his resurrection and glorification. The New Testament texts amply evidence this fact. For instance, in the letter to the Romans, St. Paul writes, "the gospel concerning his Son, who was descended from David according to the flesh and designated Son of God in power, according to the Spirit of holiness, by his resurrection from the dead, Jesus Christ our Lord" (Rom 1:3-4).[174] In his first address on the day of Pentecost, Peter said: "This Jesus, God raised up … [b]eing, therefore, exalted at the right hand of God, and having received from the Father the promise of the Holy Spirit, he has poured out this which you see and hear. For David did not ascend into the heavens, but he himself says: 'The Lord said to my Lord, sit at my right hand…'" (Acts 2:32-35; see also Ps

---

171. Montague, *The Holy Spirit*, 266.

172. McDonnell, *The Other Hand of God*, 68.

173. Congar, *I Believe in the Holy Spirit*, 3:171.

174. See also Rom 1:4; 1 Tim 3:16; 1 Pet 3:18. Here, not only the constitution of Jesus as the Son of God, but also his glorification was described as by the work of the Holy Spirit.

101:1). Peter's proclamation before the Sanhedrin that "the God of our fathers raised Jesus whom you killed by hanging him on a tree. God exalted
him at his right hand as Ruler and Savior" (Acts 5:30-31). This Jesus who
was raised became the life-giving spirit. As St. Paul states,

> what is sown is perishable, what is raised is imperishable. It [the body] is
> sown in dishonour, it is raised in glory. It is sown in weakness, it is raised in
> power. It is sown a physical body, it is raised a spiritual body. ... Thus it is
> written, "the first man, Adam, became a living being;" the last Adam became
> a life-giving spirit (1 Cor 15:42-45).

Congar observes two states in the life of Jesus, namely, the state of *kenosis*
and the state of exaltation.[175] In the incarnation and the ministry, Christ received the Spirit and was sanctified by him and acted in the Spirit. In the
resurrection and his glorification, he was raised by the Spirit and was seated
at the right hand of God. He entered into the divine communion and was
assimilated to God and united to the Spirit to the extent that St. Paul could
say, "the Lord is the Spirit" (2 Cor 3:17). The divine communion raised Jesus
to the heights of glory and power so that the Risen Lord even breathes the
Spirit on the disciples: "Receive the Holy Spirit" (Jn 20:22). According to
Augustine, Jesus was anointed by a mystical and invisible anointing in the
womb of the Virgin Mary. Jesus gives the same Spirit that he received as
man.[176] Basil the Great says that the Spirit was, first of all, present to the
Lord's flesh when he made himself the "unction" of that flesh and was made
the inseparable companion of the Word, as is written: "'Upon whom thou
shalt see the Spirit descending and remaining on Him', the same is 'my beloved Son'; and 'Jesus of Nazareth' whom 'God anointed with the Holy
Ghost'."[177] Jesus was united to the Spirit as the Christ, as well as the Risen
Lord. Aquinas also points out how the Spirit was inseparably united to Christ
in his kenotic, as well as glorified stages. The same Spirit who was given to
Christ and who dwelt in him and moved him also dwelt in and moved his
followers, the members of his Body.[178] Thus, the inseparable unity between

175. Congar, *I Believe in the Holy Spirit*, 3:169.

176. Augustine, *The Trinity*, trans. Stephen McKenna, The Fathers of the Church, 45
(Washington, DC: Catholic University of America Press, 1963), 15:46.

177. Basil, "De Spiritu Sancto," 16: 39. See also Irenaeus, "Against Heresies," in *The
Ante-Nicene Fathers*, ed. Alexander Roberts and James Donaldson (Edinburgh: T & T Clark,
1996), 3:9,3.

178. Congar, *I Believe in the Holy Spirit*, 3:170.

Christ and the Spirit helps us to understand their missions in the economy as complementary.

4.1.2. Complementary Missions of the Word and the Spirit

There is an intimate and inseparable connection between the Word and the Spirit from the first to the last book of the Bible.[179] As a summary note of his entire work on the theology of the Holy Spirit, Congar writes, "no Christology without Pneumatology and no Pneumatology without Christology."[180] There is mutuality between Pneumatology and Christology. This mutual relationship between the two divine missions is a "relationship-in-autonomy."[181] The mutuality and complementariness of the missions of the Word and the Spirit was upheld by the Fathers of the Church, presenting them as the "two hands" or "two eyes"[182] of God. As Irenaeus writes, "it was not the angels who made and formed us ... as though he (God) did not have his own hands ... for he always had before him the Word and the Wisdom, the Son and the Spirit." God created the world with "his two hands, the Son and the Spirit, the Word and the Wisdom."[183] Irenaeus also incorporates a distinctive understanding of Spirit Christology according to the synoptic gospels and a Pneumatology dependent on Christology according to John, Paul and the Acts. He says,

> [t]he Spirit shows forth the Word, and therefore, the prophets announced the Son of God, and the Word utters the Spirit, and therefore, is Himself the announcer of the prophets, and leads and draws man to the Father. ... it is not a man who speaks the prophecies, but the Spirit of God, assimilating and likening Himself to the persons represented [here it is David], speaks in the prophets, and utters the words, sometimes from Christ, and sometimes from the Father ... For he was named Christ, because through him the Father anointed and adorned all things; and because on His coming as man, He was anointed

179. Congar makes a survey of the biblical texts linking the Spirit with the Word. See Congar, *The Word and the Spirit*, 15-20.

180. *Ibid.*, 1.

181. Amos Yong, *Discerning the Spirit(S): A Pentecostal-Charismatic Contribution to Christian Theology of Religions* (Sheffield: Sheffield Academic Press, 2000), 70.

182. Athanasius held a view which is quite similar to that of Theophilus of Antioch and Irenaeus about the Son and the Spirit as the two eyes of God. Richard Patrick Crosland Hanson, *The Search for the Christian Doctrine of God: The Arian Controversy 318-381* (Edinburgh: T & T Clark, 1988), 426. See also Athanasius, "Expositio in Psalmum," in *Patrologia Graeca*, ed. J.P. Migne (Paris: Seu Petit-Montrouge, 1857), 32:18d, p. 166.

183. Irenaeus, "Against Heresies," 4:20,1 See also 4:7,4.

with the Spirit of God and his Father. As also by Isaiah, He says of Himself: *the Spirit of the Lord is upon me...*"[184]

McDonnell observes that "the whole economy is given over to the Spirit in the way that all of God's self-giving comes to us through Christ in the Spirit, and the only way we can go to God is through Christ in the Spirit."[185] We cannot understand the mission of the Word and the mission of the Spirit as entirely separate entities having no bearing on each other, or mutually exclusive entities. The New Testament attests to a radical unity between the activity of the Spirit and that of the Risen Lord. Even though the Spirit and the glorified Lord are distinct in God, both Christ and the Spirit are functionally united in such a way that we experience them together. It is in this sense that St. Paul uses the expressions "in Christ" and "in the Spirit" interchangeably (1 Cor 15:45).

However, it seems that in some way a temporal priority has been attributed to the mission of Christ over the Spirit, especially in the gospel of John. According to John 15:26 and 16:7, Christ sends the Holy Spirit. The Spirit functions as an agent or mediator of Christ's mission (Jn 14:26; 16:14). However, this does not obscure a radical unity between the missions of the Word and the Spirit, because it is also significant to note that according to John, Jesus promises the Paraclete so that his followers are not left as orphans (Jn 14:3,18). Functionally, it is through the Spirit that Jesus continues to be with us without leaving us as orphans.[186]

The East has been more successful in accommodating the Spirit and his mission as equal to that of the Son, as well as integrating the Spirit in the whole theological process. According to Lossky, there is a mutual and inseparable connectedness between the economic activities of the Son and the Spirit.[187] He goes on to explain that the coming of the Son into the world is not without the co-working of the Spirit. Similarly, the coming of the Spirit is not without the working of the Son. This is seen throughout salvation history. The salvific activity of the Son is present in the world from the very moment

184. Irenaeus, *The Demonstration of the Apostolic Preaching*, ed. W.J. Sparrow Simpson and W.K. Lowther Clarke, trans. J. Armitage Robinson, Translations of Christian Literature (New York: Macmillan, 1920), nos. 5,49,53. To some extent, the teaching of Irenaeus on the Holy Spirit is indebted to Justin Martyr, because it is probable that Justin's works were available to him. See Robinson, "Introduction: Doctrine of the Holy Spirit," *ibid.*, 24-68.

185. McDonnell, *The Other Hand of God*, 195.

186. Congar, *I Believe in the Holy Spirit*, 2:12.

187. Lossky, *Mystical Theology*, 167.

of creation, but is made present in a perfect visible and tangible manner in the incarnation. So, too, we may say that the outpouring of the Spirit at Pentecost is the new and perfect manifestation of the Spirit, otherwise never absent. Nikos Nissiotis emphatically points out that the activity of the Holy Spirit is equally important to that of Christ. The whole events in the history of salvation, beginning from the incarnation and the reconciliation in Christ and the commitment to Christ in faith, are actualised solely through the work of the Holy Spirit. Without the work of the Spirit, he says, "nothing can exist in history, neither the reality of the Incarnation and reconciliation in Christ, nor the personal commitment to him in his community of faith. Everything degenerates into easy generalization and docetic abstractions."[188] So, neither the personhood, nor the mission of the Spirit can be considered as secondary, compared to that of Christ.

Nonetheless, when explaining the role of the Spirit in relation to that of Christ, we should be aware of the tendency to downplay the centrality of Christ in the economy of salvation. While drawing attention to such a tendency prevailing to some extent in Eastern theology, John Breck points out that orthodox Pneumatology, which is based on the scriptures, should be essentially Christological. He argues that the person and mission of Christ "determine, constitute, and communicate the mystery of the Spirit."[189] As he observes,

> separated chronologically, Pascha and Pentecost cannot be separated logically, "economically." The Trinitarian unity of essence, will and operation make of both moments, both festal celebrations, complementary elements of one and the same salvific work. The economy of the Spirit, then, is one with the economy of the Son.[190]

In this connection, it is important to notice that, based on the traditional model corresponding to the inner procession of the Trinity, Heribert Mühlen ascribes the order of temporal priority to Christ, rather than to that of the Spirit. For him, the procession of the Spirit from the Father has a logical priority to the procession of the Spirit.[191] However, we purport to argue that

188. Nikos Nissiotis, "Pneumatological Christology as a Presupposition for Ecclesiology," *Oecumenica: Jahrbuch für ökumenische Forschung* (1967): 239.

189. Breck, "'The Lord Is the Spirit'," 120.

190. *Ibid.*, 120.

191. Heribert Mühlen, *Der Heilige Geist als Person: Beitrag zur Frage nach der dem Heiligen Geiste Eigentümlichen Funktion in der Trinität, bei der Inkarnation und im Gnaden-*

emphasis has to be laid on the centrality of Christ, while acknowledging the equality and complementariness of the mission of the Spirit along with that of the Son. The question of the temporal priority of the missions is secondary, compared to their unity and equality. As Basil writes,

> [w]hen we speak of the dispensations made for man by our great God and Saviour, Jesus Christ, who will gainsay their having been accomplished through the grace of the Spirit? ... the things done in the dispensation of the coming of our Lord in the flesh; all is through the Spirit. In the first place, He was made an unction [at baptism], and being inseparably present was with the very flesh of the Lord ... After this every operation was wrought with the co-operation of the Spirit.[192]

Here, Basil seems to place the Pneumatological moment prior to the Christological moment along the lines of synoptic gospel tradition; the centrality of Christ in the work of salvation and the active role of the Holy Spirit in the economy is sufficiently stressed.

We cannot but admit the equality of the double missions (Gal 4:4-6; Jn 7:37-39; 14:26; 15:26; 20:21-22) of the Son and the Spirit. They originate from the Father by the fact that the mission of the Son comes from the Father (Gal 4:6; Jn 3:17; 5:23; 6:57; 17:18), while the Spirit is sent by the Father (Gal 4:6; John 14:16, 26).[193] Therefore, the Pneumatological theology that we outline should be mindful of the mutuality of the double mission of the Word and the Spirit in God's outreach to the world.

Traditionally, the East and the West cleave to dissimilar opinions about the mission of the Holy Spirit, based on the distinction between the two processions in the immanent Trinity.[194] The Eastern Churches consider that a proper mission belongs to the Holy Spirit, in contrast to the mission that is ascribed to the Word in the West. For this reason, in the East, the Holy Spirit is ascribed with an active role in the sanctification of persons, which also admits a definitive role of the Spirit in the sacraments. The Western Church traditionally held that only the mission of the Word is properly personal, and

bund, Münsterische Beiträge zur Theologie, 26 (Münster: Aschendorffsche Verlagsbuchhandlung, 1963), 260.

192. Basil, "De Spiritu Sancto," 16: 39.

193. Other references that refer to the sending of the Spirit do not imply that the mission of the Spirit is subordinate to the mission of the Son when understood in the light of the economy of salvation that is unfolded in the whole New Testament. The understanding of the Spirit as "sent by the Son" (Lk 24:49; John 15:26; 16:7), can be interpreted that the Son sends the Spirit who is from the Father.

194. Kilmartin, *Christian Liturgy*, 114.

the economy is the work of the Godhead acting as a single principle. The work of sanctification is ascribed to the Holy Spirit by "appropriation."[195] Evidently, Western sacramental theology took a Christo-centric dimension, compared to the Pneumatological dimension of the East. Even though both the East and the West use the procession model of the Trinity to argue in favour of their claims, they are on contrary poles in the understanding of Pneumatology and Christology. However, as we have seen, there is sufficient ground to argue, based on biblical evidences, for the mutuality and complementary understanding of the missions of the Word and the Spirit. Therefore, we argue that re-constructing the processional relationship of the Trinitarian persons, so as to represent the Christological and Pneumatological dimensions, as revealed in the scriptures, would be theologically significant in the understanding of the Church and the Sacraments. We propose to begin this endeavour, first, by re-visiting the procession model and the descending Christology as its corollary, second, by considering the bestowal models and its advantages in comparison with the former.

4.2. The Procession Model and the Descending Christology

The procession model, along with its descending Christology (Jn 1:14), reveals God's mystery of salvation realised in Jesus of Nazareth. The origin of this model can be ascribed to the reflection on, and an awareness of, the implications of the salvific missions of the Word and the Spirit, as attested by biblical evidences. Thus, the starting point of the procession model is the reflection on the mission of the Word and the Spirit in the economy of salvation. This takes us back to the understanding regarding the procession of the Word and the Spirit from the Father. "The incarnation of the Word corresponds to the eternal generation of the Word from the Father; the sending of the Spirit corresponds to the eternal procession of the Spirit from the Father."[196] Said differently, the economic missions of the Son and the Holy Spirit find their basis in the Son's eternal generation and the inner procession of the Spirit in the Trinity.

---

195. *Ibid.*, 162. In Aquinas' theology the Spirit is ascribed a crucial role in the sanctification of the human persons. The activating of creation's movement to God is considered to be the work of the Holy Spirit. However, the work of grace and sanctification is not attributed to the Holy Spirit as a person of the Trinity in the strict sense. On the contrary, grace is understood to be the work of God, but appropriated to the Spirit. See Groppe, *Congar's Theology of the Spirit*, 38.

196. Kilmartin, *Christian Liturgy*, 125.

As we have seen, the diverse understanding of the procession of the Spirit in the immanent Trinity gave rise to varied emphases of Pneumatology in the East and the West. The processional relationship of the Spirit to other divine persons as understood by the *Filioque*, favors a Christologically-conditioned Pneumatology. Colwell charges that Augustine's mutual love theory, which is based on the *Filioque*, reduces the Trinity to a "duality," or "binity," de-personalising the Spirit as love, the Spirit as the love between the Father and the Son.[197] He argues that God defined as love, presupposes a lover, beloved and love. Augustine's understanding of God as love, implies a dynamic of loving, a plurality of subject and object. Identifying the Spirit as love implies a reduction of the personhood of the Holy Spirit. As Veli-Matti Kärkkäinen observes, this mode considers the Spirit only as an "impersonal divine field," or "common life of the Father and the Son," to the extent of de-hypostatising the Holy Spirit who is also the "personal centre of activity."[198] Thus, the Western addition of the *Filioque* creates an imbalance in the understanding of the persons and minimises the person and work of the Holy Spirit.[199] The personhood of the Holy Spirit remains perceptibly eclipsed by that of Christ, generating a Pneumatology that is Christologically-textured. On the contrary, the Eastern way of understanding the procession of the Spirit seems to produce a Pneumatologically-conditioned Christology, implicating a subordination of Christ to the Spirit.[200] According to biblical testimony, both of these approaches are defensible.

197. Colwell, *Promise and Presence*, 21. Augustine is well known for his mutual love theory. According to Augustine, while proceeding from the Father and the Son, the Spirit also communicates the "common love by which the Father and the Son love each other. In other words, in proceeding from the Father and the Son, the Spirit proceeds as the love between them, i.e., the love of the Father for the Son and the love of the Son for the Father." Augustine, "*De Trinitate*," 15: 27-31, esp. 27. Augustine's mutual love theory was elaborated more fully by Aquinas, and became very influential to the extent that it characterised the Trinitarian theology of the Christian West for centuries.

198. Kärkkäinen, *Pneumatology*, 120.

199. Burgess, *Holy Spirit: Eastern Traditions*, 13.

200. Vladimir Lossky strongly argued that the *Filioque* subordinates the Spirit to the Son, consequently shaping an ecclesiocentrism in the West, whereas in the East, ecclesiology is informed by both Pneumatology and Christology, based on the distinctive missions of the Word and the Spirit. Lossky, *Mystical Theology*. While acknowledging the criticism of "Christomonism" in Catholicism at face value, Congar warns against making artificial constructions according to one's likes and dislikes. He says, "[w]e should not, surely, simply make a list of what we like and call it 'Pneumatology', and then of what we dislike, and call it 'Roman Catholic juridicism'!" Congar, *The Word and the Spirit*, 117.

However, both the Eastern and Western ways of explaining the procession of the Spirit in the Godhead do not satisfactorily explain the active agency of the Spirit along with the mission of the Son, in the economy of salvation as revealed in the New Testament. Therefore, alterations have been proposed in the creedal statement so that the procession of the Spirit in the Godhead may be better explained as corresponding to the person and the activity of the Holy Spirit in the economy of salvation.[201] Essentially, this would concern retaining the personhood of the Spirit, along with the Father and the Son. The question should also be asked as to how we should accommodate the biblical notion of the Spirit as sent by the Son? This also involves the challenge of rectifying both the primacy of the Father that is lacking in the *Filioque*, and also the Christological inadequacy prevailing in the Eastern representation of the procession of the Spirit.[202] Those who try to reformulate the processional relationship of the Spirit in the Godhead seem to differ in their approaches. A proposed viable solution, which is also ecumenically relevant, is to explain the Spirit as coming "from the Father through the Son." In addition to that, an extra amendment has also been suggested: that the Son "is begotten of the Father through the Spirit," in order to highlight the Son's dependence on the Spirit. We will briefly consider these amendments, while bearing in mind their implications in the understanding of the role of the Spirit in the sacraments.

4.3. The Bestowal Model and the Ascending Spirit Christology

A Spirit Christology, in accordance with the framework of the bestowal model of the Trinity, helps us to understand the person and mission of the Spirit as being manifested in Christian revelation. The bestowal model of the

---

201. Del Colle even goes to the extent to say that the confession of the Holy Spirit as the "Lord and life-giver," since the Council of Constantinople does not reflect well the modality of the hypostatic origin of the Spirit and his dynamic nature as the one who has spoken through the prophets, and was active in the economy of salvation and our faith in terms of eschatology. Del Colle, "The Holy Spirit," 325. Five alternative formulae were presented by the Faith and Order Commission of the World Council of Churches to resolve the issue in a memorandum. They are as follows: The Spirit proceeds from the Father of the Son, the Spirit proceeds from the Father through the Son, the Spirit proceeds from the Father and receives from the Son, the Spirit proceeds from the Father and rests on the Son, the Spirit proceeds from the Father and shines out through the Son. For the text of the memorandum, see Vischer, ed., *Spirit of God, Spirit of Christ*, 3-18.

202. Smail, "The Holy Spirit in the Holy Trinity," 164.

Trinity,[203] as proposed by David Coffey tries to reconstruct the processional relationship of the immanent Trinity and examines how this model is able to overcome the limitations of the procession model which is based on Logos Christology. Coffey's bestowal model explains God's self-communication in the Word and the Spirit and how the Spirit accounts for the sanctification of human beings.

4.3.1. Reconstruction of the Intra-Trinitarian Relationship

According to Coffey, the New Testament not only attests to Christ's sending into the world, but also to his return to the Father with us in the Spirit. Christians are united to the Son through the Holy Spirit. The incarnation of Christ and the sending of the Spirit after the resurrection are the extension of their own processional relationships in the Trinity.[204] According to the New Testament, the Spirit of Christ bears the mission of uniting us with Christ by faith and sharing in his divine sonship and fellowship with God.[205] The whole aim of salvation is to reconcile sinful or alienated humanity to God himself. The work of Grace through the Spirit is to bring about our return to God, overcoming this alienation. As Paul writes to the Ephesians, God has "made known to us the mystery of his will, according to his good pleasure that he set forth in Christ, as a plan [*oikonomia*] for the fullness of time, to gather up all things in him" (Eph 1:9-10). Thus, the economy of salvation implies God's movement towards humanity and humanity's return to God, which can be explained by a "descending" and "ascending" theology, respectively. According to Coffey, the Western theology of the *Filioque* and the Eastern theology of *per Filium* and Monopatrism can be accommodated within a "descending" theology. However, the return of Jesus to the Father and the return of ourselves can be explained only within the scope of an "ascending" theology.[206] Therefore, Coffey feels the need to reconstruct the traditional model

---

203. Coffey called this model in his early writings the "bestowal model," which was later changed to the "return model" in contrast to the "procession model." David Coffey, *Deus Trinitas: The Doctrine of the Triune God* (New York: Oxford, 1999), 5; Coffey, "Spirit Christology and the Trinity," 326.

204. Del Colle, *Christ and the Spirit*, 101.

205. Coffey, *Deus Trinitas*, 36. Congar expresses more or less the same view that the incarnation of the Word of God, his death and resurrection and the sending of the Holy Spirit has opened the way for a deepened communion of God with humanity. Groppe, *Congar's Theology of the Spirit*, 56.

206. David Coffey, "The Holy Spirit as the Mutual Love of the Father and the Son," *Theological Studies* 51 (1990): 193; Kilmartin, *Christian Liturgy*, 160.

in such a way that the ascending and descending movements of the economy can be satisfactorily explained.

Coffey claims that the bestowal model serves the purpose of accommodating the descending and ascending dimensions of the economy. In this scheme, there is an inversion of the traditional order of the revelation of God: Father-Son-Spirit to Spirit-Son-Father to accentuate the Christian experience of the Spirit in Christ and their ascent to the Father.[207] Coffey cites an example from Ephesians 2:18: "[T]hrough him [Christ] both of us [Jews and Gentiles] have access in one Spirit to the Father."[208] The divine persons approach us in the order of: Father, Son and Holy Spirit, yet we respond to God in the Holy Spirit, through the Son, and to the Father.[209] Coffey says, "… God's outreach to us through Christ and the Spirit (taxis: Father-Son-Holy Spirit) makes contact with us through the Spirit, and leads us back through Christ to the Father (taxis: Holy Spirit-Son-Father)."[210] In other words, in the intra-Trinitarian relationship, the Word proceeds from the Father, and the Spirit proceeds from the Father "through the Son" or "and the Son."[211] And in the extra-Trinitarian relation, "The Father sends the Son in the Spirit to save and transform the world and the Church, and lead them in the Spirit, through Christ, back to God."[212] The saving work of the triune God in its entirety is undivided, though it is presented in a differentiated unity.[213] The Father sends the Son, who assumes the humanity of Jesus of Nazareth, and the Spirit is sent by the Son to sanctify humanity, both of which are analogous to the intra-Trinitarian procession. In this schema, the order of sanctification of the

207. Coffey, *Deus Trinitas*, 36; Coffey, "Spirit Christology and the Trinity," 324. Here Coffey asserts that the entry of the eternal Spirit into God's plan of salvation is through Christ. In this sense Coffey calls the entering of the Spirit into the history of salvation in terms of incarnation, which he expresses by "Incarnation of the Holy Spirit."

208. David Coffey, "The "Incarnation" of the Holy Spirit," *Theological Studies* 45 (1984): 466; Coffey, *Deus Trinitas*, 36; Coffey, "Spirit Christology and the Trinity," 324.

209. Walter Kasper explains that the ancient Christian Doxology was not to the Father, Son and Holy Spirit, but rather in the Spirit through Christ to the Father (… *an den Vater durch den Sohn im Heiligen Geist*). Walter Kasper, *Jesus der Christus* (Mainz: Matthias-Grünewald, 1974), 202.

210. Coffey, *Deus Trinitas*, 36; Coffey, "Spirit Christology and the Trinity," 325.

211. Kilmartin opines that "the bestowal model provides a way of speaking about the procession of the Spirit in which "through the Son" and "and the Son" are complementary ways of conceiving the origin of the Spirit." Kilmartin, *Christian Liturgy*, 139.

212. Kilian McDonnell, "A Response to D. Lyle Dabney," in *Advents of the Spirit: An Introduction to the Current Study of Pneumatology*, ed. Bradford E. Hinze and D. Lyle Dabney (Milwaukee, WI: Marquette University Press, 2001), 263.

213. Hilberath, "Identity through Self-Transcendence," 286.

people is reversed, in contrast to the order in the Trinitarian procession, namely, the Spirit is bestowed, by which persons are justified and united with the Son and made the sons and daughters of the Father. This order corresponds to the bestowal model of the immanent Trinity, and not that of the procession model. Coffey expatiates this with the Mutual Love theory of Augustine.

4.3.2. The Spirit as the Mutual Love between the Father and the Son

Relying on the Mutual Love theory of Augustine, Coffey explains the intra-Trinitarian relationship.[214] For him, the manner of procession is important to understand the relationship between the Trinitarian persons. He explains the relationship of the persons of the economic Trinity in his model as follows: "the Father bestows the Holy Spirit *ad extra* as his love in a radical act that brings Jesus into being as the Son of God in humanity; Jesus, in response, returns the Holy Spirit as his own love of and to the Father; the Holy Spirit is the mutual love of the Father and Jesus his Son."[215] Thus, in the order of the economy, the Father bestows the Holy Spirit in a creative act in which Jesus comes into being as the Son of God. This seems to contradict the order in the immanent Trinity in which the Father generates the Son on whom he bestows the Holy Spirit, the Father's self-love. In the immanent Trinity, however, the Father's love by which the Son is generated precedes the Father's love for the Son, which is the Holy Spirit.[216] Here, Coffey really distinguishes between the "love of the Father" and the "Father's love for the Son," the Holy Spirit. If this distinction is not made, it would imply that the Son is generated also through the Holy Spirit in the immanent Trinity. The Father's love that generates the Son cannot be the Holy Spirit, because the Holy Spirit is the Father's love for the Son. The love of the Father is nothing but the Father's self-love, which precedes his love For the Son, the Holy Spirit. For Coffey, the love of the Father (primary love) by which the Son is generated, is his self-love identical with the Father himself. But acting in his total self-possession, which is his self-love, identical with himself, the Father generates

---

214. The Mutual Love theory, originally found in St. Augustine, entered into scholastic theology by the twelfth century in the expression of Richard of St. Victor and carried down to the present day. Coffey claims that he is the one to use the Augustinian concept of the mutual love theory for developing a Trinitarian model. Coffey, "Incarnation," 471; Coffey, *Deus Trinitas*, 5; Coffey, "Spirit Christology and the Trinity," 326; Del Colle, *Christ and the Spirit*, 97.
215. Coffey, *Deus Trinitas*, 48. See also Del Colle, *Christ and the Spirit*, 107-108.
216. Coffey, *Deus Trinitas*, 49.

the Son, whom he "then" loves (secondary love), which is the Holy Spirit."[217]
Coffey perceives a problem in this relation. If the Holy Spirit is the mutual
love of the Father and the Son, how can the Holy Spirit be the love of the
Father for his Son? Does it not imply that the Holy Spirit is constituted even
before the realization of the love of the Son for the Father? Coffey says the
Filioque solves this problem by explaining the procession of the Holy Spirit
as from one principle and by a single spiration.[218] Coffey summarises it in the
following way:

> The Holy Spirit … is precisely the objectivisation of the mutual love of the
> Father and the Son. The initial personal love of the Father for the Son is iden-
> tical with the Father's own person. Similarly, the purely personal answering
> love of the Son for the Father would be identical with the Son's own person,
> were it not for the fact that in the meeting of the two loves, their mutual love,
> the objectivisation that takes place becomes a reality that transcends its con-
> stituent elements, that reality being the person of the Holy Spirit proceeding
> from the Father and the Son. Henceforth, according to the taxis, the Father's
> love for the Son and the Son's love for the Father are each to be identified
> with the Holy Spirit.[219]

Hence, the order follows: the generation of the Son by the Father coincides
with the bestowal of the Holy Spirit on the Son, the bestowal of the same
Spirit by the Son on the Father. The Holy Spirit is the objectivisation of their
mutual love. This double bestowal of the love of the Father and the Son constitutes only a single act of love, although the former has a priority, which
Coffey calls the *prevenient* act of the Father, to which the latter is a response.[220] The answering love of the Son, that renders the love mutual, is
identified with the Holy Spirit, but not with his person, whereas the *preve-*
nient love of the Father is identified with his hypostasis.

217. *Ibid.*, 49.

218. Thomas Aquinas, *Summa Theologiae*, ed. Ceslaus Velecky, vol. 6 (London: Blackfriars, 1965), 1a.28: 4. See also Walter Farrell, *A Companion to Summa*, vol. 1 (New York:
Sheed & Ward, 1945), 139-160. According to Coffey, the Father and the Son spirate the Spirit
as their undivided act of mutual love of the Father and the Son. He makes a distinction between the begetting of the Son and the manner of procession of the Spirit. The Spirit, as constituted, proceeds from the Father and the Son, while the Father bestows the Spirit on the Son
and the Son bestows the Spirit on the Father, as mutual love is non-constitutive of the Spirit.
See Kilmartin, *Christian Liturgy*, 131.

219. Coffey, *Deus Trinitas*, 50. Here the acts do not mean the acts of knowing and willing,
as in the Augustinian tradition. On the contrary, it refers to the acts proper to God, rather than
particular divine persons. See Coffey, *Deus Trinitas*, 54.

220. *Ibid.*, 49.

In proposing the bestowal model, Coffey does not reject the procession model as meaningless, but considers it as prior to, and as the foundation for, the return model. The bestowal model is complementary to the procession model, but not a substitute for it.[221] Coffey imports and transforms the *Filioque*, which originally belongs to the procession model. Thus, for Coffey, the Holy Spirit is the objectivisation of the mutual love of the Father and the Son. In his words, "to put [it] simply, the *Filioque*, which emerges from the procession model, is the mutual love theory of the return model, that is, the theology according to which the Holy Spirit is the objectivisation of the mutual love of the Father and the Son."[222] Coffey claims that the bestowal model accommodates two orders of the immanent Trinity, namely, the ascending and return movements. He points out that the mutual love of the Father and the Son has two aspects: the Father's love towards Jesus, and the love of the Son to the Father. The Father's love has priority in order compared to the love of the Son towards the Father, because the Son comes from the Father. The love of the Son is a return, or answer, to the love of the Father, invoked by the love of the Father's love for him. In this model, the Holy Spirit is, in the strict sense, the Father's love for his Son, which rests on the Son, its proper object.[223]

Coffey claims that his model can be an effective move towards a reconciliation of Monopatrism and Filioquism, which, in his opinion, are both one-sided. Monopatrism holds that the Holy Spirit proceeds from the Father alone, with no mentioning of the Son. As we have seen, the Nicene-Constantinopolitan Council also follows this by stating, "...the Holy Spirit proceeds from the Father," whereas the interpolation of it (*Filioque*) implies the subordination of the Spirit. Coffey attempts to reconcile these diverse positions. He writes,

> The *Filioque* itself can accommodate Monopatrism, that is, inasmuch as the Son himself proceeds from the Father, but only provided that Monopatrism does not exclude a secondary role for the Son, that is, if its key statement be interpreted in the sense that "the Holy Spirit proceeds *ultimately* from the Father alone." ... [therefore] a more balanced statement would be that "the Holy Spirit proceeds from the Father and receives from the Son."[224]

221. Kilmartin, *Christian Liturgy*, 133.
222. Coffey, *Deus Trinitas*, 52.
223. Coffey, "Spirit Christology and the Trinity," 326.
224. Coffey, *Deus Trinitas*, 5.

Coffey is here demonstrating that the integration of these models results in an amicable, formulaic expression of the Trinitarian faith, stemming from both biblical and patristic roots, finding an element of its outward expression in the statement, "the Holy Spirit proceeds from the Father and receives from the Son."[225] As such, he believes that the monarchy of the Father (Monopatrism) and the role of the Son (*Filioque*) can be appropriately integrated into a new formula. He further suggests, "...the West needs to be more mindful of the monarchy of the Father, while the East needs to acknowledge the Son a role in the origination of the Holy Spirit."[226] His formula contains two statements, namely, "the Holy Spirit proceeds from the Father and the Son as from a single principle," and "the Holy Spirit proceeds from the Father and receives from the Son."[227] The second fraction of the statement is the elucidation of the first. This, he believes, would be a balanced statement, acceptable to the East and the West. The first statement of the formula is deduced from the procession model and the second from the return model. The first statement employs the *Filioque* and maintains the distinction of persons, while the second statement stresses the relation between the Trinitarian persons. Coffey claims that this line of understanding the Trinitarian procession will prepare the ground for the understanding between the East and the West. Coffey opines that the expression "proceeds from the Father and receives from the Son" implies that *per Filium* is suggestive of two things, namely, the Holy Spirit proceeds from the Father and *through* the Son, and also the Holy Spirit proceeds from the Father *alone*.[228] Despite his inventive reconstruction, Coffey does not claim that the model answers all questions concerning Trinitarian processions.

An important benefit of this model is that it accommodates the primacy of the Father as the source of the eternal procession of the Spirit, while retaining a Christological link by the addition of "through the Son." This is in accordance with the traditional understanding of Eastern Fathers and the New Testament testimony of the Spirit as coming from the Father, and sent by the Son. The alternative expression "through the Son" makes the relationship of

---

225. *Ibid.*, 52.

226. *Ibid.*, 53. Badcock draws our attention to the opinion of the Faith and Order Commission of the World Council of Churches when he writes that "the cause of theological reconciliation might be best served, not by a re-examination of the two ancient and divergent traditions, but by an advance to a new standpoint which somehow comprehends the concerns of both." Badcock, "The Anointing of Christ and the Filioque Doctrine," 242.

227. Coffey, *Deus Trinitas*, 53.

228. *Ibid.*, 53.

the Spirit to the Son in the procession, as well as in the economy, clearer than
does the *Filioque*. Therefore, representing the procession of the Spirit
"through the Son" reduces the Christological inadequacy prevailing in traditional Eastern Trinitarian theology without threatening the monarchy of the
Father in the procession of the Spirit. As Colwell observes, the adapted version of the creedal formula "who proceeds from the Father through the Son"
would reconcile the disparities that exist between the East and the West, and
seems to express more appropriately the relatedness of the Spirit to the Father and the Son.[229] Nevertheless, this model does not clearly delineate what
precisely is the role of the Spirit as far as the origin of the Son is concerned.
However, the amendment Coffey has made over simple Filioquism regarding
the relation between the Father and the Son is not totally satisfactory, and his
integration suffers the same inadequacies of Filioquism, with respect to the
origin of the Son and his relationship with the Spirit. Therefore, we hold that
a different model that harmoniously represents the mutual relationship of the
Son and the Spirit is required to understand the role of the Spirit in the economy of salvation.

4.4. Begetting of the Son "through the Holy Spirit"?

Despites the advantages of representing the processional relationship of the
Spirit "from the Father through the Son," the model conveys nothing about
the Son's dependence on, and relatedness to, the Spirit. Tom Smail is not
fully satisfied with the mere addition of "through the Son," although he totally agrees with the effect of this amendment in emphasising the primacy of
the Father over the Son in the procession of the Spirit, as well as the Son's
distinctive role in the sending of the Spirit. He argues that if we believe that
the Trinitarian relationship revealed in history, as presented in the New Testament, is the manifestation of the eternal relationships in the Godhead, we
have to say that the Holy Spirit proceeds "from the Father through the Son."
Moreover, he points out that the New Testament speaks also of the Son's
coming through the intervention of the Spirit. Therefore, he claims that just
as the mediatory aspect of the generation of the Spirit is brought out by the
addition of "through the Son," so, too, the mediatory nature of the Son's incarnation should also be brought to light by an inclusion of "through the Spirit," because the New Testament account implies, not only that the Spirit

---

229. Colwell, *Promise and Presence*, 45.

comes "from the Father through the Son," but also the Son "from the Father through the Spirit."[230] As he puts it,

> [i]f then, we are to be true to the total New Testament witness on this matter, we must say not only that the Spirit comes from the Father through the Son, but also that the Son comes from the Father through the Spirit. There is not just a one-sided dependence of the Spirit on the Son, as the West has taught, but a mutual dependence of the two upon each other. Both have their source in the Father, but each does what he does and is who he is in relation to and dependence upon the other. Their relationship is described better as a co-ordination of the two, than as a subordination of the one to the other.[231]

Thus, Smail proposes a twofold alteration in the Nicene-Constantinopolitan Creedal statement in such a way that this mutual dependence between the Son and the Spirit may be made clearer. Accordingly, the new formula would declare that "the Spirit proceeds from the Father *through the Son*" and that the Son "is eternally begotten of the Father *through the Spirit*."[232] Smail claims that these alterations jointly explain the biblical notion of the mutual

---

230. In this regard, we may notice what Rahner says while discussing "mutuality" and "utterance." He holds that there is no mutual love between the Father and the Son, because mutuality implies two acts. However, since only the Logos is uttered, he is not the one who utters. Rahner, *The Trinity*, 106. Torrance charges that in saying so, Rahner is mislead in applying the analogy of human-connections into the inter-personal relationship of the Godhead at the expense of ignoring the biblical revelation that attests to the mutual knowledge and loving between the Father and the Son, and vice-versa. In discussing Trinitarian relations we should not treat them in mere logical order. Torrance, *Trinitarian Perspectives*, 91.

231. Thomas A. Smail, *The Giving Gift: The Holy Spirit in Person* (London: Hodder & Soughton, 1988), 141. Jürgen Moltmann argues in favour of a mutual relationship between the Son and the Spirit that determines one another, although they proceed from the Father. He states: "If instead, we note the experience of the Spirit out of which Christ himself comes and acts, and ask about the Trinitarian structure which can be detected in that, we discover that the Spirit proceeds from the Father and determines the Son, rests on the Son and shines through him. The roles of Son and Spirit are then exchanged. The Son proceeds from the Father and has the impress of the Spirit. We might say that Christ comes *a patre spirituque*, from the Father and the Spirit – though in fact it is better to avoid any undifferentiating "and" in the Trinitarian structure altogether." See Moltmann, *The Spirit of Life*, 71. Congar says that there is a relationship between the Sonship of Jesus in the economy and the eternal Sonship. He affirms that the "Word proceeds *a Patre Spirituque*, from the Father and the Spirit, since the latter intervenes in all the acts or moments in the history of the Word *incarnate*. If all the *acta et passa* of the divine economy are traced back to the eternal begetting of the Word, then the Spirit has to be situated at that point." Congar, *I Believe in the Holy Spirit*, 3:93.

232. Smail himself seems to be sceptical about venturing into this innovative amendment, although he is rather positive about the scope of reflecting on the Trinity in this way, as being supported by the gospel testimony of the Holy Spirit.

dependence on each other that exists between the Son and the Spirit. Smail makes a graphical presentation of his suggested model as follows:

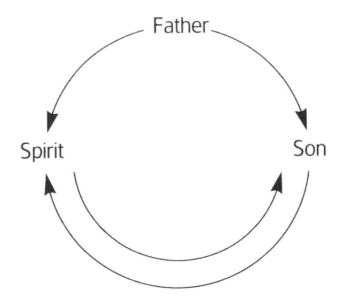

As figure indicates, both the Son and the Spirit are related to the Father as the source of origin. The Son and the Spirit are related to each other by a mutual dependence to the other. This is a relationship of co-ordination, rather than subordination. This model seems to have the potential for effectively reconciling the disparities that exist between the Eastern and Western understanding of the Trinitarian relationship, because it duly acknowledges the monarchy of the Father without falling short of the personhood of Christ and the Spirit. This way of understanding the intra-Trinitarian relationship would help us to view the persons and missions of the Son and the Spirit as equal and complementing each other, without subordinating one to the other, or dissociating one from the other.

Having discussed different models of representing the relationship between the Trinitarian persons, we are now disposed to recapitulate the outcome of our study in regards to Pneumatological theology. A fully meticulous examination of the scope and limits of the divergent models and their subsequent consequences for the East and the West, regarding the procession of the Spirit and its representation in creedal formulation is beyond the purview of our examination. However, as we have noted, the model proposed by Coffey attempts to rectify the limitations of the traditional models of the East and the West through a reconciliation, all the while emphasising the role of the Son in the processional understanding of the Spirit. It seems that due to Coffey's adherence to the mutual love theory, the personhood and the mediatory aspect of the Holy Spirit continues to be dubious. Admittedly, one may be a little reluctant to support the amendment of Smail in its original fashion owing to the countless foreseeable consequences, some of which could serve to counteract the creedal statements and their interpretations held by different churches. However, the immense emphasis that Smail lays on the Spirit's dependence on the Son is successful in rectifying what is lacking in the bestowal model of Coffey. This model is in agreement with a Pneumatologically dependent Christology. As a result, the one-sided emphasis on Christology in representing the intra-Trinitarian relationship is somehow overcome. Consequently, the mutuality of persons and missions of the Son and the Spirit are effectively represented as being manifested in the economy of salvation. Furthermore, we hold that the personhood of the Holy Spirit, as portrayed by Smail, is counteractive and remedial to the mutual love theory of Augustine, which would enhance our understanding of sacramental presence from a Pneumatological perspective. Moreover, a broader understanding of sacramentality, in the light of the overwhelming presence and the activity of the Spirit in creation, the unfolding of the universe, and the entire history of grace which culminates in Jesus of Nazareth, can be robustly located within this model. Now we shall examine the implications of a Pneumatologically-dependent Christology, as recommended by Smail, and its enrichment of our understanding of the Church and the sacraments.

5. The Church and the Sacraments

A prominent notion of the Church that has come to the theological vocabulary since Vatican II is the concept of the Church as the sacrament of Christ. The Christological foundation of such an understanding is quite evident and undisputable, especially in the West. However, having emphasised the complementariness of the mission of the Spirit with the mission of Christ in salvation, consistent with a Pneumatologically-dependent Christology, questions must be asked as to what is the role of Pneumatology in relation to

Christology in the understanding of the Church. Acknowledging the active role of the Spirit as constitutive of the identity of the person and the mission of Christ, the post-resurrectional presence and the activity of Jesus cannot be viewed as "Spirit-less." The idea of the Church as the saving presence of Christ has to be interpreted Pneumatologically. This would provide us with the key to the understanding of the sacraments of the Church as well. Before entering into this discussion, it is crucial to explain the implications of our study for defining the identity and function of the Spirit in relation to that of Christ.

5.1. The Holy Spirit as Person and Mediation

The divinity of the Holy Spirit is no longer a contentious issue in contemporary theological discussions. However, what is controversial and remains to be explored, even today is the personhood and the role of the Holy Spirit.[233] The Holy Spirit is often described by impersonal metaphors denoting his activity or functions in relation to the world. In other words, the Holy Spirit has been understood in more terms of what he does, rather than what he really is. As Yves Congar rightly observes, "[t]he Spirit is without a face and almost without a name. He is the wind who is not seen, but who makes things move. He is known by his effects."[234] Do these and similar characteristics of the Spirit which escape our general concepts of personhood permit us to confer a personal identity on the Holy Spirit? It is true that the biblical witness to the personhood of the Holy Spirit is ambiguous, as compared to the personhood of Christ who reveals himself in visible and tangible forms in historical space-time. However, the understanding of the term 'Spirit' as the Holy Spirit and as the third person of the Trinity, in a restricted sense, distinct from

---

233. There are two ways of conceiving the Spirit, namely, "God as Spirit," and "the Holy Spirit." The first expression refers to the nature or modality of God in himself and in relation to the world (the essence of God in God's very self, and in the immanent action outside himself). The second expression implies the Spirit as the third Person of the Trinity, as differentiated as well as related to the Father and the Son in the immanent and economic mission. See Del Colle, "The Holy Spirit," 323; Haight, *Jesus Symbol of God*, 447-448; Pannenberg, *Systematic Theology*, 370-378. The question regarding the personhood of the Holy Spirit is whether he can be understood as the power and action of the Father and the Son towards and in us, or he can be understood as a distinct personal subject, but never independent, who authentically participates in the Trinitarian life of God. Smail, "The Holy Spirit in the Holy Trinity," 152.

234. Congar, *I Believe in the Holy Spirit*, 3:144. In this sense, the Spirit is understood in functional terms as metaphorically representing God's actions outside the immanent Trinity. So, the Spirit seems to have been expelled from the selfhood of God.

the Father and the Son, was developed alongside the development of Trinitarian theology, especially through the working out of a Trinitarian theology by the Cappadocians and Augustine. As was pointed out earlier, the personhood of the Spirit is overshadowed by Christological prominence. Nevertheless, ascribing personal identity to the Spirit is fully in agreement with the Trinitarian faith of Christianity, although various Christian traditions differ in their respective understanding of the Spirit in relation to the Father and the Son. As previously noted, the Pneumatology that developed according to the *Filioque* model minimised the personhood and role of the Holy Spirit as manifested in the scriptures. The way in which we have explained the processional relationship of the Spirit in the triunity of God favours the ascribing of personhood on par with that of Christ and a personal and proper mission, which is not less than that of the mission of Christ. In this connection, we will examine the precise role that can be ascribed to the Spirit in the light of the Pneumatological understanding that we have developed in our study.

5.2. The Holy Spirit as "Mediated Immediacy"

In contemporary theology, there seems to be a general consensus in ascertaining the role of the Spirit in relation to Christology. A Pneumatologically-dependent Christology, that we have proposed in our study, provides us with the means for assigning personal "status" to the Spirit and for explaining the role of the Spirit as mediatory. One of the purposes of this approach is to counteract the demerits of the mutual love theory of Augustine. John Colwell shows how the aforesaid model proposed by Smail has potential enough to correct the depersonalising tendency of the mutual love theory that tends to consider the love between the Father and the Son and their self-giving as unmediated, thereby collapsing the distinction of the Lover and the Beloved.[235] He attempts to bring in a shift in the understanding of the Spirit as the love between the Father and the Son, to the Spirit as the mediation of the love between the Father and the Son. Therefore, it is the Spirit who mediates the love of the Father to the Son and the love of the Son to the Father; he is not simply the love, or bond of love, between them. Colwell claims that it is the mediatory aspect of this mutual love and self-giving that keeps the distinctiveness of the persons who indwell each other (*perichoresis*) intact. Therefore, conceiving the Holy Spirit as the personal mediator of love, rather

---

235. Colwell, *Promise and Presence*, 39-40.

than mere love between the Father and the Son, retains the unity and distinctiveness in the immanent Trinity.

Colwell bases his argument on the relational aspect of the Trinitarian persons in the economy of salvation as manifested in the Bible. The gospel narrative of the Trinity has a relational structure.[236] According to Colwell, God's revelation is always mediated. There is no unmediated epiphany or divine presence. As he puts it, "God is revealed to us … in and through the flesh of a Nazarene carpenter. … all that God is and does here is done by the mediation of the Spirit through the flesh assumed by the Son."[237] According to him, the story of Jesus narrated in the gospels is not merely the story of Jesus, but the story of his relatedness to the Father through the Spirit and the Father's relatedness to the Son through the Spirit. Therefore, the gospel story presents the Spirit as the agent of mediation between the Father and the Son. The words and actions of the Son are the words and actions of the Father mediated by the Spirit. They are the words and actions of the whole Trinity through the mediation of the Spirit. Similarly, both Jesus' ministry and his proclamation of the Father's Kingdom, is in the power of the Spirit. Jesus' sacrificial death, his self-offering to the Father, as well as his resurrection and the raising of the Son from the dead by the Father, are all mediated by the Spirit. Thus, he concludes that the relatedness of the Son to the Father, as narrated in the gospel story, is a relatedness that is mediated by the Spirit, i.e., it is a mediated relatedness.

In representing the Spirit as the mediating person of the mutual love between the Father and the Son, Colwell accentuates the personhood of the Holy Spirit in relation to the Father and the Son. Identifying the Spirit as a mediating person in the Godhead is not splitting the Trinity into three deities, because in mediating the Father and the Son, the Spirit is not acting as a third party standing isolated from, and independent of, the other two persons, but rather, the Spirit mediates the love between the Father and the Son without ceasing to be the love between them. Thus, in mediating the love, the Spirit remains as the bond of love, as the principle of unity and difference. Therefore, we purport to argue that the mediatory aspect of the Spirit emphasised by Colwell is complementary to the Augustinian notion of the Spirit as the bond of love. In this sense, the mediating function of the Spirit can be called

---

236. Moltmann, *Trinity and Kingdom*, 64.
237. Colwell, *Promise and Presence*, 56.

"mediated immediacy."[238] In mediating the love between the Father and the Son, the Spirit makes immediate the presence of the Father and the Son each to the other and mediates his own immediate presence to the other two as well. Thus, the Father, the Son and the Holy Spirit remain in immediate presence to each other (mutual indwelling). Similarly, when we speak about the mediating role of the Holy Spirit in relation to Christ in the economy of salvation, as witnessed by the New Testament, we should understand the Spirit's role as "mediated immediacy." In mediating the immediacy of God's presence in the person of Jesus Christ, the Spirit is united to Christ as the Spirit of Christ. In mediating God's presence through the words and actions of Jesus of Nazareth, the Spirit is not simply a "mediator," i.e., a third party who stands in isolation outside "mediation" itself, but rather, he *is* the mediation of the mediator. In mediating Christ, the Spirit is co-present as the Spirit of Christ. Therefore, there is an intrinsic unity and distinctiveness, as far as the personhood and the missions of the Son and the Spirit are concerned. For this reason, the understanding of the role of the Spirit as "mediated immediacy" helps us to understand the mutuality of the Son and the Spirit in the economy of salvation and in the understanding of the Church and the sacraments.

Like Colwell, on the Catholic side, Heribert Mühlen, Walter Kasper, Edward J. Kilmartin, etc., all emphasise the interrelationship between Christology and Pneumatology and develop the mediatory role of the Holy Spirit. According to Mühlen, the Spirit who anoints Jesus in the incarnation continues to mediate salvation by mediating between the risen Christ and the Church. The role of the Spirit is a mediatory role in mediating God's salvific work in time.[239] Mühlen lays emphasis on the presence of the Spirit from Jesus' conception to his death, resurrection and exaltation. According to him,

---

238. Kilmartin develops the notion of "mediated immediacy" to explain the role of the Holy Spirit in bringing the Church to Christ and Christ to the Church. He opines that the notion of "mediated immediacy" guards against falling into either overdrawn separation, or identification between them. See Edward J. Kilmartin, "The Catholic Tradition of the Eucharist. Towards the Third Millennium," *Theological Studies* 55 (1994): 435.

239. Mühlen, *Der Heilige Geist als Person*, 151. Mühlen systematically develops the personhood of the Holy Spirit, formulating a "personalist" doctrine of the Trinity in this praiseworthy work. He explains the relationship of the Trinitarian persons as *Ich-Du-Wir* relationship (Father – *Ich*, Son – *Du*). The Spirit is the bond of love and peace between the Father and the Son. The three divine persons jointly constitute *Wir*. In spite of his attempt to uphold the personhood of the Spirit, the inward relationship of the Spirit to the other two divine persons seems to be weak. See Moltmann, *The Spirit of Life*, 14.

it is the "unction" of the Spirit that is at work in the personal history of Jesus. In developing the presence and activity of the Spirit throughout the life and activity of Jesus, Mühlen overcomes the defect inherent in confining the anointing of the Spirit solely to the hypostatic union.[240]

The Spirit is the point of entry into the mystery of Christ and the Father, and also the meeting point of God and humankind. As Walter Kasper says, "the Spirit as the mediation between Father and Son is, at the same time, the mediation of God into history."[241] Kasper further expatiates this saying, "the Spirit is, therefore, in every respect the mediation, in freedom, of love, unity and distinction."[242] According to Mühlen, the Spirit mediates us with God and with one another. However, the Holy Spirit is not a mediator between Christ and us, as Christ is between the Father, but he is the "mediated imme-diacy" (*die sich selbst vermittelnde Vermittlung*) between Christ and us.[243] The personhood of the Holy Spirit is identical with that of Christ, and con-cretely experiential, but not identical with Christ in his human nature, be-cause the Spirit is represented as "wind," "dove," "tongues of fire," etc. There is no immediate contact with God, or with others, other than through the Spirit. Mühlen writes in an analogical way:

> One cannot say that the Logos is in the strict sense one and the same in the Father, in his human nature, and in us, for that would mean the 'extension' of the hypostatic union also to us. Still less can one say … that the Father is in the strict sense one and the same in the Son, in the Holy Spirit, and in us. The Holy Spirit, however, is, in the strictest sense, one and the same in the Father,

---

240. Scholastic theology primarily related the anointing of the Spirit with the "substantial" sanctification minimising the activity of the Spirit in the life and ministry of Jesus. Mühlen tried to extend it to give the Spirit a role in the salvation-historical dimension. See Gary D. Badcock, *Light of Truth & Fire of Love: A Theology of the Holy Spirit* (Grand Rapids, MI, Cambridge, UK: Eerdmans, 1997), 146-153.

241. Kasper, *Jesus the Christ*, 250.

242. *Ibid.*, 268.

243. Heribert Mühlen, *Una Mystica Persona: Die Kirche als das Mysterium der Heilsge-schichtlichen Identität des Heiligen Geistes in Christus und den Christen: Eine Person in Vielen Personen* (Paderborn: Ferdinand Schöningh, 1967), 70-82; Heribert Mühlen, "Das Christusereignis als Tat des Heiligen Geistes," in *Mysterium Salutis: Grundriss Heilsge-schichtlicher Dogmatik* (Einsiedeln: Benziger, 1969), 514-515. The expression "sich selbst vermittelnde Vermittlung" has generally been translated into English as "mediated immedi-acy." See, for instance, Kilmartin, "Catholic Traditon of the Eucharist," 435. However, in a discussion with Stijn Van den Bossche he expressed the view that he would prefer to render it as "self-mediating mediation." We retain the common English translation, "mediated immedi-acy."

in the Son, in the human nature of Jesus, and in us! The Spirit is, without qualification, the universal mediation which, on the basis of the Spirit going out from the Father and the Son, mediates all with all."[244]

Employing the Pneumatology of Heribert Mühlen, Kilmartin tries to explain the role of the Spirit in the liturgy as "mediated immediacy" in mediating Christ and the Church. "The unity between Christ and the Church is personal and immediate because it is mediated by one Spirit. The Holy Spirit is not 'mediator' between Christ and us, but rather mediation of the mediator, because the Holy Spirit is the Spirit of Christ whom he shares with us."[245] According to Rahner, in God's self-communication, there remains a remoteness, unless it is mediated by God himself. The Spirit as the mediated immediacy, as the gift of God, removes this remoteness, the role which is proper to the Spirit. "In God's *self*-communication to the creature, radically understood, the mediation itself must be God and cannot amount to a creaturely mediation ... God must mediate to himself and through himself."[246] In other words, the Holy Spirit bridges the gap between God and humankind. God's immanence comes to the world in the Spirit.

The view that the Holy Spirit brings Christians into contact with God was also held by some Fathers, although they expressed it in different terms. The Spirit is ascribed with a "contact function." The function of contact and mediation of the Spirit is indicated by the following statement of Basil as an explanation for the reverse order of the Trinitarian persons in 1Corinthians 12:4-11: "For the apostle has been inspired by human relations: When one receives a gift, we thank first the one who brings the gift, then the one who sent the gift, and finally, one ascends in thought to the source and the cause of the gift."[247] Athanasius affirms the mediatory role of the Spirit when he says, "there is nothing which is not originated and actuated through the Word in the Spirit."[248] Gregory of Nyssa says that the whole body of Christ is anointed with the Spirit in such a way that no one can approach Christ other

---

244. Mühlen, *Una Mystica Persona*, 70-82; Mühlen, "Das Christusereignins als Tat des Heiligen Geistes," 514-515. Translation from McDonnell, *The Other Hand of God*, 112.

245. Hall, *We Have the Mind of Chris*, 83-84; Kilmartin, *Eucharist in the West*, 357.

246. Karl Rahner, "Oneness and Threefoldness of God in Discussion with Islam," in *Theological Investigations* (London: Darton, Longman & Todd, 1984), 116, 118. Each of the divine persons communicates in personal particularity. The indwelling of the Spirit as the one who sanctifies, consecrates, moves etc. belongs to the Spirit in a particular and proper way. Rahner, "The Scholastic Concept of Uncreated Grace," 343-346.

247. Basil, "De Spiritu Sancto," 16:35.

248. Athanasius, "Letter to Serapion," 1:31.

than through the Spirit. He writes, "On all sides, the Holy Spirit is met by those who, by faith, approach the Son."[249] The Theological-Historical Commission has sufficiently emphasized this patristic notion as follows: "It is impossible to have any contact with God if not in the Spirit. ... The Spirit is the place for experiencing God-in-us and God-for-us."[250] It is in the Spirit that we encounter God. Understanding the role of the Spirit as mediation helps us to understand grace in a new light. McDonnell hints at the possibility of interpreting the contact and touch function of the Spirit in terms of grace. As he puts it, "the contact function of the Spirit extends as the order of nature and grace. If Jesus is the universal mediator, the Spirit is the universal mediation."[251]

Once the role of the Spirit is described as "mediated immediacy" certain consequences are bound to follow, especially in the understanding of the Church and the sacraments. The first consists in explaining the mediatory role of the Spirit in making the Church the sacrament of God's immediate presence; whereas, the second explains the active role of the Holy Spirit in mediating God's immediate presence in and through the sacraments.

5.3. Ecclesial Mediation

Ascribing a mediatory role to the Holy Spirit necessarily leads us to think of the sacramentality of the Church in terms of Pneumatology. This is because we cannot formulate a sound theology of the Church without considering Easter and Pentecost as integrally united events. Understanding the Church as the body of Christ present in history invites us to acknowledge the role of the Spirit in making the presence of Christ real in the Church, which makes it the Church of Christ, or the sacrament of Christ. That is why Eastern theology thinks of the "church as the body of Christ and the fullness of the Holy Spirit."[252] Therefore, the Pneumatological theology that we have proposed underscores the activity of the Spirit at the origin and ongoing life of the Church.

---

249. Gregory of Nyssa, "Against the Macedonians," in *Nicene and Post-Nicene Fathers*, ed. Philip Schaff and Henry Wace (Edinburgh: T & T Clark, 1996), 16.

250. Theological-Historical Commission, *The Holy Spirit, Lord and Giver of Life* (New York: Crossroad, 1997), 116.

251. McDonnell, *The Other Hand of God*, 115.

252. Kärkkäinen, *Pneumatology*, 109.

5.3.1. The Spirit as Co-instituting Principle of the Church

Pneumatological theology encourages us to reflect on the identity and mission of the Church, balancing the Christological and Pneumatological aspects, without diminishing the centrality of Christ. The Pneumatological and ecclesiological insights of Zizioulas and Congar, interpreted along the lines of the ecclesiology of Luke-Acts, provide us with innovative insights in this regard. Accordingly, we can differentiate two movements, i.e., "institutive" and "constitutive," in the origin of the Church. As Zizioulas articulates, the Church is "instituted by Christ" and "constituted" by the Holy Spirit. The Spirit is far from being a mere animator of the already existing Church, but as he puts it, "Pneumatology does not refer to the well-being of the Church but to the very being of the Church."[253] Thus, for Zizioulas, Pneumatology becomes the very ontology of the Church. In this sense, Pneumatology is unquestionably an ontological category of ecclesiology.

Yves Congar's ecclesiology also emphasises the role of Christ and the Spirit as essential components of a balanced ecclesiology.[254] He insists that there should be a balance between the Christological and Pneumatological aspects in speaking about the birth and continuing life of the Church. The origin of the Church is attributed to the Incarnate Word and his mission, as well as the activity of the glorified Lord, the indwelling of his Spirit.[255] Thus, the Church is dependent on the two missions of the Word and the Spirit. The Church, as a historical and visible reality, was founded by Christ, who is alive and active in it. The role of the Spirit is to vivify the Church and make it the body of Christ. However, the Spirit has a determinative role in the origin, life, and continuation of the Church. Congar says, "[t]he Spirit did not come simply in order to animate an institution that was already fully determined in all its structures, but that he is really the 'co-instituting' principle."[256] In this sense, the Spirit is constitutive of the identity of the Church. Moreover, the Spirit pervades the entire spheres of the Church, animating and leading it to its ultimate goal. McDonnell unambiguously expresses this overwhelming presence and activity of the Spirit as follows:

---

253. Zizioulas, *Being as Communion*, 131-132.
254. See Yves Congar, *Sainte Église: Études et approches ecclésiologiques*, Unam Sanctam, 41 (Paris: Cerf, 1963), 12.
255. Congar, *The Word and the Spirit*, 79.
256. Congar, *I Believe in the Holy Spirit*, 2:9.

... the Spirit is the principle of the church's identity. If the Spirit is divided from eschatology, then awareness that the church is on the move to a God-given goal is lost. Without the principle of movement, the church is in danger of turning from a pilgrimage people into a structure standing still. When this happens, glory is in stasis. In the splendor of its institutions, in the beauty of its liturgies, in the radiance of its saints, the earthly church is its own static end – in a word, triumphalism. The parousia has a sign hanging around its neck stamped not "delayed," but "cancelled."[257]

In contrast to the Eastern ecclesiology, there developed in the West a Christocentric ecclesiology with marginal attention to the activity of the Spirit in the origin and continuing life of the Church. Even in the documents of Vatican II, we cannot find a solid Pneumatological thread in the reflection on the Church. It is remarkable to see that the role of the Spirit is relegated merely to the animating function of the already existing Church. The Council states:

> When the work which the Father gave the Son to do on earth (cf. Jn 17:4) was accomplished, the Holy Spirit was sent on the day of Pentecost in order that he might continually sanctify the Church, and that, consequently, those who believe might have access through Christ in one Spirit to the Father (Eph 2:18).[258]

So, the origin of the Church is located exclusively on a Christological foundation. This places the mission of the Spirit in a temporal succession after the mission of Christ. Actually, there exists a temporal succession, as far as the visible missions of Christ and Spirit in the history of salvation are concerned; however, this has to be interpreted without implying a consequent Pneumatology, which would be possible only by presenting the "invisible mission of the Spirit" as simultaneous with the visible mission of the Son in the incarnation. However, optimistically, we observe a minute, but noticeable change in *Ad Gentes* (no. 4) in accepting the role of the Spirit, even before the glorification of Jesus, while speaking about the mission of the Church.

---

257. McDonnell, *The Other Hand of God*, 53.

258. *Lumen Gentium*, no. 4. The documents of Vatican II, especially, *Lumen Gentium, Dei Verbum and Ad Gentes*, have innumerable references to show the presence and activity of the Spirit in and outside the Church; the institution of the Church, however, is solely attributed to Christ (See, for instance, *Gautium et Spes*, 3b,201; 40b,238; 78a,290; *Unitatis Redintegratio*, 1a,341; *Ad Gentes*, 1a,584; 5b,589; *Lumen Gentium*, 5d,18; 8d,24). The role of the Spirit is confined merely to the functional aspect. Bonaventure Kloppenburg presents an exhaustive list of the passages that show the various functions of the Holy Spirit. See Bonaventure Kloppenburg, *The Ecclesiology of Vatican II*, trans. Matthew J. O'Connell (Chicago, IL: Franciscan Herald Press, 1974), 30-36.

Notwithstanding these developments, the ecclesiology of Vatican II, in general, is not sufficiently Pneumatological. It is the task of theologians to highlight the significance of Pneumatology in the understanding of the Church and the sacraments. Therefore, we now turn our attention to study the role of the Spirit in relation to the Church for the understanding of sacramentality.

5.3.2. Sacramental Mediation

The identity of the Church as the sacrament of Christ and the understanding of the Church as the locus of individual sacraments are well accepted in Catholic theology. Such developments are, by and large, based on Christology. As Rahner observes, "the sacramentality of the church's basic activity is implied by the very essence of the church as the irreversible presence of God's salvific offer in Christ."[259] The sacramentality of the Church consists in expressing the definitiveness of God's love and grace, and thereby making present the ongoing story of salvation.[260] This is achieved in and through the celebration of the sacraments. "… [t]he Church is something that springs from the essence of Christianity as God's self-communication to humankind made manifest and effectively expressed in Jesus."[261] According to the understanding of Rahner, the Church is the sacrament or *Realsymbol* of the ongoing visible and tangible presence of God's grace in the world. The symbolic function of the Church consists not only in proclaiming God's relationship to itself, but also in symbolising God's relationship to the world.[262] As Rahner understands, the history of the world and the history of human beings are a history of grace. Accordingly, the world and its history are the primary sacraments of God's relationship to the world, because it is in human life that one encounters God before encountering God in the Church and its sacraments.

259. Rahner, *Foundations*, 413.

260. John Carmody, "The Realism of Christian Life," in *A World of Grace: An Introduction to the Themes and Foundations of Karl Rahner's Theology*, ed. Leo J. O'Donovan (Washington, DC: Georgetown University Press, 1995), 144.

261. Michael A. Fahey, "On Being Christian Together," in *A World of Grace: An Introduction to the Themes and Foundations of Karl Rahner's Theology*, ed. Leo J. O'Donovan (Washington, DC: Georgetown University Press, 1995), 128.

262. William V. Dych, "Theology in a New Key," in *A World of Grace: An Introduction to the Themes and Foundations of Karl Rahner's Theology*, ed. Leo J. O'Donovan (Washington, DC: Georgetown University Press, 1995), 15.

The symbolic function of the Church in manifesting the salvific presence
of God in history has a two-fold mission, namely, to make present the redeeming love of God and to receive the gift of God and offer a response of
faith and love, in the Holy Spirit.[263] The Church is the venue of a "divine
commerce" (*divinum commercium*), a place whereby God's gift of presence
becomes realized, and a human response in faith and worship takes place.
God's love awakens a response, a return gift, a response in love and faith.
However, the only perfect return gift or response was given by Christ. The
Church, as a community joined with the offering of Christ, offers a return gift
in love and faith through a personal commitment.[264]

In this connection, there arises a question as to what is the fundamental
principle upon which the liturgy and sacraments are grounded. Otto Semmelroth recalls that Henry de Lubac said more than a half decade ago that "all
sacraments are essentially sacraments of the Church."[265] Accordingly, the
individual sacraments make present the sacramental reality which the Church
symbolizes and mediates as a visible body. Later, Semmelroth made an exposition of the theme: "the Church as the original sacrament [*Ursakrament*]."[266] Rahner brings a shift in this understanding by bringing in a clear
distinction in applying the term *Ursakrament* for Christ and *Grundsakrament*
for the Church.[267] Therefore, the Church, as the foundational sacrament,
communicates Christ's life through the celebration of the sacraments. Christ
is the only sacrament of God; as Schillebeeckx says, "the one and the only
saving primordial sacrament ... the one and only sacrament of God."[268] The
Church mediates the sacramentality of Christ in and through the sacraments.
Such being the case, the sacramentality of the Church and the place of the
sacraments in the Church are intertwined. However, the Pneumatological
dimension is as important as the Christological in making the Church what
the Church really is, and in mediating Christ's presence in and through the
sacraments of the Church.

We argue that the role of the Spirit as "mediatory," which was outlined in
our discussion, could also be applied in explaining the Church and the sacraments, because the Spirit mediates Christ to the Church and the Church to

263. Lukacs, "Communication – Symbols – Sacraments," 208.

264. Schillebeeckx, *Christ the Sacrament*, 91-132.

265. Henri de Lubac, *Catholicism: A Study of Dogma on Relation to the Corporate Destiny of Mankind* (London: Burns, Oates & Washbourne, 1950), 496.

266. Otto Semmelroth, *Die Kirche als Ursakrament* (Frankfurt: Josef Knecht, 1955).

267. Rahner, *The Church and the Sacraments*, 18.

268. Schillebeeckx, *Christ the Sacrament*, 40.

Christ. The definitive role that the Spirit exercises between Christ and the Church can be described as "mediated immediacy." In other words, the mutual presence between Christ and the Church becomes immediate through the mediation of the Spirit. It is in the Spirit that Christ encounters the Church and the Church encounters Christ. The unity and mutual presence that is established between Christ and the Church is "immediate" in that the Spirit does not act as a "mediator" standing outside, or isolated from this encounter, but rather, the Spirit is co-present as the interior principle of it. Therefore, the role of the Spirit is "mediation," which can rightly be called "mediated immediacy." The mutual presence that is realised by the Spirit between Christ and the Church is ultimately oriented toward the realization of the salvation accomplished in Christ.

The concept of "mediated immediacy" also underscores the unity and difference in the dynamics of the mystery of salvation.[269] The Vatican Council also considers the Holy Spirit as the principle of unity and difference between Christ and the Church. The Spirit is the principle of unity between Christ and the Church, who makes the Church the "sacrament of salvation."[270] Similarly, Kilmartin says that the Church is the "[s]acrament of Christ in the Holy Spirit."[271] It is the Spirit who mediates God's free offer of salvation in and through the Church. As McDonnell says, in the order of salvation, the Spirit has "an immediacy proper to His person."[272] The same notion is expressed by Heribert Mühlen when he says that the Spirit is "itself the unmediated, mediating immediacy of our standing over against Christ."[273] In the history of salvation, the Spirit functions as the "point of entry" where, through Christ, the Father enters history and humankind ascends to the mystery of the Father through Christ.[274] Irenaeus also conveys the same idea when speaking about the salvation of the faithful that they advance "by degrees; first, by the Spirit they mount to the Son, and [then], by the Son (they ascend) to the Father."[275] According to the Spirit theology of Barth, the Holy

269. Kilmartin, "Catholic Eucharistic Theology," 435.

270. *Lumen Gentium*, no. 48b.

271. Hall, *We Have the Mind of Christ*, 116. Hall opines here that in this regard Kilmartin slightly differs from W. Kasper who says that the Church is "the place of the Holy Spirit."

272. McDonnell, "Theology of the Holy Spirit," 209.

273. Mühlen, "Das Christusereignins als Tat des Heiligen Geistes," 514-515. Cf. n. 243 above.

274. *Ibid.*, 208.

275. Irenaeus, "Against Heresies," in *The Ante-Nicene Fathers*, ed. Alexander Roberts and James Donaldson (Edinburgh: T & T Clark, 1996), 3:24,1.

Spirit has a mediating function. The Spirit is understood as mediating God's revelation to humankind. He parallels the Spirit's function of mediating revelation to humankind to the activity of the Spirit in the incarnation, in the uniting of the Son of God to the humanity of Jesus. According to him, the Spirit is the point where the Father, through his Son, reaches out to history, and thereby, the Spirit is the point of entry into the mystery of Christ and the Trinity.[276] Basil has also insisted on the role of the Spirit in mediating the knowledge of the mystery of Christ and the Trinity. The Spirit reveals the glory of the Son and leads through him to the indescribable source of this glory, the Father.[277] This process goes in tune with the liturgical dynamics, namely, in the Spirit, through Christ to the Father. Now, we move on to the discussion of the role of the Spirit in the sacraments and liturgical celebrations.

5.4. Sacramental Efficacy

As was mentioned in the first chapter, the pertinent question that inhabited the minds of scholastic theologians was the efficacy of the sacraments, which later assumed a new shape in the debate over "mystery presence" that has dominated the theological arena since the 1920s. Even now, the same question arrests our attention as requiring a better sacramental hermeneutics. The question of sacramental efficacy is, in fact, the question concerning the *how* of the sacraments, the question as to how to relate the presence of Christ and his saving deeds with the Church's liturgical celebration. In other words, how does the sacramental celebration of the Church effectively make present the reality signified by the sacramental symbols? How does the celebration of the Church here and now in historical space-time, realize what it signifies and symbolically represents? Bearing these questions in mind, we shall now see exactly what insights Pneumatology may give us regarding the question of sacramental efficacy.

The discussion pursued throughout the present chapter was in view of discovering the role of the Holy Spirit in the sacramental event. With this purpose in mind, we proposed a Pneumatological theology, a way of doing theology from a Pneumatological perspective, within the theological framework of God's self-communication, whereby we brought into focus a Pneumato-

---

276. Philip J. Rosato, *The Spirit as Lord: The Pneumatology of Karl Barth* (Edinburg: T & T Clark, 1981), 17-21.

277. Basil, "De Spiritu Sancto," 18:47.

logical string that runs through the history of God's engagement with the world, specifically, by delineating the overwhelming presence of the Spirit that human beings experience at the core of their being and in the experience of the universe. The Christian revelation of the Holy Spirit has to be understood in the lineage of this experience of the Spirit in creation as the life-breath, the creative and animating power of God. Even though the revelation of the Holy Spirit as the Third Person of the Trinity was intensely manifested only in the New Testament, the Spirit's presence and activity have been perceived and experienced by various religious traditions and peoples of God. So the phenomenon of the Spirit is at the origin of God-thought and the reflection on creation and its unfolding, directed towards its final destiny. This experience of the Spirit that pervades the history of God's encounter with the world was crystallised in the New Testament, in the person of Christ, in the Christ-event which was actually a "Spirit-event." As it becomes clear from the Pneumatological Christology outlined in this study, the experience of the Spirit was the basic phenomenon constitutive of his personhood, life and mission. In the post-Pentecostal era of the Church, we see the vivacious activity and experience of the Spirit as Christ is experienced in the Spirit. Today, the presence and activity of Christ that the Church realizes and mediates becomes tangible in the sacramental mediation of the Spirit. Thus, the fundamental basis of the sacramentality of creation, the mystery of Christ and the Church, and of the sacraments, is the same Holy Spirit. Without understanding this uninterrupted lineage and overpowering resonance of the Spirit in the history of God's self-communication, the reflection on sacramentality and sacramental presence would be faulty and incomplete. The theological backbone that supported our arguments in this regard is the personhood of the Spirit that we have defended through the re-construction of the Intra-Trinitarian relationship.

Accordingly, Pneumatological theology helps us to affirm that the role of the Holy Spirit is of primary importance in the understanding of the efficacy of the sacraments, and to locate sacramental presence within the context of God's self-communication or gift of himself, which is essentially Trinitarian. God communicates his salvific presence in and through the sacramental event through the mediation of the Spirit, who is the "mediated immediacy" of our standing-over against Christ. A sacramental hermeneutics based on Pneumatology cannot reduce the sacraments to mere instrumental causes, or juridically constituted signs for the conferral of grace, but rather, the celebration of the sacraments itself must be understood as the participation in the mystery of Christ, the reception of God's gift of himself made available in Christ and mediated by the Spirit. Thus, sacramental presence, understood in this manner, manifests a clear lineage of the presence of God in the Spirit, beginning with creation, culminating in the mystery of Christ, and continuing unceasingly in the intense presence and activity of the Spirit which is concretely experienced in the Church, particularly in the celebration of the sacraments.

6. Conclusion

In the present chapter, our aim was to re-discover the role of the Holy Spirit for a better hermeneutic of sacramental efficacy. In this endeavour, we proposed a pnuematological theology alongside a Pneumatologically-dependent Christology within the theology of God's self-communication *ad intra* and *ad extra*. Accordingly, we defended the personhood of the Holy Spirit and described the role of the Spirit as mediation, specifically identifying the Spirit as "mediated immediacy." Moreover, we have defended the equality of the role and mission of the Spirit without subjugating or forfeiting the mission of Christ. Furthermore, we have pointed out that the Spirit has a determinative role in mediating the salvific presence in the sacraments of the Church in the trajectory of God's self-communication. As we have pointed out, this self-communication of God is made possible through the sacraments, and emphasises the mediatory role of the Spirit in mediating sacramental presence with the support of a Pneumatological theology.

Alongside the Pneumatological dimension, what is equally relevant is the question of symbolic efficacy, because in the sacramental celebration, there comes into play an array of symbolic elements, whose significance has been brought to light through the developments in the study of language and symbols. How do we understand the liturgical and sacramental dynamics that come into play in our sacramental celebrations? For instance, how does the pronouncement of the formula, together with the specific actions performed at baptism, make one Christian? Or how does the recitation of the words, together with the actions performed over the bread and wine and other ritual enactments of the liturgical celebration, derive their efficacy? Is the efficacy that the Church believes to be realized and teaches to be effective, based on the magical efficacy of symbols? How do we explain the efficacy of symbols in the sacramental event? Is it by the power inherent in the rituals? Or is it by the power of human action? Is it by the power of Christ's passion, as the scholastics explained?

The task of addressing these and similar questions has to be undertaken, being attentive to postmodern sensibilities, without falling into metaphysical temptation. Therefore, it is important to discover a non-metaphysical approach in which God's self-communication can be explained, avoiding meta-narratives. We propose to do this within phenomenology, employing the notion of givenness. In the following chapter, we will develop a theological-phenomenological construct such that God's giving in the sacraments can be interpreted by giving proper attention to both the Christological and Pneumatological dimensions.

CHAPTER THREE

THE PHENOMENON OF GOD'S SELF-COMMUNICATION

In the preceding chapter, we have formulated a Pneumatological theology of God's self-communication that sheds light on the importance of Pneumatology in the understanding of the sacramental event. In the present chapter, we will attempt to fill the Pneumatological deficit that lies within contemporary sacramental thinking which tries, in general, to explain sacramental presence in terms of the phenomenology of symbols and language. Therefore, the main issue that is addressed in this chapter will be how to correlate between philosophy and theology, phenomenology and Pneumatology, which are of two different domains. In this regard, the phenomenology of Jean-Luc Marion seems to provide us with the key to explore the possibilities of reflecting on revelation within phenomenology, whereby the revelation of the Spirit can be placed alongside the revelation of Christ. In fact, employing the vocabulary of Marion, God's self-communication in the Word and the Spirit can rightly be translated into the language of the gift.[1] Therefore, this chapter undertakes a rather extensive study of Marion's phenomenology of givenness and its theological implications for thinking of God's self-communication as God's gift in Christ and the Spirit, in view of explaining the sacraments. The thrust of this chapter is to develop a sacramental hermeneutic using a phenomenological concept of God's self-communication as gift that will take Pneumatology, seriously. This chapter will take up Marion's phenomenology of givenness, especially as developed through the categories of the icon and the idol. This in turn provides a phenomenological framework from which it is possible to understand the sacraments as iconic-symbols. While Marion never explicitly works out a sacramental theology, the purpose of the current

---

1. The sender, message and receiver constitute the process of communication ("someone" says "something" to "someone"). In the same way, the paradigm of the gift implies the giver, gift and recipient/givee ("someone" gives "something" to "someone"). However, an absolute separation between the giver and the gift is not applicable to God's giving, because God gives himself.

inquiry is to explore the underlying thread woven through his philosophical and theological project, and how it can provide a phenomenological construct for developing a sacramental hermeneutics within the context of postmodern thinking.

1. Metaphor of the Gift

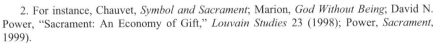

Giving and receiving are basic human actions that govern the relationships of individuals and communities. Human life, from its origin and throughout its growth to the end, can be seen as the sum of "giving" and "receiving." Our belongingness to the human family involves a life of connectedness characterised by giving and receiving. Human beings give and receive life, commodities, services, love, time, etc. Therefore, the metaphor of "the gift" can be considered the fundamental aspect of being human. The interest that various disciplines have taken in studying the phenomenon of gift points to its importance, as well as to the complexities involved in identifying its nature and function as expressing and constructing relationships.

The phenomenon of the gift models, not only human relations, but also divine relations. The concept of giving is also ascribed to God, as the supreme giver, which is considered under the rubric of divine action. Gift-giving and its implications provide a format for reflecting on the relationship between God and the world in creation, the incarnation, the gift of the Spirit, and the sacraments, particularly the Eucharist. Thus, the anthropological and phenomenological notion of the gift has become a paradigm in contemporary theology.[2]

Upon looking into the structure of the gift, we are struck by the diversity and the multiplicity of viewpoints under which acts of giving and receiving are understood. Initially, and in general, we tend to understand gifts as presents. Gifts are presented by someone to someone. There are three constitutive elements in the scheme of gift-giving.[3] They are: someone gives, something is given, and someone receives. The practice of gift-giving implies that a gift is given in the form of a present by someone to someone; it has to be freely given away and freely received. The word "freely" expresses

---

2. For instance, Chauvet, *Symbol and Sacrament*; Marion, *God Without Being*; David N. Power, "Sacrament: An Economy of Gift," *Louvain Studies* 23 (1998); Power, *Sacrament*, 1999).

3. Stephen H. Webb, *The Gifting God: A Trinitarian Ethic of Excess* (New York: Oxford University Press, 1996), 13.

the fact that there is no compulsion on the part of the giver or receiver. However, in receiving the gift, the presence of it ought to be acknowledged, if by nothing else, at least by a gesture of gratitude. It seems to be impossible to acknowledge a gift without a "return gift" of gratitude, or some form of repayment, however menial it may be. Can a gift be thought of in its free givenness if it already implies a return of some kind? Does the gift, in order to be a pure gift, need to be freed from any form of return or repayment? Does the fact that a gift is liberated from presence, from its external manifestation lead to the conclusion that a gift can never be a present? Attempts at answering these questions have generated several diverse theories of the gift and giving in anthropology, social sciences, and philosophy.

1.1. The Gift Economy

The classical idea of the gift comes from Aristotle whereby the gift is described as "something given without recompense."[4] It was Marcel Mauss who brought the topic of the gift into public discussion, highlighting its prominence in governing individual and social relationships. In his classical work, *Essai sur le don, forme archaique de l'Exchange*, published in 1924, he describes the practices of gift-giving and gift-receiving in ancient societies.[5] Mauss analyses the complex social rules which governed the gift-giving practices in archaic societies. The gift exchange in such societies operates basically on three obligations, namely, the obligation to give, the obligation

---

4. Aristotle, "Topics," in *Aristotle: Selected Works*, ed. Lloyd P. Gerson (Grinnell, IA: Peripatetic Press, 1982), 125a.18. See also Risto Saarinen, *God and the Gift: An Ecumenical Theology of Giving* (Collegeville, MN: The Liturgical Press, 2005), 6; Calvin O. Schrag, *God as Otherwise Than Being: Toward a Semantics of the Gift*, Northwestern University Studies in Phenomenology & Existential Philosophy (Evanston, IL: Northwestern University Press, 2002), 106.

5. Mauss refers to Ralph Waldo Emerson's (1803-1882) pioneering essay "Gifts," written in 1844, which already raised the paradoxical and problematic character of the gift in their interconnectedness between the object given and relationship. Marcel Mauss, *The Gift: The Form and Reason for Exchange in Archaic Societies*, trans. W.D. Halls, Routledge Classics (London: Routledge, 2002), 65. See also Ralph Waldo Emerson, "Gifts" (1844), available from http://www.bartleby.com/5/113.html (accessed August 16, 2008); Bronislav Malinowski and Calude Lévi-Strauss are also eminent figures remaining in the trajectory of Mauss. Claude Lévi-Strauss, *The Elementary Structures of Kinship*, ed. Rodney Needham, trans. James Harle Bell and John Richard von Sturmer (London: Eyre, 1969); Claude Lévi-Strauss, *Introduction to the Work of Marcel Mauss*, trans. F. Baker (London: Routledge & Kegan Paul, 1987); Bonislaw Malinowski, *Argonatus of Western Pacific* (New York: E.P. Dutton, 1961). However, modern reflection on gifts and gift-giving was initiated by Mauss.

to receive, and the obligation to repay.[6] Even before the use of money, there existed a market economy which was based on the mutual exchange of gifts. This was a means of acquiring goods and obtaining social services. Based on exchange, an economic hierarchy was created, and thus, having the power or capacity to give gifts was related to one's social status. In other words, one's social status was determined, based on the perceived ability to give gifts. This process can be seen as giving rise to competition, even escalating into war and violence. The whole exchange process was a vicious circle. The gift-exchange in such societies, however, did not serve utilitarian ends, due to the fact that the counter-gift tended to exceed the original gift, even though gift-giving was often motivated by the desire for ensuring better social status, protection, and so on. It served the purpose of mutuality and security in need. Therefore, the giving of the gift, always put the receiver into obligation, or debt, even if it was not explicit, rejecting the possibility of a "free gift." Although Mauss has distinguished this from the gifts and services of market economies, traditional societies operated on the basis of loosely defined principles of exchange.[7] Various tribes were bound to give and receive gifts which put them under an obligation to return the favor in some fashion. Nearly all of the studies based on archaic societies explain the concept of the gift within the scheme of reciprocity. In such systems, the gift does not contradict exchange, albeit the gift obligates a return. The notion of obligatory reciprocity does not dismiss gratuitousness, even though there can be the vestiges of power and domination.

Attempting to give a moderate interpretation to Mauss' views, Jacques Godbout argues that human beings can give gifts with genuine intention.[8] The gift (the giftness of the gift) is not cancelled out because of the idea of obligation that prevailed in ancient societies. There can be gift-giving unconditionally and irreducibly without being subject to legal obligation or economic utility. Examples such as these include the generous giving involved in family life, humanitarian aid programs, Christmas or birthday presents, etc. Thus, he tries to uncover the genuine act of giving in the paradigm of the gift. He argues that the genuineness and gratuity in such cases cannot be

6. Lévi-Strauss, *Introduction to the Work of Marcel Mauss*, 43; Mauss, *The Gift in Archaic Societies*, 1-23.

7. Schrag, *Semantics of the Gift*, 106; Allan D. Schrift, ed., *The Logic of the Gift: Toward an Ethic of Generosity* (New York, London: Routledge, 1997), 4.

8. Jacques Godbout and Caillé Alain, *The World of the Gift*, trans. Winkler Donald (Montreal, Quebec: McGill-Queens University Press, 2000).

ruled out, even though most givings are contaminated by reciprocity in various forms, namely, gratitude, a sense of fulfillment prompting further giving, etc. Without extirpating gift from the domain of economic-exchange, with its forms of reciprocity and return, Godbout emphasises the non-calculable, free, and unselfish motive of giving.

Pierre Bourdieu provides a different explanation of the gift without referring to the subjective intentions of the donor.[9] He emphasizes the time factor between the gift and the counter-gift. In day-to-day living, we find that it is improper to reciprocate a gift with a counter-gift without a time frame. If the recipient returns a gift without a suitable time frame, it can be seen as amounting to a refusal of the gift. It is equally insulting to return the same, even if at a later time. However, immediately reciprocating with an equal return (counter-gift) belongs in the domain of commerce, an act of buying and selling. Therefore, according to Bourdieu, a counter-gift must be both deferred and different.[10] Bourdieu's analysis of the gift is understood according to the logic of practice in archaic forms which runs counter to the principles of economic exchange.[11] In such exchanges, there exist "symbolic goods," or "symbolic capital" which is beyond material value. A "symbolic alchemy" is at work in such societies that are beyond economic reason and exchange.[12] A theory of practice underlies the manner of giving and reception and the goals that they achieve in maintaining relationships, status, honor, etc.

A common theme underlying the theories of both Godbout and Bourdieu is the discovering of the reason for the giving of the gift other than economic reason. Bourdieu is less optimistic than Godbout regarding true generosity despite his accommodation of generosity within the framework of some conditions that exist in society which he calls "symbolic alchemy." Godbout is more optimistic about gratuity and generosity, especially in selfless giving, as being operative in altruistic actions.

---

9. Pierre Bourdieu, *The Logic of Practice*, trans. Richard Nice (Stanford, CA: Polity Press, 1990), 80-141. Here Bourdieu explains a logic of practice which is different from the logic of the logician. It is an "economy of logic" operated by a minimum logic that is required by the needs of practice. It often contradicts the "logical logic." *Ibid.*, 86-87, 92. Allan D. Schrift reproduces important parts of the *Logic of Practice*. See Alan D. Schrift, ed., *The Logic of the Gift* (New York, London: Routledge, 1997), 190-230.

10. Bourdieu, *The Logic of Practice*, 98-111.

11. *Ibid.*, 112-121.

12. Schrift, ed., *The Logic of the Gift*, 14.

The anthropological and sociological analysis and discussions on gift gained momentum in the philosophical arena, especially within deconstructionist thought, where theorists sought to shed light on the limits of the explanation and knowledge of the gift. However, the question of the gift continues to be discussed at length in contemporary philosophical theology. Recently, the works of Jacques Derrida, Jean-Luc Marion, and others have brought to light the import of it in academic theology and the philosophy of religion. The discussions are augmented, based on the critique of "free/pure gift," which can even challenge the Christian concept of God's gift as freely given and gratuitous. This seems to put in question the "free gift" of God (God's gift of himself) which we believe that the sacraments are guaranteed to bestow. The seeming impossibility of a "free gift" puts the theological claim of God's gift at stake, contaminating it with the implied notions of the exercise of power and domination, subjecting human beings to an irrevocable dependence and debt. Therefore, employing the language of the gift in explaining God's relation to the world will be ambiguous and confusing, without clarifying the meaning and significance we attach to its theological use.

1.2. Gift and Presence

As mentioned at the outset, the purpose of this work is to explore an alternative way of understanding sacramental presence; in scholastic language, this translates into how the sacraments are "realized," or how they become "effective." How does the divine of the Holy become present in the ritual performance of the sacraments? This question is relevant, because in order for the ritual performances to become sacramental, the divine ought to be present in the ritual performances in some way. In this sense, the *how* and *what* of the sacramental "presence" is at issue. According to Derrida, the gift has a close connection to the present, and also to the presence of the present. As he puts it, "a gift is called a present, that 'to give' may also be said 'to make a present', 'to give a present'."[13] In the reflection on the gift also, the notion of presence is at issue. The connection between the gift and the present, when extended to sacramental presence more fully elucidates the understanding of God's gift in the sacraments, and helps to answer some of the questions raised above.

---

13. Jacques Derrida, *Given Time: 1. Counterfeit Money*, trans. Peggy Kamuf (Chicago, IL: University of Chicago, 1992), 10. Originally published in French as *Donner le temps*, this is a translation from the Edition Galilée, 1991.

Again, in what sense is the divine present in the sacraments if a metaphysical understanding of presence is rejected? The metaphor of the gift offers plausible answers to such questions, because in proceeding with the metaphor of the gift, the idolatry of metaphysics in understanding presence is actually overcome. Thus, the approach remains in the trajectory of overcoming the metaphysics which has been pursued all through the present discussion. Moreover, the phenomenology of the gift requires that it be freed from the confines of Being, Good, and Levinas' ethics of responsibility.[14] However, in reflecting on the gift, the temptation remains to submit the gift to the economy of exchange relations which, in turn, transforms the gift into reciprocity and return, even though it is merely simple gratitude. But thinking of the gift necessarily implies that something gracious has been rendered which the recipient could, in herself, not do. Thus, the recipient is, in some sense, lessened before the giver. Gratitude and the receiving of the gift serve to elevate the status of the giver, while degrading the givee to the status of servitude. As such, the gift-giving in the scheme of exchange is infected by reciprocity which forfeits the notion of the pure gift. Therefore, the current challenge of this project is to consider: is there a gift and giving possible, without being infected by reciprocity? Will the concept of a pure gift oppose the Christian concept of God's self-communication as gift and the human response demanded of us? As a preliminary step towards addressing these issues, the discussion will turn to the philosophical challenge that questions the very possibility of the gift. It will then be possible to discuss, in detail, the phenomenology of givenness and the gift as a hermeneutical framework in which the Christian revelation, God's gift and the sacramental gift, can be thought. Hence, a plausible concept of the gift will be developed that can enlighten the understanding of the self-giving God and, ultimately, the understanding of God's giving in the sacraments.

1.3. The Gift Aporia

Jacques Derrida raises fundamental challenges to the philosophical notion of the gift. He summarily presents the philosophical aporia of the gift in his works, *Given Time: I: Counterfeit Money* and the *Gift of Death*.[15] In *Given*

---

14. Schrag, *Semantics of the Gift*, 104.
15. Derrida, *Given Time*; Jacques Derrida, *The Gift of Death*, trans. David Wills (Chicago, IL, London: The University of Chicago Press, 1995).

Time, Derrida raises questions concerning the very possibility of the gift.[16]
He argues that gift-giving, in a network of economic exchange relations,
virtually negates the gift, as gift. Derrida's arguments are as follows: if I give
you a gift, then I look good and put you in debt. But if the gift is genuine,
"there must be no reciprocity, return, exchange, counter-gift, or debt."[17]
There is absolutely no giving back, whether it is sooner or later, whether it is
the same or a different thing. The very notion of counter-gift, or return, annuls the gift, as gift. In giving the gift, the social status of the giver is increased automatically, and the givee is placed in a debt of gratitude. Within
the scheme of economic exchange, a gift inevitably incurs indebtedness, at
least in the form of a customary thanksgiving, which is "actually" an acknowledgement that something has been done for someone, and that same
someone is obliged to give something back. Derrida argues that a genuine
gift, in order to be pure, must be forgotten in the very moment that it is given
and received. However, in contrast, in the moment a gift is given, it suc-
cumbs to the vicious circle of exchange relations.[18] Thus, all gifts become, in
practice, counterfeit. As he says,

> [t]he moment the gift, however generous it be, is infected with the slightest
> hint of calculation, the moment it takes account of knowledge [*connaissance*]
> or recognition [*reconnaissance*], it falls within the ambit of an economy: it
> exchanges, in short it gives counterfeit money, since it gives in exchange for
> payment.[19]

The recognition of a gift *as* gift, its appearance *as such*, its presence *as
present*, suffices to annul the gift.[20] Therefore, Derrida argues that the "con-

---

16. Derrida shows the problematic nature of the gift, analysing gift-giving on the basis of
two factors (freedom and the present) that pertains to the idea of the gift. He rules out the
possibility of the gift, analysing the notions of the "giver," "gift" and "givee," owing to the
fact that both the gift and giving tend to be reduced to the domain of economy. For a concise
treatment of the topic, see Robyn Horner, *Rethinking God as Gift: Marion, Derrida, and the
Limits of Phenomenology* (New York: Fordham University Press, 2001), 4-18. See also Jean-
Luc Marion, *Being Given: Toward a Phenomenology of Givenness*, trans. Jeffrey L. Kosky
(Stanford, CA: Stanford University Press, 2002), 74-78.

17. Derrida, *Given Time*, 12.

18. Derrida places himself against the gift concept of Mauss. According to him, Mauss'
study on the gift-exchange in archaic societies clearly shows this vicious circle which actually
fulfils the conditions of the gift. For Derrida, they are the conditions that impel the annulment
of the gift. Therefore, Derrida opines that Mauss "speaks of everything but the gift." Derrida,
Given Time, 24.

19. Derrida, *The Gift of Death*, 112.

20. Derrida, *Given Time*, 13.

ditions of [the] possibility of the gift … designates simultaneously the conditions of the impossibility of the gift," which according to him, is the fundamental aporia of the gift. Strictly speaking, a gift can neither be given nor received. The ambivalence of gift-giving is that the act of giving adds something to the donor by way of return, rather than to the recipient, "which is the opposite of what the gift was supposed to do."[21] Derrida goes deep in his analysis of the gift, saying that a mere recognition of the gift as a gift by the recipient, itself annuls the gift, because by acknowledging the intention of the gift, the recipient gives back a symbolic gift in the form of recognition, which adds to the honor of the donor, which as a result, destroys the gift, as gift. Something similar happens on the part of the donor as well. As soon as the giver knows that he is giving a gift, or intends to give, the giver is starting to pay himself a symbolic recognition. The donor begins to think, as he intends to give, "to pay himself, to gratify himself, to congratulate himself, to give back to himself symbolically the value of what he thinks he has given or what he is preparing to give."[22] Therefore, in order that the gift can be given, both the giver and the givee are to forget it immediately, which means, the gift must not appear as a gift, because knowing the truth of the gift as a gift annuls the gift.

As distinct from the analysis of Mauss and others, it is not essentially a social or economic domain, but rather, a philosophical problem. In arguing this way, Derrida is not rejecting the possibility of the gift, but draws attention to the discrepancy between the common notion of the gift and the philosophical impossibility regarding the attainment of a perfect definition of the gift. For Derrida, "the gift is another name for the impossible; we still think it, we name it, we desire it," even though we can never encounter it. He goes on to say that "a theory of the gift is powerless by its very essence." What is possible for us is to think of the "transcendental illusion of the gift."[23] We see the trace of the gift, but in close examination, we do not encounter the gift, but only an illusion of it. So, the gift is a philosophical aporia, according to Derrida. Even though the thought of the gift is an impossibility, Derrida emphasises the relevance of the gift as unknowable. He claims not to have said that there is no gift, but he does insist, is that "its possibility is possible as

21. John D. Caputo and Michael J. Scanlon, eds., *God, the Gift and Postmodernism* (Bloomington, IN: Indiana University Press, 1999), 4.

22. Derrida, *Given Time*, 14.

23. *Ibid.*, 29.

impossible."[24] He argues that the gift cannot be known as such, "but it can be thought of. We can think what we cannot know ... [T]here is something in excess to knowledge."[25]

The anthropological and philosophical discussions on the gift do not specifically concern the notion of God as giver. However, extending these notions to God would imply that God's gifts are "counterfeit."[26] Nevertheless, Jean-Luc Marion has in recent years developed a phenomenology of givenness in which the gift can be thought of. He tries to provide a philosophical possibility of thinking about the gift within a phenomenological construct, going back to the philosophical tradition of Martin Heidegger, and especially Edmund Husserl. Thus, he tries to portray an image of God experienced through giving which is yet, not a "counterfeit" giving. In the following section, we make a detailed study of Marion's phenomenology of givenness in view of understanding its implications for the understanding of God and God's self-communication as gift, which becomes concrete for us in the sacraments of the Church.[27]

2. The Phenomenology of Givenness

The "theological turn" in phenomenology provides theologians with the means to liberate theology from the categories of Being and a metaphysically idolatrous God.[28] Marion has made considerable contributions in this regard,

---

24. It has to be remembered that Derrida does not deny the gift, but the phenomenological impossibility of knowing a gift as such. As he puts it, "I never said that there is no gift. No. I said exactly the opposite. What are the conditions for us to say there is a gift, if we cannot determine it theoretically, phenomenologically?" Jacques Derrida and Jean-Luc Marion, "On the Gift: A Discussion between Jacques Derrida and Jean-Luc Marion, Moderated by Richard Kearney," in *God, the Gift, and Postmodernism*, ed. John D. Caputo and Michael J. Scanlon (Bloomington, IN: Indiana University Press, 1999), 60.

25. Derrida and Marion, "On the Gift," 60.

26. John Martis, "Postmodernism and God as Giver," *The Way* 36 (1996): 240.

27. For the implications of Marion's phenomenology for theology, particularly for sacramental theology, see Stijn Van den Bossche, "God Does Appear in Immanence Afterall: Jean-Luc Marion's Phenomenology as a New First Philosophy for Theology," in *Sacramental Presence in a Postmodern Context*, ed. Lieven Boeve and Lambert Leijssen (Leuven: Leuven University Press, 2001), 325-346.

28. Dominique Janicaud affirms that there has been a theological turn in French phenomenology. Dominique Janicaud, "The Theological Turn of French Phenomenology," in *Phenomenology and the "Theological Turn": The French Debate*, ed. Dominique Janicaud, *et al.* (New York: Fordham University Press, 2000). This was originally published in French as

pushing phenomenology to its limits and by opening avenues for theology in considering God's engagement with the world in terms of givenness (rather than Being).[29] In the following section, we shall discuss the phenomenological understanding of givenness in such a way that it helps to understand and articulate God's self-communication in terms of gift.

2.1. Transcendence as Given

The fundamental notion of Marion's phenomenology is that the phenomenon is given. In *Being Given*, Marion gives a detailed account of pure givenness in dialogue with Husserl and Heidegger.[30] Against the "constituting subject," retained by Husserl and Heidegger, Marion argues that phenomena are given, rather than constituted by the subject according to the conditions imposed on them by the subject. Therefore, he argues that a phenomenon "gives itself," "appearing itself," and "imposing itself" on the recipient. As such, Marion defines the phenomenon as that which shows itself, in itself, and on the basis of *itself*. The phenomenon shows itself more than anything else, in that it gives itself on the basis of itself.[31] In other words, phenomenality refers to something that shows itself as itself *from itself*. Accordingly, Marion understands the status of self as purely given. The origin of one's being precedes oneself, so one is absolutely indebted to what is given. In other words, it is the extremely rich givenness of the phenomena, the overflowing givenness of the phenomena that primarily encounters the human person.

Dominique Janicaud, *et al.*, eds., *Le tournant théologique de la phénoménologie française* (Paris: Éditions de l'Éclat, 1991).

29. As Stephen Webb lauds, "Nobody has done this in a more original way than Jean-Luc Marion, who does not subordinate the gift to the question of reality, but rather, interrogates the idea of "what is" from the perspective of the gift." Webb, *The Gift Giving God*, 129. "Givenness" is the English translation of the term *donatio*) and German *Gegebenheit*. See Jean-Luc Marion, *The Idol and Distance*, trans. Thomas A. Carlson (New York: Fordham University Press, 2001), xxi. *Givenness (donation* – German *Gegebenheit*), signifies four things: 1) its act (to give, *donner*); 2) what is at stake (gift, *don*); 3) the actor (giver, *donateur*); 4) the gift given (given, *donné*). See Marion, *Being Given*, 61. For an etymological and semantic study of the terms referring to givenness, gift, reception, etc., in German, see Martin M. Lintner, *Eine Ethik des Schenkens: Von einer Anthropologischen zu einer Theologisch-Ethischen Deutung der Gabe und ihrer Aporien*, Studien der Moraltheologie, 35 (Wien, Berlin: LIT Verlag, 2006), 33-40.

30. Marion, *Being Given*, 221. Here he relies more on the Heideggerian notion of phenomenality, rather than that of Husserl who understands phenomenon as intuition. *Ibid.*, 138, 201.

31. *Ibid.*, 17-18.

Marion's phenomenology is different from Husserlian phenomenology which rests on intuition; it is a hermeneutical phenomenology which allows the transcendent to give itself in immanence. Accordingly, phenomenology is concerned with, not merely "seeing," but "seeing-as" and what is given in "seeing-as" is determined by what is taken.[32] There is no originary presence; presence is mediated by that which is present prior to the presencing. The understanding of presence, in this sense, as Ricœur explains, is the result of "the dispossession of consciousness as the place and origin of meaning."[33] The dispossession of consciousness in hermeneutical phenomenology comes into play in two ways: first, in interpretation, which includes a detour through cultures and text, and is guided by prior interpretations; second, the hermeneutic of suspicion. The dispossession of consciousness that is characteristic of hermeneutical phenomenology means, "[w]e must really lose hold of consciousness and its pretension of ruling over meaning … reflection, in order to get at the root of desire, must let itself be dispossessed of the conscious meaning of discourse and displaced to another place of meaning."[34] According to the norm of hermeneutical phenomenology, intersubjectivity does not consist in a subject-object encounter, but rather, in the experience of being looked at. The *Sinngebung* or constitution of meaning comes from the experience of being looked at. In other words, meaning comes from without in the experience of being looked at. It is going beyond intentionality and freeing phenomenology from the confines of objectification and representation.[35] Thus, Marion tries to free his thought from the confines of Being or subjectivity by developing a hermeneutical phenomenology of givenness. As John O'Donohue observes:

> "Givenness" is both the source and the force at the heart of Marion's "ontology"; it is the originary impulse that projects, propels, and structures what is. It precedes identity; indeed, it confers identity. In a deft phenomenological manoeuvre, Marion is able to claim the "delay" in the initial self-activation of

---

32. Merold Westphal, "Vision and Voice: Phenomenology and Theology in the Work of Jean-Luc Marion," *International Journal of Philosophy of Religion* 60, no. 117-137 (2006): 119.

33. Paul Ricœur, *Freud and Philosophy: An Essay on Interpretation*, trans. D. Savage (New Haven, CT: Yale University Press, 1970), 42.

34. Ricœur, *Freud and Philosophy*, 422, 424.

35. Westphal, "Vision and Voice," 121.

subjectivity as a key instance of the generosity and the prevenience of "givenness."[36]

As Stijn Van den Bossche observes, according to the *a posterior*-principle of
reduction the given is neither *object* nor being, but the object and being are
given. The thing is reduced from object and being to the given. Marion's
reduction removes all that hinders the phenomenon from showing itself, or
demonstrating itself. The appearance of phenomena is possible without having recourse to Being, but in terms of givenness. In other words, the being of
every being is being-given.[37] His phenomenological principle is: "the more
reduction, the more givenness," which, according to him, ensures the possibility for the reality to show itself, or to let the other appear independent of
the subject.[38] So, the reality appears as given. In other words, the phenomenon, reduced to givenness, is no longer perceived as object or being, but manifests itself as given. "Marion's subject enjoys full epistemological capacity,
but it is an epistemological capacity awakened and conferred by the prevenient activity of "givenness": the more the subject is willing to receive, the
more it comes to know."[39] Thus, Marion's phenomenological reduction considers givenness as the first principle of the phenomenon, even prior to the
presencing of the phenomenon. This provides theology with a philosophical
framework in which God's self-communication can be thought of as givenness. However, the question may be posed: is it possible to think of something as purely given or, in other words, what are the conditions of something
which can be reduced to pure givenness?

2.2. The Notion of the Pure Gift

Marion presents the gift as a paradigm of the phenomenon. He stresses that
everything is given as a phenomenon. He claims that phenomenology can
penetrate into the essence of gifthood and explain the essence of phenomenality as givenness. Thus, he upholds the possibility of pure gift.[40] Taking

36. John O'Donohue, "The Absent Threshold: An Eckhartian Afterword," in *Givenness
and God: Questions of Jean-Luc Marion*, ed. Ian Leask and Eoin Cassidy, Perspectives in
Continental Philosophy (New York: Fordham University Press, 2005), 278.

37. Jean-Luc Marion, "Metaphysics and Phenomenology: A Relief for Theology," *Critical
Inquiry* 20 (1994): 583.

38. Van den Bossche, "God in Immanence," 332.

39. O'Donohue, "The Absent Threshold," 279.

40. For an account of Marion's arguments in defence of the possibility of the gift, see
Jean-Luc Marion, "Sketch of a Phenomenological Concept of Gift," in *Postmodern Philoso-*

Derrida's charges seriously, Marion goes on to consider: Does a pure gift exist or does a gift as self-gift exist? To elucidate: One of the conditions of a pure gift is that it is not ruled by causality and the economic scheme of exchange and value. According to him, the gift cannot be understood in the domain of metaphysics, according to the principle of causality and sufficient reason. If the gift is explained in terms of causality, then it would imply that the gift is something that has been received or given to serve a goal or an end.[41] Therefore, he argues that the gift is possible only outside the domain of metaphysics, and the gift itself is that which gives account of itself. Accordingly, a phenomenon appears in its own horizon as purely given, a phenomenon reduced to givenness. Marion retains the notion of the pure gift and interprets it by applying the principle of reduction to the instance of the experience of the giving and the receiving of a present. In this way, the gift becomes "present," not in its objective value, or in what it really is, but consists in the gesture (the gift), irrespective of the object-value of it. According to Marion, the gift gives itself without "presence."[42] In this connection John Milbank differs from Marion.

John Milbank, a philosophically interested theologian, holds a view of gift which is quite different from that of Marion. He wants to incorporate ontology in his understanding of gift, calling attention to its significance in theology: the necessity of seeing the gift in terms of gift-exchange.[43] He is critical of a unilateral "puritan gift" as retained by Marion. In the vein of Mauss and others, he argues that a good and sensible gift does receive something back.

---

phy and Christian Thought, ed. Merold Westphal (Bloomington, IN: Indiana University Press, 1999), 122-143; Marion, *Being Given*, 71-118; Jean-Luc Marion, "The Reason of the Gift," in *Givenness and God: Questions of Jean-Luc Marion*, ed. Ian Leask and Eoin Cassidy, Perspectives in Continental Philosophy (New York: Fordham University Press, 2005), 101-134.

41. In the metaphysical scheme, givenness is formulated in terms of a giver, a gift given and a give, and the gift is governed by the principle of identity and sufficient reason.

42. Van den Bossche, "God in Immanence," 336.

43. For a comprehensive understanding of the gift according to Milbank, see John Milbank, "Can a Gift Be Given? Prolegomena to a Future Trinitarian Metaphysics," *Modern Theology* 11 (1995): 119-122; John Milbank, *Being Reconciled: Ontology and Pardon*, ed. John Milbank, Catherine Pickstock, and Graham Ward, Radical Orthodoxy Series (London, New York: Routledge, 2003), esp. 154-161. In *Being Reconciled*, Milbank argues that the true gift involves always gift-exchange. He explains the ethical and theological dimensions of reconciliation against the background of the discussion of the gift in response to the works of Derrida, Levinas, Marion etc. See also John Milbank, "The Soul of Reciprocity, Part One: Reciprocity Refused," *Modern Theology* 17 (2001): 335-391; John Milbank, "The Soul of Reciprocity Part Two: Reciprocity Granted," *Modern Theology* 17 (2001): 485-507.

In response to Derrida's problematising of the gift, he develops a theological response, utilising the notion of *agape* as "purified gift-exchange," as "delay and non-identical repetition," purifying the stains of all "archaic components of gift giving."[44] His idea of the gift is also characterised by a reciprocity that accommodates deference (time-gap) and difference (non-identity). He argues that the notion of a "purified gift-exchange" can be applied to the Christian notion of *agape*. But a unilateral puritan gift, held by Marion, cannot be applied to the notion of *agape*. However, he agrees with the fact that, in a sense, nothing can be given back to God for the divine gift. Nevertheless, he argues that even the supreme model of unilateral giving involves some form of return. He tries to reconcile absolute gratuity with absolute exchange.[45] If the gift fails to evoke some form of return by acknowledgement, the gift is simply not there, and therefore, cannot be given. In the same way, the divine gift, in order to be given, both distance and reciprocity are essential, and it takes place, subject to delay and difference.[46] Even though Milbank acknowledges much of Marion's understanding of gift, he distances himself from Marion regarding the existence of a purely unilateral gift. He is against the construal of gift in terms of what he calls a "modern purism."[47] For Milbank, Marion's attempt to liberate the gift from being, alongside the notion of pure givenness, does not work. A gift without being cannot be a gift of anything. According to Milbank, in order that the gift be truly there, the gift must be reciprocal, but at the same time, "asymmetrical," or "non-identical," operating under the mode of "repeated exchange."[48]

In this analysis of the discussion of gift, two currents have been identified. The main difference can be acknowledged as the question of reciprocity and return. Marion and Derrida take an anti-ontological stance, arguing in favour of a strictly unilateral gift without reciprocity. However, they distance each other on the question of the possibility of such a gift. Marion affirms the possibility of the pure gift, while Derrida champions its impossibility. Milbank retains the possibility of the gift within an ontological construct by purifying gift-exchange with gratuity, thus meriting the social, economic, and anthropological theories of gift-exchange. The diverse understanding of the gift also has implications for shaping different theologies. Marion's under-

---

44. Milbank, "Can a Gift Be Given?," 131.
45. Saarinen, *God and the Gift*, 32.
46. Milbank, "Can a Gift Be Given?," 133-135.
47. *Ibid.*, 141-144.
48. Milbank, *Being Reconciled*, 157.

standing of the phenomenon as given and the possibility of gift-giving seem to give us input for developing a theology of givenness in order to explain the gift of God in the divine economy which finds expression in the sacraments. Moreover, his defence of pure gift helps us to retain the independent and gratuitous character of God's gift. Nevertheless, there seems to be a challenge in reconciling the notions of gratuity and return/response in terms of God's giving and our response, even while subscribing to a unilateral gift outside economic exchange. We will address this issue in the final pages of this chapter. A detailed examination of the manner in which Marion develops his phenomenology of givenness will equip us for this purpose. It is this we turn to now.

2.2.1. Gift as Givenness

According to Marion, givenness vanishes as soon as reciprocity transforms it into exchange. Therefore, is it possible to understand the gift as gift, as pure givenness? Marion argues that it is possible outside the horizon of exchange and economic reason, i.e., considering the gift as irreducible to exchange and economy.

2.2.1.1. Existential Aspect of Givenness

According to Marion, giving and receiving are ordinary phenomena of human experience. He points out that constantly "we give without account," "*without ceasing*," "*without measure*" and "*without … consciousness* [(being conscious of)]" the fact that we are giving.[49] The giving which Marion discusses is a giving that is not governed by the principle of sufficient reason as compared to economic or market exchange, but rather a giving for its own sake. In other words, sense, it is a giving for giving. The phenomenality of such "givings," operative in day-to-day life, is pure givenness. "The gift implies a perfect and pure gratuity, in which it is necessary to give for nothing, without there ever being a return."[50] However, the gift ceases to exist in the scheme of exchange. He explains how the giver (*le donateur*), the givee (*le donataire*), and the gift (*le don donné*) can be abolished which governs the scheme of exchange.[51] In the scheme of exchange, the giver is abolished in

---

49. Marion further elaborates this notion. See Marion, "The Reason of the Gift," 101-102.
50. *Ibid.*, 105.
51. *Ibid.*, 102-105, 109-112.

terms of return, the givee is abolished in terms of indebtedness, and the gift by commodifying it. The economic exchange is operated according to sufficient reason and value which always obligates rendering, an account. In the process of economic exchange, gratuity is annulled to the point of ceasing the gift to exist. He concludes that no explanation of the gift is possible in the horizon of economy.

2.2.1.2. Reduction to Givenness

Having annulled the possibility of the pure gift in the economic exchange, Marion further considers whether there is any other horizon in which we can think of the gift. As will be discussed in the following pages, through a phenomenological reduction of the gift to givenness, Marion argues in favour of the possibility of the pure gift employing the threefold objections of Derrida as reasons for transcending the conditions of economic exchange.[52] Marion claims that the gift is possible by reducing the gift to givenness by starting from the origin of the gift before getting dissolved into the economic exchange scheme, or to the economy's sufficient reason. As he says, the phenomenon of the gift is possible, "by maintaining it in itself; that is, by reducing the gift to itself, hence to givenness, which is the gift's own proper horizon."[53] In other words, this means starting from the gift itself placing the phenomenon of the gift within the horizon of givenness: "a phenomenon that could never allow itself to be recaptured by the economic horizon, a gift that is always already reduced and drawn back to givenness, free of any degradation into economy, born free of sufficient reason."[54] So, the possibility of thinking about the gift is the phenomenological reduction of the gift to givenness. Thus, he proposes a possible first principle of phenomenology: "As

---

52. Marion, *Being Given*, 83ff.

53. Marion, "The Reason of the Gift," 113. It has been argued that exchange is not as easily assimilated into commercial exchange as Marion thinks. Gift-exchange has also a logic which, in many cases, resembles the logic of givenness. However, gift exchange also differs from givenness in many respects. See Kathryn Tanner, "Theology at the Limits of Phenomenology," in *Counter-Experiences: Reading Jean-Luc Marion*, ed. Kevin Hart (Notre Dame, IN: University of Notre Dame Press, 2007), 214. We will take into account Tanner's concern by showing how reciprocity and return gift can be considered under the rubric of a more positive perspective, other than mere economic or business exchange in terms of Marion's understanding of the gift, as we will see later.

54. Marion, "The Reason of the Gift," 117.

much reduction, as much givenness,"[55] by which he overcomes the limitations of the Husserlian principle of phenomenology. Marion argues,

> [n]o givenness without reduction, no reduction that does not lead to given-
> ness. Now, reduction eliminates all transcendence, that is to say, the inten-
> tional ecstasy of consciousness toward its objective, which alone allows
> knowledge of it, but also incertitude, error, illusion, and so on; thus the given-
> ness of the given, on the express condition that it is already reduced, reduced
> to the pure given, becomes absolutely indubitable.[56]

Marion says that the interconnection that exists between reduction and givenness defines the principle of phenomenology. According to him,

> [w]hat appears gives itself, that is to say, it appears without restraint or re-
> mainder; it thus comes about [*ad-vient*], happens, and imposes itself as such,
> not as the semblance or the representative of an absent or dissimulated in-
> itself, but as itself, in person and in the flesh; what appears is emptied totally,
> so to speak (with its essential being [*estance*], its innermost depth of sub-
> stance, its material individuation, and so on), to the point of passing from the
> rank of image, from simple seeming or bereft appearance, to the one unique
> thing at stake.[57]

So, givenness gives the given with certainty, without doubt. Therefore, Marion opens the possibility of gift, reducing it to givenness which always precedes the gift. This saves the gift from dissolving into exchange. The gift is
liberated from any social process or calculable, ethical behavior, by obliterating the condition of exchange, because the giver gives without a givee to
acknowledge the gift; the givee receives without a giver to honor, bringing
about the gift absolutely, and *as such*.[58]

Thus, Marion considers thinking about the possibility of the gift in a
scheme in which the gift can be thought about without falling under the
scheme of the giver, the givee, and without giving any object that is subject

55. Jean-Luc Marion, *Reduction and Givenness: Investigations of Husserl, Heidegger, and Phenomenology*, trans. Thomas A. Carlson (Evanston, IL: Northwestern University Press, 1998), 203; Marion, *Being Given*, 1; Jean-Luc Marion, *In Excess: Studies of Saturated Phenomena*, ed. John D. Caputo, trans. Robyn Horner and Vincent Berraud, Perspectives in Continental Philosophy (New York: Fordham University Press, 2002), 17.

56. Marion, *In Excess*, 18.

57. *Ibid.*, 19.

58. Marion, "The Reason of the Gift," 113. Italics mine. In this connection, we must take into account Derrida's emphasis on the impossibility of the gift "as such." He argues: "So the gift as such, is impossible. I insist on the 'as such'." Derrida and Marion, "On the Gift," 60.

to exchange value.[59] The death of the giver creates the possibility of the gift in its givenness, which calls for neither recognition, nor reimbursement. The givee is abolished in two ways: The gift is given for the gift's sake, while the giver and the givee remain anonymous to each other. In the same way, the gift remains in its perfect form when given to an enemy. As Marion writes, "[i]t is only to an enemy that I can make a gift without risk of finding it taken up in an exchange, or trapped in reciprocity. Paradoxically, only my enemy takes care of the gift by protecting it from a relationship of giving-giving. Whoever gives to his enemy does so without return, without anything coming back, and without sufficient reason, incontestably."[60] Moreover, the possibility of the gift can also be thought of in terms of "non-objective gifts" or "*nothing.*"

> For in giving these nonobjective gifts, which elude being either understood or possessed, which supply no gain or assignable return, and which really provide nothing (*nothing real; ne rem*), I in fact give myself in my most complete selfhood. In giving this *nothing*, I give all that I have, because I am not giving something that I possess apart from myself, but rather that which I am.[61]

In summation, Marion transposes "the gift away from economy and toward givenness" by "bracketing" the giver, the givee, and the objectivity of the gift. In the process of giving, it is the "givability," the self-decision and openness of the giver that makes the gift possible. According to Marion, the gift and the gift-object are not identical. The gift object may be an inadequate way of signifying the gift.[62] "The gifts which give the most give literally nothing," because the self-decision of the giver is fundamental to giving. For instance, in a lover's giving of a ring, it is not the ring that finally counts, but the self-decision of the giver which the ring is a symbol. When a ruler endows power, the objects given are the symbols of giving the most he can give.[63]

59. Marion, "The Reason of the Gift," 113-116. Marion, *Being Given*, 79ff.

60. Marion, "The Reason of the Gift," 15.

61. *Ibid.*, 115.

62. Horner, *Rethinking God as Gift*, 131.

63. Marion, *In Excess*, 131-133. The symbolic aspect of gift giving is very well expressed by Ralph Waldo Emerson in his essay on "Gifts." As he puts it, "[o]ur tokens of compliment and love are for the most part barbarous. Rings and other jewels are not gifts, but apologies for gifts. The only gift is a portion of thyself. Thou must bleed for me. Therefore the poet brings his poem; the shepherd, his lamb; the farmer, corn; the girl, a handkerchief of her own sewing. This is right and pleasing, for it restores society insofar to its primary basis, when a man's

2.3. Re-imagining God as Givenness

Husserl's phenomenological analysis never starts with the assumption of a transcendent God.[64] In such a phenomenological reduction, a prior givenness cannot be thought of, nor can one apprehend givenness as God, due to Husserl's placing of God within "brackets." However, Marion's phenomenological project opens the possibility of explaining the phenomenality of God as pure givenness. His thinking is motivated by a religious intentionality. Accordingly, he develops a biblical figure of God who is givenness before Being, and is not caught in the language of metaphysics which subjects God to Being.

Marion himself tried to develop the implications of his phenomenology of givenness, especially in his theological works. His phenomenological project of gift begins with the thought of "God without Being," which he develops in dialogue with Heidegger.[65] *God Without Being* presents God as gift. He introduces the gift of God, a giving that is not exhausted within Being, but surpasses Being. According to Marion, God gives himself as gift. Phenomenologically, God is "the being-given par excellence according to the notion of donation."[66] He is gift before Being. "[H]e comes to us in and as gift."[67] Marion's phenomenological project lays emphasis on an *a priori* gift, or givenness, the author of which, or the infinite source of which, is God. God, as the "given par excellence" gives "without restriction, without reserve, without restraint."[68] He rejects the Heideggerian insistence that the divine needs Being as the precondition, or possible place of appearance, and develops a concept of the gift as the self-giving gift of Being, while the giver remains absent. There exists two ways of understanding gift. First, gift is understood as appropriation, which can be understood in terms of Heidegger's *es gibt*.

biography is conveyed in his gift, and every man's wealth is an index of his merit." Emerson, "Gifts," available from http://www.bartleby.com/5/113.html.

64. Ruud Welten, "Saturation and Disappointment: Marion According to Husserl," *Bijdragen: International Journal in Philosophy and Theology* 65 (2004): 80.

65. The thesis of "God Without Being" is not to reject the existence of God, but rather, he claims that our thesis about the existence or non-existence of God falls infinitely short of the picture of a Christian God of revelation whose name is designated as Love. In arguing this, Marion's theological critique is two-directional, namely, a theological critique of ontotheological conceptions of God in the history of metaphysics, and a critique of ontotheological conceptions of human subjectivity of modernity.

66. Marion, "Metaphysics and Phenomenology," 588.

67. Marion, *God Without Being*, 3.

68. Marion, "Metaphysics and Phenomenology," 588.

Accordingly, the gift is just "there," with the giver remaining absent. This understanding of the gift is entirely philosophical, according to the dynamics of Being and beings. The second way of understanding the gift is entirely theological, and pertains to the scheme of the Bible which presupposes a divine Giver ruled by distance and dispossession. As Marion puts it,

> [b]etween the gift given and the giver giving, giving does not open the (quadri-) dimension of appropriation, but preserves distance. ... This other model of the gift, since it unites only to the extent that it distinguishes, can precisely, distort Being/being by disappropriating in it what the *Ereignis* appropriates.[69]

Marion thinks of the giver without being transcendent within the scope of phenomenology. He argues in favour of the possibility of immanent givenness whereby the phenomenon becomes its own giver, i.e., the phenomenon gives *itself*. The self-giving of the phenomenon is possible prior to the involvement of the subject. The phenomenological understanding of givenness opens the possibility for a consideration of the biblical image of God as pure givenness, as manifested in Christian revelation. Therefore, it is important to study how Marion opens phenomenology to consider the God of revelation. It is to this the discussion will turn now.

3. The Phenomenon of Revelation

In the strict sense, the figure of God that Marion traces out in the phenomenology of givenness remains a God of the philosophers. However, the theological motif is self-evident. Therefore, it has been argued that, in doing so, he is entering into the realm of theological discourse, into the field of revelation (*die Offenbarung*), rather than that of the presumably pure manifestation of phenomenology (*die Offenbarkeit*).[70] Marion patterns a theological strategy based on the reality of revelation as the pure gift, as the excess of givenness. He re-defines phenomenality in such a way that it allows possibility for the revelation of Christ. He seeks to construct a phenomenology remaining open to transcendence; however, it is not within the ambits of conventional

69. Marion, *God Without Being*, 104.
70. Graham Ward, "The Theological Project of Jean-Luc Marion," in *Post-Secular Philosophy*, ed. Philip Blond (New York: Routledge, 1998), 229-230, 233-234. Ward's charge is mainly that by putting his phenomenology at the service of a "Conservative-Catholic theology," Marion has diluted the authenticity of phenomenological work.

phenomenology, but "within the framework of a phenomenology that is pushed to its utmost possibilities."[71]

3.1. Re-configuring Reduction

According to Husserl, "every originary intuition is a legitimising source of cognition, that everything originarily offered in intuition be accepted as it presents itself."[72] Marion's phenomenological project unfolds the full consequences of this supreme principle of phenomenology. Marion's third reduction (phenomenological reduction), the primacy of givenness, is drawn out of this primary principle of phenomenology. He considers phenomenon as phenomenality. He argues that if intuition is freed from intentionality and objective representation, then givenness would appear in its originality without *a priori* conditions. In other words, the phenomenon goes beyond the limits of metaphysical reckonings. As he puts it, in the appearance of phenomenon as givenness, the principle of sufficient reason is overcome by the "principle of sufficient intuition" and the "principle of insufficient intention."[73] Thus, intentionality is overwhelmed by intuition opening the possibility of "bedazzling" excess so that the phenomenon might appear without boundaries, which is called the "saturated phenomenon." Phenomenality is absolutely irreducible. The givenness, in its own right, ensures its visibility. Thus, the saturated phenomenon is an unconditional and irreducible givenness, according to the norm of maximum phenomenality.

3.2. Beyond Surplus

The underlying principle of Marion's key concept of the saturated phenomenon is the Husserlian notion of surplus. Therefore, in order to comprehend Marion's understanding of surplus, one should know how the notion of surplus structures Husserl's thought. Husserl understands every form of consciousness as an act of consciousness which has a multiple structure, namely,

---

71. Marion, *God Without Being*, xxii.

72. Edmund Husserl, *Ideas Pertaining to a Pure Phenomenology and to a Phenomenological Philosophy*, trans. Fred Kersten (Dordrecht: Kluwer, 1982), 1:24, p. 44. See also Ian Leask, "The Dative Subject (and the 'Principle of Principles')," in *Givenness and God: Questions of Jean-Luc Marion*, ed. Ian Leask and Eoin Cassidy, Perspectives in Continental Philosophy (New York: Fordham University Press, 2005), 182.

73. Marion, *In Excess*, 105.

every act of consciousness aims (intention) at its fulfilment.[74] Within the structure of intention and fulfilment, he identifies a particular moment which is called the *surplus* (*Überschuß*).[75] Explained in more concrete terms, during the act of perceiving something, there is already a surplus intuition. So, according to Husserl, "the things we see are always more than what we see really and actually of them."[76] In other words, we see things as they are through a surplus intuition. However, in contrast to Husserl, Marion considers the possibility of a phenomenon whereby intuition exceeds intention. He is searching for the possible phenomenal link between intention and fulfilment, which is not marked by a deficiency, but rather, by excess or abundance; a saturated phenomenon which is not merely fulfilment, but rather excess of fulfilment.[77] In doing so, Marion's motive is theological. His concept of the saturated phenomenon goes beyond the Husserlian structure of intention/fulfilment in that the intention is not merely fulfilled, but saturated. It crosses the borders of maximum fulfilment, and thereby, it crosses the borders of fulfilment.[78] However, the question remains as to how to adequately understand any kind of fulfilment apart from the intentionality of consciousness. So, from a Husserlian point of view, there is no need for rejecting intentionality in explaining the phenomenality of the saturated phenomenon. As such, Marion explains saturation from a Husserlian point of view as "over-fulfilment" or "excess" which does not fulfil one's own (the subject's) expectations. In this sense, "saturation is not only more than intentionality, more than fulfilment; it traverses intentionality."[79]

74. Welten, "Saturation and Disappointment," 84.

75. 'Surplus' is the English rendering of Husserl's term *Überschuß*. It is translated into French as *excédent* or *surcroît*. See Marion, *Being Given*, 191. It can also be translated as "augmentation" and "excess." See Welten, "Saturation and Disappointment," 83.

76. Edmund Husserl, *The Crisis of European Sciences and Transcendental Phenomenology* (Evanston, IL: Northwestern University Press, 1970), 87.

77. Marion, *Being Given*, 267.

78. Husserlian phenomenology differs from Marion in the sense that in Husserl, intentionality strives for fulfilment, whereas, for Marion saturation is not possible without going beyond intentionality. Welten, "Saturation and Disappointment," 90.

79. Welten, "Saturation and Disappointment," 90. Marion develops his concept of the saturated phenomenon through a reversal of intentionality which was largely influenced by Levinas' thinking that "it is not the active, nominative consciousness and language who sets the conditions under which the phenomenon appears, but much rather the unconditional and irreducible givenness of the phenomenon that first gives birth to a radically passive, vocative, and dative 'subject.'" See Thomas A. Carlson, "Blindness and the Decision to See: On Revelation and Reception in Jean-Luc Marion," in *Counter-Experiences: Reading Jean-Luc Marion*, ed. Kevin Hart (Notre Dame, IN: Indiana University Press, 2007), 155.

According to the Husserlian understanding, there is no correspondence between intuition and intention. In other words, for a phenomenon to appear, the intuition of the thing should coincide with the intention of it, which, according to Husserl, never occurs. For example, in the case of a cube, one only has partial intuition of it, as a cube.[80] Marion, on the other hand, argues that every phenomenon is calibrated with a surplus intuition over against intention. The intuition of a phenomenon exceeds the intention that constitutes the phenomenon as an object. In fact, in giving itself, the phenomenon as such, is saturated with intuition which surpasses our subjective, conceptualising gaze.[81] Regarding the saturated phenomenon, there is an excess of intuition which is beyond the concept and the meaning of the subject that surpasses the structure of intentionality.

Marion explains further that the saturated phenomenon entails a duality between "intention (signification)" and "intuition (fulfilment)." He says, "intuition gives (itself), in exceeding what the concept (signification, intentionality, aim, and so on) can foresee of it and show. I call these saturated phenomena, or paradoxes."[82] Intentionality is actually "reversed" in such a way that the "intuition submerges all intention."[83] The phenomenon is not subjected to one's own intentionality or signification, but rather, one is subject to the gaze of the phenomenon. It is a "reverse intentionality" in the sense that,

> my look is submerged, in a counter-intentional manner. Then I am no longer the transcendental *I* but rather the witness, constituted by what happens to him or her. Hence, it is the para-doxa, inverted *doxa*. In this way, the phenomenon

---

80. There is a gap between what is seen and what is originally visible. For instance, I never *see* a cube, but I "constitute" it, attributing three other sides, based on what is already seen. There is a difference between the fulfilling intuition and intention, the sign and the referent. Jean-Luc Marion, *The Crossing of the Visible*, trans. James K.A. Smith (Stanford, CA: Stanford University Press, 2004), 55.

81. Van den Bossche, "God in Immanence," 339.

82. Marion, *In Excess*, 112. A saturated phenomenon is a phenomenon that is saturated with givenness. In a saturated phenomenon, intuition outweighs or saturates every understanding of the phenomenon through intentionality in such a way that the phenomenon shows itself as given, prior to its being conceived as an object. See Marion, *Being Given*, esp. 20, 189-198.

83. Marion, *In Excess*, 116. This radical reversal of intentionality is theologically significant for overcoming the metaphysical impasse in God-thought, and in developing a perspective of the sacraments in terms of givenness, as we will see later.

that befalls and happens to us reverses the order of visibility in that it no longer results from my intention but from its own counter-intentionality.[84]

Briefly speaking, a phenomenon is saturated when the excess of intuition, over signification, reproaches the constitution of an object. For this reason, the subject is the latecomer, and remains "dative."[85] In other words, the subject is reformulated in the dative case, i.e., the subject is constituted and not constituting. In the face of the saturated phenomenon, "[t]he *I* loses its anteriority and finds itself, so to speak, deprived of the duties of constitution, and thus is itself constituted: a *me* rather than an *I*."[86] I cannot intend saturation; it comes over me, reversing my intentionality. The saturated phenomenon can, therefore, be explained as a phenomenon that I do not really expect; hence, it is paradoxical. Marion expresses it as a totally unforeseeable event.[87] The coming of the Messiah does not exactly fulfil our expectations (Jewish), but surpasses or exceeds them. In a sense, it disappoints human concepts and expectations by traversing them.

3.2.1. The Saturated Phenomena Par Excellence

The excess of the phenomenon over-fulfils intentional consciousness by saturating it. For this reason, Marion names this phenomenal appearance, the "saturated phenomenon par excellence." The phenomenon of revelation can be thought of only in terms of an excess of phenomenal appearance or excess of givenness.

Marion tries to consider the possibility of the phenomenon conceived within the mystical theology of Dionysius. He points out that mystical theology is often misunderstood as a negation, rather than considering it as the "third way" which goes beyond affirmation and negation to the "experience of incomprehension." Marion achieves this by using Husserl's dual category of intention/intuition (signification/fulfilment) as a third relational possibility according to the third way.[88] Accordingly, "[t]he intention (the concept or the signification) can never reach adequation with the intuition (fulfilment), not

84. Marion, *In Excess*, 113.

85. The term 'dative' is borrowed from grammar where the dative case signifies passivity as compared with the activity of the nominative case (subject). This analogy is employed for explaining the 'trans-formation' of the (constituting) 'I' to the (constituted) 'me'.

86. *Ibid.*, 119.

87. Marion, *Being Given*, 225.

88. Marion shows that the theological concepts of *apophasis* and *kataphasis* can be illustrated, employing the dual categories of intention and fulfilment.

because the latter is lacking, but because it exceeds what the concept can receive, expose, and comprehend."[89] "[T]he excess of intuition overcomes, submerges, exceeds – in short, saturates – the measure of each and every concept."[90] This is what Marion calls "the saturated phenomenon."[91] The impossibility of knowledge of the phenomenon arises, not because of the lack of intuition, but owing to its *excess* which "neither concept nor significa-tion nor intention can foresee, organize or contain."[92] Marion claims that this third relation, that he establishes between intention/intuition, can be well-situated in the third way of apophatic theology. He states that Dionysius

> denies first that negation itself suffices to define a theology, next that negation
> opposes affirmation while pretending to invert it. In short, Dionysius always
> thinks negation exactly as he thinks affirmation as one of the two values
> truths can have, one of the two forms of predication which is precisely a mat-
> ter of transgressing completely, as the discourse of metaphysics. With the
> third way, not only is it no longer a matter of saying (or denying) something
> about something, it is also no longer a matter of saying or unsaying, but of re-
> ferring to Him who is no longer touched by nomination. It is solely a matter
> of de-nominating.[93]

The saturated phenomenon cannot be identified with negative theology, be-cause it is not unknowable, yet it exceeds our capacity to know (incompre-hension). As Welten observes,

> like saturation, disappointment has nothing to do with negative theology. On
> the contrary, as intentional modalities, they (saturation, disappointment) are
> … the acts of our consciousness in a positive way, not by means of negation.
> Saturation is not an intentional modality of positive consciousness because of

---

89. Marion, *In Excess*, 159.

90. Jean-Luc Marion, "In the Name: How to Avoid Speaking of 'Negative Theology'," in *God, the Gift, and Postmodernism*, ed. John D. Caputo and Michael. J. Scanlon (Bloomington, IN: Indiana University Press, 1999), 40; Marion, *In Excess*, 159.

91. Marion, *Being Given*, 24-25, 225-228. His concept of the "saturated phenomenon" generated a great deal of criticism. For example, see John D. Caputo, "Apostles of the Impos-sible: On God and the Gift in Derrida and Marion," in *God, the Gift and Postmodernism*, ed. John D. Caputo and Michael J. Scanlon (Bloomington, IN: Indiana University Press, 1999), 185-222; Horner, *Rethinking God as Gift*; Janicaud, *et al.*, *Phenomenology and the "Theologi-cal Turn"*, 3-106.

92. Marion, *In Excess*, 159.

93. Marion, "In the Name," 28.

its over-fulfilment; instead, like disappointment, it is a positive description of a mental state of intentional consciousness.[94]

As he explains, Marion's point is that "if God appears to us without the possibility of reducing his appearing to noetic conditions, he must overwhelm our play of intention and fulfilment." Thus, according to Marion, "from the point of view of revelation, the saturated phenomenon has to be, fundamentally, disappointment; whereas, from the point of view of phenomenology, this phenomenality is always en route to its final fulfilment."[95]

Marion integrates the phenomenological construct of the saturated phenomenon with the discussion on the giving and the showing of the phenomenon. He investigates the possibility of an unconditioned and irreducible phenomenon which goes beyond the Kantian and Husserlian limitation of the phenomenon within the horizon of apparition and constituting subject, *I*. According to them, phenomenality is the phenomenon reduced to the status of finite objectivity by reducing it to the finitude of its own horizon and to the *I* that it constitutes. Marion, on the contrary, argues that there is the possibility of an unconditioned and irreducible phenomenon, which he explains according to the notion of the saturated phenomenon. Accordingly, intuition saturates every concept or signification in such a way that the phenomenon appears in a mode by saturating the intuition, the gaze, to which the phenomenon gives itself. The givenness of the saturated phenomenon determines knowledge, and not the other way round. For this reason, Marion is speaking about the *saturated* phenomenon, not of the *saturating* phenomenon.[96] Marion shows that the saturated phenomenon passes beyond the Kantian categories and principles of such an understanding by inverting them, and describing the saturated phenomenon as invisible according to quantity, unbearable according to the terms of quality, unconditioned in terms of relation, and irregardable according to modality.[97]

94. Welten, "Saturation and Disappointment," 94.
95. *Ibid.*, 96.
96. Marion, *Being Given*, 197, see also p. 362, n. 37.
97. Marion explains the four modes in which the phenomenon appears, namely, according to quantity, quality, relation and modality. Marion, *Being Given*, 199-233. Marion makes a distinction between "to see" (*voir*) and "to gaze" (*regarder*) although they are equivalent and go together. To gaze implies much more than merely "to see." Seeing is the process of perceiving something by the senses of sight as it shows in visibility. Gazing, on the other hand, involves keeping that which is seen under the control of the seer. It is the process of construing the visible within the limits of concept. In other words, gaze reduces the visible to objectness. See *ibid.*, 214.

As was mentioned, in the saturated phenomenon, the intuition submerges the expectation of the intention; intuition surpasses intention. Therefore, the saturated phenomenon is a paradox in the sense that intuition sets forth a surplus that the concept cannot organize. Neither can intention foresee it, nor can intention control or master it. Freed from it, intuition establishes itself and precedes every intention and signification. Givenness breaches into intuition prior to intention in such a way that it is not intentionality that constitutes an object defined by its own horizon. The *I* remains passive. The phenomenon shows itself because it gives itself first. Givenness comes first, unconditioned and without being limited by a horizon. Phenomenality is ruled by givenness in the sense that "the phenomenon no longer gives itself in the measure to which it shows itself, but shows itself in the measure (or eventually, lack of measure) to which it gives itself."[98] Marion claims that the saturated phenomenon remains within the definition of phenomenality, because what Marion does is "nothing other than push the universal determinations of the given beyond their limits," submerging every horizon and reverting the *I* into a witness.[99] Therefore, the saturated phenomenon is a phenomenon in its own right. The saturated phenomenon is that which fulfils, excessively, the definition of the phenomenon. As Marion puts it, "it [the saturated phenomenon] alone truly appears as itself, of itself and starting from itself."[100] As Welten observes, "Marion's contribution to contemporary phenomenology lies in his description of a kind of phenomenality that aims at going back to givenness in its purest, most radical form, and encloses the whole scope of possible phenomenology."[101]

In Marion's view, the saturated phenomenon entails what he calls "a paradox." He presents the paradoxical phenomenon of the "impossible" that bedazzles the ego through an excess of intuition over the intention of the conceptuality of the subject. This is the superabundance of givenness. The *I* can see it, but its excess renders it irregardable, in that the *I* can no longer master, or keep it as a mere object. The experience of the excess of intuition can be sometimes felt and experienced as a disappointment, because there can be experiences which surpass our understanding. It is a paradox in that

98. Marion, *Being Given*, 226.

99. *Ibid.*, 227.

100. Cited in Felix O Murchadha, "Glory, Idolatry, Kairos: Revelation and the Ontological Difference in Marion," in *Givenness and God: Questions of Jean-Luc Marion*, ed. Ian Leask and Eoin Cassidy, Perspectives in Continental Philosophy (New York: Fordham University Press, 2005), 78.

101. Welten, "Saturation and Disappointment," 79.

the phenomenon suspends the constituting *I*. The subject (*I*) is not only able to constitute the phenomenon, but the *I* also becomes constituted by it, and becomes a mere witness to it. The excess of intuition that comes to the subject submerges it so as to lose its status as the gazing *I*, and become the gazed *I* (by the phenomenon). The nominative *I* turns dative in becoming the passive recipient of the call that precedes it.

Marion distinguishes four types of saturated phenomena according to their diverse modes of phenomenality. Throughout Marion's writings, one sees an opposition between the idol and the icon, which (both) belong to the category of the "saturated phenomenon." In contrast to the idol, in the icon saturation is accomplished as irregardable and irreducible. It is that type of phenomenon in which the Other shows itself as the icon. A detailed understanding of the distinction between the icon and the idol is of great significance in order to understand Marion's theology and its potential for understanding God's givenness in the sacramental event.

3.2.2. Phenomenological/Theological 'Categories' of Marion

Having defined God as givenness, and the identity of the subject as gifted, Marion further develops certain "categories"[102] that come into play in his theological and philosophical thinking. Of these, "idol" and "icon" are of great significance for theology.

3.2.3. Idol and Icon

A recurring theme in the works of Marion is the discussion about the categories of the idol and the icon. In *God Without Being*, Marion introduces two closely related, but sharply different, phenomenological ideas: the idol and the icon. He employs these phenomenological ideas in order to distinguish two different ways of talking about God.[103] Marion explains how the idol and

102. Strictly speaking, employing the term "category" to the philosophical and theological notions of Marion is untenable, because of its metaphysical overtones. However, as we have already mentioned, they are, in fact, "non-categorical" categories. Therefore, when we use the term "category" we simply mean "notion," "view," "perspective," "meaning," etc. of the icon, and not the so-called structured, systematic, rigid and defined category in a metaphysical sense.

103. A few examples are: Marion, *God Without Being*; Marion, *The Idol and Distance*; Marion, *Being Given*; Marion, *Prolegomena to Charity*; Marion, *The Crossing of the Visible*. He introduces the category of the icon, in contrast to the idol and applies them both to theology for explaining how the notion of the icon helps us to overcome metaphysical idolatry. For

the icon differ from each other. The nature of the idol is self-sufficiency whereas that of the icon is infinitude.[104] An image becomes an idol when one sees nothing beyond the image; one's gaze is dazzled, absorbed by the object.[105] The icon is not to be confused with the image. The icon is not determined by the way one looks at it, but it provokes infinite vision, and determines itself, without being gazed at idolatrously.[106] The icon draws the viewer from what is seen to what is unseen, beyond the represented image. In contrast to the idol, the icon refers to the invisible and brings the invisible to visibility without representing it *as such*, but as an opening to it.[107]

The idol is visible and knowable. The idol captivates the gaze only in as much as the gaze can envisage it. It is the gaze that makes the idol, not vice versa. Visibility fills the intentional gaze. The gaze stops in/on the idol without passing beyond the idol. The idol functions as an invisible mirror reflecting or imaging the scope of the intentional gaze. The advent of the divine is realised according to the human gaze. Divinity is manifested and measured according to the amount a gaze can bear. The idol consigns the presence of the divine to the measure of human gaze. Idolatry comes into play when the concept functions exactly as an idol, forming the conceptual idol. The measure of the concept of the divine is determined by the aim of the gaze. It consists in naming or defining of God, which is obviously equating God with the concepts of subjective intentionality.[108]

The icon, on the contrary, does not result from the gaze, but forms it. The icon renders visible the invisible *as such*. The icon summons the gaze, not

---

a brief understanding of the contrasting notions of the idol and the icon, see Marion, *God Without Being*, 7-24. See also Philip Blond, "The Primacy of Theology and the Question of Perception," in *Religion, Modernity, Postmodernity*, ed. Paul Heelas (Oxford: Blackwell, 1998), 281-313.

104. Charles Lock, "Against Being: An Introduction to the Thought of Jean-Luc Marion," *St. Vladimir's Theological Quarterly* 37 (1993): 373.

105. Graham Ward, "Introducing Jean-Luc Marion," *New Black Friars* 76 (1995): 319.

106. Ward, "Introducing Marion," 373-374.

107. Marion, *God Without Being*, 8-9. In developing his theology of the icon, Marion is influenced by John of Damascus. John of Damascus positioned himself against iconoclasts who undermined the use of images. He advocated the power of the icon to relate the visible to the prototype, and encouraged the veneration the divine images. See John of Damascus, *On the Divine Images: Three Apologies against Those Who Attack the Divine Images*, trans. David Anderson (Crestwood, NY: St. Vladimir's Seminary Press, 1980), 20. As Lock opines, Marion obliquely admits an awareness of Orthodox theology, especially in his treatment of the concepts of the idol and the icon. See Lock, "Against Being," 373.

108. Marion, *God Without Being*, 29.

surpassing or "freezing" the visible. The icon's gaze allows the intention of the invisible to appear visibly. The icon envisages the gazing gaze and takes it back from the visible to the invisible. The givenness of the icon rests on the invisible that saturates the visibility of the face with meaning. Thus the icon functions as the visible of the invisible.

So, the difference between the self-givenness of the icon and the idol depends on the perceiving subject. The vision is dazzled to the point that it collapses as it mirrors the capacity of the gaze.[109] The icon results from an invisible source in the process of the surrendering gaze.[110] "It no longer offers any spectacle to the gaze and tolerates no gaze from any spectator, but rather, exerts its own gaze over that which meets it. The gazer takes the place of the gazed upon."[111] The icon is designated as saturated phenomenon par excellence, because it is in the icon that all the characteristics of the three preceding types are crystallised. The phenomenon of the icon is, yet remains phenomenon, because it "shows itself in and from itself, only insofar as it gives itself in and from itself."[112] The idol remains proportionate to the anticipated desire of the gaze, whereas the icon exceeds the scope of expectation, inverting the intentional gaze of the subject.[113] This is illustrated by the diverse ways of looking at a painting. The givenness of the painting appears, according to the way one looks at it, and not according to the objectivity or thingness of the painting.[114] Paradoxically, it is the invisibility which makes the phenomenon visible. In this regard, Marion argues for the possibility of other things, such as time, life, one's word, etc., which may be thought upon without reference to objectivity. Marion is claiming that there exists a new class of phenomena which can be reduced to pure givenness.[115] According to him, there can be givenness without a given. In this sense, the par excellence of donation (givenness) comes in bedazzlement, thus God shines in his ab-

---

109. Marion, *Being Given*, 315.

110. Marion, *God Without Being*, 78.

111. Marion, *Being Given*, 232.

112. *Ibid.*, 233.

113. Marion, *The Crossing of the Visible*, 33. This kind of "idolatry" comes into play in modern communication strategies. For example, the tele-visual image, in order to be seen, must be conformed to the measure of limits and demands of the viewer, which means, every image must be made an idol of the viewer. So, the tele-visual idol appears as much as it is valued by the viewer. See *ibid.*, 51.

114. Marion, *Being Given*, 64-66.

115. *Ibid.*, 79-85.

sence, turning donation to abandon.[116] In this context, Marion situates revelation as a potentially invisible, but possible phenomenon.

3.2.3.1. The Visible and the Invisible

The visible and the invisible embrace each other in the icon so as to become the divine face which shows itself for humanity.[117] The dialectic of the visible and the invisible, in showing the divine face, can rightly be understood in light of the epiphany found in Exodus 3:2-6.[118] This shows how phenomenology and transcendence can be correlated. Here, God appears not as the First Cause, but as the First Speaker: the First *Sinngeber*. God reveals himself, and Moses is engulfed by a new horizon of experience which replaces mystery with transparency. The invisible becomes visible; the Numinous assumes phenomenality. Moses was able to recognize God's presence when the visible became voice (not sound, but speech).[119] Westphal says that the story of the epiphany in Exodus serves as the hermeneutical key for the understanding of the phenomenology of Marion, especially the themes of the icon and the idol and the notion of the saturated phenomenon, which is ruled by the dialectics of the visible and the invisible.[120] "[I]t was only through the voice that the visible became, not merely a curiosity, but the face of God from which Moses hid his own face."[121] Marion accepts the Husserlian insight that "[t]o understand is ultimately to see. To speak of something [is] in order to make it visible."[122] Accordingly, for Marion, "seeing" does not merely pertain to the senses, but it stands as the metaphor for intellectual conception. Similarly, "intuition" involves a "seeing" of both the senses and the intellect, despite the fact that God is incomprehensible, because any claim of comprehension affirms the possibility of incomprehensibility. As he puts it,

116. Marion, "Metaphysics and Phenomenology," 589.
117. Marion, *The Crossing of the Visible*, 87.
118. Westphal, "Vision and Voice," 131.
119. The dialectic of the visible and the voice also constitutes the New Testament theophanies, as we will see, particularly at the baptism of Jesus, and Pentecost.
120. Westphal, "Vision and Voice," 132.
121. *Ibid.*, 135.
122. Marion, "Metaphysics and Phenomenology," 580; Jean-Luc Marion, "Metaphysics and Phenomenology: A Summary for Theologians," in *The Postmodern God*, ed. Graham Ward (Oxford: Blackwell Publishers, 1997), 285; Marion, *Reduction and Givenness*, 33.

[f]or the one we comprehend would always remain less than and below the one we do not comprehend. Incomprehensibility therefore belongs to the formal definition of God, since comprehending him would put him on the same level as a finite mind ... As soon as one tries to catch sight of God, the relation must be inverted; knowledge holds only if comprehension ceases.[123]

Therefore, the excess of God's givenness consists, not in transparency, but rather, in incomprehensibility, which is also ruled by the logic (non-logic) of distance.

3.2.3.2. The Distance

According to Marion, distance is something essential that rules every relationship. Distance is understood as a separation or spacing that makes love and relationship possible. Distance prevents the reduction of relationships to one's own imagination.[124] Distance rules both divine (Inter-Trinitarian and Extra-Trinitarian) and human (interpersonal) relationships.[125] There is a radical and unbridgeable gap, or distance, that separates God and human beings, which no concept or image can cross.[126] Paradoxically, it is distance and

---

123. Marion, "In the Name," 37.

124. Horner, *Marion*, 60.

125. The divine relationship that we refer to is twofold: First, the relationship that exists within the Trinitarian being of God (immanent Trinity); second, the relationship that exists between God and human beings (economic Trinity). By human relationship, we mean the relationship between human beings.

126. Jean-Luc Marion, *The Idol and Distance*, trans. Thomas A. Carlson (New York: Fordham University Press, 2001), 17. Marion uses "distance" in various contexts with different meanings. Nevertheless, he basically uses this term in order to designate "the relationship of creature to the Creator." See Jean-Luc Marion, "Distance et béatitude: sur le mot capacitas chez Saint Augustin," *Résurrection* 29 (1968): 59. This relationship is understood to be that of "absolute difference between God and humanity." Horner, *Marion*, 51. The idea of distance in Marion seems to have been influenced by the idea of distance in Hans Urs von Balthasar who understands it in four different dimensions, of which two are human and two divine. According to him, there exists a natural distance between God and human beings (as creatures). There is also a sinful distance created by the sinfulness of human beings. The natural distance (*distasis*) is basic to biblical religion, a basic presupposition of understanding and appreciating the unity that grace brings about. In contrast to this, sinful distance (a deeper *distasis*) is that which separates humans unnaturally from God. Horner, *Marion*, 52. See also Hans Urs von Balthasar, *Explorations in Theology*, trans. Brian McNeil, 4 vols. (San Francisco, CA: Ignatius Press, 1993), 173; Marion, *The Idol and Distance*, 155. Marion's understanding of distance can be considered to have been influenced by Levinas' concept of irreducible distance or difference that forms relationships. For Levinas, distance characterises relationship in the sense that while I am in relation to the other, I cannot reduce that other to my own dimensions

proximity at the same time. This dialectic of distance and proximity comes into play in the Trinitarian relationship and the relationship between God and human beings. Marion illustrates how the dialectics of distance and withdrawal and the divinity's coming into presence comes into play in the paschal mystery:

> The paschal mystery shows Christ's divinity in two such moments: on the Cross, the distance of withdrawal is seen as his complete distinction from the Father; and in the Resurrection, the distance of withdrawal is seen as his complete unity with the Father. What this means for the disciples is that manifestation only ever coincides with disappearance. Disclosure is only ever offered subject to a distance that forbids recuperation.[127]

The dialectic of distance and proximity is fundamental to the understanding of presence. According to Marion, God enters into thought as distance; he gives the thought of Godself over to contemplation in the icon, only to be known as love and through love, particularly as a gift of love.[128] In Marion's terms, this God, as giver, would be manifest as withdrawn from even the traces of Being of his gift, i.e., of himself as given by, as *re-presented* in, gift.[129]

Marion makes a clear distinction between "distance" and "ontological difference," in that the former makes the Absolute present, whereas the latter makes the referent disappear.[130] However, presence assumes the mode of invisibility; it appears as the invisible. Distance makes room for the transcendence to become immanent. As O'Donohue puts it,

> "Distance" … guarantee[s] Otherness. The metaphor of "distance" also suggests a continuity with the Faraway that allows him to exploit a dynamic of separation that never becomes alienation and a dynamic of nearing that can never claim the Absolute. "Distance" becomes the root of possibility, the ground of longing, and the spur and the invitation to participation; it is not merely a transcendental regulative principle that delivers a bare arithmetic of

of thought. So he says, "the *sway* [*pourvoir*] of the I will not cross the distance marked by the alterity of the other." Lévinas, *Totality and Infinity*, 38.

127. Horner, *Marion*, 56. See Marion, *The Idol and Distance*, 118-120.

128. Horner, *Marion*, 51.

129. John Martis, "Thomistic *Esse* – Idol or Icon? Jean-Luc Marion's God Without Being," *Pacifica* (1996): 64.

130. Marion, *The Idol and Distance*, 153-154.

logical space. Ironically, it is precisely "distance" that creates the fecund
space where the Absolute can become present.[131]

The icon upholds the distance between the image and the imaged, making the
invisible present (absent) in the visible. So, the icon partakes in the imaged
reality, although it does not reproduce it. In Christian revelation, the power of
the icon consists in making visible the invisible mystery of the Word Incarnate. The icon brings to visibility, the invisible reality of God. This takes
place through a crossing of the gazes on the "face."

3.2.3.3. The Face

Marion explains the "face" as a saturated phenomenon, employing the insight
of Levinas describing the phenomenality of "the face as icon addressing a
call ... as envisaging me."[132] The face is a phenomenological category of the
visible and the invisible, a paradox. The paradox of the face finds its expression in the paradox of Christ.[133] The paradox is generated by the intervention
(crossing) of the invisible in the visible, for instance, the divine-human nature of Christ. With the face (painting) iconically understood, we have a
crossing of the gazes in the icon (in the visible), i.e., the (invisible) gaze of
the one in prayer (*l'adonné*) and the gaze (invisible) of the benevolent one.
Thus, two invisible gazes cross in the icon of the face.[134]

3.3. The Possibility of Revelation

As has been previously shown, Marion develops an iconic perspective on the
immanence of God through the fundamental principle of the phenomenology
of givenness. According to Marion, givenness exceeds phenomenology, and
the amount to which givenness exceeds Husserlian phenomenology is illustrated in the concept of the *excess*, or the saturated phenomenon.[135] In doing

---

131. O'Donohue, "The Absent Threshold," 280.
132. Marion, *In Excess*, 115-119.
133. Marion, *The Crossing of the Visible*, 1.
134. *Ibid.*, 20-23.
135. Welten, "Saturation and Disappointment," 81. In contrast to Heidegger, Marion insists on the saturated phenomenon as a revelation which is beyond all frames of reference,
horizons and language. Heidegger insists that revelation can make sense only in reception and
response to what is given in, and by language. See Brian Elliott, "Reduced Phenomenon and
Unreserved Debts in Marion's Reading of Heidegger," in *Givenness and God: Questions of
Jean-Luc Marion*, ed. Ian Leask and Eoin Cassidy, Perspectives in Continental Philosophy
(New York: Fordham University Press, 2005), 95-96.

this Marion employs a contra-method as compared to the Husserlian (given as *object*) and the Heideggerian (given as *being*) phenomenological reduction.[136] Marion's understanding of Being as given goes beyond Husserl and Heidegger to the extent that he redefines phenomenality in such a way that it opens the possibility for the revelation of God. Thus, admitting the revelation of God as a genuine phenomenological possibility implies freeing phenomenality from the confines of objectivity (Husserl) and of Being (Heidegger).[137] For this reason, Marion has been criticised for crossing the limits of phenomenology, because phenomenality, in its radical form, is only possible through intentionality.[138] However, Marion's phenomenology is not concerned with a particular kind of phenomenon, but it pertains to phenomenality itself, which can be seen as being very close to revelation. The saturated phenomenon is not the phenomenon of something, not even of God, but the appearance of phenomenality itself.[139] The phenomenon always remains within the bounds of consciousness itself. The saturated phenomenon is of something *surplus*, in the sense that it is merely a correlate of consciousness.[140]

The poignant question here is whether the phenomenon of God (Revelation) can be thought of within the limits of classical phenomenology. Marion attempts to answer this criticism by distinguishing between revelation as possibility and Revelation as historicity.[141] Phenomenology can identify the possibility of the saturated phenomenon (revelation), within the scope of giveness, but associating that givenness to the givenness of God as charity belongs to the territory of revealed theology.[142] Our study of Marion's phe-

---

136. Van den Bossche, "God in Immanence," 331.

137. Marion, *Being Given*, 242.

138. Marléne Zarader levels charges against the phenomenology of Marion as such, especially the reversal of the subject to inhabit "unconditioned givenness." Accordingly, she charges that Marion's "subject has been smuggled in through the back door." Westphal, "Vision and Voice," 125. Janicaud charges that the religious interests of French phenomenology creates a "rupture with immanent phenomenology." Janicaud, *et al.*, *Phenomenology and the "Theological Turn,"* 16-17. According to him, "phenomenology has been taken hostage by a theology that does not want to say its name." *Ibid.*, 43. These and similar charges levelled against Marion are not of little significance. Even though Marion's theological motif can easily be discerned, as we shall see, he tries to make a borderline between the domain of theology and philosophy.

139. Welten, "Saturation and Disappointment," 82.

140. *Ibid.*, 83.

141. The variant use of the word "revelation/Revelation" distinguishes revelation as possibility according to phenomenology, whereas "Revelation" pertains to revealed theology.

142. Marion, "Metaphysics and Phenomenology," 590.

nomenology of givenness suggests that saturation is the most plausible means of understanding our relationship to God, outside onto-theology. Marion gives new insights in his phenomenology by not fulfilling the intention, but by saturating it. However, the understanding of the saturated phenomenon within the confines of phenomenology does not certify God's appearance, but only offers a possibility. So, the phenomenon of Christ (revelation) remains a *possibility*.[143]

Marion is not hesitant to confess the theological implications of his phenomenological construct. He acknowledges the unsurpassable primacy of Christian revelation. Marion's phenomenology opens a way for theologians to reflect on revelation from a phenomenological perspective, thus liberating the self-revelation of God from the metaphysical concept of Being fashioned through thought and language. Marion's remarkable contribution consists in establishing a link between theology and phenomenology within the confines of postmodern thinking. As Van den Bossche points out, Marion's importance for theology lies in solving the problem of the conflict between *theologia rationalis* and *theologia revelata*.[144] This is achieved by setting phenomenology upon grounds which are open to the possibility of revelation according to the biblical account of the revelation of Jesus. Thus, Marion allows the invisible God to appear for reason. As Kathryn Tanner opines, Marion's phenomenological vocabulary is of great significance as an "enormously suggestive resource for theologians."[145] The import of Marion's phenomenology of givenness for theological discourse lies in its ability to understand God's givenness in Christ and the Spirit. Thus, it provides the insights to situate God's self-communication in terms of the givenness of God in Christ and the Spirit. In what follows, we will explore the Christological (1) and the Pneumatological (2) facets that constitute the totality of the phenomenon of Christian revelation.

4. God's Gift-giving in Christ: The Phenomenon of Revelation (1)

The phenomenon of revelation, as a particular case of phenomenon as opposed to other phenomena, is characterised by an excess of intuition, which

---

143. Marion, *Being Given*, 95.
144. Van den Bossche, "God in Immanence," 345.
145. Tanner, "Theology at the Limits of Phenomenology," 201.

saturates all meaning. In other words, it appears itself as a gift.[146] Perhaps
Marion's unique contribution to theology is "to conceive and to speak of
revelation as inconceivable and ineffable because [it is] unconditionally self-
giving."[147] Marion's phenomenology provides God with the possibility of
revealing himself in his own way, rather than being subject to the limits of
human experience and reason. Marion's phenomenology of givenness helps
us to consider revelation in terms of self-giving phenomenality, as unconditional and that which exceeds all horizons.

4.1. Phenomenality of Revelation

Marion succeeds in situating, revelation within phenomenality through the
analysis of the "saturated phenomenon," and by presenting revelation as the
highest form of saturated phenomena. By introducing the notion of the saturated phenomena, he shows that the givenness of intuition (revelation) precedes and exceeds the intention, or the conception of the subject, while con-
forming to the norms of phenomenality. As he puts it,

> [i]f an actual revelation must, can or could have been given in phenomenal
> apparition, it could have, can or will be able to do so only by giving itself ac-
> cording to the type of paradox par excellence … If revelation there must be
> (and phenomenology has no authority to decide this), then it will assume, as-
> sumes, or assumed the figure of paradox of paradoxes, according to an essen-
> tial law of phenomenality. In this sense, since revelation remains a variation
> of saturation itself, a variation of the phenomenality of the phenomenon in as

146. Marion, "Concept of Gift," 122. Balthasar seems to have exerted considerable influence on the theology of Marion in understanding Revelation as a phenomenon, and in his
understanding of the theology of the gift. Marion himself acknowledges his admiration for
Balthasar's work. Marion, *The Idol and Distance*, 13. According to Balthasar, God "shows
and bestows himself" in Jesus Christ, the Word made flesh. God is seen and known through
Jesus Christ. Hans Urs von Balthasar, *The Glory of the Lord: A Theological Aesthetics*, trans.
Erasmo Leiva-Merikakis, vol. 1 (San Francisco, CA: Ignatius Press, ²1982), 153. Hence, he
understands Christ as a phenomenon that can be known and seen by those who consent themselves to be recognised by the phenomenon. *Ibid.*, 131.

147. Carlson, "Blindness and the Decision to See: On Revelation and Reception in Jean-
Luc Marion," 153. The interrelationship between the revelation and the gift consists in *showing*, because "the gift becomes gift in revealing. The theology of gift is sustained by a structure
of givenness where the phenomenon shows itself as and for itself." Horner, *Rethinking God as
Gift*, 177. It is in this sense that Marion can open the possibility of revelation in phenomenology.

much as [is] given, it still remains inscribed within the transcendental conditions of possibility.[148]

Having affirmed the phenomenality of revelation, he goes on exploring the possibility of a phenomenon which gives itself according to a maximum of phenomenality. In his opinion, the phenomenon of revelation confounds, although paradoxically, all types of saturation in such a way that it can be described as the saturation of saturation, or saturation par excellence. Marion explains that if the phenomenon of revelation could appear, it would be possible only according to the figure of the paradox par excellence (paradox of paradoxes), according to the law of phenomenality (that which shows itself; gives itself). He interprets the figure of Christ as manifested in the New Testament as the "saturated phenomenon," the "saturation of saturation," and the "paradox of paradoxes."[149] He further examines, phenomenologically, the manifestation of Christ as the paradigm of revelation according to the four modes of saturation.

4.2. Phenomenality of Revelation: A Key to Theology of Revelation

Marion is positive about the relationship between theology and phenomenology. In this regard, he makes a distinction between metaphysical theology and revealed theology. While shaping phenomenology, he is hesitant to encroach on the field of theology. What he does is to give a hint as to the possibility of revelation. Nevertheless, he is not uncertain about the possibility of the theology of revelation within the range of phenomenology. He claims that

> [r]evealed theology, by the very fact that it is based on given facts, which are given positively as figures, appearances, and manifestations (indeed, apparitions, miracles, revelations, and so on), takes place in the natural field of phenomenality and is therefore dependent on the competence of phenomenology.[150]

Marion wants to preserve the identity of both phenomenology and theology without crossing their boundaries, by simply highlighting the phenomenon of revelation as a possibility. As he states, "The phenomenon of revelation remains a mere possibility. I am going to describe it without presupposing its

---

148. Marion, *Being Given*, 235.
149. *Ibid.*, 235-236.
150. Marion, *In Excess*, 28.

actuality, and yet, all the while, propose a precise figure for it."[151] He is refraining from speaking of Revelation as actuality, implicitly leaving it to the
task of theology. "To be sure, Revelation (as actuality) is never confounded
with revelation (as possible phenomenon). I will scrupulously respect this
conceptual difference by its graphic translation."[152] While remaining within
the norms of phenomenology, he acknowledges the primacy of theology in
speaking about revelation as actuality, which would imply that, as Emmanuel
Falque observes, "just as phenomenology goes beyond metaphysics, (revealed) theology goes beyond phenomenology in the requisites of its saturation, and in this way, opens, to the *theologian philosopher* or the *philosopher
theologian* …, a path, that this time, it belongs to him in his own right to
occupy.[153] Thus, he assigns full right for the theologian in developing a theology of revelation meriting his phenomenological thinking, which he elucidates in his theological works. Thus, as Van den Bossche opines, "[t]he hat
trick of *God Without Being* is now that Marion, in an extremely anti-modern
move, tries to force this second, religious, indeed creational understanding of
reality as the crown upon reason, hence placing theology as a crown upon
philosophy, in an Augustinian move of usurpation of reason by faith."[154]

151. Marion, *Being Given*, 235.

152. Marion makes it clear that phenomenology describes only the possibility of revelation, but not the actuality of it. As he puts it, "If God were to manifest himself (or manifested
himself), he would use a paradox to the second degree. Revelation (of God by himself, *theological*), if it takes place, will assume the phenomenal figure of the phenomenon of revelation,
of the paradox of paradoxes, of saturation to the second degree. To be sure, *R*evelation (as
actuality) is never confounded with *r*evelation (as possible phenomenon)." Phenomenology
lacks the means to do so. Anything beyond it pertains to revealed theology. See Marion, *Being
Given*, 367 n. 90. Marion seems to forbid himself from intersecting the borders of philosophy
and theology. Nevertheless apparently he authorizes and exhibits an intersection or encounter
between them. Interestingly enough, Marion has targeted his interlocutors in his key note
lecture at the Simon Silverman Symposium on Phenomenology in April 2009, at Duquesne
University, Pittsburgh, PA which I attended. He posed the question "who" or "what philosophy" has the reason to set a limit to phenomenology? He has also cited from the history of
theology and philosophy that the separation between theology and philosophy came at a very
later period.

153. Emmanuel Falque, "*Larvatus pro Deo*: Jean-Luc Marion's Phenomenology and Theology," in *Counter-Experiences: Reading Jean-Luc Marion*, ed. Kevin Hart (Notre Dame, IN:
University of Notre Dame Press, 2007), 190-191.

154. Stijn Van den Bossche, "From the Other's Point of View: The Challenge of Jean-Luc
Marion's Phenomenology to Theology," in *Religious Experience and Contemporary Theological Epistemology* (Leuven: Leuven University Press, 2005), 69.

Marion's theological motive becomes clearer, in his presentation of the figure of the Christ crucified, as the iconic manifestation of God's love.

4.3. The Iconic Figure of Christ

Revelation occurs phenomenally. Marion emphasises the phenomenological
place of theology, and calls for reading the Judeo-Christian Revelation as a
rightful phenomenon. Thus, he accentuates the possibility and necessity of a
phenomenological reading of the events of revelation narrated in the scripture, particularly in the New Testament, apart from the existing forms of
hermeneutics.[155] Marion himself takes the initial steps in reflecting upon
revelation, phenomenologically based on the New Testament.

According to Marion, as the New Testament witnesses, Jesus Christ is the
historical paradigm of revelation as possibility.[156] The phenomenon of revelation becomes a historical actuality in Jesus of Nazareth. The high point of
Christ's manifestation, the pure phenomenality of Christ, is disclosed in the
paradox of the Cross, his humiliating death. So, God reveals himself in the
paradox of faith. The revelation of God consists in his revelation in Christ,
which is pure gift and givenness that dispels any understanding of revelation
in terms of being.[157] As Marion observes, "in the revelatory figure of Jesus
Christ, the Father enters into an absolute epiphany, through filtered, through
finitude."[158] In the paradoxical figure of the Cross, the excess of Love bedazzles; a Love which only the gaze that loves can bear and recognise, as the
figure of God in his *kenosis*.[159] He goes on saying that "love alone accedes to
Love, because only the gaze that bears the visible can abandon itself to the
infinite depths of the Christ, [the] Paschal icon of the Father."[160] He explains

---

155. Marion, *In Excess*, 29. Marion encourages theologians "to read phenomenologically
the events of revelation ... instead of always privileging ontic, historic, or semiotic hermeneutics." *Ibid.*, 201.

156. Van den Bossche gives a summary picture of Marion's explanation of the possibility
of revelation. See Van den Bossche, "God in Immanence," 340-343. It is significant to note
that Marion does not say that Christ is "*the* example" or "the *only* example" of the manifestation of the phenomenon of revelation, leaving it to a Catholic theologian to do so. Stijn Van
den Bossche, "A Possible Present for Theology: Theological Implications of Jean-Luc
Marion's Phenomenology of Givenness," *Bijdragen: International Journal in Philosophy and
Theology* 65 (2003): 73.

157. See Marion, *The Idol and Distance*, 273.

158. Marion, *Prolegomena to Charity*, 66.

159. *Ibid.*, 66-67.

160. *Ibid.*, 68-69.

how the figure of Christ, as described in the New Testament, can be seen as the saturation of saturation, according to the four modes of saturation, highlights how they inhabit the revelation of Jesus as witnessed in the biblical narratives.[161]

Marion acknowledges in his theological works the unsurpassable primacy of Christian revelation. He explains how the revelation of Christ, as manifested in the New Testament, suitably fits into the four modes of saturated phenomena whose excellence is in the icon. According to quantity, Christ is the phenomenon that cannot be anticipated, a theme Marion explains with reference to the incarnation and the second coming of Christ. This meets the conditions of the event. Again, with regard to quality, the intuition that saturates Christ as a phenomenon exceeds the limits in such a way that no phenomenological gaze can bear it. The unbearable nature of Christ's phenomenon is illustrated in the light of the accounts of the Transfiguration and Jesus' command not to touch him after the Resurrection. This nature of the superabundance, which is unbearable, falls under the conditions of the idol. From the perspective of relation, Christ is presented as the phenomenon that saturates every horizon of conceptuality of the constituting *I*. The multiplicity of titles ascribed to Jesus and the non-worldliness of his kingdom, reveal the inadequacy of a limiting horizon. This is actually the saturation of the flesh. Lastly, Christ is a saturated phenomenon according to modality. This operates according to the figure of the icon. So, the phenomenon of Christ constitutes the one who adores him, rather than being constituted. According to Marion, no one can see the Face of God without dying. "God cannot be seen, not only because nothing finite can bear his glory without perishing, but

---

161. The icon chrystalises all the other modes of phenomenality whose example is seen in the icon of Christ. As he explains, the Incarnation and the second coming of Christ are paradigmatic of the event. According to *quantity*, Jesus manifests himself as the unsurveyable event (*invisible*). Marion explains the experience of humans with Jesus as unforeseeable, indeterminable and incalculable. In this sense, Jesus' revelation escapes the concepts according to quantity. According to *quality*, Jesus is beyond the quality of human experience, beyond touching and no-touching, beyond reunion and departure, etc. Humans cannot support the true Christ and the intuition reaches the point whereby that exceeds the gazing gaze. According to *modality*, Christ cannot be gazed at; he constitutes Ego as witness, as an icon, he gazes first at the Ego. Marion explains this especially with the narrative of the rich young man (Mk 10:17-22). According to modality, the figure of Christ becomes the icon who "regards me in such a way that He constitutes me as his witness, rather than some transcendental 'I' constituting Him to its own liking." Marion, *Being Given*, 236-241. It is significant for our purpose to elaborate on how the revelation of Christ can be explained in terms of icon. For the sake of brevity, we do not make an extensive study of the other modes of phenomenality.

194 *Chapter Three*

above all, because a God that could be conceptually comprehended would no longer bear the title 'God'."[162] However, God appears as visible in the disfigured humanity of Christ. In contrast to image, the icon manifests the invisibility of God. If one looks at the icon, one feels oneself being seen by the icon. The invisible and envisaging gaze of the icon crosses the gaze of the one who looks at it.[163] The icon allows the gaze to be transpierced, forfeiting the prestige of the visible from its face, its glory. In this sense, Christ displays the logic of the iconic image in sacrificing his visage and his glory to be the trace of the invisible God (Col 1:15).[164] This takes place in the incarnation (Jn 1:14). Christ becomes the authentic icon of the Father, surrendering his own will to the point of death.[165] According to Marion, the Cross characterizes this par excellence. The iconic value of the Cross rests, not in offering any spectacle or resembling image of Christ, but rather in disqualifying even the smallest trace of reproducing the original glory in its visibility. "The Cross gives a figure of Christ only under the paradox of a secret glory, thus a concealed visibility; further, the Cross, renouncing for itself any similitude, cannot be guaranteed, even "approximately," by similarity to other types, thus to other icons."[166] The radical unity of Christ with the Father was guaranteed in the hypostatic union so that Christ could even say: "The one who has seen me has seen the Father" (Jn 14:9). The iconic figure of Christ is the saturated phenomenon par excellence, whereby God's givenness assumes maximum phenomenality (Revelation).[167] He further expatiates this with the parable of the rich young man (Mk 10:17-22), the election of persons (Mt 19:16-30), etc. In all these instances, the *I* becomes constituted and made a witness by a redoubled saturation that meets the conditions of the icon. Thus, Christ becomes the saturated phenomenon par excellence.

162. Marion, "In the Name," 34.

163. Marion, *The Crossing of the Visible*, 59.

164. *Ibid.*, 61-62. Marion presents the Cross as the paradox par excellence. On the Cross Christ kills his own image, creating an abyss between his appearance and infinite glory. Like the centurion (Mk 15:39; Mt 27:54), only those who cross this abyss can recognise the invisible meaning of the Cross, or see the trace of the invisible God. The centurion interpreted the corpse of Christ as the sign of God. See *ibid.*, 72.

165. Marion, *The Crossing of the Visible*, 62.

166. *Ibid.*, 71.

167. As will be explained later, the givenness of God in the disfigured figure of Jesus is integrally linked to the gift of the Holy Spirit (Revelation of the Spirit). Therefore, in the icon of the Cross, the image of the self-giving God in the Son and the Spirit appear in maximum phenomenality.

4.4. The Trace of an Agapic God

Marion develops the concept of the icon as a means of overcoming metaphysics. Looking at God idolatrously means thinking of God as in philosophical theology, or as *causa sui*. Thinking of God iconically means considering God as the God of the Bible, who was revealed in Jesus as love. The category of the icon is significant in the thought of Marion, because it frees theology from the idolatry of metaphysics, and creates a rupture between Being and becoming. In his approach to God, Marion attempts not only to think of God non-onto-theologically, but also seeks to overcome thought as such, considering theology as a different kind of thought. Thus, what Marion aims to achieve is to prepare the ground for transgressing Being, in order to give room for the God of the scripture, who is beyond Being.[168] The theological significance of the icon consists in making it possible to think of God through the mystical lens of love, without falling into the idolatry of metaphysics that is based on Being. This is seen in *God Without Being*. In contrast to the idol, which tends to reinforce the identity of the *ego*, the icon empties the *ego*, thereby liberating one from the danger of the inherent tendency of metaphysics to master, grasp, and control everything.[169]

The categories of the icon and idol are theologically important, because, for Marion, the icon, in contrast to the idol, is the sublime paradigm of the saturated phenomenon that encompasses all other modes of the saturated phenomenon. They signify two distinctive modes of apprehending the divine.[170] The icon helps to overcome the notion of a transcendent God, a radically Other, whose immanence is subject to the conditions of reason and perception. Marion achieves this by describing "the icon and the saturated phenomenon as the possibility that what is present either to sense or to intellect presents itself as pointing beyond itself to what cannot be grasped or encompassed by their sense or intellect, image or concept."[171]

Marion's distinction between the idol and the icon comes into play in his understanding of revelation. The idol explains the phenomenal way in which we grasp revelation. Accordingly, "we grasp it [revelation] in such a way that the grasped object does not reveal us God himself, but just ourselves grasp-

---

168. Ward, "Introducing Jean-Luc Marion," 320.
169. Horner, *Marion*, 64.
170. Marion, *God Without Being*, 9.
171. Westphal, "Vision and Voice," 132.

ing the object."[172] So Revelation is the mirroring of the subject's desire for self-transcendence. In the iconic understanding, there is a reversal of the order in the way of grasping the Revelation. Thus, "it [Revelation] is not so much that I perceive God revealing Himself; rather, it is that I perceive my-self being perceived."[173] According to this order, one's gaze is subjected to the gazing gaze of the Revealing God.[174] In contrast to the idol, the icon functions as manifesting the invisible God.[175] As Horner puts it, the icon works as a kind of "negative theophany."[176] The idol maintains the proximity of the divine, whereas the icon protects the distance of the divine.[177] Concep-tually speaking, the idol functions in creating conceptual images of the divine as in onto-theology, whereas the icon allows a distance for the divine to over-flow beyond conceptual idolatry.[178]

Marion develops a theological critique of metaphysics through the catego-ries of the idol and the icon by which he explains two distinctive approaches when looking at the divine.[179] His critique of "onto-theology" becomes clear-

172. Rico Sneller, "Incarnation as a Prerequisite: Marion and Derrida," *Bijdragen: Inter-national Journal in Philosophy and Theology* 65 (2004): 42.

173. Sneller, "Incarnation," 42.

174. In *The Idol and the Distance*, Marion illustrates the function of the idol not as the personification of the deity, but as referring to the human experience of the divinity. Marion, *The Idol and Distance*, 19-22.

175. St. Paul names Christ as the "icon of the invisible God (Col 1:15)." Marion writes, "The depth of the visible face of the Son lets the invisibility of the Father be seen as such. The icon manifests neither the human face, nor the divine nature such that no one would be able to envisage, but, theologians of the icon would say, the relationship of the one to the other in the hypostasis, the person." Marion, *The Idol and Distance*, 23. See also Marion, *God Without Being*, 17. The method of the figuration of Christ as the icon involves a paradox of the look, a "contra-intentionality," an intentionality weighing on me, rather than the intentionality of the *I* that objectivises the other. See Jean-Luc Marion, "'Christian Philosophy': Hermeneutic or Heuristic?," in *The Question of Christian Philosophy*, ed. Francis J. Ambrosio (New York: Fordham University Press, 1999), 259. There is a crossing of gazes in Christ which extends to the invisibility of the Father. "Christ Jesus offers not only a visible image of the Father who remains invisible but even a (visible) face of the invisible itself (the Father), a visible image of the invisible *as invisible*." Marion, *The Crossing of the Visible*, 58.

176. Horner, *Rethinking God as Gift*, 160.

177. Marion, *The Idol and Distance*, 23-24.

178. Marion speaks vehemently against the metaphysical idolatry in the West. Marion, *God Without Being*, 16.

179. Marion's categories of the idol and the icon are said to be quasi phenomenological, because within the ambit of phenomenology, they imply nothing more than a signalling of the divine. However, in Marion's treatment, they are theologically motivated. Marion writes, "the icon has a theological status, the reference of the visible face to the intention that envisages,

er in placing the idol and the icon in contrast to one another as diverse approaches to the divine. In the idol, the vision of the divinity is determined by the prior conditions and limitations of the consciousness of the subject. The idol is the self-created image of God, the best that human beings can make of God.[180] According to Marion, the metaphysical concept of God, or Being, falls within this category. The idolatrous representation of God is parallel to the God of onto-theology which is preconceived, well-defined, and determined by conceptual consciousness, whereas the iconic representation of God stands for the God of faith who exceeds the limits of any definition, predication, or concept. Accordingly, the idolatrous vision of the divinity becomes the result of an indirect or invisible mirror of one's own thinking, which delimits the definitive otherness and incomprehensibility of the divine. The idol represents the primacy of the subject's intentional consciousness, whereas with the icon, one finds radical disrupt or reverse intentionality.[181] In the idol, one sees the invisible mirroring of one's own thought, whereas in the icon one is envisaged by the irreducible other, prior to one's own thought.[182] The gaze in the idol contemplates the representation of its own *Ego*. The metaphysical concepts of God, or idols of God, fail to present the God of Revelation. Therefore, being confronted with the impossibility of thinking about God as such, Marion looks to the language of theology which is suitable to a way of thinking about God that exceeds the conditions of Being/beings. This he finds in Christian theological tradition and the Bible where God is articulated first, not as Being, but as love. In this regard, the theological question of the divine names and the language of praise of Dionysius serve Marion as powerful sources for the overcoming of the language

culminating in the reference of the Christ to the Father: for the formula *eikon tou theou aoratou* concerns first the Christ. It would remain to specify in what measure this attribution has a normative value, far from constituting just one application of the icon among others." Marion, *God Without Being*, 23-24.

180. Idolatry comes from the word εἴδωλον. In classical Greek philosophy, especially in Plato it means a deceiving image. In Christianity, it came to designate false gods. Murchadha, "Glory, Idolatry, Kairos," 69.

181. Thomas A. Carlson, *Indiscretion: Finitude and the Naming of God* (Chicago, IL: University of Chicago Press, 1999), 191.

182. Marion is indebted to the ethics of Levinas for this "reversal of intentionality," and applies it to all phenomena in general. For the theological implications of the categories of the idol and the icon, see Marion, *God Without Being*, chs. 1-2. For Marion the idol denotes the metaphysical concept of God, conceived as the Supreme Being or *causa sui*, which reveals the limits of thought and definition.

of knowing and predication.[183] Therefore, Marion points beyond onto-theology, claiming that the advent, or the presence of God, can only be thought as possible through an absence that cannot be presented or contained within a concept. The category of the icon reflects this figure of God who precedes Being, and is beyond naming or predication. Thus, the gaze is transferred with the notion of the icon. The entire scheme is conceived in a reverse order in which the total reality is seen through the lens of the Other who gazes at us. As compared to the idolatrous mode, the iconic mode of visibility is characterised by a reversal of intentionality that results in a radically different vision of the divinity. So, the reality is given to us. In the icon, the vision of the divine precedes and exceeds the limits of prior conditions and limitations of the intentional consciousness of the subject. In this mode of iconic vision, the subject does not constitute the vision of the divinity, but the subject is envisaged by, and constituted by, the divine otherness that exceeds the intentionality and subjectivity.

4.4.1. Love Other than Being

The "death of God" does not mark the disappearance of God, but reveals the failure of thought and language to define or comprehend a God who surpasses every concept and definition.[184] According to Marion, idolatry constitutes "the subjection of the divine to the human conditions of the experience of the divine."[185] Marion's theological project is to free the Christian God from such idolatry. The death of the metaphysical idol will open the space for a "negative theophany," whereby one can encounter the visibility of the invisible. Marion's phenomenology opens a way for the appearance of the phenomenon of revelation, a phenomenon in the full sense, which "appears truly as itself, of itself, and on the basis of itself, since it alone appears without the limits of a horizon or reduction to an *I*, but constitutes itself, to the

183. Marion, *The Idol and Distance*, 138-195. Marion's use of the non-predicative language of prayer/praise is from Dionysisus' hymnic form of language. This signifies that when the language assumes the form of prayer, it becomes possible to go beyond affirmation or negation about the essence of God, but rather one is directed towards the divine (excess). Thus, the subject is capable (incapable) of receiving more than that which the predicative language and thought can contain.

184. Marion discusses extensively the Nietzschean concept of the "death of God." See Marion, *The Idol and Distance*, 27-78.

185. *Ibid.*, 6.

point of giving *itself* as a *self*."[186] In the theological sense, it can be applied to the God of Revelation, who is revealed unconditionally as Love. As Thomas A. Carlson states, according to Marion's theology, "God loves even those who do not love him, shows himself even to those who do not yet see him. And just as my will to see phenomenal givenness would itself be a function of that givenness itself, so here my eventual capacity to love and to see God would be given first, and only by God's love for me."[187]

However, according to Marion, Being, as understood by Heidegger, hinders the possibility of a revelation which escapes the dimension of Being.[188] The difference regarding the question of revelation between Heidegger and Marion is this: Heidegger sets conditions under which revelation is possible. Accordingly, for Heidegger, God has to comply with Being itself in order to open up the possibility of revelation. So God's revelation is within the confines of Being and reveals himself as *a* being. On the other hand, Marion opens the possibility of revelation without having to comply with Being and without Being. Marion's criticism of Derrida is sharper than those raised against Heidegger, because according to him, Heidegger conceded the possibility of revelation under the restraint of Being, while Derrida left no option for it (revelation).[189] Marion distinguishes himself, both from Derrida and Heidegger, by presenting the Christian God as the Father who manifested himself in biblical revelation, characterised not by the norms of Being, but solely and absolutely by love. It is in and through love that God gives all, and identifies himself as givenness.[190] Marion's Christian God is the one who generously gives himself, not to be proved conceptually, but to be received in love and contemplation.

Marion defends his theological stance. According to him, theology presupposes the historical actuality of revelation in the person of Christ, which can only be understood through theological thinking, which begins with God's unconditional self-revelation. In this way, his understanding of revelation is focused on a Christian Father-God who gives himself only in distance. This is a theme which he explains through the categories of the idol and the

---

186. Marion, *Being Given*, 219.
187. *Ibid.*, xxx-xxxi.
188. Sneller, "Incarnation," 44.
189. *Ibid.*," 49.
190. Marion laments that philosophy has abandoned speaking about love, which culminates in an abandoning of speaking about God's Christian Name. Van den Bossche, "From the Other's Point of View," 62.

icon.[191] Marion contends that God's way of revealing himself is through the icon. In the iconic way of revelation, the perceiver, who perceives, is also being perceived. As such, intentionality can be said to be reversed. The icon provides the condition (simultaneously its non-condition) for the crossing out of the conceptual idol of God, making room for the crossed out God, whose name is YHWH (Ex 3:4),[192] *Agape*, to appear. According to Marion, the name YHWH is a paradox, and says nothing about the essence of the divine. God escapes every concept and definition, as he illustrates, based on Dionysius' Theology of Divine Names.[193] Marion writes,

> [a]mong the divine names, none exhausts ~~God~~ or offers the grasp or hold of a comprehension of him. The divine names have strictly no other function than [to] manifest this impossibility. More positively, they function to manifest the distance that separates (and hence unites) all the names of ~~God~~ – all, for in distance all can merit the qualifier divine. Here, predication must yield to praise – which, itself also, maintains a discourse.[194]

Marion explains, in what sense, God is Love before Being in the light of the parable of the prodigal son (Lk 15:11-32) highlighting the aspect of God's giving.[195] The parable shows how the gift can easily be lost into the sphere of economic exchange, or to an economy of idolatry, unless operated by love. The attitude of the son is that of appropriation or possession of the gift given by the Father, and not that of disappropriation. The son fails to see the father as the giver; he possesses and spends the gift. For him the gift has only finite, monetary value. The prodigal son considers the gift, his inheritance, as disposable property that can be commodified. So, unlike his father, he sees the gift through the perspective of economic exchange. However, as gift, it has to be understood, not in terms of monetary value, nor in terms of being, what *is*, but rather, in terms of givenness (*donation*).[196] This parable shows how

---

191. One can clearly see that, in Marion's works, theology and phenomenology inform each other. This we see especially in the treatment of his idol and icon. The factuality of revelation that he ascribes to theology has been presented as a possibility in phenomenology. In this sense, we can say that Marion's phenomenology is not devoid of theological motives.

192. Marion, *God Without Being*, 73ff.

193. *Ibid.*, 76ff.

194. *Ibid.*, 106.

195. Marion, *God Without Being*, 95-100. The parable of the prodigal son is the single instance in the whole New Testament where the philosophical term *ousia* is used. See David Moss, "Costly Giving: On Jean-Luc Marion's Theology of the Gift," *New Blackfriars* 74 (1993): 392-399.

196. See Marion, *God Without Being*, 99.

commodification of the gift can frustrate the infinite depth of giving. As Moss puts it, "the Gift – the gift of place, meaning and legitimacy, once shared by Father and Sons alike – [is annulled] into a mode of dissipation, lubricated by the younger son's desire."[197] There is no ground for the gift, other than love. Marion says,

> [t]he father is not fixed on the *ousia* because with his gaze he transpierces all that is not inscribed in the rigor of a gift, giving, received, given: goods, common by definition and circulation, are presented as indifferent stakes of those who, through them, give themselves to each other in a circulation which is more essential than what it exchanges.[198]

Ironically, everything is transformed by the outpouring of the father's love. In the end, one sees that the salvation of the younger son takes place in his return to the logic of the pure gift: *don-abandon-par-don*. As Marion puts it, "[f]inally, the moment of pardon comes; the father recognizes his son from afar, embraces him, and takes him in; what does the father say, give and forgive? No doubt, he returns humanity (in washing, clothing), but above all he returns filiation."[199]

According to Marion, giving oneself means giving oneself in terms of love, which is, in fact, a *kenosis* governed by dispossession and unconditionality. Thus, as Van den Bossche observes, by translating Being into love and givenness according to the logic (non-logic) of love, he achieves two things: he develops an iconic figure through which God gazes at us (iconic gaze), and the figure of the pure gift that makes present God's transcendence in immanence, according to the logic of the Bible. God is not the one whom we see (or do not see), but he is the one who sees us. The kernel of Marion's phenomenology is this: "[T]ruth in it adopts a strictly immanent character, and hence, needs no longer be founded by [a] transcendent God or one of His transcendental surrogates."[200] In other words, the immanent truth is found in observing that things are (being) given to us from elsewhere, and not from our gazing gaze, but rather, being given, and we stand as recipients responding to it. Therefore, God's self is phenomenologically given through the iconic figure of Christ.

However, according to the scheme of Christian economy, God's givenness in Christ can only be understood alongside God's givenness in the Holy

---

197. Moss, "Costly Giving," 396.
198. Marion, *God Without Being*, 99.
199. *Ibid.*
200. Van den Bossche, "God in Immanence," 344.

Spirit. Marion's theological phenomenology of givenness does not sufficiently account for the revelation of God in the Spirit. The givenness and gift of the Spirit is a point that Marion hardly develops, although he understands the Trinitarian dimension of the self-giving God. Hence, it remains the task of theologians to discuss the givenness and gift of the Spirit, which is integral to the New Testament revelation. God's excessive giving, in the iconic figure of Christ, is closely linked to the excess of the givenness of the Spirit after the resurrection. In the vein of the discussions that has been pursued so far, we will explain God's givenness as the gift of the Holy Spirit, and how the excess of the gift of the Spirit can be understood in terms of the notion of the saturated phenomenon.

5. Gift of the Holy Spirit: The Phenomenon of Revelation (2)

The agapic God, whose excess of love made manifest in the gift of the Son, also pours out his love in the third person of the Trinity. The excess of God's givenness is the Holy Spirit.[201] As Paul writes, "God's love has flooded our inmost heart through the Holy Spirit he has given us" (Rom 5:5; see also Acts 2:37-38; 10:44-46; 11:15-17). Just as the Spirit legitimates the unity in the Trinitarian communion, both in the immanent and economic manifestations of God, it is the Spirit who urges one to access the invisible in the icon. As Marion puts it, "[t]he Trinitarian basis opens up a definitive and unsurpassable distance, which only the Spirit can cross without respite, and yet without movement … He alone renders possible the confession of Christ and the veneration of the icon."[202] Therefore, the gift of the Spirit and Christ belong to the Trinitarian mode of God's givenness in the economy of salvation in an integral way. From a phenomenological perspective, one can say that the New Testament bears witness to the gift of the Spirit, in excess, in maximum phenomenality as the saturated phenomenon.

5.1. The Excess of the Spirit in Jesus

In the second chapter, the role of the Spirit in the life of Jesus was discussed from a biblical-theological perspective. Now, we shall explain Jesus' experience of the Spirit as excess as exemplified at his baptism, and how the gift

---

201. According to Augustine, the supreme name of the Holy Spirit is *donum*. Milbank, *Being Reconciled*, ix.

202. Marion, *The Crossing of the Visible*, 84.

of the Spirit is closely associated with the iconic figure of God's self-giving on the Cross from a phenomenological perspective.

5.1.1. The Jordanian Event

One can understand the epiphany in the Jordan from a phenomenological point of view. The baptismal event is a phenomenon that gives itself in maximum phenomenality, irreducible to any horizon of human conceptuality. It is an iconic event in which God's givenness was manifested in the Spirit and Christ. God shows (manifests) himself in and of himself, by himself, phenomenally, in "visible" form and "voice." The dialectic of the visible and the voice of the Old Testament theophanies characterise the baptismal event as well. The "vision" of the Spirit descending from the Father in the form of a dove, and the voice of the Father announcing Jesus as the eternal Son, reminds one of the close association with the "visible" and the "voice" in the Old Testament figure of God's appearance, where God speaks out of fire (Deut 4:36; cf. Deut 5:4; Ex 20:18).[203] Hilary of Poitiers writes, "[h]e (Jesus) is designated Son by the voice and the vision."[204] It is the anointing by the Spirit and the voice of the Father that declares Jesus as the eternal Son of God. The givenness and the gift of the Spirit are manifested in Jesus' baptism. It is actually the givenness of the Father in the gift of the Spirit, because in giving the Spirit, the Father was reassuring the Sonship of Jesus.

According to the synoptic gospels, the Holy Spirit descends upon Jesus as the sovereign intervention of God. The baptism of Jesus was the revelation of Jesus as the eternal Son of God, which assumed a Trinitarian mode in which the three persons of the Trinity come into play. From a phenomenological perspective, it was an event of the excess of the Spirit. The "immersion" in the water and the descent of the Spirit manifest the excess of the givenness of the Spirit bestowed on Jesus. Hilary's exegesis sufficiently draws attention to the dimension of the excess of the Spirit with which Jesus was anointed. As he puts it, "[i]n effect, after he had been baptised, the gates of heaven opened, the Spirit is sent and is recognised under the appearance of the dove, and he

---

203. The connection between the "visible" and the "voice" can also be seen in the transfiguration of Jesus (Lk 9:28-36).

204. Hilary of Poitiers, "On Matthew," in *Nicene and Post-Nicene Fathers*, ed. Philip Schaff and Henry Wace (Edinburgh: T & T Clark, 1979), 2:6.

(Jesus) bathes in this sort of unction of the Father's love."[205] Hilary's technical use of the term "bath," to denote the unction of the Spirit, points to the abundance of the Spirit with which Jesus was filled.[206] McDonnell points out that it is significant to note that John indicates twice that the Spirit came down and "remained" upon Jesus (John 1:32,33; see also Mk 1:10). This reveals the fullness of the Spirit that Jesus possessed, so that he could impart the Spirit after the resurrection (Jn 20:22).[207] At Pentecost, one sees this outpouring of the Spirit in abundance, out of the abundance of the Spirit he himself possessed. The excess of the Spirit was also manifested in the life and ministry of Jesus. In his commentary on Psalm 64:9, Hilary speaks of the Spirit as the "[r]iver of God [which] is full of water." He justifies this in light of John 4:14 and 7:39. The abundance of the water makes the river overflow. The gift of the Spirit overflows in the life of a Christian. As he puts it, "we are inundated with the gifts of the Spirit. That fountain of life, which is the river of God, spills over in us."[208] In regards to the messianic role of Jesus (Isa 11:2), the baptism of Jesus is seen as an experience of the excess of the Spirit, whereby the "long drought of the Spirit is over, and the silence of God's voice ended."[209]

The Spirit of Jesus is not something that Jesus merely receives, but the Spirit is that which Jesus receives, communicates, and acts upon others.[210] According to Mark, the excess and power of the Spirit was manifested in his "new teaching" (1:22), his charismatic ministry of healing (1:32-34), and forgiveness of sins (2:10), especially in his exorcisms (1:22-28; 5:1-20; 7:24-30; 9:14-29; see also Mk 3:11, 22-30). The excess of the Spirit in Jesus is also witnessed by Luke in his summary statement, "how God anointed him with the Holy Spirit and with power" (Acts 10:38). Not only does Luke take over all the healing and exorcisms of Mark, but also adds three of his own, namely, "a spirit of infirmity" (13:10-17), the man with dropsy (14:1-6), and

205. Hilary of Poitiers, *On Matthew*, 2:5. The sequence of events, namely, that of "immersion" and the "descent of the Spirit" are to be understood as a single unit that constitutes the event of baptism.

206. In the ordinary sense as compared to "pouring out" or "sprinkling," "bath" and "immersion" connote richness and abundance.

207. Kilian McDonnell, *The Baptism of Jesus in the Jordan: The Trinitarian and Cosmic Order of Salvation* (Collegeville, MN: Liturgical Press, 1996), 11.

208. Hilary of Poitiers, "Tract on the Psalms," in *The Nicene and Post-Nicene Fathers*, ed. Philip Schaff and Henry Wace (Edinburgh: T & T Clark, 1979), 64:13,14.

209. McDonnell, *The Baptism of Jesus*, 10.

210. McDonnell and Montague, *Christian Initiation*, 7.

the ten lepers (17:11-19). It is also significant that Luke puts the entire ministry of Jesus under the seal of the Holy Spirit (4:18-19) whose excess we see in the prophetic and charismatic ministry of Jesus. The same Spirit that was given to Jesus in his baptism, and was manifested in his ministry, is endowed to the community at Pentecost.

5.1.2. Gift of the Spirit and the Disfigured Figure of Christ

The Markan understanding of the baptism of Jesus has an allusion to the scandal of the Cross within the plot-development of the gospel.[211] Jesus' reference to the *cup* and *baptism*, as a reply to James' and John's request to sit at the right and the left of Jesus respectively, contains an allusion to his passion (Mk 10:38-39; see also Mk 14:36; Lk 12:50). Therefore, the language of "baptism" is a metaphorical reference to the passion into which Jesus will be immersed. As G.R. Beasley-Murray writes, "[h]e [Jesus] is to be plunged, not into water, but into calamity unto death."[212] This indirectly relates the gift of the Spirit, to the salvific death of Christ, and clearly indicates that the Spirit can only be given through Jesus' death on the Cross.

This connection becomes more evident in the gospel of John. As compared to Mark, John directly relates the gift of the Spirit to the death of Christ. It is through the death of Jesus that the Spirit is given. The giving of the Spirit is proleptically attributed to the last breath of Jesus (Jn 19:30) and to the pierced side of Christ (19:34; see also Jn 7:37).[213] According to John, the

---

211. *Ibid.*, 10-11.

212. G.R. Beasley-Murray, *Baptism in the New Testament* (New York: Macmillan, 1962), 72. J.D.G. Dunn argues that according to "Q" tradition, the baptism of Jesus with "the Holy Spirit and fire" has to be fulfilled in his passion. Luke 12:49-50 associates the image of fire with baptism with a reference to the passion. See J.D.G. Dunn, "The Birth of a Metaphor – Baptised in the Spirit," *Expository Times* 89 (1978): 134-138.

213. It is interesting to note how John connects 19:30 and 34. Apparently παρέδοξεν τὸ πνεῦμα (he gave over/up his spirit) in 30 refers to the anthropological giving up of his life force. Gerhard Friedrich, "πνεῦμα," in *Theological Dictionary of the New Testament* (Grand Rapids, MI: Eerdmans, 1968), 438 n. 714. This may be in tune with other similar usages in John (11:33; 13:21). However, Karotemprel argues, this can be understood proleptically as referring to the Spirit since, according to John, the gift of the Spirit being the fruit of the Cross. Sebastian Karotemprel, "The Glorification of Jesus and the Outpouring of the Spirit," in *The Promise of Living Water* (Bombay: Asian Trading Corporation, 1977), 63-82. The actual giving of the Spirit (Jn 20:22) after the resurrection (Jn 19:30) can only be taken as symbolic or proleptic. Nevertheless, this does not downplay the gift of the Spirit and its connection to "the hour." Raymond E. Brown makes it clear, saying, "[t]he symbolism here is proleptic and serves to clarify that, while only the risen Jesus gives the Spirit, that gift flows

gift of the Spirit is the fruit of Jesus' glorification on the Cross (20:22). Therefore, there is a close relationship between God's gift of himself, in Christ, on the Cross and the gift of the Holy Spirit. As Burge describes, "the Spirit of Jesus which departs at the cross in the death is the same Spirit which brings life at Pentecost."[214] Thus the pneumatic baptism of which John prophesied (Jn 1:33; Mk 1:8) is realised through the agency of Jesus' death.[215] Therefore, the revelation, or the gift of the Spirit, is closely linked to the disfigured figure of Christ. In other words, the excess of the givenness of the Spirit is closely related to the Cross.

5.2. The Excess of the Spirit at Pentecost

A closer look at the event of Pentecost shows that the revelation of the Holy Spirit is an event of excess and abundance. Therefore, the event of Pentecost can be seen as a saturated phenomenon, whereby the Spirit was manifested through the charisms of tongues and prophecy. This premise will be briefly explained through a cursory survey of the first two chapters of the Acts where we see the core of Lukan Pneumatology in the Acts.

5.2.1. Acts 1:1-8

The "promise of the Father" of Luke 24:49 and Acts 1:4 is realised in the Pentecostal event.[216] Of the three references (vv. 2,5,8) that Luke makes when he refers to the promise of the Holy Spirit (1:1-8), verses 5 and 8 indicate the excess of the givenness of the Spirit. In v. 5, by presenting the coming of the Spirit as in baptism, Luke draws attention to the baptismal rite of John which is "immersion."[217] The term "immersion" is in tune with the commonly used term "filled" with the Holy Spirit of the Acts (e.g. 2:4; 4:31).

---

from the whole process of glorification in 'the hour' of the passion, death, resurrection and ascension." Raymond E. Brown, *The Gospel According to John*, Anchor Bible Commentary (New York: Doubleday, 1970), 2:951.

214. Gary M. Burge, *The Anointed Community: The Holy Spirit in the Johannine Tradition* (Grand Rapids, MI: Eerdmans, 1987), 95, 100.

215. Aidan Kavanagh, *The Shape of Baptism: The Rite of Christian Initiation* (Collegeville, MN: The Liturgical Press, 1991), 15.

216. "And [behold] I am sending the promise of my Father upon you; but stay in the city until you are clothed with the power from on high" (Luke 24:49). The word "clothed" also indicates the abundance of the Spirit that is bestowed on the disciples at Pentecost.

217. George T. Montague, *The Holy Spirit: Growth of a Biblical Tradition* (New York, Paramus, NJ, Toronto: Paulist Press, 1976), 272.

These technical terms jointly refer to the excess in which the gift of the Spirit (2:38) is received. V. 2 is of Trinitarian significance, introducing the gift of the *Spirit* as the promise of *my* (Christ's) *Father* as recalling the epiphany in Jesus' baptism. In v. 8, the coming gift of the Spirit is mentioned as the gift of "power," that will make them witnesses beyond boundaries (to the ends of the earth).[218]

5.2.2. Givenness of the Theophany in Acts 2:1-13

The phenomenon of Pentecost takes place with miraculous wind, sound, and tongues of fire. They were "filled with the Holy Spirit" beyond intention and the power of the Spirit was imposed in such a way that the excess of the phenomenon, or the gift of the Spirit, unfolds in the charismatic dimension it assumes. The *power* from on high, which is referred to in Luke 24:49, is manifested in the charismatic experience of tongues and prophecy (see also Acts 19:6), accompanied by miraculous conversion. It is the excess of the Spirit that Jesus promised to give to those who ask for the gift (Luke 11:13).[219]

The first part (Acts 2:1-3) describes the giving of the phenomenon where one sees the phenomenological dimensions of the gift of the Spirit. Luke explains the elements of the theophany. There came a "sound" from heaven like the "rush of a violent wind" (v. 2). The word echoes the Old Testament theophanies (Ex 19:16; 1Sam 4:5; Ps 45:3; 12:19; 19:18) of which noise/sound is a common phenomenon. In v. 3 the proper Pentecostal phenomenon is seen. The tongues of fire appeared to those who were gathered and a tongue rested on each of them. Like the sound, the Old Testament theophanies are frequently accompanied by wind and fire (e.g. Isa 4:4; 2Sam 22:16; Ps 50:3; Jer 30:23; Isa 66:15). But for Luke, the tongues of fire symbolize the gift of the Holy Spirit which is manifested in the gift of tongues (v. 4). The close association with the "visible" and the "voice," as in the Old Testament figure of God's appearance, reveals a God who speaks out of fire

---

218. This recalls the nature of Jesus' kingdom: "He will reign over the house of Jacob forever, and of his kingdom there will be no end" (Lk 1:33). This happens through the power of the Holy Spirit (Lk 1:35).

219. "If you then, who are evil, know how to give good gifts to your children, how much more will the heavenly Father give the Holy Spirit to those who ask him." Here the Holy Spirit is referred to as gift, and the giving in excess.

(Deut 4:36; cf. Deut 5:4; Ex 20:18) in the Pentecostal event.[220] As Montague explains, by the tongues "*as of* fire," Luke means something really visible as in the Sinai tradition, whereby the people "*seeing* the voice," stay at a distance (20:18-21).[221] *Visibility* is essential to the manifestation of the Spirit. The effect of the Spirit, the "infilling" of the Spirit, began to be manifested in the gift of tongues (cf. Acts 2:6-11). The phenomenon of speaking different languages has symbolic and theological meanings. From a phenomenological perspective, this refers to a non-conceptual or pre-conceptual language as in 1Cor 12:1-11, the language of prophecy and tongues, whereby it is not *I* who speak, the word is given to me.

The idol and the icon are integral to the understanding of the phenomenon of the Spirit at Pentecost. The idolatrous gazes (of the people) interpret the gift of tongues and prophecy as drunkenness. Pentecost becomes the gift of the Spirit only when the phenomenon is allowed to show and manifest itself. The abundance of the Spirit that imposes itself upon the disciples empowers them to be powerful witnesses of Christ, receiving the gift of the Spirit. The Spirit constitutes the disciples as powerful witnesses. Here, the constituting *I* is transformed to the one who is constituted, and receives a new identity as witness.

The Spirit can be thought of only in terms of the gift. The Spirit can only be received (Acts 8:17); it cannot be obtained with money (8:20). The aspect of a reception can also be found in the gospel of John. According to John, the Spirit can only be *received* as indicated by phrases such as "Receive the Holy Spirit" (Jn 20:22).[222] John also introduces the Spirit as the fulfilment of the eschatological gift of the Spirit (14:26; 15:26; 16:7). Therefore, the Spirit is a gift that is to be received, whereby the subjects are only recipients.

The "Little Pentecost" of Acts 4:23-31 must also be explained in connection to Acts 1:1-8. This event is reminiscent of Luke 11:13, whereby the Spi-

---

220. As was mentioned, the connection between the "visible" and the "voice" can also be seen at the baptism of Jesus. Here the descent of the Spirit in the form of a dove who, resting on Jesus, accompanied by the voice of the Father is parallel to the coming of the Spirit in the form of fire accompanied by the voice.

221. Montague, *The Holy Spirit*, 278.

222. John's use of λαμβάνειν (receive) goes in tune with the ancient Christian formula of receiving the Spirit. A few examples are: Jn 7:39; Rom 8:15; 1Cor 2:12; 2 Cor 11:4; Gal 3:2, 14; Acts 1:8; 2:38; 8:15, 17, 19; 10:47; 19:2) See Rudolf Bultmann, *The Gospel of John*, trans. G.R. Beasley-Murray (Oxford: Blackwell, 1971), 616 n. 3. For a discussion on the chronological problem between Jn 20:22 and Luke's account in the Acts, see Burge, *The Anointed Community*, 114-149.

rit is bestowed upon the disciples in answer to prayer. The shaking of the place in which they were gathered echoes the first Pentecost. Besides, the same expression, "they were all filled with the Holy Spirit," (Acts 2:4), and the boldness with which they spoke the word of God points to the excess of the phenomenon of the gift of the Spirit as in the first Pentecost. According to Luke, the charismatic signs, especially those of tongues and prophecy, have a privileged place. As Montague puts it, "the Spirit cannot be known to have poured *in* unless it somehow pours *out*."[223] From a phenomenological perspective, the manner in which the giving of the Holy Spirit, as attested by the scriptures, undergirds the aspect of the excess and abundance of the revelation of the Spirit that surpasses all understanding, calculations, concepts, and language.

5.3. The Excess of the Spirit in the Nascent Church

Jesus gives the Spirit from the excess that he himself experiences, the gift of the Spirit is not rationed (Jn 3:34). The excess of the Spirit is manifested in the life of the disciples, according to the promise of Jesus that his disciples will do greater works than he did (Jn 14:12). This is realized in the life of the Church after Pentecost. The saturated phenomenon of the Spirit is being unfolded in the vibrant activity of spreading the gospel and the expansion of the Church. The gift of the Spirit, which was manifested as given once-and-for-all, manifests his all-pervasiveness in weaving the life of the Church. The Spirit-events continue as the story unfolds in the Acts through healing and exorcisms (e.g. Acts 3:1-10; 9:32; 8:7; 14:8-13; 16:16-18; 9:36-42). The effects of the Spirit is manifested also in the preaching (Acts 3:11-26), signifying the advent of the messianic age (Isa 35:3, 6) and the availability of the new life of the resurrection (Acts 4:2). A summary statement concerning the signs and wonders performed by the apostles (Acts 5:12-16) and of the healing and exorcisms of Paul in Ephesus (Acts 19:11-12) allude to the charismatic activity in which the early Church experienced the excess of the gift of the Spirit. However, the activity of the Spirit is not in isolation to the activity of Christ. It is significant to note that Peter interprets the event of Pentecost in terms of Jesus, and by affirming the necessity of being baptised in the name of Jesus for receiving the Holy Spirit (Acts 2:38). The relationship of the name of Jesus and the Holy Spirit shaped the life experience of the budding Church. As Montague elucidates, the charismatic gifts of tongues and

---

223. McDonnell and Montague, *Christian Initiation*, 40.

prophecy belong to the Holy Spirit (Acts 2; 10:46; 19:6), whereas the cures, and exorcisms, as with preaching, are primarily attributed to the name of Jesus (Acts 3:6,16; 4:7,10,12,30; 16:18; 19:13,17).[224] The life and teaching of Jesus (Acts 10:39) and the reality of his resurrection (Acts 1:8,22; 10:41; 5:3) constituted the preaching and testimony. It was the power of the Spirit that enabled them to bear witness (Acts 1:8; 4:29-33) to Jesus Christ, even risking their lives.[225] In brief, the gift of the Spirit patterns the concrete and experiential life of the Church in such a way that the age of salvation can rightly be called the age of the Spirit. Therefore, the God who gives himself in Christ gives also Pneumatologically through the gift of the Spirit.

The understanding of God's self-giving in Christ and the Spirit, God's self-communication to humankind, which has been developed according to the phenomenology of Marion, suggests that God's giving in the sacraments can be explained only by placing the revelatory giving in Christ and the Spirit on equal footing. Therefore, a phenomenological understanding of God's self communication, as has been designated in the present chapter, God's giving of himself, goes in line with the Pneumatological theology that was outlined in the second chapter. Thus, it can now be argued that a phenomenological and symbolic understanding of the sacraments should also inhabit the activity of the Holy Spirit along with that of Christ, which will be discussed towards the end of this chapter. In order to achieve this task, it is important to outline a possible theology of the gift that reconciles the notions of gratuity and return, which are essential to the Christian understanding of the divine-human relationship, while addressing the charges posed against a unilateral and puritan gift as retained by Marion.

6. A Theology of the Gift

In response to the current research on gift in philosophy, anthropology, and amongst other social sciences, theologians have the task of discerning "how God's gift giving is radically different from patterns of giving among human persons and communities."[226] This turns the attention to the gift of God in Christ and the Spirit. The practices of gift exchange, as enunciated by Mauss,

---

224. Montague, *The Holy Spirit*, 289.

225. We see this concretely in the martyrdom of Stephen. At the time of his martyrdom he was "filled with the Holy Spirit," and was given a vision of the "glory of God and Jesus standing at the right hand of God" (Acts 7:55).

226. R. Kevin Seasoltz, *God's Gift Giving: In Christ and through the Spirit* (New York: Continuum, 2007), 1.

do not function in the dynamics of God's economy of the gift. This would imply that God's gift of creation, the incarnation, the gift of the Spirit, and the gift of God in the sacraments are given to us so that we may return our lives to God, and as such, exalt God as a generous benefactor. It remains a fact that human beings can never adequately or equally reciprocate the gifts of God. Moreover, from a Derridian point of view, the impossibility of the pure gift also puts into question the very possibility of divine gifts.

Nevertheless, the paradigm of the gift has been used in the Christian tradition and theology.[227] Christian teaching cannot undermine the possibility of the gift, because human persons relate to others, as well as to God, on the basis of God's ultimate gift in Christ. According to Jewish and Christian traditions, there is an eminent sense in which God is the one who requires love, allegiance, and servitude above all else. Moreover, the variety of activities ranging from simple acts of generosity and altruism to heroic deeds of self-sacrifice and martyrdom can be accommodated within the framework of giving. Therefore, the impossibility of the gift questions the logic of the Christian understanding of gift-giving, in general. Taking into account these concerns, it is required that a plausible theology of the gift is developed.

6.1. Theologizing of Givenness

The phenomenological understanding of the gift becomes important for theology, because it is an attempt to get to the heart of what it means for God to give Godself. As Horner points out, the language/category of the gift is theologically compelling, because it basically refers to what essentially takes place in the relationship between God and human beings. As has been explained in the present chapter, Marion attempts to theologise givenness, thereby, opening the possibility of a phenomenality of Christian Revelation. It is possible to speak of a theology of the gift in the light of God's gift in Christ and the Spirit. However, the challenging question is whether it is possible to

---

227. For instance, Hans Urs von Balthasar explains God's self-revelation and our human response in terms of gift-giving and the return gift. God's self-giving love finds its great manifestation on the Cross of Christ. God's self-gift in Christ can only be embraced through an appropriate response of a dispossession of ourselves in imitation of God. According to Balthasar, we can appropriate God's expropriation only through our own expropriation. Moreover, when we receive the gift of life, it obliges us that we not only receive the ability to bear fruit for God's sake, but also for others. God's superabundant generosity has to be outpoured into the lives of others. Hans Urs von Balthasar, *The Glory of the Lord: A Theological Aesthetics*, ed. John Riches, trans. Brian McNeil, vol. 7 (Edinburgh: T & T Clark, 1989), 389-484.

develop a Christian theology of giving, which is gratuitous and reciprocal, in terms of the unilateral and non-reciprocal concept of the gift retained by Marion. Marion's theological project takes into account the Christian understanding of reciprocity without contradicting the gratuity and graciousness of God. In this regard, Marion seems to be closer to Milbank, although he does not hold Milbank's ontology of the gift.

6.1.1. Giving and Being

Marion's contribution to theology is significant because he develops a consistent theology of giving and the gift, modelled on the Trinitarian pattern of giving. As he says, "to unravel this thought of the gift as such, it would be necessary to engage in an examination of Trinitarian theology, outside the scope of phenomenology, as well as of metaphysics."[228] He gives an indication that the three persons of the Trinity, the Father, the Son, and the Holy Spirit, "fulfils in its own way all three functions (giver, givee, givability/ receivability)" of givenness.[229] Accordingly, there is a possibility of reflecting on the Christian concept of giving in terms of gratuity, as well as reciprocity, which has to be distinguished from economic exchange. Therefore, it essentially pertains to the concept of grace with all its implications which makes this relationship possible.

Marion's credit rests in giving a consistent theology of treating the reality of God in terms of givenness and the gift. Naming God as *agape*, he equates givenness with charity. Therefore, God is love before Being; God is givenness before Being. So, as Webb opines, for Marion, "to be" and "to give" are interchangeable in God. As he writes, "[i]f, to begin with, 'God is love', then God loves before being, He only is as He embodies himself, in order to love more closely that which and those who themselves, have first to be."[230] Thus, Marion reinvests the title that revelation gives: that God is, as God gives. He even tries to liberate God from the vestiges of the "Being of beings," as well. By doing so, Marion is not denying being for God, but rather, as Webb puts it, God's "Being is gift, and the real name of God is charity. God's giving does not explain or minimise the mystery of Being; on the contrary, the gratuity of God's giving is that mystery."[231] God gives God's self. Therefore,

---

228. Marion, *Being Given*, 114-115.
229. *Ibid.*
230. Webb, *The Gift Giving God*, 128.
231. *Ibid.*, 130.

God has to be received and named in terms of giving: givenness of God as manifested in the economic revelation through the gift of the Son and the Spirit. The icon and the idol are two contrasting modes of receiving God, a God who is *agape*, against metaphysical idolatry. "The icon recognizes no other measure than its own infinite excessiveness [*démesure*]."[232] "By definition and decision, God, if he must be thought, can meet no theoretical space to his measure [*mesure*], because his measure exerts itself in our eyes as an excessiveness [*démesure*]."[233]

In the second chapter an extended study of God's self-communication, based on the Rahnerian axiom has been made. The fundamental principle of this axiom is that God *in se* is God *pro nobis*. The God who communicated himself in the economy is not a God of Being, but a giving God. In fact, it is givenness that patterns the mode of Trinitarian giving, both in the immanent and economic Trinity, because God gives without being subject to objectification. The excess of givenness does not allow for any limited objectification. Therefore, Marion stands close to negative theology, and suggests that what characterises God to humanity is not God's being, but rather, the givenness, or "the name." In this regard, Marion is in line with LaCugna who says, "[t]he incomprehensible God *is* God by sharing, bestowing, diffusing, expressing Godself. The gift of existence and grace that God imparts to the world is not produced by efficient causality, largely extrinsic to God; the gift is nothing other than God's own self."[234] The Trinitarian God is givenness in Godself. Relying on Dionysius and Bonaventure, LaCugna states that "goodness is self-diffusive, not self-contained."[235] The classical notion of *perichoresis*, or the mutual indwelling of the Trinitarian persons, which defines the inner life of the Trinity, is characterised by an excess of love and mutual self-giving. Thus, LaCugna emphasises that God's being is in giving. However, she does not present a systematic consideration of God's precedence in terms of giving as Marion does.

---

232. Marion, *God without Being*, 21.

233. *Ibid.*, 45.

234. LaCugna, *God for Us*, 210-211. This can be compared with the Trinitarian understanding of God held by M. Douglas Meeks as the One who shares abundantly. Accordingly, "God owns by giving." To be more precise, "God is not a self-possessor. God is rather a community, a community of persons united in giving themselves to each other and to the world." M. Douglas Meeks, *God the Economist: The Doctrine of God and Political Economy* (Minneapolis, MN: Fortress, 1989), 115, 111.

235. LaCugna, *God for Us*, 353.

Ascribing givenness as originary to the being of God helps to explain the Trinitarian dynamics of mutual giving outside the scheme of exchange or reciprocity. In the Trinitarian giving, the giving of each of the divine persons must be understood as pure giving without being contaminated by reciprocity. Therefore, the manner of giving that governs the Trinity is originary and in excess itself, so much so, that it is irreducible to any sort of return. This is a love that expects nothing to be given back. It is from the very nature of the Trinitarian persons that any mutual giving becomes possible, in the first place. A similar relationship constitutes the divine-human relationship as well.

6.1.2. Givenness and the Gift of the Call: The Dative Subject

According to Westphal, the phenomenology of religion seeks to describe the believing souls as the "subject" in relation to the holy or the sacred which is described as the "object."[236] Therefore, the phenomenological notion of the gift and givenness is theologically nuanced, as far as the relationship between the self-giving God and human beings as gifted, are concerned. Marion's phenomenology of givenness also assigns a status and function to the "subject" which can be said to be in the least, other than the metaphysical subject. In this regard, Heidegger's account of *Gelassenheit* allows one to replace "constitution" with "reception," and to accept the attitude of passivity in relation to alterity.[237] This recalls the issue of reversed-intentionality which was discussed earlier. It is not the abolition of the subject as such, but the *I* within oneself that lays hold of the "object." Hence, it can be said that one is not advocating any kind of "experience without a subject," but rather, "experience without a certain kind of subject."[238] One is still left with a subject, but a subject that is incapable of fully delimiting that which is beyond limits and horizons.

Marion speaks of givenness at the very "beginning." Obviously, this refers, not to an empirically determined temporal sequence, but to that which is prior to any reckoning whatsoever, including a preconceived giver. In this sense, the phenomenon can be said to give and show itself, independent of the subject. The presencing of the phenomenon, in this manner, can be

---

236. See Merold Westphal, *God, Guilt, and Death: An Existential Phenomenology of Religion* (Bloomington, IN: Indiana University Press, 1997), 1-12.
237. Westphal, "Vision and Voice," 124.
238. *Ibid.*, 125.

called, "immanent otherness." In presencing itself, the phenomenon, which is at a distance, becomes internal to the phenomena (itself); it shows itself phenomenally.[239] Marion refers to the subject as the one "to whom has been given" (*l'adonné*), i.e., "the gifted-devoted."[240] The phenomenal world is given or shows itself, and one as *l'adonné* (only) responds to it. Here, the subject has no logical priority, but only epistemological priority, because phenomenality begins not with the gaze of the subject, but rather, the subject only makes the phenomenon visible as to whom it has been given, or to whom the phenomenality shows itself. The subject retains epistemic priority over the "reality," surrendering logical priority as the receiver to whom it is given.[241] Thus, Marion re-defines the metaphysical *ego* as *l'adonné*. The basic experience of the subject is the experience of being given, gifted or loved.[242]

It is important to discuss whether or not the portrayal of the subject as the gifted in a mute and passive mode endangers the Christian concept of revelation and the demand for a free and voluntary response of faith. Therefore, the crux of the issue lies in explaining the notion of return/response in terms of the "phenomenological theology" of givenness. Now, we will discuss how far Marion's "puritan gift" inhabits the dimension of the call and the response which is fundamental to the understanding of revelation and faith.

6.2. The Question of Return

The problematization of the gift pursued by Derrida invites one to consider whether or not an application of the puritan notion of the gift developed by Marion can be used in order to explain God's gift of himself in Christ and the Spirit, in terms of unconditional charity as gift. How can the notion of God's gift to human beings be reatined, freeing that notion from the law of exchange and the circle of return? Does not God's giving necessarily engage an obligation, contract and covenant? If it does, how can it be said that God's giving is pure? Does the notion of obligatory return annul the gift as such? Such questions are relevant also in terms of the sacramental gift.

---

239. Van den Bossche, "From the Other's Point of View," 72.

240. Van den Bossche explains the subject as the one to whom a call is given by the Other. See Van den Bossche, "A Possible Present for Theology," 55, 57.

241. *Ibid.*, 57; Van den Bossche, "From the Other's Point of View," 72.

242. *Ibid.*, 74-75.

Milbank argues that Christianity has combined the sacrificial and reciprocal character of giving.[243] The modern purism regarding the gift, which is unilateral (sacrificial) and non-reciprocal, is the child of a rigorous theological thinking of *agape* in a self-defeating manner, dissociating *agape* from the giver's own happiness and well-being.[244] Milbank shows another face of Christian giving which also takes into account the giver. He proposes a purified gift exchange over and against the notion of a unilateral and sacrificial giving. Although Milbank does admit to the sacrificial aspect of giving portrayed in the gospels as "letting oneself go," he still affirms the return which comes in the form of receiving back an abundance of life (cf. Jn 11:25; 12:24).[245] He also understands the gift of Christ in the incarnation in terms of the return of humanity to the Father. Furthermore, he extends the notion of reciprocity to the gift of the Holy Spirit, because he understands, the Holy Spirit as the gift that results from the mutual relationship between the Father and the Son.[246] It is God who gives the Spirit, but the Spirit is the relationship between the Father and the Son. Milbank also looks at the Christ event through the lens of return and argues that the mystery of Christ is fulfilled in his resurrection and return to the Father. It is the same mystery that is celebrated in the liturgy through the offering of the bread and wine. The scheme of return is operative in the celebration, because the worshiping community consumes the gifts returned to them as the gift of his body and blood.[247] For Milbank, what distinguishes the gift from the contract is neither absolute freedom, nor the aspect of the gift characterised as non-being, but rather, the "asymmetrical reciprocity" and "non-identical repetition" that governs the logic of counter-gift.[248] In contrast to Derrida, for Milbank, reciprocity makes the gift possible.

---

243. For instance, Milbank traces back to the reciprocity or bilateral nature of the Old Covenant and the message of sacrificial love (love of enemies) which is unilateral, expecting no return (Luke 6:32-35). In contrast to this, he also cites John as presenting a love which circulates among friends (disciples). See Milbank, *Being Reconciled*, 160. Martin M. Lintner undertakes an elaborate study of the different understandings of the gift (*Geist der Gabe*) in the life and teachings of Jesus, especially regarding his self-giving on the Cross (*Opfer und Gabe*) in view of its implications for a theological ethics. Lintner, *Eine Ethik des Schenkens*.
244. Milbank, "Can a Gift Be Given?," 132.
245. Milbank, *Being Reconciled*, 155.
246. Milbank, "Can a Gift Be Given?," 137; Milbank, *Being Reconciled*, 160.
247. Milbank, *Being Reconciled*, 160-161.
248. *Ibid.*, 156.

Marion's understanding of pure givenness apparently rejects a return in any form. In spite of Marion's attempt to avoid reciprocity, reciprocity or reception forms an important element of his phenomenology of givenness. This presupposes a favourable reception in return to givenness that gives itself unconditionally. He overcomes the limits of reciprocity and return by introducing the notion of the pure gift which is unveiled on the Cross whose name is Love, because only love gives without any expectation or return. Marion says that only "love loves without condition, simply because it loves" and for love's sake.[249] Therefore, only love has the capacity to break the vicious circle of exchange, and enable one to give without return, without giving being reduced to economic exchange. Therefore, God other than Being, Love other than Being, breaks the law of return through the law of charity. One cannot say that Marion rejects return as such. According to him, God who reveals or gives himself as Love in Jesus Christ can be reached only by receiving him by love. As he puts it, "God, who gives himself as Love only through love, can be reached only so long as one receives him by love, and to receive him by love becomes possible only for he[him] who gives himself to him" by a self surrender.[250] Therefore, what makes the gift distinctively Christian is nothing but the aspect of love.

Studies on the question of gift also pay attention to the necessity of return as an essential form of receiving gift. In this regard, Kathryn Tanner remarks that "[o]ne receives gifts only in giving them back to the giver in the same way one has been given them."[251] Marion does not seem to be on a different pole, as far as the question of reception is concerned. Nevertheless, the distinctive character of Marion's understanding of reception lies in an acceptance that yields the givee to praise. As Marion puts it, "[p]resence of Christ, and therefore, also that of the Father, discloses itself by a gift; it can, therefore, be recognized only by a blessing. A presence which gives itself by grace and identifies itself with this gift, can, therefore, be seen only in being received, and be received only in being blessed."[252] Thus reception and praise fit into the language the gift without any contradiction. Tanner emphasises the unconditionality of God's giving in that we receive the gift of God unde-

249. Marion, *God Without Being*, 47.

250. Marion, *Prolegomena to Charity*, 61.

251. Tanner, "Theology at the Limits of Phenomenology," 222. See also Marion, *God Without Being*, 104; Marion, *Being Given*, 282-288.

252. Marion, *The Idol and Distance*, 155.

servedly, even before the gift turns us into faithful witnesses or lovers.[253]
Tanner's stress on unconditionality upholds the gratuitousness of God's giving intact. Nevertheless, it is untenable to view God's giving and human reception in temporal sequence as she does.

Marion's notion of the pure gift does not reject the notion of return *as
such*, but a return of the same, while allowing room for a *response* that surpasses the domain of exchange. In a personal communication to the author,
he writes, "there is no *return* of the gift, strictly speaking, but another gift, in
the other direction, as gratuitous and unilateral than the first: it is not [a] return of the same, but an answer, different, to the first."[254] Van den Bossche's
explanation of *l'adonné* as a particular kind of subject seems to inhabit a
response based on the notion of originary givenness. Marion speaks about a
call that is always, already given which remains unknown in its origin, but
known from the response. The call is anonymous which comes to us as a
gift.[255] The caller is identified in the response of the devotee. In the phenomenological scheme of givenness, the subject is in the position of the receiver, without mastery.[256] There is an appeal and a response. The subject is
called to respond. However, there is no temporal priority for the appeal, because the call is known only in response, and the capacity to respond is inseparable from the givenness of the call. As Van den Bossche points out, Marion's phenomenology of givenness renders truth an immanent character according to the mode of love, defining the subject as the gifted (*l'adonné*). Two
things come into play here: first, phenomena are given from elsewhere; and
second, phenomena give themselves to us, invoking an inevitable answer.

It is true that God cannot be adequately reciprocated with an equal return
when we take into consideration God-given gifts. Marion retains the possibility of the pure gift, because the remarkable feature of God's giving is that he
goes on giving, in spite of our refusal. His understanding of gratuity also
involves an exchange, although not in an extreme or rigorous form. So it

---

253. Tanner, "Theology at the Limits of Phenomenology," 223. Here Tanner also observes
that, in spite of Marion's attempt to delimit the gift from being conditioned by the reception of
the subject, an aspect of reciprocity recurs on another level. He does this by introducing the
notion of passive recipient who is unable to control making room for the givenness to manifest
itself. This "precondition" is an empty yielding to the givenness' inexorable influence. See
ibid., 223-224.

254. I am thankful to Prof. Marion for his personal response to my questions concerning
the gift and the return, by email (8 April, 2008).

255. Marion, *Being Given*, 282-287, 296-308.

256. Murchadha, "Glory, Idolatry, Kairos," 82-83.

cannot be called, in the strict sense, a return. However, he incorporates the return in "some sense." As he observes,

> [t]he giving traverses distance by not ceasing to send the given back to the giver … [T]he self-withdrawal of the giver in the gift may be read on the gift, in the very fact that it refers back absolutely to the giver … The gift gives the giver to be seen, in repeating the gift backwards … God requires receiving the gift, and since the gift occurs only in distance, returning it.[257]

Therefore, one should take extraordinary care not to reduce Marion's subject into a scheme of exchange, because, as O'Leary observes, the frontier between the economy and the gift is so narrow that it rules out the notion of a purist claim of the gratuitous gift.[258] Marion's understanding of the pure gift consists in thinking of givenness before and beyond the thought of reciprocity. One can understand God's gift to human beings only as prevenient and originary. As Tanner observes, "[t]he unconditionality of God's giving simply means that God gives before any such return on our part, and that God continues to give, even when that return fails to be made, indeed, even if any such return were never to be made, for the sake of enabling it."[259] In what follows, a theology of the gift employing the notion of "excess" and the "fatherhood image," integrating the approaches of Stephen Webb and Calvin O. Schrag into the framework of God's giving, by reconciling the notions of gratuity and return will be developed.

257. Marion, *God Without Being*, 104, 107.
258. Joseph S. O'Leary, "The Gift: A Trojan Horse in the Citadel of Phenomenology?," in *Givenness and God: Questions of Jean-Luc Marion*, ed. Ian Leask and Eoin Cassidy, Perspectives in Continental Philosophy (New York: Fordham University Press, 2005), 144. O'Leary also explains that Marion has not acknowledged the plurality of gift exchange that exists in archaic societies outside the realm of economic exchange. According to him, the commodity exchange that exists in the domain of the social mechanism has to be distinguished from the gift exchange that exists in the language of the community. O'Leary, "The Gift," 142-147.
259. Tanner, "Theology at the Limits of Phenomenology," 221-222. In fact, Tanner observes this as a criticism against Marion, contending that Marion rejects any form of return. For she argues that exchange is not easily assimilated into commercial exchange as Marion thinks. Gift exchange can have a logic which, in many cases, is identical to the logic of givenness. She also states that gift exchange also differs from givenness in many respects. See Tanner, "Theology at the Limits of Phenomenology," 214. We agree with Tanner that reciprocity and the return gift can be considered in a more positive light than a mere reduction to economic or business exchange, as we will see later. We hold that Marion would principally agree with the above statement of Tanner, because Marion's main emphasis is the placing of givenness at the beginning of any God-thought in the understanding of our relationship with God.

6.2.1. Theo-Economics *of Giving*

Marion considers the possibility of the gift outside of economic exchange relations. A gift, genuinely given cannot be reduced to a commodity, or given an exchange value. It would annul the very conditions of genuine gift-giving. Therefore, genuine giving and the gift require that the recipient be freed from the obligation of reciprocation, or the incursion of debt. Marion tries to overcome these problems by transcending the requirements of reciprocity through the notion of *agape*, which is different from *eros* or *philia*.[260] This is a love that expects nothing to be given back. In this sense, the true gift is the gift of love, because it is the gift which incurs no reciprocity or return. According to Derrida, the inner dynamics of giving a gift imply the destruction of the gift itself. The gift is annihilated at giving and reception. However, according to Marion, the gift operates according to the norm of *agape*, whose icon is seen in the love of God, whose love was made manifest in the figure of Christ. Under the scheme of non-reciprocal gift-giving, one finds that the initial givenness does not call for a counter-gift, but rather, the givee responds to the gift in an ethical engagement with others.

Those who uphold the impossibility of the gift in contemporary discussions of the gift seem to presuppose a choice between excess and exchange, because exchange presupposes a symmetrical relationship, whereas excess, an asymmetrical one. Stephen Webb proposes a *theo-economics* which overcomes the necessity of making a choice between them, by bringing together the notions of excess and exchange. He claims that this approach explains the Christian understanding of giving, and it takes excess and mutuality, seriously. He finds a theological paradigm, a theological model of gifting, in the Christian doctrine of the Trinity, arguing that God's gift-giving exhibits both the characteristics of excess (surplus) *and* reciprocity. Thus, he shows how gifting combines excess and exchange without annihilating their differences.

---

260. Schrag, *Semantics of the Gift*, 110-111. In this regard, it is important to notice the distinction between *epithymia* (sensual love), *philia* (friendship) and *eros* (intellectual love, but often viewed identical to sensual love) and *agape* (Latin *caritas*). In contrast to *agape*, the other three notions are preferential, possessive and conditional. Furthermore, they also require a symmetrical relationship and reciprocity as the necessary conditions of their functioning. *Agape* operates non-preferentially, non-possessively and unconditionally, outside the norms of symmetry and reciprocity. See Schrag, *ibid.*, 132.

6.2.1.1. Asymmetrical Reciprocity

God's giving perpetuates giving. God's gift determines identity, enabling one to give to a community of givers who are empowered by an original abundance accelerating the gift in a mutual exchange. Webb makes a theological account of God and the Church as a community of givers as the paradigm for an account of gift and giving, bringing excess and exchange without polarisation. He claims that there is a Christian grammar of gratuity and gratitude that empowers rather than humiliates. Webb argues that "divine gift giving is both excessive and reciprocal, or rather, it is reciprocal precisely because it is excessive ... God's giving is an abundance, an excessive giving that initiates, sustains, and solicits a response from the one to whom God gives."[261] Against the puritan claims regarding the gift, he argues that "[t]rue gifts create return gifts, but it does not follow that giving, therefore, is always controlled by a logic of equivalence, of measuring this for that. For the return response to be solicited, the gift itself must be excessive, wonderful, unexpected."[262] To understand the relationship between the gift of God and the subsequent human response, Webb introduces the notion of *excess* and *reciprocity*, in other words, the notion of "asymmetrical-reciprocity."[263] Thus, Webb attempts to formulate a theological construct using this very notion, explaining the concept of the Trinity as a "Gifting God" who is constituted essentially by excess and reciprocity. As he puts it,

> [m]y governing insight is the following: *divine excess begets reciprocity.* Without excess, reciprocity becomes calculation, bartering, exchange; without reciprocity, excess becomes irrelevant, anarchic, and wasteful ... In the end,

---

261. Webb, *The Gift Giving God*, 90.
262. *Ibid.*
263. Schrag, *Semantics of the Gift*, 126. The notion of "asymmetrical reciprocity" was brought to prominence by a feminist political and social theorist, Iris Marion Young. She argues that we cannot understand others' experiences by imagining ourselves in their place, or in terms of symmetrical reciprocity, but rather, a reciprocity which expresses itself in moral respect and asymmetry which arises from people's greatly varying life histories and social positions. See particularly Iris Marion Young, "Asymmetrical Reciprocity: On Moral Respect, Wonder, and Enlarged Thought," *Constellations: An International Journal of Critical Democratic Theory* 3 (1997). However, La Caze argues that Young's articulation of asymmetrical reciprocity in terms of wonder and the gift involves certain problems. By discussing friendship and political representation, she shows how taking self-respect into account complicates asymmetrical reciprocity. See Marguerite La Caze, "Seeing Oneself through the Eyes of the Other: Asymmetrical Reciprocity and Self-respect," *Hyptia: A Journal of Feminist Philosophy* 23 (2008).

what God gives is the power of giving itself, the possibility that we can all participate in the movement of giving with the hope that such generosity will be enhanced, organized, and consummated in God's very own becoming.[264]

Webb distinguishes three moments in God's giving, considering God as "the Giver, the Given and the Giving," which is parallel to the three elements that constitute gift-giving, namely, the giver, what is given, and the givee. God, as the Divine Gift, in its Trinitarian expression is at once the Giver, the Given, and the Giving. Moreover, God's giving imparts to the givee the power of giving herself, which finds expression in further giving (progressively), acknowledging the excess of the gift she received. Thus, being given, the givee becomes the giver herself in the society. Those who deny the gift fail to acknowledge the genuineness of generous acts by portraying gift-giving as totally opposite to exchange, excluding even the least form of gratitude or reciprocity.

What Webb emphasises is the prevenience of God's giving. God gives excessively in order to be passed along. As such, excess implies mutuality by responding to giving with further giving, creating relationships of obligation and responsibility. Therefore, it is not the starting point, but the end point. As Webb says, "[t]he end point of gifting … should not be read into the beginning of the process. God does not want us to give, so that God does not give for no purpose, but God wants us to give – not [to] save or consume – as God gives, excessively."[265] St. Paul says, "[w]hat do you possess that was not given to you? If then, you really received it all as a gift, why take the credit to yourself?" (1Cor 4:8). Therefore, giving is, itself, multiplied as further giving.

God's giving in Jesus is the paradigm for the totality of God's giving. It shows the excess of God's giving. As St. Paul writes, God "did not spare his own Son, but gave him up for us all; and with this gift how can he fail to lavish upon us all that he has to give?" (Rom 8:32). The logic (non-logic) of God's giving is superabundance, superabundance itself, of which conceptuality cannot explain nor clarify. God's giving in abundance on the Cross reveals that giving can come in the form of "losing," but "losing" in this sense, is closely connected with gaining. In God's giving in "Jesus Christ, the giving of God is both sacrificed and revealed, hidden and made manifest, squandered and returned, denied and reborn."[266]

---

264. Webb, *The Gift Giving God*, 90-91.
265. *Ibid.*, 139.
266. *Ibid.*, 144.

The aspect of asymmetry and reciprocity can also be found in the thought of Milbank. In addition to that, he accepts the notions of deferral and difference from Bourdieu. He opines that "if a gift can be given at all, it must be within the *logos* or measure of a necessary *delay* (whose term is indeterminate, though not infinite) and of *non-identical repetition* between the gift and the counter-gift."[267] Accordingly, the gift always involves a "giving back," if not to the individual donor, at least by way of "a giving in return" or "a passing on" to the social circle that the individual is part of. This operates asymmetrically and non-identically in an unpredictable time to unpredictable recipients. Even though gift-exchange is contractual, it preserves an element of gratuity, irreducible to contract.[268] Milbank's attempt to retain the gratuitous character of the gift is, indeed, admirable. Nevertheless, the time factor involved in his explanation of the gift cannot be applied to God's giving, modelled on the Trinitarian giving. In this respect, Webb's exposition of the gift goes better in par with Marion, and it seems to be more promising for developing a theology of gift. Presenting Webb in conjunction with Marion, however, is not intended to simplify the distinctive and unilateral (pure) character of the gift according to Marion, but rather, to show how his puritan gift can be enriched by introducing the notion of return/acknowledgement, emphasizing the gratuitous and reciprocal dimension of divine-human relationship entertained by Christian theology.

6.2.1.2. *Acknowledgement and* Re-turn

Having lauded Marion's approach of conceiving God's being in terms of the gift, Webb sees Marion's portrayal of gift-giving as a docile and humble beholding, providing no room for an active return.[269] This seems to be the logical consequence of Marion's whole process of thinking, which seeks to safeguard a puritan gift through the obliterating of any sign of either a giver, or a receiver. It is true that, in the strict sense, Marion is not concerned with return or reciprocity. However, as has been pointed out, he translates return into the language of praise: "To return the gift, to play redundantly the unthinkable donation, this is not said, but done. Love is not spoken, in the end, it is made. Only then can discourse be reborn, but as an enjoyment, a jubila-

---

267. Milbank, "Can a Gift Be Given?," 125.
268. *Ibid.*, 126.
269. Webb, *The Gift Giving God*, 133.

tion, a praise."[270] In this regard, one may ask if Marion's understanding of gift can accommodate the Christian notion of the gift which demands a response, or the same form of reciprocity. Can asymmetry and reciprocity be integrated to Marion's phenomenology of the gift? Can the full practical applications of God's giving, a giving which itself proliferates further giving, be accommodated within the context of Marion's thought? These are realisable possibilities under a thinking which translates *return* into re-*turn*. We intend to achieve this by taking the image of fatherhood employed by Marion to a horizontal direction, employing the insights of Schrag.

Marion explains *fatherhood* as an exceptional phenomenological symbol, the highest form of givenness, because fatherhood gives itself and shows itself and in principle, manifests more than itself.[271] The gift that is given in fatherhood shows how the gift is reduced to givenness by virtue of the impossibility of a return gift, quite unlike in the scheme of economic reason or exchange. The giving in fatherhood is without reciprocity and within excess.[272] Marion argues that the reduction of the given to givenness does not contradict the possibility of the phenomenon of the gift in its own right (the given).

The language of the gift should pervade God-thought. The concept of the gift developed by Marion can be applied to theology for explaining the reception of divine gifts. As Schrag suggests, this can be explained through a "hermeneutic of acknowledgement," rather than an "epistemology of recognition," which can be accomplished by bringing a horizontal dimension to the notion of return, as is found in the incarnation. Translating the incarnation into the language of the gift would mean that God's gift comes to presence in the historical visibility and tangibility in which God made himself known. This knowledge, as Schrag points out, is not an epistemological recognition based on metaphysics, but rather, a knowledge informed by a "hermeneutic of acknowledgement as attestation."[273] For this reason, the gift can be thought of as transgressing the "epistemology of recognition," that obligates the alleged aporia of acknowledging the gift with a "thank you." Gratitude, within the economy of exchange, is considered as return, but it does not

270. *Ibid.*, 107.
271. Marion, *Being Given*, 26, esp. 266ff. See also, Marion, "The Reason of the Gift," 116-122.
272. The scheme of exchange obligates an equal return according to the principle of identity. On the contrary, the reduced gift always gives more than itself, allows for a thing not being equal to itself. Marion, "The Reason of the Gift," 124.
273. Schrag, *Semantics of the Gift*, 117.

necessarily belong to the domain of exchange relations. In fact, one's gratitude in response to the divine gifts surpasses the vicious circle of economic exchange. Such a response is appropriate in the reception of divine gifts, and it belongs to the circuit (flow) of the gift, rather than the circling back of the gift to the giver, as a return, or reward. The circuit is not directed to the giver, but rather, to others. In this sense, one's response to the divine gifts is *re-turn* rather than return. The course is *re-turned* to the other, one's neighbour, as charity. As Schrag rightly observes, acknowledging a gift is "not to return something to the giver, but rather, to give to the other – to the third person, the neighbour, to the one who is nearby, both in physical and social space, and thus *continue* the giving."[274] Marion's metaphor of fatherhood is the example par excellence for such a *re-turn* of the *return*. This is the manner of return that we make in receiving the gift of God and the sacramental gift; the gift is *re-turned* as ethical engagement. "It is in this manner that giving is perpetuated as an expenditure, without return, enhancing the quality of life among the inhabitants of the earth in a drive toward justice and social solidarity."[275] In fact, it is the acknowledgement of the unconditional love that expects nothing in return. It can also assume the form of doxology, of liturgical praise. It is not as a return, but a response that spontaneously overflows from the heart, not out of obligation, but from gratitude. It is beyond the scheme of economic exchange relation, and belongs to the grammar of faith. The gift is beyond the structures of being. The gift in the Logos transcends the reciprocating economy of exchange relations.

The gift of God that generates further giving and empowers one to give is the grace of God, the gift of the Holy Spirit. It is the Holy Spirit who propels further giving. "The Spirit is the vehicle that is self-effacing, leading us further toward the perfect relationship of excess and mutuality in God."[276] The Holy Spirit is, at the same time, the gift, and that which mediates further giving. The excess of God's grace does not dissipate in the recipient, but the excess of the gift takes shape in the life of those who respond to it, by giving the gift further. Thus, excess takes the form of mutuality. The Christian understanding of giving does not negate the excess of giving, but affirms the extravagance of giving. The gift circulates in mutuality and sharing, living in and for/with each other (Acts 4:32-35; 2:42). Therefore, the return is not a symmetrical return to God which is humanly impossible, but a transfer of the

---

274. *Ibid.*, 119.
275. *Ibid.*, 120.
276. Webb, *The Gift Giving God*, 155.

gift as a response to God's giving which is gratuitous. The original gift of God's love cannot be repaid; it does not frighten one with a demand for infinite praise or reimbursement, although praise can be an appropriate gift to the gratuitous gift. Gratitude has to be purified from the scheme of economic exchange relations into a process of begetting further giving that perpetuates the gift itself, while not substituting it with thanksgiving. In other words, gratitude must find expression in joyous participation in the life of the gift. The gift itself is referred to as thanksgiving (2 Cor 9:11-12), and it is with real gratitude that one may increase and propagate the gift (Mt 25:14-20) by further giving (e.g. fatherhood/life). Nevertheless, the Christian concept of the gift solicits praise which leads to action, an attitude that translates into action.

7. A Sacramental Theology of Givenness

The language of the gift became widely accepted in contemporary discussions on the sacraments. The possibility of understanding Christian revelation in terms of givenness through the iconic figure of Christ, and the excess of givenness in the Spirit, helps one to reflect on the sacraments through the lens of givenness. God's givenness in the icon of Christ and the iconic experience of the gift of the Spirit as the fruit of the Pasch, constitute the self-giving image of God, whose givenness finds expression in the sacraments of the Church. Along with the theology of God's self-communication developed in the second chapter, it has been shown that the self-communication is continued in and through the Church and the sacraments. Much emphasis was laid on the Pneumatological dimension as foundational to the sacramentality of the Church. When we render it into the language of giving, it follows that it is the excess of the Spirit that is given to the Church that makes the Church a sacrament. The Church, as the icon of God's self-giving, contains and mediates the givenness of God in Christ and the Spirit. An idolatrous view confines one's understanding of the Church to an image of one's own making. It may lead to a tendency to identify the Church with an institutionalised Church accompanied by all its paraphernalia and blemishes, according to the limits of one's conceptual horizon. The iconic approach, on the other hand, takes one beyond and beneath, to the sacramental aspect which surpasses the splodge and scars of the Church as an earthly reality. Only when one arrives at a thinking wherein the possibility of envisioning the invisible is opened, may one come to really experience the incomprehensible mystery of the Church that mediates the presence of God. In fact, there takes place a crossing of the visible and the invisible, as in the icon, in the sacramental under-standing of the Church.

7.1. Sacramental Economy of the Gift

As has been shown, the giving and receiving involved in human relationships is patterned by the law of reciprocity and return. The concept of the gift has received diverse meanings and implications in the phenomenological, socio-logical and anthropological perspectives, even challenging the possibility of the gift. The very possibility of the gift has been challenged by Derrida, tak-ing into account the burden that gift-giving imposes upon the receiver, a bur-den which comes in the form of a return gift. The gift-giving that existed in traditional societies also demanded a return gift in smaller or greater degree, while acknowledging the status of the donor. Thus, an expected return, in any form, annuls the pure gratuity of gift-giving, despite the fact that the ex-change of gifts guarantees the ordering of the social and economic life of the society. This being the case, can the paradigm of the gift be applied in terms of God's giving? We must also acknowledge the fact that, as human beings, we can never make an adequate return to God. There is no proper sense in which the Church gives anything back to God. However, generally speaking, immaterial gifts such as reverence, praise and worship in the language of liturgy and sacrifice are considered to be various forms of gifts given to God. Nevertheless, can the pattern of economic exchange be applied to divine-human relations? Can we entertain a gift-exchange paradigm in God's giving in the sacraments? If we can, how do we understand the sacramental gift and our return, without conflicting the gratuity and graciousness of God? The diversity inherent in the notion of the gift itself points to the complexity of this issue.

7.1.1. The Mode of "Gift-exchange" in the Sacraments

The phenomenology of givenness and the gift provide a language divorced from that of Being and causality to explain the event that takes place in the sacraments. Contemporary sacramental theologians such as Chauvet, Power, and Marion incorporate the language of the gift in their sacramental theolo-gy.[277] In the following section, a sacramental understanding of the gift in

---

277. However, it has to be said that, apart from the commonalities, they differ in many re-spects in their understandings of the gift. As will be explained, Chauvet uses the concept of

dialogue with Chauvet, Marion, and Power will be proposed, drawing on, and applying the insights of the phenomenology of givenness. At the same time, this will be accomplished in a Pneumatological fashion. However, first, we will take up the issue of the gift-reception-return paradigm in contemporary sacramental theology, followed by the Pneumatological paradigm.

As has been pointed out, Chauvet's enunciation of the sacraments in terms of language and symbol, instead of instrumental causality, develops "*a fundamental theology of sacramentality*."[278] He applies this scheme to the understanding of Christian sacramental identity.[279] Accordingly, the Scripture is the Gift, the Sacraments fall under reception, and Ethics is seen as the return gift. This triple movement is a symbolic exchange over and against the market exchange which is a double movement.[280] In the scheme of Chauvet, that of gift-exchange, the logical structure is gift/reception/return gift. He understands the sacraments as mediations (against instruments), symbols (against signs) where God inscribes God's self in the human person and gives identity to the human person as believing subject, placed in a network of relationships, brotherhood and sisterhood. For him, liturgical language and symbols are the primary means for, and functions of, defining the identity or receiving oneself (grace), rather than understanding grace as an object we receive. Grace cannot be explained as an object that comes to the human person. Nonetheless, it can be understood as something that takes place internally and in relation to God and one another. To quote Chauvet:

> We can express [grace] only in the symbolic labor of birth it carries out in us: the labor of the ongoing passage to 'thanksgiving' – in this way we come forth as children of God – and to a 'living' – in this way we simultaneously come forth as brothers and sisters for others – which makes us co-respond to this God who gives grace and is revealed in Jesus.[281]

Chauvet appropriates into his sacramental theology the anthropological notion of the gift-exchange which existed in traditional societies. Chauvet's use

---

gift-exchange which is worked out in anthropological and sociological research, particularly the gift-exchange in the trajectory of Mauss and Lévi-Strauss.

278. Chauvet, *Symbol and Sacrament*, 1.

279. *Ibid.*, 267.

280. Chauvet explains how this triple structure forms Christian reality by re-reading the scriptural narratives and Church tradition (liturgy). See Chauvet, *Symbol and Sacrament*, 161-170, 268-277.

281. *Ibid.*, 446.

of Mauss and Strauss[282] in sacramental theology is based on the assumption that there are exchanges in society which transcend the order of utilitarian value. Employing this archaic notion to sacramental theology, he raises exchange to a symbolic order, over and against utility and market value, where the whole structure is entangled in obligatory generosity. Thus, he tries to reconcile reciprocity and generosity in the divine-human exchange that takes place in the sacramental exchange. He emphasises the superabundance and graciousness involving in gift-exchange. The "automatic laws" that govern the phenomenon of exchange, according to the cycle of reciprocity by Strauss, are the unconscious principles of the obligation to give, the obligation to return a gift, and the obligation to receive.[283] Bourdieu goes beyond Strauss and Mauss in arguing that, in practice, the cycle of reciprocity can be interrupted by ingratitude or rejection. There can be occasions in which the gift is confronted with non-acceptance or non-return, stagnating the intentional meaning of giving.[284] The flow of the cycle that operates in different stages of the exchange can be interrupted, obliterating the cycle of reciprocity. As Bourdieu points out, "[i]n reality, the gift may remain unreciprocated, when one obliges an ungrateful person; it may be rejected as an insult, inasmuch as it asserts or demands the possibility of reciprocity, and therefore, of recognition."[285] From the point of view of Bourdieu, Chauvet's application of gift-exchange does not take into account the possible interruption of the cycle of reciprocity which shatters the very possibility of the gift. For, according to Bourdieu, the act of gift-giving can always be "liable to fall flat and so, for a lack of response, to be stripped retrospectively of its intentional meaning."[286] Bourdieu calls our attention to the uncertainty that exists in the exchanges initiated in ordinary life, even regarding little gifts given between persons. Therefore, one cannot take it for granted that every gift obligates a return gift automatically. According to Bourdieu, "[t]he simple possibility that things might proceed otherwise than is laid down by the 'mechanical laws' of the cycles of reciprocity, is sufficient to change the whole experience of practice and, by the same token, its logic."[287]

---

282. Mauss, *The Gift in Archaic Societies*; Marcel Mauss and Clauve Lévi-Strauss, *Sociologie et anthropologie* (Paris: Presses Universitaires de France, 1950).

283. Lévi-Strauss, *Introduction to the Work of Marcel Mauss*, 43.

284. Bourdieu, *The Logic of Practice*, 98.

285. *Ibid.*

286. *Ibid.*, 105.

287. *Ibid.*, 99.

Also, there exists a power factor in the scheme of gift-exchange, which Bourdieu describes as symbolic power or symbolic violence. Thus there is a symbolic power in symbolic exchange, "an 'invisible' power which is 'misrecognized' as such and thereby 'recognised' as legitimate."[288] The concept of the gift that Chauvet employs in his sacramental theology is quite different from that of Marion, in that Chauvet advocates an obligatory generosity which implies an obligatory return gift, reducing the symbolic exchange into an economic exchange ruled by power and domination.[289] This seems to have the tendency of assuming the motives existing in market exchange. The market exchange is monitored by a direct transaction (a double movement). In fact, as Pilario contends, Chauvet's obligatory generosity reflects the inherent mechanism of power in the scheme of exchange, even though he tries to overcome it by raising exchange to the order of symbolic exchange. Therefore, gift giving is, in fact, power-laden. Chauvet has not taken into account the exercise of asymmetric power relations in material or symbolic exchange.[290] There is an intervening time between the gift and the return gift, wherein one finds an acknowledgement of the gift as gift, without a reduction of it to debt, which Pilario points out that both Chauvet and Bourdieu agree with. According to Chauvet, it is this intervening time factor that raises exchange to the realm of the symbolic. On the contrary, Bourdieu sees this intervening moment as the mystifying moment in which both power and domination appear through the back door.[291] Therefore, we purport to argue that, as far as the divine gifts are concerned, the free nature of God's gift and the human response cannot adequately be represented in such a scheme. In applying the scheme of exchange, as enunciated by Chauvet, to represent the divine *commercium* in the sacraments, we must hold certain reservations.

David N. Power develops a sacramental theology which is not grounded on the thought and the language of Being, but is based on the language of the

288. Pierre Bourdieu, *Language and Symbolic Power*, ed. John B. Thompson, trans. Gino Raymond and Matthew Adamson (Cambridge, U.K.: Polity Press, 1991), see introduction by Thompson, p. 23.

289. Daniel Franklin Pilario contents the model of gift-exchange as inadequate for a sacramental theology in the light of Pierre Bourdieu's critique of the anthropological understanding of gift-exchange ruled by a cycle of reciprocity. Daniel Franklin Pilario, "'Gift-Exchange' in Sacramentology: A Critical Assessment from the Perspective of Pierre Bourdieu," in *Contemporary Sacramental Contours of a God Incarnate*, ed. Lieven Boeve and Lambert Leijssen (Leuven: Peeters, 2001), 85-101.

290. Pilario, "'Gift-Exchange'," 89. See also Lintner, *Eine Ethik des Schenkens*, 61-62.

291. Pilario, "'Gift-Exchange'," 98.

gift.[292] He uses the metaphor of the gift in order to explain what is given and done in the sacramental worship, viewing sacramental dispensation as an economy of the gift.[293] Power tries to emphasize the gratuity of God's gift in the sacraments, reversing the order of giving by placing stress on the gratuitous initiative, as in the incarnation. Thus, the employment of the expression *commercium* to designate God's gift-giving is distinct from economic exchange. The sacramental economy of exchange is different from economic exchange, because the gifts that the people bring are not the offer of something to God, but rather, so that the gifts be taken up into the divine exchange that takes place in the incarnation. Power is aware of the complexities pertaining to the phenomenological and philosophical discussions on the gift and the aporia of a pure, free and gratuitous gift. He argues that the category of the gift can be used to explain divine gifts, especially the sacramental gift. The language of gift was commonly used to explain the gift of grace in the sacraments. However, an indiscriminate application in the present context of discussion regarding the phenomenon of the gift will obscure the gift of God in the sacramental economy. In this regard, Power cautions the need for freeing the use of the gift from the thought of obligatory return and reciprocity, thereby creating room for God's gratuity in the divine gift.[294] It seems that Power has woven a theology of the sacraments in terms of the language of the gift, integrating the phenomenological insights of Marion, and reconciling the Christian understanding of reciprocity and gratuity in a consistent manner.

---

292. Power acknowledges the mediatory function of language, and considers the sacrament as a language event. According to him, "[a]ll reality is given to us through language that is embedded in being and culture." Power, *Sacrament*, 76. He emphatically points out the relevance of having recourse to phenomenology in contemporary sacramental thinking. As he says, "[i]n philosophy and theology ... there is the move from metaphysics to phenomenology and hermeneutics, preferring the interpretation of language to the self-assured guidance of thoughts and ideas." *Ibid.*, 15.

293. Power prefers the term "economy" to "exchange" from liturgical history and its richness in designating the wonderful exchange that takes place in the sacraments. He examines how the English word "economy" (Greek *oikonomia*, Latin *commercium*) refers to an exchange or sharing in the gift, which ultimately, maintains the ordering of the community. See Power, "Economy of Gift," 145-148; Power, *Sacrament*, 276-277.

294. Power, "Economy of Gift," 154.

7.1.2. Graciousness and Gratuity

If the metaphor of the gift is employed in the understanding of the sacramental gift, does it obliterate the notions of graciousness and gratuity in God's giving? Power explains how Hélène Cixous' insight of a "womanly" gift[295] helps to explain the sacramental economy in terms of the gift. According to Cixous, the gift is possible based on gratuity, because it is based on freedom. She emphasises the freedom the recipient exercises in acting or living out the gift, independent of the nature of the gift itself or the expectation of the donor. The recipient acts responsibly, entirely out of an appreciation for the gift as such. Nevertheless, in living out from the gift, there is also a mutuality, owing to the fact that the gift has been passed from the giver to the recipient, which, in some way, gives room for an exchange and participation in the gift. The analogy of "motherhood" or "parenthood" explains the possibility of such a gift, which allows room for gratuity. In giving birth, the mother gives life. The real reception, as far as the child is concerned, is to live this gift of life freely, not as a return gift to the mother or parents out of obligation, but rather, through an appreciation of that gift. The enhancement of life may continue by perpetuating this gift by giving to others from the gift the child has received. The "womanly" gift parallels Marion's "fatherhood" image.

Power uses the image of the gift of life in his understanding of the gift.[296] While applying this analogy to the sacraments, he emphasises the phenomenon of giving, because the image of motherhood or fatherhood is a gift which is irreducible to mere biological factors, but is, rather, a constant giving. According to Power, the gratuity and the generosity of the gift can be retained, only by preserving the distance between the giver and the gift. In the ordinary understanding of gift-giving, there is a tendency to identify the gift with the giver, or the giver is conceived as being represented by the gift. Also,

---

295. Power, *Sacrament*, 279-280. Cixous develops a "feminine" notion of generosity and gratuity in contrast to the "masculine" notion. The law of return underlying classical economies is masculine. She draws attention to the maternal gifts that escape the logic of appropriation. The masculine is animated by the fear of "expropriation," whereas the feminine is characterised by her "capacity to depropriate without self-interest." Hélène Cixous, "Sorties: Out and Out: Attacks/Ways Out/Forays," in *The Logic of the Gift: Toward and Ethic of Generosity*, ed. Alan D. Schrift (New York, London: Routledge, 1997), 151, 159. See also Verena Andermatt Conley, *Hélène Cixous: Writing the Feminine* (Lincoln, NE: University of Nebraska Press, 1984). Marion's explanation of "fatherhood" as a phenomenological symbol in order to explain givenness, as explained above, is complementary to Cixous's "womanly" gift, disregarding the gender consciousness of both authors.

296. Power, *Sacrament*, 280.

there is no fusion between the giver and the gifted (givee), even though there is mutuality and participation. Besides, the response of the gifted consists, not in a giving back, but rather, in accepting from the giver and finding union with the giver. This way of applying the notion of the gift to sacramental gift is actually in line with the theology of the gift that has been developed using the insights of Marion, Webb and Schrag. Therefore, the response of the "gifted" in the reception of the sacramental gift is nothing other than a *return* in living out the grace that is given in the sacraments, not as a giving back, but in the manner of further givings, not out of obligation, but out of pure appreciation of the gift *as such*.

7.1.3. The Gifted (l'adonné)

The gift is irreducible to the given. The pure gift can be thought of under the rubric of exchange relation between humans, provided the distance and otherness of the giver and the gifted remain intact, ensuring the freedom of the recipient to live out the gift given appreciating the gift for its own sake. The metaphor of life in its pure form is an example for this, as Power explains it.[297] He distinguishes three qualities in giving, which he borrows from Marion which provide an analogy of what is taking place in the sacraments.[298] They are: 1) the analogy of motherhood which symbolises a continuous giving without obscuring the distance between the giver and the givee while allowing participation and mutuality without obligating a return, 2) a gratuitous giving which moves towards futurity, enhancing life (not 'present'), a giving that increases the measure of giving as it proceeds toward the future, and 3) giving and the gift as parallel to the saying and said, without fusing or identifying them, invoking a response from whom the call is addressed. According to this analogy of giving, sacraments can be interpreted as God's giving in the Word and the Spirit. The gift of life, forgiveness, the communion with Christ and the gift of the Spirit are given, giving a share in God's life of love, but at the same time, retaining the distance of God as incomprehensible mystery which is beyond conceptualisation and naming. The sacramental gift does not consist merely of the present, but is oriented towards eschatological fulfilment and the giving increases in measure each moment. The *divine commercium* implies this participation and mutuality in

---

297. *Ibid.*, 279-280.
298. *Ibid.*, 280-281. See also Marion, *Being Given*, 124-152; Marion, *Prolegomena to Charity*, 79-118; Marion, "The Reason of the Gift," 101-134.

God's gift of himself, a covenantal relationship with God and the people and the life into the fullness of that relationship. Through the sacraments, the believing subjects are not repaying or returning anything back to God, but by receiving the life in Christ, enter into the mainstream of love, by entering into a communion with the Father through Christ and the Spirit. The response is not by way of returning anything to God, but rather, as bestowed upon, the believers become bestowers, as the gifted become givers or witnesses of that love, living a life of love for love. It only acknowledges the gift given and lives out of it. It is relational, Trinitarian in character. This is not a responsibility to be met in justice, nor an obligation to give back, but only a freedom to go forth, to live out of the communion in love that is God-given.[299] Thus, briefly speaking, the giving is perpetuated by a gracious living in love for love's sake, a giving irreducible to return, a *re-turn* to the other.

8. Conclusion

In the present chapter, we have made an attempt to situate God's self-communication in Christ and the Holy Spirit within the framework of the phenomenology of givenness, as developed by Marion. In so doing, we have extended the scope of phenomenology to the reflection of the revelation of God in Christ and the Spirit, an innovation which Marion himself has initiated. It has been shown that God's gift of love that gives in *excess* (saturated phenomenon) in the figure of Christ and in the phenomenon of the Spirit, constitutes a single event of God's revelation. Different notions of the gift have been discussed, with the view of sorting out a plausible theology of the gift within which God's givenness in the Word and the Spirit and in the sacraments of the Church can be explained. Accordingly, the notion of pure gift against the problematisation of the gift and the question of return has been retained. Moreover, it was also argued that the Christian notion of return (response) can be well situated within the framework of the pure gift, rather than within the scheme of symbolic-exchange, with its offshoot of obligatory generosity. The concept of the gift that has been defended in this chapter has the benefit of developing a theology of the gift, upholding the

---

299. Power, *Sacrament*, 156. In this regard, it seems to me that one can question Power's expression "economy of gift," because "economy" or *commercium* implies reciprocity that governs relationship. This expression sounds more in tune with Chauvet, while in details, as he explains, it is more filial to the gift-giving according to Marion, which goes in line with the image of fatherhood.

graciousness and gratuitousness of God's giving and the free response of human beings. It can be claimed that the theology of the gift that has been sketched out so far offers us the possibility of reflecting on sacramental presence and grace, in terms of the gift outside the metaphysical scheme. This task will be taken on in the following chapter with special reference to the Eucharist.

CHAPTER FOUR

THE SACRAMENTAL GIFT

The primary interest of this work has been that of the realization of the sacraments against the background of the notions of sacramental efficacy as symbolic efficacy and the efficacy by the Holy Spirit. Having defined the role of the Spirit, through systematic reflection on, and a phenomenological reading of, God's self-communication in preceding chapters, it is now possible to formulate a plausible theology of the sacraments integrating Pneumatological and symbolic dimensions. Therefore, in the present chapter, the main task will be to develop a theology of sacramental presence and grace, in terms of gift from both a Pneumatological and phenomenological perspective. To be more precise, as delineated in the third chapter, we understand symbolic as iconic, as distinct from the traditional understanding of symbol that is made in contrast to sign, metaphor, etc., although the icon encapsulates many of the features shared by them. Therefore, this chapter envisages an explanation of the sacraments as "iconic-symbols" and symbolic efficacy as "iconic-efficacy." For the sake of lucidity and precision, the scope of this study will be limited, particularly, to the key notions of sacramental presence and grace, with special reference to the sacrament of the Eucharist.

1. Gift of Presence

Thus far, it has already explained how the notion of the gift is connected to the concept of presence: the relationship between the present and the presence. In the ordinary sense, the gift is understood as present, the gift given. Therefore, the question of sacramental presence pertains to the question of the given in the present, the gift of presence.[1] In other words, it relates to the fundamental question of the *how* and *what* of the sacramental presence or in

1. "Present" designates two things for us, namely, present as gift and present (the given) as "here" and "now" with reference to the past and the future. Therefore, "presence" refers to what is given in the present (gift/temporality).

other words, the relationship between the visible and the invisible which has become the basic question of this project. Marion's phenomenological insights, discussed at length throughout this work, allow for the possibility of re-visiting the sacramental gift and the gift of presence as opened up by Marion himself.[2]

1.1. Beyond "Metaphysics of Presence" and "Negative Theology"

Marion develops a non-metaphysical concept of presence according to the post-modern sensibility. Employing the Pseudo-Dionysius' notion of God as beyond affirmation (metaphysics of presence) and negation (negative theology), he ascribes presence, the full capacity to appear itself in excess, as in the icon. In fact, the basic stance that has been taken in this work distances us from the "metaphysics of presence" which is based on the ultimacy of Being and human conceptuality. On the contrary, presence cannot be reduced to mere absence either. In this regard, Marion opens the means for overcoming the two traditional ways of explaining presence, namely, the language of affirmation (*kataphasis*) and negation (*apophasis*), which according to Marion, fall under the impasse created by metaphysics of presence, assigning full capacity to the notion of the icon. Accordingly, the category of the icon (in contrast to the idol) opens up the possibility of a "third way," (the way of not-naming or de-nomination) within which sacramental presence can be thought of as beyond affirmation and negation.[3] Marion contends that the

2. Marion, *God Without Being*, 161-182; Marion, *Prolegomena to Charity*, 124-152. The phenomenology of givenness proposed by Marion opened the floor for serious discussions among theologians. A few examples are: Stijn Van den Bossche, "A Possible Present for Theology; Gerard Loughlin, "Transubstantiation: Eucharist as Pure Gift," in *Christ: The Sacramental World*, ed. David Brown and Ann Loades (London: SPCK, 1996); Mitchell, "Mystery and Manners;" Nathan D. Mitchell, *Meeting Mystery* (New York: Orbis Books, 2006); Philipp Wolfram Rosemann, "Postmodern Philosophy and J.-L. Marion's Eucharistic Realism," in *The Mystery of Faith: Reflections on the Encyclical Ecclesia de Eucharistia*, ed. James McEvoy and Maurice Hogan (Dublin: Columba Press, 2005).

3. Marion, "In the Name," 24-42. See also Mitchell, *Meeting Mystery*, 271. In developing the notion of presence, Marion relies on the so-called "negative theology" of Dionysius. He rejects the general proposition of identifying Dionysius with an *apophatic* theology. According to him, what Dionysius does is not make a choice between *apophatic* and *kataphatic* theologies, but rather, opts for a "third way" which understands God beyond Being. So what Dionysius does is to establish a triplicity of eminence, cause and incomprehensibility, rather than make a choice between *apophatic* and *kataphatic* modes of speaking about the reality. Marion writes, "de-nomination ... does not end up in a 'metaphysics of presence' that does not call itself as such. Rather, it ends up as a pragmatic theology of absence – where the name is

critique of the metaphysical concept of presence is actually not the rejection of the presence of God, but rather, a corrective to a totalitarian concept of presence. According to him, the death of the idolatrous concept of God makes an "empty space of a new presence."[4] Therefore, the abyss created by the "disfigured figure of Christ" is not mere "emptiness," but an "empty space" which is saturated with "presence, whose visibility opens up to an "absence." The self-giving God gives himself in maximum phenomenality in the abyss of the Cross and the resurrection. Thus, what Marion advocates is a "pragmatic theology of absence." Therefore, presence can no longer be subjected to metaphysical idolatry, nor can it be left to be informed by a negative theology. By the "pragmatic theology of absence," Marion does not attempt to establish the non-presence of God, but rather, to protect God from the "metaphysics of presence." "By theology of absence … we mean, not the non-presence of God, but the fact that the name that God is given, the name which gives God, which is given as God … *serves to shield God from presence...*and offers him precisely as an exception to presence."[5] Marion continues, "the Name does not name God as an essence; it designates what passes beyond every name. The Name designates what one does not name and says that one does not name it."[6] Therefore, the function of Name is no longer to incarnate God into predicative language, but by naming, the believing subjects are inscribed in the very horizon of God, according to Marion, as it happens at baptism.[7] In brief, the mode of presence that Marion develops through his theological works is a presence that goes *beyond* affirmation and

---

given as having no name, as not giving the essence, and having nothing but this absence to make manifest; a theology where hearing happens." Marion, *In Excess*, 155. Marion says, "the paradox or paradoxes [the saturated phenomenon/phenomenon of revelation] does not have to choose between [k]ataphasis and apophasis any more than between saturation and shortage of intuition; it uses them all in order to push to its end the phenomenality of what shows itself only insofar as it gives itself." Marion, *Being Given*, 245.

    4. Marion, *The Idol and Distance*, 36. In this sense, Marion interprets the "death of God" of Nietzsche as the death of the idolatrous concept of God. He writes, "what the last (or next-to-last) metaphysical word calls the "death of God" does not signify that God passes out of play, but indicates the *modern* face of his insistent and eternal fidelity." "[N]o "death of God" goes as far as the desertion of Christ by the Father on Good Friday; and from the bottom of the inferal abyss that opened at the very heart of our history, once and for all, there issues the insurpassable filiation that eternally confesses the paternity of the Father." Marion, *The Idol and Distance*, xxxv.

    5. Marion, "In the Name," 37. See also Marion, *In Excess*, 156.

    6. *Ibid.*, 157.

    7. *Ibid.*

negation, a presence that gives itself in absence.[8] Furthermore, presence is given in the mode of the icon, and according to the principle of distance.

1.2. Iconic Presence

The iconic mode of presence that Marion sketches out, along the lines of the phenomenology of givenness, is over and against the metaphysical notion of presence. It has necessary concomitant results for the understanding of sacramental presence in general. The fundamental principle upon which Marion's phenomenology operates, which has gained wide acceptance, is the notion of distance whereby the giver retains his identity in gift-giving. In other words, as Martis expresses, the act of giving involves a withholding on the part of the giver. It is a "distance-in-nearness," according to the norm of the icon.[9] Applying this notion to God would imply that God, as the giver, gifts his presence sacramentally, without forfeiting his divine identity in the given. This is not a concept of presence that rules out God's presence, but rather, allows room for God's unconditional and free self-giving, regardless of human conceptual and linguistic horizons.[10] In this sense, presence cannot be identified with the "present" (the gift/the given), despite the inseparable relationship existing between them. Therefore, as Power explains, God's gift of himself in the Word and the Spirit, realized for the Church, in the sacramental gift, consists, not in the present or in the given; but in giving himself. The divine remains a mystery, without being possessed by the human person.[11] Thus, the iconic mode of presence explains presence as givenness *as such*, before being subject to one's own conceptual and linguistic affirmations.

Marion explains the "withdrawal of the divine" as the ultimate manifestation of the phenomenon of revelation, as in the paradigmatic figure of Christ.[12] The paradoxical absence of the divine on the Cross and in the Resurrec-

8. We lay emphasis on "beyond" in the sense that the concept of presence that we develop relying on Marion, is not a middle position "between" *kataphasis* and *apophasis*.

9. John Martis, "Postmodernism and God as Giver," *The Way* 36 (1996): 241; R. Kevin Seasoltz, *God's Gift Giving: In Christ and through the Spirit* (New York: Continuum, 2007), 8-9.

10. Seasoltz, *God's Gift Giving*, 9.

11. Power, *Sacrament*, 280.

12. Marion, *The Idol and Distance*, 80. Marion explains how the theme of the withdrawal of the divine in Hölderlin and the twilight of the idols in Nietzsche mark the mode of divine manifestation in absence, and its conformity to Dionysius and the biblical revelation and operates in terms of distance. He makes a detailed exposition of this theme with reference to

tion turns into the manifestation of divine presence through withdrawal.[13] Moreover, the gift of the Spirit turns the profound sadness of the disciples into triumphant joy. Hölderlin writes:

> Therefore he sent them
>
> The spirit, and mightily trembled the house.[14]

The Eucharistic teaching of Christ (Lk 24:27,30) makes the disciples realize the necessity of the effacement of his flesh as well as the corporality of the consecrated bread. The eventual disappearance that follows indicates how the appearance coincides with apparent disappearance. However, remarkably, true ascent to the faith in the presence occurs through the gift of the Spirit at Pentecost. It is the Holy Spirit who allows one to endure the emptiness of withdrawal. As Marion states,

> God's present is not inscribed in a presence that a possessive gaze could bind. The present reveals itself in the withdrawal of presence, because that withdrawal harbors in itself, and delivers by a gift, the only presence of the present, and the sole present of a presence. It is only in such a withdrawal that presence and the present can be conjoined. This is what is rendered thinkable by the recourse to the Spirit, this is what the disciples miss. The latter do not reach, even after the gift of the Spirit … [because] the insistent and poorly received gift of the Spirit becomes familiar only if the withdrawal, at first, that of Christ, is opened to us, as a danger and as a salvation.[15]

The theme of withdrawal and distance gives an impetus to contemporary sacramental theology to favour a "pragmatic theology of absence."[16] As Lambert Leijssen points out, God's presence can be thought of and experienced only "in terms of absent/present, veiled/unveiled, transcen-

---

Friedrich Nietzsche, Johann Christian Hölderlin and Dyonisius. See, Marion, *The Idol and Distance*, 27-197. Hölderlin (1770-1843) is a renowned German lyric poet who blended classical and Christian themes in his works. Both Heidegger and Nietzsche were fascinated and influenced by the works of Hölderlin. *Johann Christian Friedrich Hölderlin*, available from http://www.kirjasto.sci.fi/holderli.htm. (2003, accessed April 12, 2008).

13. Marion, *The Idol and Distance*, 118-120.

14. Friedrich Hölderlin, *Patmos*, available from http://hor.de/gedichte/friedrich_hoelderlin/patmos.htm. (Gemeinfreie Gedichte, accessed September 2, 2008).

15. Marion, *The Idol and Distance*, 119-120. Marion says that Hölderlin understands the full and definitive gift of the Spirit as an eschatological event. However, we may argue that the fullness of the empowerment of the gift of the Spirit takes place after the withdrawal of Christ as the fruit of the resurrection at Pentecost.

16. Mitchell, "Eucharist in Post-Modern Theology," 135.

dent/immanent, invisible/visible."[17] He explains, further, that God's presence emerges as "present-absent," "as a continuous glimpse (*glimmer*, not glitter)" of the withdrawing Mystery.[18] As Van den Bossche clarifies, however, God's withdrawal, or distance must not be understood as non-presence, but rather, as the eternal and faithful presence. Therefore, the real presence of God is by right of distance, withdrawal, or absence. The Judeo-Christian religion provides us, not with the image of an absent Invisible God, but we encounter the Invisible Himself in immanence without any distance.[19] The view of God's presence in terms of withdrawal and absence is located at the center of the Christian message, the mystery of Christ, as manifested in revelation with Easter as the point of departure. It is important to see that, as in Hölderlin, both for Chauvet and Marion, the Emmaus story functions as the interpretive key for the understanding of sacramental presence after Easter.[20] As Chauvet states, believing in the Eucharistic presence after Easter is possible only by consenting to an "absence" which is symbolically, "the presence-of-the-absence of God."[21] The innovative notion of sacramental presence is the understanding of a "real presence" as atemporal and non-empirical.[22] Thus, the concept of real presence is no more reduced to a "thing," but rather, relocated from a "thing" to the gift which the assembly as such, receives. Therefore, the divine gives itself in the icon, as maximum phenomenality, as excess, and as the saturation of saturation, according to the norm of withdrawal and distance, without being limited by subject and language. The divine gives itself in the icon, because the icon has a theological status, as it first and foremost refers to the iconic figure of Christ.[23] Therefore, in what follows, we will

17. Lambert J. Leijssen, *With the Silent Glimmer of God's Spirit: A Postmodern Look at the Sacraments*, trans. Marie Baird (New York/Mahwah, NJ: Paulist Press, 2006), 24.

18. Leijssen, *The Silent Glimmer*, 26.

19. Stijn Van den Bossche, "From the Other's Point of View: The Challenge of Jean-Luc Marion's Phenomenology to Theology," in *Religious Experience and Contemporary Theological Epistemology* (Leuven: Leuven University Press, 2005), 65.

20. Chauvet, *Symbol and Sacrament*, 161ff; Louis-Marie Chauvet, "The Broken Bread as Theological Figure of Eucharistic Presence," in *Sacramental Presence in a Postmodern Context* (Leuven: University Press, 2001), 236-262; Marion, "They Recognised Him," 145-152.

21. Chauvet, *Symbol and Sacrament*, 405.

22. Marion, *Prolegomena to Charity*, 124.

23. "The icon has a theological status, the reference of the visible face to the intention that envisages, culminating in the reference of the Christ to the Father: for the formula *eikon tou theou aoratou* concerns first the Christ. It would remain to specify in what measure this attribution has a normative value, far from constituting just one application of the icon among others." Marion, *God Without Being*, 23-24.

develop a concept of presence which accedes to withdrawal and distance, according to the mode of the icon. It can be argued that the theological status of the icon enables us to explain the sacraments as iconic-symbols whereby God's self-gift is realized in maximum phenomenality as the saturated phenomenon. This will be discussed with special reference to the Eucharist.

1.3. The Eucharistic Gift

The Eucharist is generally regarded as gift. The Eucharistic gift is the perfect model for every gift, because "the Eucharist is the pure gift of God."[24] In the sacrament of the Eucharist, Christ gives himself to the community unconditionally and unreservedly. However, is it possible to understand the Eucharistic gift against the backdrop of the "problematisation" of the gift? Can we articulate God's unconditional giving in the sacraments, particularly in the Eucharistic gift (present), in the light of the theology of givenness? Can we retain the notion of "real presence" according to a theology which cancels out the giver, givee, and the gift? Does the giving of Christ, as self-giving love in the Eucharist, entangles human persons in an irrevocable contract and infinite debt (covenantal aspect)? How do we explain the "reality" of Eucharistic gift and presence, according to the notion of pure gift as retained by Marion? The present reflection, in this regard, has to do with the question of transubstantiation. However, in pursuing these discussions, the intention is not to reject the legitimacy and weight of explaining the Eucharistic presence. Instead, the current argument does insist on is the inadequacy of delimiting "presence" in a closed system. Therefore, emphatically, we stress the real presence, which is primarily a matter of faith, as the "champion of transubstantiation," honestly confessed.[25]

Within the context of the discussions concerning the problematisation of the gift, the Eucharistic gift can be thought of solely in terms of an *a priori* givenness that precedes the gift, before being dissipated into the circle of return. In other words, the originary givenness of God is to be located prior to the Eucharistic gift. In what follows, we will develop a plausible way of

24. Gerard Loughlin, *Telling God's Story: Bible, Church and Narrative Theology* (Cambridge: Cambridge University Press, 1996), 226.

25. In this connection, we are reminded of the attitude that Aquinas, the champion of transubstantiation entertained toward the Eucharistic mystery. At the beginning of the account of transubstantiation, Aquinas reminds us that "we could never know by our senses that the real body of Christ and his blood are in this sacrament, but only by our faith which is based on the authority of God." Aquinas, *Summa Theologiae*, 3a.75:1.

understanding sacramental presence, in terms of givenness, addressing the aforementioned questions seriously.

1.3.1. Eucharistic 'Present' and 'Presence'

Marion's thought is "[E]ucharistic in its very core."[26] His phenomenology of givenness provides a better explanation of the relationship between the visible and the invisible aspects of the sacraments, without yielding to idolatry. Accordingly, Eucharistic presence can be interpreted as Christ's presence in the present (gifts of bread and wine), as making presence in the present here and now. In other words, presence cannot be identified with what is present (the given). Mitchell writes, "[s]acraments are situations in which Christ's mode of presence is perceived as "absence," since, by their nature, sacramental signs are self-effacing, kenotic; they draw us beyond themselves to a reality they may embody, but never exhaust."[27] Therefore, the "coming-into- presence" can be understood in terms of "excess," as incomprehensible. As Marion points out, the task is entirely theological, and it consists of examining the following question, "can the Eucharistic presence of Christ as consecrated bread and wine determine, starting from itself and itself alone, the conditions of its own reality?" Furthermore, this, he claims, can be done reflecting on the Eucharistic presence, starting "from the present, but the present must be understood, first, as a gift that is given." The manner of presence under consideration does not pertain to "the *here* and *now* of the present," but rather, "*of the present, that is to say of the gift*."[28] The crux of the issue consists in articulating presence, starting from the gift that realises "presence in the present."

The Eucharist gives itself paradoxically, as in the paradoxical figure of Christ on the Cross. The way in which the Eucharist gives itself, in the "anteriority, exteriority, and materiality of the sacrament" is exposed to idolatry.[29] Indeed, the Eucharist, understood iconically, as the "visible" of the "invisible," reinforces the irreducibility of God's presence, Christ's presence to one's own horizons, because Eucharistic presence is fundamentally marked by an "absence" in the mode of the icon. God's gracious gift of the Eucharist discloses itself while concealing it, retaining the radical difference and other-

---

26. Rosemann, "Postmodern Philosophy," 231.
27. Nathan D. Mitchell, "'But Only Say the Word'," *Worship* 80 (2006): 455.
28. Marion, *God Without Being*, 171.
29. Chauvet, *Symbol and Sacrament*, 402.

ness of God. As Chauvet explains, the Eucharistic presence is not "simple *esse* of a mere thing," but Christ's *"coming-into-presence"* in the Eucharistic under the mode of *absence* of the *sacramentum* of the bread and wine, in the emptiness of the broken bread.[30] Thus, the Eucharist is the *"paradigmatic figure of the presence-of-the absence of God."*[31] In the Eucharist, the gracious gift of God is received in the species of bread and wine. As Chauvet puts it, "by offering it, the Church recognises it as the gift of God's very self, as the *autocommunication* of God's very self in Christ."[32] As will be explained, what is given in the present, here and now, is given by the past and the future.

1.3.2. Critique of the 'Real Presence'

Marion attempts to liberate the notion of presence from the so-called "metaphysics of presence" which epitomises the Western understanding of sacramental presence, especially Christ's "real presence" in the Eucharist. Marion's interpretation of presence begins pointing out, to what the sacramental presence should not be reduced. His first objection is against the understanding of substantial presence that reduces Eucharistic presence to a delimited thing that is at one's disposal. Confining sacramental presence to a place implies limiting the excess of God's giving in the sacraments, the body and blood of the risen Christ, to a natural and manipulable thing.[33] Marion cautions about two forms of idolatries which arise from the mistaken notion of presence. The first idolatry is *metaphysical* which consists of a mistaken notion of transubstantiation that "fixes and freezes" Christ's presence in an "available, permanent, handy and delimited thing." The danger involved in

---

30. *Ibid.*, 404-408. Leijssen calls the emptiness that enthralls the broken bread as *kenosis*. Leijssen, *The Silent Glimmer of the Spirit*, 26, 28. The presence-absence dialectics of sacramental presence as enunciated by Chauvet is not strictly identical with that of Marion's understanding of presence in terms of the icon. However, it is important to note that Chauvet is aware of the idolatry which is likely to occur in experiencing the divine. He explains this in terms of the notions of the icon and the idol. See Chauvet, *Symbol and Sacrament*, 216-220.

31. *Ibid.*, 405.

32. *Ibid.*, 398.

33. Aquinas answers the question whether Christ was present in the bread and wine "as in a place," with a definitive "no." *Utrum corpus Christi sit in hoc sacramento sicut in loco? He responds: Corpus Christi non est in hoc sacramento secundum proprium modum quantitatis dimensivae, sed magis secundum modum substantiae* ("The body of Christ is not in this sacrament according to its own natural mode of quantitative dimension, but rather according to the mode of substance"). Aquinas, *Summa Theologiae*, 3a.60:5.

this metaphysical thinking is a sort of idolatry, whereby the community construes the real *presence* as something at their disposal. As Marion observes, the community

> seeks to place "God" [in contrast to the crossed out God] at its disposition like a thing, its thing, to reassure its identity and strength, its determination in that thing. Of this "God" made thing, one would expect precisely nothing but *real* presence: presence reduced to the dimensions of a thing, a thing that is as much disposed to "honor by its presence."[34]

In this way, transubstantiation can be misrepresented as "the imposture of an idolatry that imagines itself to honour "God" when it heaps praises on his pathetic "canned" substitute (the reservation of the Eucharist), exhibited as an attraction (display of the Holy Sacrament), brandished like a banner (processions), and so on."[35] Therefore, it is necessary to go beyond this distorted, idolatrous concept of the real presence.

The second idolatry which Marion identifies is *psychological*, which replaces presence from a "thing" to the "consciousness of the community"; what he rejects is transposing the real presence into the human subject. He rejects this, because, according to this notion, the presence of Christ is not received as a gift through the priest who acts *in persona Christi*, but rather, Christ's presence is dependent on the subjective consciousness, words, acts, and intentions of the community.[36] Thus, presence is *made* through a "calculating will," as Chauvet expresses it.[37] Accordingly, presence is relocated from the bread and wine to the collective consciousness of the community. In this sense, presence is measured by the will, attention or consciousness of the community. This leads to a minimalist understanding of presence that en-

---

34. Marion, *God Without Being*, 164.

35. *Ibid.*, 164. Marion neither rejects nor underestimates the traditional liturgical practices, but only suggests a proper understanding of real presence is of high significance in order to appreciate Eucharistic contemplation, adoration and other liturgical practices. Rosemann, "Marion's Eucharistic Realism," 233.

36. Such an understanding of sacramental presence as Marion refers to are particularly those progressive ideas (transcriptions of transubstantiation) called transignification, transfinalisation etc. For a concise treatment of these notions, see Paul H. Jones, *Christ's Eucharistic Presence: A History of the Doctrine* (New York: Peter Lang, 1994), 90ff; Powers, *Eucharistic Theology*, 11-179; Edward Schillebeeckx, *The Eucharist*, trans. N. D. Smith (New York: Sheed & Ward, 1968), 89-151. The "psychological idolatry" can be compared with the worship of the divine in Hinduism. The image of the deity becomes presence of the divine only insofar as the divine is invoked on the idol by the priest or the devotee. The deity is present to the devotee as long as she is present to the divine.

37. Chauvet, *Symbol and Sacrament*, 61. Italics mine.

dures as long as the community is present. Therefore, in brief, both these idolatries are to be rejected, because their result is a "God held hostage by bread or by folk, that is, a God who no longer gives freely, sovereignly, excessively, and inexhaustibly."[38] Explaining sacramental presence in terms of givenness enables one to overcome the aforesaid mistaken notions of sacramental presence.

1.3.3. The Real Presence as Given

The Church's Eucharistic faith calls us to believe in a unique and mystical reality in the consecrated species, although the species remain bread and wine. Is it possible to explain this mystery of faith, according to the phenomenology of givenness as enunciated by Marion? In order to remain faithful to the Eucharistic teaching of the Church, a plausible theology of presence that maintains the true, substantial and real presence of Christ in the Eucharist must be developed. Marion's phenomenology of givenness helps us to understand the Eucharist as the saturated phenomenon, in which God's givenness gives itself in maximum phenomenality. He himself is convinced of the opening to reflect even on the sacramental presence through the category of saturated phenomenon. This is clear from Marion's address to a group of bishops in June 2000 in Lourdes at the colloquium on the Eucharist: "[W]e are, exactly, before *this*. We are even before an *exemplary case* of the *saturated phenomenon*."[39]

Having unveiled the erroneous interpretations of Eucharistic presence in order to overcome them, Marion develops a plausible theology of real presence in terms of the gift. Nevertheless, the question of presence is legitimate, and it requires adequate explanation, but what is important is the utmost priority of the gift before any conceptualisation or explanation. "A gift, and this is one above all, does not require, first, that one explain it, but, indeed, that one receive it."[40] Marion upholds the "objective reality" of Christ's presence in the Eucharist.[41] He considers the real presence as the culmination of a

---

38. Mitchell, *Meeting Mystery*, 271.

39. Jean-Luc Marion, "Réaliser la présence réelle," *La Maison-Dieu* 225 (2001): 26. Translation from Emmanuel Falque (ed.), *Larvatus Pro Deo: Jean-Luc Marion's Phenomenology and Theology*, ed. Kevin Hart (Notre Dame, IN: University of Notre Dame Press, 2007), 195.

40. Marion, *God Without Being*, 162.

41. John Paul II, *Encyclical Letter Ecclesia de Eucharistia: On the Eucharist in Its Relationship to the Church* (Boston, MA: Pauline Books and Media, 2003), no. 15. The encyclical

progressive manifestation of the Infinite (theophany of God's infinite love) in the finite, which finds expression in creation, in the history of Israel and, radically, in the Word Incarnate. The mystery of transubstantiation is the concrete expression of God's infinite love, poured out through God's Son. The love of God enters the finite world in the form of lowly food. In all these theophanies, God's entering into the finite, in order to offer or communicate God's love, is entirely a gratuitous gift, a gift made possible by abandoning his divinity. God's abandoning in the incarnation and in the Eucharist is very radical in the sense that "in the former, Christ abandons his life for our salvation, subjecting himself to humiliation, torture, and death; in the latter, God's 'gift of self goes right to the point where he abandons himself as a thing'."[42] Thus, in the Eucharist, the reality of Christ is conjoined to the finite things: the species of bread and wine, without being absorbed into the sign (the species remain only as accidents). In this connection, it is significant to note that Marion tries to overcome the idolatry of localising presence to a thing, by distinguishing between the "given" and the "present" (here, the bread and wine). The given exceeds what is given in the present.

Marion's concept of real presence pivots on the dialectics of the terms real and presence that compose the expression, "real presence."[43] They are two closely related, but distinct aspects of Christ's body and blood in the Eucharist. In contrast to the idolatrous gaze, Marion advocates a "theological gaze" that helps to understand the Eucharistic present as "mystical." According to Marion, there exists a distinction between the reality of Christ's body and blood (*res*) in the Eucharist, and his presence in the sacrament, and also between the species of bread and wine and the divine person. The mystical character of the Eucharistic present reverses the "real" from the "species" to the "sacramental," i.e., "the [E]ucharistic present as gift that itself is given as mystical." Accordingly, Christ is given sacramentally in the transubstantiated bread and wine (*res*); at the same time, they still remain as the purely sacramental body in relation to the ecclesial body (mystical body), the Church. Thus, Marion says, that the "real" of the Eucharistic present is that which is invisible to the ordinary gaze (mystical), i.e., "the Body of the Christ and his ecclesiastical body."[44] It is the distance that separates and unites between

---

describes the real presence as an "objective reality." In this sense, Marion is in conformity with the position of the Church on real presence.

42. Rosemann, "Marion's Eucharistic Realism," 234.

43. *Ibid.*, 233.

44. Marion, *God Without Being*, 180-181.

"reality" and "presence" that allows for the ability to discern the presence of God in the given, or to see through the accidents of bread and wine, the Christ who appears behind them.[45] What is foundational to this distinction is the two kinds of gaze (*regard*) of the real, according to the manner of the idol and the icon. The idolatrous gaze disseminates the distance generating a metaphysical concept of the thing, thus, identifying presence to the species, whereas the iconic gaze preserves the distance generating a concept of presence that surpasses the former and opens up to the presence of Christ who appears behind them. In order to assume the true meaning of the Eucharistic present in this manner requires a disposition of contemplation and prayer that consents distance and the conversion of one's idolatrous gaze.[46]

1.3.3.1. Temporalisation of the Eucharist

Marion develops a broader understanding of presence based on a non-metaphysical concept of time as given. He makes a distinction between two modes of temporalisation according to the manner of the difference between the iconic and idolatrous concepts of presence, namely, "metaphysical" and "Christic" temporality.[47] In the ordinary understanding, "present" is defined negatively, in terms of the "past" and the "future," both past and future as non-present and non-time. Accordingly, present begins when the past ends, and the future begins when the present ends. Instead, the understanding of time, as given, helps to recognize the present, as given by the past and the future. So time is considered non-metaphysically, as that which is given, rather than that which gives. The metaphysical understanding of time gives rise to an idolatrous concept of presence that limits presence to the present moment, or to the here and now, as long as the reality is present to the consciousness in the present moment. On the contrary, Marion insists that the Eucharistic gift is not determined as the presence of the present moment alone. Therefore, a non-metaphysical concept of time encourages one to think about the reality as given from the whole, the past and the future. As Rosemann puts it, the metaphysical conception of time understands "the whole from the present," whereas the "gifted concept of time ... understands

---

45. Rosemann, "Marion's Eucharistic Realism," 237. This requires faith from us. See n. 25 above.

46. Marion, *God Without Being*, 182.

47. *Ibid.*, 169-172. See also Loughlin, *Telling God's Story*, 237-241; Mitchell, *Meeting Mystery*, 273-276; Rosemann, "Marion's Eucharistic Realism," 237-242.

the present from the whole."[48] Thus, presence should be thought of as beginning from the gift, a presence given in terms of the past and the future. In this sense, the presence of the Eucharist must not be construed to a presence from the here and now, but from the past, the future, and finally, the present. It is the memory (anamnesis) that constitutes the here and now in relation to the past event as well as an eschatological announcement in terms of the future. The presence as "dailyness and viaticum" assumes full meaning only when the temporalisation of the Eucharist is understood in reference to the past as well as the future. As Marion puts it,

> [t]he present of the eucharistic gift is not at all temporalised starting from *here and now* but as a memorial (temporalisation starting from the past), then as eschatological announcement (temporalisation starting from the future), and finally, and only finally, as dailyness and viaticum (temporalisation starting from the present).[49]

Approaching Eucharistic presence, in terms of the gift, implies that the community does not construct presence at its disposal, but instead the presence is a gift which can only be welcomed and received as gift. The gift as given by Christ, is welcomed and received through the mediation of the priest who acts *in persona Christi*. The community that receives the gift, find themselves nourished and gathered together by it. The presence, thus, is neither confined to a mute thing, nor transferred to the conceptual consciousness and making of the community; instead it has to be accepted as, and only, as a gift from God. So, Marion accentuates the need for choosing between idol and distance. Christ's presence can be recognised in the exteriority of the present only by those who can open themselves to *distance*.[50] In this sense, according to Marion, Christ's presence in the Eucharist is not exhausted by his objectification in the bread and wine, which makes him available here and now, like a thing with its concomitant idolatry. This is contrary to the metaphysical concept of presence which is governed by the ordinary concept of time that reduces presence to something available in the present, here and now. Hence, theologically speaking, the Eucharistic gift that Christ makes of himself in the species of bread and wine, has to be understood in its past, future and temporal dimensions. Thus, "Christic temporalisation," the understanding of the Eucharist from the Christic perspective, helps us to overcome the meta-

48. Loughlin, *Telling God's Story*, 239.
49. Marion, *God Without Being*, 172.
50. *Ibid.*, 169.

physical conception of time, which construes the past as "no-longer-present," and the future as the "not-yet-present."[51] The present is thus understood, in terms of the past and the future, as the gift given by the past and the future.

Marion attempts to traverse the "blackouts" which are created by the notion of presence as *here* and *now* through the notion of an *a priori* gift that is anterior to the present. This involves thinking "presence as a present," presence as the gift always-already given, operated by anamnesis and *epektasis* (temporalisation by the future). Thus, according to Christian temporality, the present is realised by the past and the future. The past and present are not non-present, in terms of the present, according to the ordinary concept of time, but they are determinants of the Eucharistic present. Marion understands the Eucharist as the gift that comes from Christ in the present, in the dailyness. The notion of presence, conceived in this manner, is in opposition to the metaphysical mode which reduces presence to "an available permanence" at the neglect of the future and the past, but rather, "as a new sort of advent," as originarily given.[52]

The Eucharistic present that gives itself in maximum phenomenality in a Christo-liturgical temporality, gives itself as an *event* saturating quantitatively our concepts.[53] The Eucharist also saturates all concepts according to quality, and gives itself as in the *idol*.[54] Accordingly, this Eucharistic understanding can be as minimised as fulfilling one's own conceptual gaze, not because the presence is delimited, but rather, the excess of intuition blinds in such a way as to equate one's conceptual idol. "In fact," the Eucharist is, "by itself, the absolute gift, whose perfection anticipates our mode of presence, surpasses our attention, dazzles our gaze, and discourages our lucidity."[55] It is a gift that can neither be welcomed nor understood. The Eucharist gives itself as *flesh* as a "unique" sacramental reality, as an absolute phenomenon saturating the human person's intention.[56] Finally, the Eucharistic givenness gives itself in maximum phenomenality as an *icon* invisible to the gazing subject. One ascends to the Eucharistic faith as far as one allows the icon to

51. Rosemann, "Marion's Eucharistic Realism," 238.
52. Marion, *God Without Being*, 172-173.
53. Van den Bossche, "A Possible Present for Theology," 75. Van den Bossche explains how the Eucharistic presence gives itself in maximum phenomenality as the saturated phenomenon according to the four modes of phenomenality, namely, in terms of an event, idol, flesh and icon.
54. *Ibid.*, 75.
55. Marion, *God Without Being*, 174.
56. Van den Bossche, "A Possible Present for Theology," 76.

gaze at oneself. Thus, in the Eucharist, there takes place a saturation of saturation according to the four modes of saturation whereby givenness gives itself in maximum phenomenality. The Eucharist becomes the *sacrament of givenness par excellence*, beyond concepts and horizons of perceiving subjects.

Marion's concept of presence is operated according to the notion of distance, in the sense that the Eucharistic presence is distinguished from the subjective consciousness the one who summons it.[57] Eucharistic presence endures beyond one's conscious attention, because it is not one's consciousness that summons the Other (Christ) in presence, but rather, it is the Other (Christ/the Spirit) who summons attention and prayer. What God gives in the Eucharist is love. Only the iconic gaze can penetrate into the infinite love that is present behind the species. The "reality," from the Christian point of view, is that the "bread and wine" are the *res* (the matter of the sacrament) and the *sacramentum* (a sacramental sign) of the body and blood of Christ and of the Church; furthermore, the iconic gaze sees in the species, the person of Christ whose gift of charity is saturated in excess.[58] Therefore, in the Eucharistic gift, the presence of Christ is fully realised in the present. Thus, the believing community is called to ascend to the iconic apparition of the Eucharistically given present under the temporality of "here and now."[59] In brief, Marion says that what is designated as "real presence" must be received on the basis of the memorial that gives it as a pledge, and appeals for its anticipation and its eschatological accomplishment.

Assigning full weight to the meaning of anamnesis in the Jewish Passover, Marion argues further that the Eucharist is not mere remembrance of a past event, as if it has nothing to do with the present and the future. He understands the anamnetic command of Christ, "Do this in memory of me" (Lk 22:19), not just as a mere "remembrance" (opposite of forgetting), recalling what is non-present, but rather, "[i]t is a question of making an appeal, in the name of the past event, to God, in order that he recall an engagement (a covenant) that determines the instant, presently given, to the believing community."[60] Therefore, the daily celebration of the Eucharist can be understood as the "re-presentation" of Christ's sacrifice, which was accomplished on the

57. See Marion, *God Without Being*, 176-177.
58. Loughlin, *Telling God's Story*, 240-241; Rosemann, "Marion's Eucharistic Realism," 240-241.
59. Marion, *God Without Being*, 174-176.
60. *Ibid.*, 172.

Cross.[61] The Church's celebration defines the present as between the accomplished reality and the awaited second coming of Christ. As Rosemann states, "[the] presence of Christ in the Eucharist renews God's pledge of Christ's full presence that we eagerly wait. In this way, the present, far from being self-sufficient, derives its meaning from the past."[62] It is the memorial that makes the past a decisive reality for the present; thus "the past determines the reality present – better, the present is understood as a today to which alone the memorial, as an actual pledge, gives meaning and reality."[63] In this sense, the Eucharistic present is the temporalisation of the past as memorial.

The understanding of the Eucharist as a memorial, essentially leads to its eschatological dimension.[64] The memorial obtains validity in terms of the pledge for an eschatological advent of the *Parousia*. Thus, the memorial of Christ has to be celebrated (Lk 22:17) "until he comes" (1Cor 11:26). In other words, the memorial aims at the *Parousia*. According to Marion, the Cross, which is the fulfilment of the covenant, embraces the promise of the *Parousia* (Mt 26:29; cf. Mk 14:25). Furthermore, Marion explains that "until he comes" does not refer simply to a period of waiting for Christ to come again, but rather, involves an appeal for, and hastening of, his return. Thus, the future determines the present as its very mode of advent. As Marion puts it, "[t]he pledge, which the memorial sets into operation, now anticipates the future, so that the present itself occurs entirely as this anticipation concretely lived."[65] Thus, just as the past is temporalised through memory, so the Eucharistic present is temporalised through the future. Thus, the Eucharistic present (gift) is constituted within a dynamic tension between the past and the present.

As was explained at length, the presence of Christ in the Eucharistic gift is fully realized in the present; presence is realized in and through what is given as present (gift). In fact, the certitude of what is given in the present pertains to the question of efficacy. The phenomenology of givenness, ac-

61. John Paul II, *Ecclesia de Eucharistia*, nos. 11, 15.

62. Rosemann, "Marion's Eucharistic Realism," 239.

63. Marion, *God Without Being*, 173. Marion explains this with reference to 1 Cor 15:17-18 where St. Paul says, "[i]f Christ has not been raised, your faith is futile and you are still in your sins ... For if for this life only [present, *tautē*] we have hoped in Christ, we are of all people most to be pitied." The past, present and future are made real through the celebration of the sacraments. *Catechism of the Catholic Church*, (London: Geoffrey Chapman, 2000), no. 1152.

64. Marion, *God Without Being*, 173.

65. *Ibid.*, 174.

cording to the mode of the icon, explains the givenness of Christ in the Eucharist, here and now, in relation to the past and the future. In the following section, it will be argued that the givenness of Christ in the present can be adequately explained only with reference to the givenness of the Spirit highlighting the role of the Spirit in realizing presence, in terms of the past and future.

1.3.4. The Spirit and Presence

Traditionally, Catholic theology ascribed the efficacy of the sacraments to Christ's own agency and power. The whole Western tradition inherited this view from Augustine and Aquinas. The following statement of Augustine is well-known:

> Even though many ministers – just or unjust – may baptise, the power of baptism should be attributed to Christ alone, on whom the dove descended and of whom it was said 'This is the one who baptises with the Holy Spirit'. Peter may baptise, but it is really Christ who baptises. Paul may baptise, but it is Christ who baptises. Judas may baptise, but still it is Christ who baptises.[66]

Even within Aquinas' explanation of sacramental efficacy, which is described in terms of sign and cause, the efficacy of the sacraments flow from the power of Christ, the Incarnate Word.[67] The official Catholic theology, even today, is loyal to this way of understanding the efficacy of the sacraments. This is clearly seen in the statement of Vatican II: "by his power," Christ is "present in the sacraments so that when anybody baptizes, it is really Christ himself who baptizes."[68] Christological dimension is quite obvious in the understanding of the sacraments. With due regard for the agency and power of Christ, we insist on the agency and the power of the Holy Spirit in the sacramental event, which we designate as "mediation," as we have described it based on a systematic reflection of the double and complementary missions of the Word and the Spirit. Therefore, the sacramental gift and the gift of presence can be duly explained, only in terms of the originary givenness of the Spirit, who mediates Christ through the language and symbols of the sacraments. In what follows, we will develop a sacramental hermeneutics of givenness, which explains the sacraments as iconic-symbols, integrating

---

66. Augustine, "Homilies on the Gospel of John," in *The Nicene and Post-Nicene Fathers*, ed. Philip Schaff (Edinburg: T & T Clark, 1991), 6:7.

67. Aquinas, *Summa Theologiae*, 3a.60:1-3.

68. *Sacrosanctum Concilium*, no. 7.

both Christological and Pneumatological aspects within the reach of the phenomenology of givenness.

1.3.4.1. Iconic Symbolization

The categories of the icon and the idol provide two contrasting perspectives
under which the sacraments can be explained, as in the dual mode of reflecting on the appearance of the divine. The idolatrous approach to the sacraments parallels the metaphysical scheme of sacramental efficacy that is operated in accordance with the notion of causality, or in terms of human subject.
Besides, the idolatrous way of thinking "sacrament" gives rise to a "real"
presence confined to a thing to be looked at, as in the mistaken notions of the
theory of transubstantiation, and the role of the priest in the sacramental
event as mechanistic and magical. On the contrary, the iconic approach of
explaining the sacraments encourages one to allow the givenness to speak for
itself and to give itself, unconditionally, and without being limited by constituting subject. The power of the icon to conceal and reveal the invisible in
the visible helps us to understand the sacrament, other than by the language
of causality.[69] In the order of the icon, presence is understood solely as "giv-
en," and not made or constituted by the subjects, but rather, they are constituted by the presence that submerges them. In the same way, individual sacraments are originally "given," and not constituted by the receiving subjects, but rather, they are being constituted by them.

The power of the icon in constructing the reality does not lie in resemblance, but rather, in non-resemblance. In this sense, Christ is the icon par
excellence, the icon of the invisible God (Father). Christ becomes the icon of
the Father in the disfigured humanity. It is in his kenosis that he manifests the
glory of the Father. In this sense, with regard to the sacraments, the iconic
symbolization consists in the power of the sacrament to reveal likes in the

---

69. George S. Worgul expresses the view that a symbol centred understanding of the sacraments runs the risk of preventing the symbol from going beyond the symbol to the reality
by hiding, rather than by revealing the symbolised by being obsessed or possessed by the
symbol itself. However, the notion of the icon helps us to overcome this limitation. George S.
Worgul, "Sacraments: Iconic Interruptions of the Loving God," in *Gods sacramentele aanwezigheid in de wereld van vandaag. Hulde aan professor dr. Lambert Leijssen bij zijn emeritaat*, ed. Thomas Knieps-Port le Roi and Lieven Boeve (Leuven, Voorburg: Acco, 2008), 165.
Our approach to the sacraments try to rectify the aforesaid limitation of symbolisation by
developing an iconic-symbolic perspective which is phenomenological, rather than based on a
transcendental metaphysical system governed by Being.

unlike, in the concealment needed to make known what is revealed. An icon is a coming to presence of the divine, without it being present as knowable in *itself*. This is true with the sacraments. Sacraments do not image, as in a mirror, the invisible reality that they contain and realize. As Power explains, the bread and wine given to the disciples at the Last Supper was not the reproductive image of Christ's self-giving and redemptive sacrifice, but rather, it was the remembrance of that event in ritual and symbolic enactment. Therefore, the sacramental symbols do not image the event as such, but keep the event in memorial.[70] For example, the symbolic elements such as bread, wine, water, oil, etc. used in the sacraments are the images of human and cosmic life, but they are not the replica of the mystery being realized through the ritual and symbolic use of them. Within the context of the celebration, the symbolic elements function as iconic so as to signify the reality on the basis of what Power calls *iconic augmentation*.

1.3.4.2. Iconic Augmentation

Power tries to explain the sacramental dynamics employing the concept of the icon as developed by Marion. He explains *how* the efficacy of the sacraments can be understood through the notion of iconic augmentation. According to him, "[t]o refer to painting, ritual, or word usage as iconic, is to recognize how, through these images, actions, and words, a meaning and truth are given to life that is gift to it, some greater force and power and hope that appears, advents, in the moment of the iconic."[71] In the sacrament, various images, actions, and words come into play, crossing each other in signifying and offering the gift which surpasses any human capacity.[72] Through the ritual actions, the cosmic elements of bread, wine, water, and oil, through the ritual action, are saturated or augmented, encompassing into the world of God's gracious, for-giving and life-giving activity.[73] However, as far as the sacraments are concerned, in order that the event may be kept in memory, the ritual enactment of the Church must be infatuated by the power and originary activity of the Holy Spirit, which can be referred to as *pneumatic augmenta-*

---

70. Power, *Sacrament*, 283.

71. *Ibid.*, 285.

72. Sacraments have been generally understood as symbolic actions that mediate the presence of God. However, this is never understood as human actions as a means to make God's presence. It is the Spirit who actualises the presence of God. Herbert Vorgrimler, *Sacramental Theology*, trans. Linda M. Maloney (Collegeville, MN: Sacramental Theology, 1992), 71-72.

73. Power, *Sacrament*, 285.

tion. Thus, the sacraments become the phenomenal events showing itself, the event of *Pasch* through the medium of rites, signs, symbols and language, but mediated by the Spirit. In other words, sacraments become the saturated phenomenon, or the icon of God's gift of himself, through Christ and the Spirit. As Caputo observes, what takes place in the sacraments is that the "present gift" (e.g., bread and wine at Eucharist) are saturated by the "hyperpresence or hypergivenness of the gifting" in its "unlimited and invisible givenness."[74] In other words, the sacraments become iconic-symbols of the givenness of God in Christ and the Spirit.

1.3.4.3. Pneumatic Augmentation

For Chauvet and Power, the event that is mediated through language is the Pasch of Christ. Marion also develops a sacramental thinking, taking the Pasch as the vantage point. While acknowledging their contribution in contemporary sacramental thinking, a more adequate explanation has to be given about the manner in which the mystery of the paschal event is mediated in and through the celebration of the sacraments.[75] The question which has been raised already, whether the language has inherent capacity to realize the gifting of God in the sacramental event, has to be taken seriously. It can be argued that from a Pneumatological point of view, the agency of the Spirit in realizing the sacramental gift, as in God's gift of himself in the economy must not be underestimated. Notwithstanding, the Pneumatological and Trinitarian emphases that both Chauvet and Power lay in their prestigious works on sacraments, they still lack a systematic weaving of the Pneumatological dimension with that of the symbolic, linguistic and anthropological.[76] Power pays sufficient attention to explain the power of the language in making present the Father's gift in Christ and the Spirit. We purport to argue that

---

74. John D. Caputo, "Apostles of the Impossible: On God and the Gift in Derrida and Marion," in *God, the Gift and Postmodernism*, ed. John D. Caputo and Michael J. Scanlon (Bloomington, IN: Indiana University Press, 1999), 136.

75. Odo Casel posed the question as to *how is the presence of Christ realized in the liturgical celebrations in and by the partaking assembly*, as early as the latter part of the twentieth century which aroused great interest and debate in the theological arena. He was of the opinion that Christ's presence in the liturgical celebration can neither be considered as flowing from the power (*virtus*) of his historical sacrifice on the Cross nor from the intrinsic capacity of signs to produce their effects (*per signum*). Casel, *The Mystery of Christian Worship*.

76. We have already pointed out in the first chapter that the Trinitarian Christology that Chauvet develops remains as an appendage to the concept of sacramental mediation developed in the preceding chapters of his celebrated work, *Symbol and Sacrament*.

Power's emphasis on the power of language relegates the role of the Spirit to the background, although he tries to acknowledge the gift of both the Word and the Spirit in the sacramental event. The validity of our argument becomes clear form what Power writes:

> What is stressed here [in the sacramental event] is that it is in the very medium of language that the event enters into human lives and history. It is through the very means of language, and within both the power and constructions of language, that the Word and Spirit are present in the paschal memorial ... The twofold mission of Word and Spirit comes from the Father *as his gift.*[77]

As noted above, he relates sacramental presence to the notion of iconic augmentation, or the manner in which the icon is saturated with the power of constructing the reality. Thus, it seems that the language and symbols, in some way, contain inherent power that is capable of effecting the reality by ritual performance. This sort of a self-contained efficacy leads contemporary sacramental theology only to transform efficacy from causality to symbolic efficacy. Even in postmodern sacramental thinking, sufficient attention has not been paid to correlate sacramental presence to the role of the Holy Spirit in a consistent manner. In other words, they somehow fail in situating the role of the Spirit in the sacramental event. Therefore, what is proposed, in particular, is the mediatory role of the Holy Spirit in saturating the celebration of the Church so that the language and symbols may contain and effect the sacrament. Thus, the emphasis is transferred from the "power of the language and symbols" to the "originary activity of the Holy Spirit" in the sacramental event.[78]

In this regard, Siobhán Garrigan's criticism of Chauvet's emphasis on body and ritual symbolisation in forming identity is worth mentioning.[79] She challenges the claim of contemporary sacramental and liturgical theology that rituality embodies a religious/symbolic efficacy, highlighting the ambivalence of ritual theorists in ascribing special power to ritual. Her critique is

77. Power, *Sacrament*, 82-83.

78. Raymond Brown, analysing the parallelism between the sayings about the coming of the Paraclete (Jn 14:15-17) and the coming *back* of Jesus (Jn 14:18-21) concludes that the presence of Jesus after his return to the Father is realized in and through the Paraclete. See Raymond Brown, *The Gospel According to John (I–XII)*, The Anchor Bible Commentary, 2 (Garden City, NY: Doubleday, 1966), 645.

79. Siobhán Garrigan, *Beyond Ritual: Sacramental Theology after Habermas* (Hampshire: Ashgate, 2004), 41-68.

particularly oriented toward Chauvet's anthropological assertion that the ritual symbolisation as such, makes the sacrament. Even though she admits the function of rituals in instituting identity, she calls into question Chauvet's anthropological assertion as its primary function.[80] Chauvet's affirmation of rituality, as having privileged access to symbolic reality/efficacy, is at stake in the wake of the criticisms raised by Garrigan. The same criticism can be levelled against Power as well.

As Garrigan further points out, there is a linguistic inadequacy which Chauvet and Power overcome by introducing the notion of the theology of grace in the metaphor of the gift/giving. It is true that postmodern sacramental theology considers the metaphor of the gift as a means of overcoming metaphysics and the language of causality. However, Garrigan does not convincingly argue how the metaphor of the gift overcomes the reduction of sacramental mediation exclusively as symbolic mediation. The Pneumatological focus that has been delineated encourages one to argue that even the metaphor of the gift remains inadequate, unless interpreted in terms of God's gift of himself, in and through Christ and the Spirit. Therefore, in what follows, we propose a hermeneutic of sacramentality of givenness enlightened by Pneumatology, without deviating from the postmodern trail and ascertaining full capacity to the metaphor of the gift and the phenomenology of givenness. This can be achieved by recognizing the mediatory role of the Spirit as integral to symbolic mediation, in the explanation of God's giving in Christ and the Spirit in the sacramental event. However, before entering into this discussion, let us examine the implications of approaching grace iconically in terms of the gift.

2. Gift of Grace

Traditionally, the sacraments are understood as perceptible and efficacious sings instituted by Christ to communicate grace.[81] Catholic tradition also holds that the sacraments confer grace and they are effective *ex opere operato*. The understanding of grace as a mechanically generated product cannot be retained any longer. Instead, the phenomenological turn in theology encourages one to re-construct the traditional notion of grace from a phenome-

---

80. *Ibid.*
81. This understanding which is expressed in the *Catechism of the Catholic Church* (no. 1127, 1084) goes back to Augustine and its continuation through the tradition of Peter Lombard, Aquinas and other medieval theologians.

nological perspective, in terms of the gift. As Joseph S. O'Leary observes, the notion of grace is one of the fundamental themes of Christian theology that survives, and can be well inserted into the phenomenological mode. He observes,

> [i]ndeed, grace – as phenomenon, event, process – could fill in for all the other notions that have become so elusive, or could provide the key for their postmetaphysical retrieval … Incarnation, redemption, and resurrection could all be "reduced" (in something like a phenomenological reduction) to an event of grace (and of course the entire vocabulary of the Spirit feeds into this reading).[82]

O'Leary finds a nexus between the notions of grace and givenness, and argues that it can be employed in interpreting other notions in theology in such a way that it can dismantle the metaphysical blockade in theology.[83] Moreover, with regard to the sacraments, explaining grace through the language of the gift upholds the basic traits of grace as both gratuitous and gracious. In this connection, Chauvet's contribution in developing a non-metaphysical concept of sacramental grace within the scheme of symbolic efficacy is admirable.

Chauvet attempts to explain sacramental grace outside the scheme of causality, integrating both graciousness and gratuitousness. He begins by showing the inadequacy of designating "grace," which refers to the sacramental relation with God, within the metaphysical scheme of causality. He proposes a "symbolic scheme" over and against the "metaphysical scheme" within which grace can be explained as "*non*-object" and "*non*-value," affirming "graciousness" and "gratuitousness" as constitutive elements of it.[84] Graciousness, which is fundamental to the notion of grace, can be designated only as non-value, incalculable and super-abundance. Sacramental grace ought to be situated within the scheme of symbolic exchange, which is in the

---

82. Joseph S. O'Leary, "The Gift: A Trojan Horse in the Citadel of Phenomenology?," in *Givenness and God: Questions of Jean-Luc Marion*, ed. Ian Leask and Eoin Cassidy, Perspectives in Continental Philosophy (New York: Fordham University Press, 2005), 136.

83. *Ibid.*, 137. Even Marion's approach cannot be considered as a total overcoming of metaphysics, although theologians consider Marion as a resource to overcome the metaphysical blockages in theology. For Marion's approach has also been looked at "as restoring metaphysics in the key of phenomenology." See *ibid.*, 137.

84. Chauvet, *Symbol and Sacrament*, 7. He finds the biblical image of manna (Ex 16:13-21), whose name itself is a question (*man hu* – what is it?), beautifully express the traits of grace which is of another order other than that of object, measure, and the logic of value. See Chauvet, *Symbol and Sacrament*, 44-45. See also Chauvet, *Sacraments*, 87-89.

sphere of non-value.[85] Chauvet argues that the Christian concept of grace must be complemented with the notion of "gratuitousness." This involves the conceiving of grace as gift: God's gratuitous gift that precedes all else. Therefore, gratuitousness essentially means "givenness." This is clear, as Chauvet says, "we are not at the origin of our own selves, but that we receive our selves from a gift that was there before us: [a] free gift, which can in no way be demanded and, which, we can in no way justify."[86] According to the scheme of symbolic exchange that Chauvet develops, the gift obliges a return-gift. In the same way as the Christian understanding of grace, on the side of human beings, should integrate both graciousness and gratuitousness. As he puts it,

> the gratuitousness of the gift *carries the obligation of the return-gift of a re-sponse*. Therefore, theologically, grace requires not only this initial gratuitousness on which everything else depends but also the *graciousness of the whole circuit*, and especially of the return gift ... beyond price, without calculation – in short, as a response of love.[87]

As it becomes clear, Chauvet regards the human response, or the return-gift as belonging to the Christian concept of grace. The gratuitousness of the gift of grace must provide room for a gracious response by the subject, because grace is not a "finished product."[88] The response is not simply to safeguard the freedom of the subject, but rather, the very nature of the grace as non-object and non-value necessitates it. Chauvet insists on the graciousness and gratuitousness of the gift of grace solely as based on God's initiative out of pure love.[89] Gift is given without necessary reason, free of charge, without calculation, without value. Graciousness pertains also to the return-gift of the believing subject. However, he argues the gratuitousness of the gift does not extirpate the possibility of a return-gift, but only obliges the human subject to return by way of an ethical engagement.[90] Chauvet argues that God's grace can be received *as* grace only by a *return-gift* by way of thanksgiving, grati-

---

85. Chauvet considers the logic of business exchange and symbolic exchange are poles apart and on two different levels. What governs the business exchange is operated under the logic of value, use and calculation; symbolic exchange is governed by non-value, non-calculation and abundance. Chauvet, *Symbol and Sacrament*, 106-107.

86. *Ibid.*, 108.

87. *Ibid.*, 108-109.

88. *Ibid.*, 109.

89. Chauvet, *Sacraments*, 123.

90. *Ibid.*, 125.

tude and love.[91] Now, the question can be asked about the status of the gift if
the obligatory return is not made by the human subject: would the gift be a
gift, or does it cease to be a gift when the gift is confronted with the lack of
return? Chauvet, does not address this issue at length, but he is more concerned with emphasizing the responsibility of the human person in the effec-
tiveness (fecundity) of the sacraments in concrete life. Nevertheless, one
cannot assume that Chauvet does deny the objective efficacy of the sacraments independently of the subject. It seems that, rather than denying objective efficacy, Chauvet is cautioning against the danger of construing sacramental efficacy solely to an automatically efficacy (*ex opere operato*) to
extent of neglecting the role of the human subject (*ex opera operantis*). The
return-gift, the gracious response of the human subject in freedom necessarily belongs to the course of grace. Therefore, Chauvet opines that infant baptism cannot be a perfect example for explaining the gratuitousness of grace in
baptism.[92] This symbolic labor of receiving oneself, what he calls grace, is
within the intra-linguistic mode which establishes a new brotherly and sister-
ly relationship between believing subjects. Therefore, "'grace' designates,
not an object that we receive, but rather, a symbolic work of receiving oneself: a work of 'perlaboration' in the Spirit by which subjects receive themselves from God in Christ as sons and daughters, brothers and sisters."[93] Pi-
thily saying, according to Chauvet, grace is the gracious and gratuitous relationship between God and the believing subjects, as well as the relationship
among them.

Within the scheme of gift-reception-return of Chauvet, the aspect of obligatory return by way of a symbolic labor of becoming believing subjects can
be accommodated without any problem. However, there seems to exist an
apparent tension between the gratuitousness and the freedom of the subjects
in Marion's scheme. It seems that, from the point of view of Marion, the
notion of the obligatory return gift annuls the gift *as such*. Hence, there remains the question of reconciling the gratuitousness and the response to the
gift of grace which human beings are called to make. Nevertheless, it can be
held that the notion of *a priori* givenness, as retained by Marion, duly accommodates the graciousness and gratuitousness of God. The notion of obli-

---

91. *Ibid.*, 124.

92. Chauvet, *Sacraments*, 126.

93. Chauvet, *Symbol and Sacrament*, 140. Chauvet develops this theme in chapter eleven.
We will explain further the role of the Spirit in the sanctification of the assembly alongside the
Spirit's role in the sanctification of the gifts.

gatory return does not fit into the scheme of Marion as it counteracts the notion of pure gift. The grace is always already there, even at the risk of rejection or forsaking. There can be no return directed in the strict sense, to God, as symmetrical to God's giving, but there can be a response by way of a *return* which is basically non-obligatory.

Chauvet's understanding of grace liberates the notion of sacramental grace from the confines of a narrow understanding of grace as understood in scholastic terms. However, the "obligatory" nature of grace to a certain extent obliterates the gift character of grace from the perspective of the "pure gift," as defended by Marion. Therefore, we hold the view that Chauvet's gift-reception-return-gift scheme that characterises his understanding of sacramental grace, in a way, diminishes the gift character of grace as gift. The phenomenology of givenness better explains grace as the excess of the givenness of God in Christ and the Spirit in the mode of the icon. The notion of pure gift and the originary activity of the Holy Spirit help to ease the apparent tension existing between graciousness and obligation in Chauvet's understanding of grace.

2.1. Phenomenon of Grace

The notion of grace is essentially a theological concept. Therefore, an understanding of sacramental grace must be situated within the Trinitarian mode of givenness in the Word and the Spirit. Nevertheless, the phenomenology of givenness and the givenness in the icon help to give a better exposition of grace in terms of givenness, and to overcome the minimalist understanding of sacramental efficacy. Accordingly, grace can be understood as a gift from God, but not as a "thing" that is received because of one's own doing good. Grace is not something that is deserved, but is needed for everyone; it is not something that is received because of one's merit, but only because of God's love. Grace is nothing but God's free and gratuitous love. The gratuitous love of God, God's grace that comes to the human person can be better represented by the icon.[94] God's gift of love, which is absolutely free and gratuitous, comes to human beings in the gift of Christ and the Spirit. Phenomenologically speaking, grace is the experience of "being-given." Being given life, human persons are called to be the children of God, a reality that takes place at baptism (*l'adonné*). As the children of God, we are given identity and relationship with God, as well as with other human persons. Nicholas

---

94. Leijssen, *The Silent Glimmer*, 29.

Lash writes, "[t]he gift is the very 'being-given', or givenness of God: God as 'donation' … God's giving never leaves God's hands, in which are held all things as 'being-given' … God's 'gift', like God's 'utterance', names an eternal relationship of origin."[95] This is a relationship that characterises one's identity as the sons and daughters, as well as brothers and sisters to each other, in Christ and the Spirit.

The effect or the grace of the sacrament has been described as the experience of salvation. The efficacy of the sacraments consists in describing how to represent the reality of God's salvation made available to a ritual participant. However, grace must not be understood as something static, material, or as a finished product. Instead, from a Trinitarian perspective, it is dynamic; it is the presence and action of God who loves in freedom; it is gratuitous.[96] In the Trinitarian theology we have developed, it becomes clear that both the Son and the Spirit are gifts, or God's givenness is realized in and through the Word and the Spirit. Both the Son and the Spirit are given in the economy so that God is given. As Loughlin explains, through the notion of the gift, the tension between the divisions "giver," "gift," and "givee," are overcome, because what is given in the present is not "something," but what is given in the sacramental gift is God himself. When God gives, "no-thing" passes from God to someone else, but God bestows himself graciously and gratuitously and draws near. "God gives only himself. When God gives, nothing passes from God to someone else; rather God draws near. Nor is God given to someone else, for the someone else is the being of the gift."[97] As John Milbank says, "[i]t is a gift to no-one, but rather, establishes creatures as themselves gifts."[98] In this sense, the gift of grace is not anything but the presence of a living person, the triune God who gives himself into a dynamic relationship between himself and the one who accepts him in faith.[99]

---

95. Nicholas Lash, *Believing Three Ways in One God: A Reading of the Apostle's Creed* (London: SCM Press, 1992), 92, 105. God's 'utterance' are the Word and the Spirit. See also Jean-Luc Marion, "Metaphysics and Phenomenology: A Relief for Theology," *Critical Inquiry* 20 (1994): 587-589.

96. Colwell, *Promise and Presence*, 29.

97. Loughlin, *Telling God's Story*, 243.

98. John Milbank, "Can a Gift Be Given? Prolegomena to a Future Trinitarian Metaphysics," *Modern Theology* 11 (1995): 135. According to Milbank, this giving is an absolute exchange governed by absolute gratuity. The understanding of "give to" and "receive from" is overcome by annulling the "neutral space" between them.

99. Worgul, *From Magic to Metaphor*, 127-128.

Accordingly, God's grace can be understood only as the givenness of God which is originary, "always already," and independent of and prior to liturgical actions.[100] Sacraments as iconic-symbols also mediate grace which precedes and surpasses human understanding and activity. In the sacramental givenness, God's givenness realises itself in maximum phenomenality, especially in the Eucharist. So the sacraments, understood according to the modes of saturation, saturate the givenness of grace, gratuitously and graciously. The nature of the grace, understood iconically, reminds one of what Chauvet explains through the analogy of manna. When we speak in general that we receive grace in the sacraments, we might not understand grace as an "object" of "value" that is given, grace as "something" to be accrued or piled up to a greater or lesser degree, in accordance with the moral disposition of the individual. According to Leijssen, the understanding of grace, as different from a "thing," as "non-calculable," and "non-value," is to understand grace "as a dynamic relation established by the Spirit." The grace proper to each sacrament is nothing other than the "many forms of the gift of the Spirit."[101] However, it is true that one has to employ the grammar of language, in terms of the subject-object relationship, when speaking of grace as the relationship with God and humanity (covenant) in the Spirit, the gift of God's self-communication, etc. However, it is important to ascend one's thoughts to its gracious and gratuitous aspects, as well as to its provenience as coming from God. This will be an appropriate attitude for receiving God's gift, in excess, which is beyond value, measure, naming, and calculation irrespective of language and grammar that one uses for designating it.

According to Paul, grace is a new relationship with God that is effected by God's gracious action in Christ (the Christ-event).[102] What struck Paul most was the love of God beyond his imagination, which was revealed to him in the crucified Jesus (Acts 9:5). He was possessed by Christ (Phil 3:12). Paul employs the term χάρις, in order to designate the boundless love that he experienced from God. So Paul claims: "The Son of God loved me and gave himself for me." Grace is not "something," but "someone"; it is the presence of the one who gives himself freely and gratuitously. The gift of love was so

---

100. In this regard, it is worth mentioning the distinction that Karl Rahner makes between prevenient grace and accepted grace. The prevenient grace, which is originarily given (offered grace) becomes accepted grace.

101. Leijssen, *The Silent Glimmer*, 36.

102. The Greek word χάρις refers to God's salvific act in Jesus Christ. Two other relative terms are 'righteousness' and 'justification'. Raymond E. Brown, *An Introduction to the New Testament* (New York: Doubleday, 1997), 441.

strong that nothing could separate him from the love of Christ (Rom 8:35-37). Paul also says that the excess of God's gift of love is mediated through the Spirit: "the love of God has been poured out into our hearts through the Holy Spirit that has been given to us" (Rom 5:5). For Paul, χάρις is actually the excess of God's love. He writes, "For Christ, while we were still helpless, yet died at the appointed time for the ungodly ... God proves his love for us in that while we were still sinners Christ died for us" (Rom 5:6,8). In other words, grace is God's favor, a participation in the life of God. Grace is God's giving of his own very self (life) to humanity. Thus, according to Paul, grace is the gratuitous and gracious love of God given in Christ and the Spirit.

God does not give himself away in the gift of his presence, but God's giving is in the mode of the icon and of distance. Therefore, sacraments can be explained as iconic-symbols that give grace. Sacraments as iconic-symbols, confer and symbolize grace (conceal and reveal).[103] In the life of a Christian, we identify, particular "moments" or "times" other than the ordinary, which we believe, are the times in which that person receives grace. Those are the moments when we experience grace "really real" or "concretely" in life. The iconic perspective of sacramental grace dissipates any thought of mastery, and defines the subjects as *l'adonné* whose lives have been "graced" by the givenness of God in excess. Nonetheless, the excess of givenness realizes itself in the sacraments iconically retaining the distance. As Colwell articulates,

> a sacrament may be the means of his [God's] presence, but it is never at our disposal; he is not capricious, but neither is he subject to necessity; a sacrament may be the means of his presence, but it is never his prison; he is freely and graciously here, but he is not confined or controllable here or anywhere else. If grace might rightly be used with reference to a gift then this one who loves in freedom remains the free Lord of the beinggivenness of that gift; God may give himself but he never gives himself away; he never becomes our possession or property.[104]

The gift of grace that the sacraments bestow can be entertained and be graced only by those who consent themselves to a self-giving God, whose givenness expresses itself in an invisible mode in the iconicity of the sacraments. In this

---

103. This is somewhat similar to the scholastic understanding that the sacraments effect grace what they signify and signify what they effect. However, the iconic understanding does not support a relationship between the icon and the reality by way of causation, and the icon does not equate with the givenness of the reality.

104. Colwell, *Promise and Presence*, 29.

gracing event, the Spirit remains as the "mediated immediacy," as the gift
and the giver, as will be explained below.

2.2. *Gift of the Spirit*

The inappropriateness of designating grace as a calculable thing has been
made clear. Nevertheless, posing a question regarding the "what" and "how"
of the phenomenon (reality) of grace that the sacraments symbolize and actualise is worthwhile. According to the Pneumatological theology that was
developed in the second chapter, the two missions of the Word and the Spirit
come into play in the sacramental economy, especially in the understanding
of grace. God's self-communication, or the gift of himself, is nothing other
than the gift of love which is visible in the figure of Christ on the Cross and
in the gift of the Holy Spirit. They constitute a single act of the givenness of
God. In the post-Pentecostal period, the givenness of God becomes concrete
and experiential in and through the Holy Spirit. Therefore, the theology of
grace ought to be based essentially on Pneumatology. In this regard, Lambert
Leijssen's contribution to sacramental theology is remarkable. He extends
the Pneumatological aspect to the entire spectrum of the seven sacraments
and to sacramental grace. He describes the grace of the sacraments as "the
gift of the Holy Spirit," "the silent glimmer of the Spirit" that permeates the
everyday lives of Christians.[105] According to him, the sacraments are the
manifold "forms of the gift of the Spirit," the "language of the self-giving
God."[106] Thus, God's gift of himself in the "corporality" of the sacraments
becomes the "real-symbolic" mediation of the presence of Christ in and
through the mediation of the Holy Spirit. In making God's gifting in the Son
possible, the Spirit plays a mediatory role, while remaining the gift himself.[107] Therefore, the Spirit is the giver and the gift in the sacramental event.
This is clearly represented in the narrative structure and dynamics of the liturgy. As Chauvet points out, the gift received in the sacraments is

> the very Grace of God or better still, God revealing God fully as grace in the
> gift of self as Son in Jesus, a gift actualised by the Spirit, as the prayers of ep-
> iclesis in the sacramental celebrations demonstrate. This is why, in the wake

105. Leijssen, *The Silent Glimmer*, 37.
106. *Ibid.*, 36.
107. As we have explained the role of the Spirit in the Trinity as "mediated immediacy,"
we have shown that in mediating Christ, the Spirit is not absent from the scene, but is present
as the mediation of the mediator. In the same way, in mediating sacramental presence and
grace, the Spirit is present identifying himself as the gift and the giver.

of the liturgy, a long theological tradition has rightly perceived in the gift of the Spirit the grace par excellence given to humanity.[108]

For it is only in and through the Spirit that we have access to the life of God. The Spirit dwells in us in mediating God's love and life. The gift of grace mediated in and through the sacraments is a gift that unfolds in the life of a Christian. For this reason, the gift of grace, which the human person receives in the Holy Spirit, entails a task as we will see now.

2.3. Gift and Task

According to Chauvet, "[g]race is always bestowed as a task."[109] He integrates into the notion of graciousness, the free human response. Accordingly, the gift of grace, received in thanksgiving (oblation), must express itself in a return-gift which implies ethics, an agapic relationship between brothers and sisters. Chauvet observes, "the sacramental reception of the free *'grace-bestowing'* of God in the symbolic *'giving-thanks'* of the oblation needs to be verified in a *'living-in-grace'* among brothers and sisters."[110] In principle, one may agree that Chauvet, in accentuating the ethical dimension that the gift of grace, engages the person's real life. Nonetheless, it seems that Chauvet's commitment to the gift-reception-return, to some extent, subjugates or compromises the gracious and gratuitous character of the gift. We argue that an iconic approach that considers the gift of grace from the perspective of love integrates grace in terms of gift and task, while retaining the gift character of grace intact.

As has already been mentioned, the gift of grace is actually the gift of love, the Spirit of love (Holy Spirit). God's givenness can be understood only in terms of love. Therefore, grace is the mystery of God's gratuitous love; it respects the freedom of the individual. Where there is love, there is freedom. Therefore, a response to the gift of God's grace in Christ and the Spirit has to be understood, not in terms of obligatory return, but rather, in terms of a reception in gratitude and thanksgiving.[111] The notion of obligatory return cannot be applied to the scheme of grace when regarded in terms of love, because love never obligates, but instead allows the freedom of response that gives room for living in love. For this reason, the task, which the gift of grace

108. Chauvet, *Sacraments*, 151.
109. Chauvet, *Symbol and Sacrament*, 277-278.
110. *Ibid.*, 280.
111. Leijssen, *The Silent Glimmer*, 41.

imposes upon the recipient, cannot be understood solely as obligatory, but rather, must be seen from the perspective of love that allows the freedom to receive and to respond to that love in love. It is a freedom to go forth; it is living in grace, living in love. The liturgical celebration of the Church realizes in concrete terms the gift of God in Christ and the Spirit in the word and the sacrament. Now we shall consider how the gift of presence and grace are realized liturgically in the sacramental celebrations of the Church.

3. Iconic-Symbolization in the Liturgy

The phenomenology of givenness and the givenness in the icon help to develop a new understanding of the sacraments as iconic-symbols. When one gives precedence to God's givenness, beyond human concept and language, sacraments can only be understood as the celebration of God's givenness in excess, in the word and the sacrament, mediated by the Spirit. The liturgy of the word and the liturgy of the Eucharist form a single event that constitutes the sacrament of the Eucharist. As Vatican II says, Christ is liturgically "present in his word."[112] Furthermore, the Council affirms, "the liturgy of the word and the eucharistic liturgy are so closely connected with each other that they form but one single act of worship."[113] In general, *Sacrosanctum concilium* affirms Christ's paschal presence in the liturgical assembly. This can be understood by examining the relationship between the presence of Christ and what the liturgical assembly actually 'does' at liturgy. In the following section, we will explain the Eucharist as paradigmatic of God's givenness in the sacraments, drawing attention to the dynamics of the liturgical event with special focus on the liturgy of the word and the liturgy of the Eucharist. This allows for an interpretation of the Eucharist as the sacrament par excellence of God's self-giving, the culmination of the phenomenality God's self-giving.

3.1. The Language Event as Spirit Event

Contemporary developments in the study of language and symbols have unquestionably ascertained the function of language and symbols in construct-

---

112. *Sacrosanctum Concilium*, no. 7. It follows *Mediator Dei* in discussing "the different modes of Christ's personal presence." See Edward J. Kilmartin, "Christ's Presence in the Liturgy," in *Bread from Heaven: Essays on the Eucharist*, ed. Paul Bernier (New York: Paulist, 1977), 102-104.
113. *Sacrosanctum Concilium*, no. 56.

ing sacramental imagination and reality. According to Power, a "ritual or sacramental event relates to an event within time past through the capacities and power of language to carry it forward and to allow it to enter afresh into lives."[114] Therefore, the sacramental signs and symbols are necessary to mediate presence. However, they neither exhaust nor realize the presence of Christ nor confer grace in themselves. Therefore, "sacraments are not self-assertive actions by autonomous human subjects (individual or collective); they are *language*, speech in its supreme sense: the symbolic self-disclosure and self-communication of One who alone utters an originating Word."[115] What is mediated through the language and symbols cannot be fully explained solely on the basis of the power of language and symbols. As was explained, in order that the reality comes into presence, they are to be augmented by the originary givenness and the activity of the Holy Spirit. The sacramental event enacted through language and symbols, realizes presence and grace mediated by the originary givenness and activity of the Holy Spirit, by making symbolic mediation truly the sacramental mediation of the presence of God. Therefore, the language event is turned to a Spirit event through the mediatory role of the Holy Spirit. However, the Spirit acts not in the "vacuum," but in the "body-ness" of the liturgy. Therefore, the celebrating assembly has to insert itself into the pre-programmed structure of the liturgy in time and space.

3.1.1. Iconicity of Liturgical Space-time

In the liturgy, there is a mixture of symbols and signs that come into play within the iconicity of worship. The signification that is made in a particular liturgy is not the imagination of an individual or a group, but is the collective memory of biblical communities which is handed down through millennia, carried in text, rite, and symbols.[116] In this connection it is important to see how Cardinal Godfried Danneels calls our attention to the "givenness" of the liturgy. He lays emphasis on the fact that liturgy is "God's work on us before being our work on God." He goes on saying that, in fact, through liturgical celebration, "the community enters into a pre-established, divine and spiritual

---

114. Power, *Sacrament*, 75.
115. Mitchell, "'But Only Say the Word'," 356.
116. Graham Hughes, *Worship as Meaning: A Liturgical Theology for Late Modernity* (Cambridge, UK: Cambridge University Press, 2003), 152.

architecture."[117] In this sense, liturgy "pre-exists"; therefore, liturgy is not the creation of the celebrating community, but rather, the members of the liturgical assembly are the servants and guardians of it. He refers to the fundamental attitude of the worshipping community as "*homo liturgicus*," which is an attitude of "orientation towards God, readiness to listen, obedience, grateful reception, wonder, adoration and praise."[118]

The community finds meaning in the celebration insofar as it can inhabit itself into the givenness of the liturgy. Hughes uses a technical term "frontier" in order to explain the reality of mediating presence in liturgical space-time.[119] According to him, frontier connotes: space, time, embodiment, movement, etc. In the liturgical celebration, one comes to the frontier, even passes beyond it and returns. A participant who comes to the frontier confines herself to a specific time and duration, and submits to the iconic significations of worship which mediates the real and the imaginary, the presence of God.[120] Noticeably, there are three successive stages in this divine-human encounter. As Hughes explains, there are: "entrance," "being in," and "departure from" God's presence. At the entrance of the worshipping space itself, there is an iconic realization of the sacred. Moreover, the liturgical dynamics come into play through locomotion, liturgical direction, temporal sequence, and meaningful progression of the events within the liturgical space-time realizing sacramental presence.

Entering into the world of symbols is necessary to understand the reality that is being realized by the dynamism of symbols. In fact, this is an entrance into the realm of a participatory knowledge, which is different from an informatory or objective knowledge. Hughes says that there is a temporal progression in the liturgical celebration.[121] Spatial and temporal dimensions are closely related. In the plot development of the liturgy, the participants enter into a space which is other than the ordinary, designated for the celebration. In the same way, they also enter into a specific time, which is the liturgical time. This is the time in which a sequence of events is enacted, and at the end, they exit from this time. The meaning of liturgy has been foreseen and realised in and through the narrative configuration, or the structured enact-

---

117. Godfried Danneels, "Liturgy Forty Years after the Second Vatican Council: High Point or Recession," in *The Mystery of Faith: Reflections on the Encyclical Ecclesia de Eucharistia* (Dublin: Columba Press, 2005), 24-25.

118. Danneels, "Liturgy," 25.

119. Hughes, *Worship as Meaning*, 153.

120. *Ibid.*, 153-154.

121. *Ibid.*, 164-169.

ment of events. It is within the configuration of the liturgical space-time that the community encounters the divine or the presence becomes realized. "The 'narrative configuration' ('emplotment'), then, which 'makes a story out of [the] actions [of the liturgy]' is the sequence: 'entrance into, presence within, and return from' and encounter with the divine."[122] Each participant has to recognise herself within the universe of the dynamics of symbols. As Mitchell Nathan puts it,

> [a] symbol is not an object to be manipulated through mime and memory, but an environment to be inhabited. Symbols are places to live, breathing spaces that help us discover the possibilities that life offers … By engaging in symbols, by inhabiting their environment, people discover new horizons for life, new values and motivation.[123]

Entrance literally means to leave one space and to pass into another. This designates, iconically, the passing of the worshiper to the space specifically designated for liturgy. According to Catherine Vincie, there is a "violent rupture required for entrance into the assembly and for dismissal from it."[124] So, the worship takes place in a space different from ordinariness of familiar space ('secular' space). Everything within this space makes the worshipper feel that it is different from other spaces, and it creates a sacred atmosphere. The architecture also is very significant.[125] According to Lathrop Gordon, the church is a symbolic space which is different from other spaces because of its unique intention. As he puts it,

> according to the classic description of this basic symbol [i.e., the liturgical assembly] this meaning is not – or ought not be – a crowd, a cheering section, a gathering to hear a lecture or a sales pitch, an audience. It is not a collection

---

122. *Ibid.*, 165. Hughes makes use of the idea of Ricœur that time becomes meaningful when it is rendered in a narrative form. Paul Ricœur, "Time and Narrative," *Critical Inquiry* (1980): esp. 169; See also Paul Ricœur, *Time and Narrative*, 3 vols. (Chicago, IL: Chicago University Press, 1984-8), 1:53. According to Ricœur, the meaning of "temporal passage" is derived from our capacity of "emplotment." Human beings make meaning out of actions configuring them in a temporal succession. See *ibid.*, 44, 65.

123. Nathan D. Mitchell, "Symbols Are Actions, Not Objects," *Living Worship* 13 (1977): 1-2.

124. Catherine Vincie, "The Liturgical Assembly: Review and Assessment," *Worship* 67 (1993): 136.

125. Gerard Lukken, *Per Visibilia ad Invisibilia: Anthropological, Theological and Semiotic Studies on the Liturgy and the Sacraments*, ed. Louis Van Tongeren and Charles Caspers, Liturgia Condenda, 2 (Kampen: Kok Pharos, 1994), 359-374. See also the introductory chapter, "semiotics of architecture."

of consumers come to an expert, a gathering of the uninvolved come to be entertained.[126]

The entrance into the worshipping space is a symbolic act pregnant with meanings. Hughes distinguishes entrance into two stages: first, a worshipper enters individually with an interior state of mind which is invisible to others; second, there is the gathering of the members into a corporate entity.[127] The locomotion of the individual is highly significant, namely, the movement of the priest to the pulpit, the choir moving to the place, the worshippers finding their seats, etc. All these movements constitute the act of entrance. When the entrance is by a ceremonial procession with the carrying of the Bible, followed by other ministers, accompanied by incense, music, etc., the leaders construct meaning by walking. This walking is an iconic representation of coming into the presence of God.[128]

Having realized the presence within, the assembly recedes or passes back across the frontier of liturgical space-time in the final blessing and dismissal. Hughes insists that this should not be reduced to an empty ritual merely to signify that "it's all finished now."[129] Instead, corresponding to the entrance to the space and time of the liturgy, the final blessing should be accompanied by an iconic representation of the solemn recession of the passing back of the people crossing the boundary into the world. The recessional rites ought to signify effectively that the people continue to live their lives from the empowerment and blessings that they receive in the liturgical space-time, in the encounter with God. Briefly speaking, the whole liturgical dynamics is very important in constructing the meaning of the liturgy. But the originary activity of the Spirit, which lies even at the root of gathering the assembly, is that which makes the Church's liturgy fecund so as to mediate presence and grace. It is to this discussion that we will turn now.

---

126. Gordon W. Lathrop, *Holy People: A Liturgical Ecclesiology* (Minneapolis, MN: Fortress Press, 1999), 23.

127. Hughes, *Worship as Meaning*, 157.

128. See Robert Hurd, "A More Organic Opening: Ritual Music and the New Gathering Rite," *Worship* 72 (1998): 294-295; Kevin W. Irwin, *Context and Text: Method in Liturgical Theology* (Collegeville, MN: The Liturgical Press, 1994), 67. See also Louis Maldonado and David Power, "Symbol and Art in Worship," *Concilium* (1980): 112-119. Besides, the entrance at the beginning of every Eucharistic celebration re-present the solemn entry of Jesus into Jerusalem, which the Church solemnly commemorates on Passion Sunday. See National Conference of Catholic Bishops of America, *The Roman Missal*, trans. The International Commission on English in the Liturgy (New York: Catholic Book Publishing Co., 1985), 122.

129. Hughes, *Worship as Meaning*, 159.

3.1.2. Iconicity of the Assembly

In the liturgy, it is not the assembly that makes the reality, but the participants, as a whole, enter the flow of the liturgy so that they may partake in the reality which is beyond their capacity to produce. Liturgy is not something that the assembly "does" or "makes," it is the arena where the Divine comes as gift, as givenness, as love manifesting itself. God's coming-to-presence has to be understood from its Trinitarian source, wherein the givenness finds its expression in the most sublime and perfect form as the gift of charity. It is the same "love given" that is seen in the dynamics of the liturgy. David Coffey helps to understand this more clearly. He states,

> [a]uthentic human love is necessarily at the same time love of God and love of neighbour. Jesus' love of the men and women to whom he was sent is therefore one with his love of the Father and identical with the Holy Spirit as Spirit of Christ. The Spirit that he pours out on humankind from the cross, the Spirit by which he is present and active for the rest of time in the Church thus brought into existence, is the same as the Spirit that on the cross he returns definitively to the Father. This Spirit, active in the Church's ministry of word and sacrament, draws those who respond into union with Christ, and thus into the ambit of activity of the same Spirit as Spirit of God, Spirit of the Father, Spirit of sonship and daughterhood, whereby they are re-created, forgiven, and sanctified by grace, and drawn into stable union with the Son, thus becoming 'son (and daughters) in the Son'. The one Spirit is simultaneously Spirit of God and Spirit of Christ. His visible action in the world as the Spirit of Christ is the 'sacrament' of his invisible action as the Spirit of God."[130]

Therefore, the basic symbolic reality of the Church is nothing other than the unconditional, non-calculable and excessive givenness of God's love in the Word and the Spirit; a love that gives itself and shows itself, and from itself, beyond one's own conceptual and perceptual limits. The efficacy of the liturgical actions, even the very act of constituting the assembly as the Church (Body of Christ), as worshipping community, is that love, the Holy Spirit. The Church is not making a "present" of its own, of its own capacity here and now, but the Spirit constitutes the Church as *l'adonné*, so as to receive presence as given. That is why Chauvet opines that the act of the assembly

---

130. David Coffey, *Deus Trinitas: The Doctrine of the Triune God* (New York: Oxford, 1999), cited in Nathan D. Mitchell, "'Christ's Presence in the Assembly'," *Worship* 80 (2006): 263-264.

who gather to celebrate liturgy is not that of self-assertion, but of *disposses-sion*.[131] Therefore, the proper attitude of the assembly must be of a "letting-be" (counter-intentional), rather than that of mastery, in order to be gifted by the excess of divine presence. As Marion says,

> it is not a question here (in the case of the sacraments) only of constituting ob-jects starting from a transcendental subjectivity, which masters them by the initiative of an intentionality and certifies them by the assurance of an intui-tive fulfilment, but of receiving phenomena that show themselves staring from Godself, contrary to our expectations, anticipations, and plans, accord-ing to the deployment of intuition 'too' strong (Mark 9:3) for our capacity, the very glory of God.[132]

Moreover, the liturgical assembly assumes a theological status as the icon. For the church is the sign raised up among the nations which draws others into the way of Christ's life. As Gordon Lathrop points out, assembly is "the most basic symbol of Christian worship."[133] Liturgy is not the new creation of any particular liturgical assembly, but rather it is carried down through the centuries in tradition.[134] So the historical connectivity makes the celebration actual. "The business of this assembly will look more than a little silly ... unless we know that the bread and wine, water and words are used here with historical intent."[135] The traditional greeting, "the Lord be with you," is in-stantaneously imbued with meaning, when the priest summons people for liturgy with it.[136] This greeting efficaciously inhabits meaning, and becomes effective through historical connectivity. However, the question of liturgical symbolism and the whole array of ritual enactments are not simply a question of effecting meaning, but rather, of actualising the reality. It is the reality that makes the celebration meaningful in the life of the Church here and now. The ritual enactments, no matter how superb they might be, remain sterile and

---

131. Chauvet, *Symbol and Sacrament*, 231-239.

132. Jean-Luc Marion, "La phénoménalité du Sacrament: Être et donation," *Communio* 40 (2001): 72. As cited in Falque, ed., *Larvatus Pro Deo*, 194. Chauvet also points out more or less the same, that as homologous to Heidegger's *es gibt*, it is the Spirit, who allows us "to let God be God and thus establish a true communion with God." See Chauvet, *Symbol and Sa-crament*, 514.

133. Lathrop, *Holy People*, 48.

134. *Ibid.*, 31-43.

135. Gordon W. Lathrop, *Holy Things: A Liturgical Theology* (Minneapolis, MN: Fortress Press, 1993), 100.

136. Hughes, *Worship as Meaning*, 179.

empty unless saturated and filled with presence by the enlivening Spirit. In
this sense,

> "presence" is best understood as an open space of passage/transit rather than
> as delimiting boundary. It belongs to the definition of all real presence to be
> limitless, like love. We can affirm Christ's always arriving "presence" in the
> celebrating community precisely because this coming – ever new – displaces
> our emptiness, making us truly the embodied site where love "delivers itself
> body and soul.[137]

The activity of the Holy Spirit makes the Church's celebration of the memorial of Jesus as sacramental memory in the historical "today" of the believing subjects.[138] Therefore, a proper explanation of sacramental efficacy
must be made, intertwining the Pneumatological and the symbolic aspects. In
what follows, it will be highlighted as to how the interplay of the Pneumatological and the symbolic in the liturgy of the word and the liturgy of the Eucharist constitutes the givenness of God in the sacraments. This will be accomplished by relying on the Eucharistic hermeneutics of Marion in the light
of the Emmaus episode.

3.2. Givenness in the Word

God's givenness expresses itself in concrete fashion in the celebration of
the sacraments. The whole liturgical celebration can be seen as given.
Through the readings and homily Christ speaks to the liturgical assembly.[139]
Christ "is present in his word since it is he himself who speaks when the holy
scriptures are read in the Church" (SC 7). The community receives the word
as given. Through the liturgy of the word, the assembly enters into an environment wherein the word is received in gratitude as the word of God, renouncing their own individual and collective horizons.

The liturgy of the word is a language event. The word is spoken, heard
and received. However, there exists a gap between the "sign" and the "referent," the "word" and the "referent." In the liturgy, the referent is Christ; the

---

137. Mitchell, "'Christ's Presence in the Assembly'," 265.

138. Chauvet, *Symbol and Sacrament*, 510.

139. The General Instruction on the *Roman Missal* specifies 'six structural units' for the
revised Order of Mass (*Ordo Missae*), namely, introductory rites, the liturgy of the word, the
preparation of the gifts and altar, the eucharistic prayer, the communion rite, the conclusion.
However, in what follows, our study is confined to a general understanding of the presence
and conferral of grace as given in the word and the Eucharist mediated by the Spirit.

event referred to is the death and resurrection of Christ, which is a past event (of history), an accomplished and foreclosed event whose traces are contained in the text. Marion explains it, figuratively, as follows:

> The word does not transmit the text, but rather, through the text, the event. The text does not at all coincide with the event; at best, it consigns the traces of it, as the veil of Veronica retains the features of Christ: by rapid imposition of the event that transpires … [t]he text does not coincide with the event or permit going back to it, since it results from it.[140]

The hermeneutics alone is unable to bridge the gap between the text and the referent. According to Marion, the referent of the liturgy can be approached only insofar as one can trans-pierce without being absorbed by an idolatrous spectacle that stops the spectator in the visibility of a "grand mass," but rather, there must take place, a "crossing of the visible by the invisible," allowing a crossing of my gaze by an invisible gaze of the Other (the referent).[141] This occurs when the worshipers allow themselves to be gazed at by the One who sees their state of being in prayer. Thus, they are liberated from an idolatrous gaze that seeks presence in the visible. In this situation, the gap between the text and the referent is not transgressed. Marion explains how this gap between the text (the word) and the referent can be transgressed through a hermeneutic of the word in the light of the Emmaus story (Lk 24:13-49).[142] This seems to be paradigmatic of receiving the word as given in the liturgy of the word, as relating the word and the referent. He explains how the Paschal event, which is a past event (Lk 24:18), for the disciples, as well as for those today, can be made present through the word. What the community has is the text, but the event referred to is lacking; what hermeneutic can bring to light is only the meaning, but not the advent of the referent. The advent of the referent is made possible through a "new event," through another hermeneutic, whereby "the referent in person redoubles," and become the interpreted and the interpreter: "The referent itself is interpreted in it as referring only to itself."[143] Just as in the Emmaus episode, "as long as the Word does not come in person to interpret to the disciples the texts of the prophets, and even the

---

140. Marion, *God Without Being*, 146.

141. Marion, *The Crossing of the Visible*, 65.

142. Marion, *God Without Being*, 146ff. We employ the "Word" in upper case to refer to Christ and "word" in the lower case to designate the preached word or the text.

143. *Ibid.*, 147. Marion cites Lk 24:15, 25-27 in order to show how Jesus interprets the Scriptures at length as referring to him. In such a way, only an adequate interpretation of the text makes possible to relate the text with the Paschal event.

chronicle of the things seen (*logoi*, Luke 24:25), they do not see what is evident (Luke 24:17)." Therefore, Marion insists that the interpreter, "*[t]he theologian, must go beyond the text to the Word, interpreting it from the point of view of the Word.*" In the liturgical celebration, the manner of reading and interpreting the scripture must be as "the self-referential hermeneutic of the texts by the Word."[144] The disciples do not understand the meaning of the text (the event) as long as the Word (the Interpreter) becomes the interpreted. In the same way, the priest who presides over the Eucharist interprets the scripture referring to Christ (as in Luke 24:27). Early Christianity understood the proclamation of the word by the bishop as divinely inspired.[145] The proclamation of the word, or the liturgical homily, manifests a two-fold faithfulness, namely, faithfulness to God and to God's people. The faithfulness to the word was guaranteed by the fidelity to the text, and the latter is implied in the right application of the word to the Church. Thus, the bishop fulfils the role as the type of Christ (*typus Christi*).[146] The letter becomes the living word insofar as the bishop becomes the type of Christ, in fidelity to God, and the people in preaching the word of God. As Marion illustrates, Christ abolishes "the gap between the speaker who states (prophet or scribe) and the sign (speech or text), namely, "the gap between the sign and the referent." In other words, "Christ does not say the word, he says *himself* the Word..., because he is said and proffered through and through. As in him coincide – or rather commune – the sign, the locutor, and the referent."[147]

In the liturgy of the word, there is a transgression of language taking place, as in the incarnation. However, it is not the power of the language that makes it a liturgical event. Marion explains this in a Trinitarian fashion. Accordingly, Christ's identification with the word involves a Trinitarian dimension, because "[t]he Word lets himself be said by the Father – in the Spirit." Jesus' identity as the Son of the Father consists in being "said by the Father" and "proffered by the breath of the paternal voice, breath, the Spirit."[148] In

---

144. *Ibid.*, 149.

145. Enrico Mazza, *The Celebration of the Eucharist: The Origin of the Rite and the Development of Its Interpretation* (Collegeville, MN: Liturgical Press, 1999), 265.

146. Mazza, *The Celebration of the Eucharist*, 265.

147. Marion, *God Without Being*, 140. In the Syro-Malabar liturgy, the celebrant solemnly proceeds to *behma* (the table of the word or ambo) holding the gospel raised as though his face is veiled from the people. It symbolises that it is not the celebrant who says the word, but Christ says *himself* the Word. See Syro-Malayar Bishops' Conference, *Syro-Malabar Sabhayude Qurbana* (Trivandrum, India: San Jos Press, 1989), 33.

148. Marion, *God Without Being*, 142.

other words, the Word becomes the Said of the Father and appears as the Son; as the Said of the Father, the Word is proffered by the Spirit, the breath, as the paternal voice of the Father (Jn 12:28; Mt 3:26; Mk 9:7). Marion portrays the Trinitarian mode of God's gift of God's self in the Word, because "[w]hen he [Christ] speaks the words of the Father, he lets himself be spoken by the Father as his Word. Thus *the Word is said as it is given*: starting from the Father and in returning to the Father. This very transference designates the Spirit."[149] In the same way, theology becomes *theo*logy of the *Logos* when we "let the Word speak us (or make us speak) in the way that it speaks of and to God."[150] The theologians' task is "of abandoning his discourse and every linguistic initiative to the Word, in order to let himself be said by the Word, as the Word lets himself be said by the Father."[151] So the right attitude is of hermeneutic, of "letting be," a docile abandonment so that God speaks in human speech. In the liturgy, when the community allows Christ himself to say the Word, the gap between the speaker who speaks and the said, or the sign, and the referent, is abolished. Interpretation referring back to the Word is made possible "by the labor of the Spirit that arranges a eucharistic community in such a way that it reproduces a given disposition of the Word referent, and is identified with the Word, interpreted according to this relation … This endless fecundity depends on the power of the Spirit that gives rise to the eucharistic attitudes."[152] As Kevin Irwin puts it,

> [w]e [the assembly] revere the books containing the readings, we proclaim selected texts, and we respond to them in faith, and in so doing we experience once more and again and again their saving power. What we hear, *happens*. What we proclaim, *occurs*. What the word says *becomes* an act of grace and favour for us here and now, for our salvation and for our more complete union with God.[153]

This happens because, in the liturgy of the word, the worshipping community goes beyond the text to the referent. When the text is read and interpreted in the assembly, it makes the invisible visible, in the sense that the text assumes a body; it is an experience of being enlivened by the Spirit. As St. Paul says, "the letter kills, but the Spirit gives life" (2Cor 3:6). It is the spirit who me-

---

149. *Ibid.*
150. *Ibid.*, 143. Marion makes a contrast between "*theo*logy" and "theo*logy*."
151. *Ibid.*, 144.
152. *Ibid.*, 157.
153. Kevin W. Irwin, *Models of the Eucharist* (New York, Mahwah, NJ: Paulist Press, 2005), 101.

diates the text to the referent in such a way that the participating assembly receives the gift of presence in the "present" of the text. The letter, or the word in the text has no capacity to mediate the referent; the transgression of the word happens in and through the Holy Spirit given to the Church. The Spirit, who gave Christ a body, gives the letter a body in the liturgical reading and proclamation of the scriptures. In this sense, it is not the community who makes presence, but rather, the community receives Christ given in the liturgical event as a gift mediated by the Spirit.

Here the text within the context of the liturgy of the word functions as the icon: the readings and interpretations of the word of God amidst the assembly, iconically understood, are saturated with the presence of Christ wherein Christ, the Said of the Father says himself the Word in the Spirit. So, the liturgy of the Word becomes a Trinitarian event. The word operates in the mode of the icon, because Christ gives himself in the word governed by the principle of distance. What is given in the word exceeds what is visibly contained in the text and the whole symbolic and liturgical dynamics. In this sense, the givenness of Christ in the word is "sacramental"; Christ comes near, but in distance; Christ becomes visible, but as invisible. This is the manner in which the divine gives itself phenomenally, in excess, without being subject to the linguistic and conceptual limits of the constituting subject. It is the gift of the Spirit that enables the assembly to consent itself to distance and absence, and to ascend to a faith in the presence.

Christ, who gives himself in the word in the Spirit as the Said of the Father, gives himself fully in the breaking of the bread. Thus, the hermeneutic is completed "in the Eucharistic rite where the Word, visibly absent, makes himself recognized in the breaking of the bread, characterises the priest as his *person*."[154] In the liturgy, "Christ speaks in the readings, makes himself seen, touched, eaten, and breathed in his Eucharistic body. Every liturgy affects the appearance of Christ and results from it."[155] Now we shall see how the word is received as given, and how the word leads the liturgical assembly to recognition in the breaking of the bread.

3.3. Givenness in the Sacrament

Furthermore, the hermeneutic itself is not sufficient to make the Word visible in the text. It should give way to the Eucharistic moment (Lk 24:28-33)

---

154. Marion, *God Without Being*, 152.
155. Marion, *The Crossing of the Visible*, 64.

where recognition takes place (Lk 24:31); in other words, a transition from the hermeneutic to the Eucharist must take place. "The Eucharist accomplishes, as its central moment, the hermeneutic (it occurs at 24:30, halfway between the two mentions in the scriptures, 24:27 and 24:32). It alone allows the text to pass to its referent, recognized as the nontextual Word of the words."[156] It is in the Eucharist that the Word interprets in person. First, the Word speaks of the scriptures as concerning him (24:27). Second, the Word "proffers the unspeakable speech" in the breaking of the bread (24:30). Thus the hermeneutic is completed by appearing the Word in person. As Marion emphatically points out,

> [t]he Eucharist alone completes the hermeneutic; the hermeneutic culminates in the Eucharist; the one assures the other its condition of possibility: the intervention in person of the referent of the text as the centre of its meaning, of the Word, outside of the words, to re-appropriate them to himself as 'what concerns him, *ta peri heautou*' (24:27).[157]

Christ, the Said of the Father, says himself the Word in the Spirit, in the Eucharistic gesture; it is Christ himself who says the word (the Eucharistic words), and himself who breaks the bread. What takes place here is a Trinitarian event. The gift of the body and blood in the Eucharist must be understood in a Trinitarian fashion (as in the hermeneutic of the word). In the Eucharistic gesture of breaking the bread, a transgression of the words and actions takes place proffered by the Spirit. Every linguistic and symbolic action is augmented by the hyper-givenness of the Spirit so that they are raised to their ultimate relational possibility. The gifts of the Church, the bread and wine, are incorporated into the self-giving of Christ being elevated into the hypergivenness of God by the Spirit.[158] Thus, the bread and the wine become the iconic-symbols of the givenness of God in Christ and the Spirit. In other words, through the intervention of the Spirit, the material elements are transformed to the sacramental body and blood of Christ. Thus, the sacramental symbols become the iconic-symbols of God's self-giving in a true, substantial and real manner.

Interpreting sacraments as iconic-symbols is theologically compelling, as far as certain predominant notions, such as the theology of the moment of

156. Marion, *God Without Being*, 151.
157. *Ibid.*, 150-151.
158. In the memorial offering prayer (Eucharistic prayer I), the celebrant prays bowing with hands joined that "your angel may take this sacrifice to your altar in heaven." See The *Roman Missal*, 546.

consecration, the role of the priest *in persona Christi*, and the epiclesis question, are concerned. In what follows, we propose a plausible way of understanding these interconnected notions from an iconic-symbolic perspective.

3.3.1. The Moment of Consecration

Up to the middle ages, the Eucharist was considered as the celebration of the assembly in which they experienced the presence of the Lord as the Host of the entire meal.[159] However, the notion of the moment of consecration, which became predominant in the Middle Ages, exhibited a tendency of reducing the presence of Christ to the species of bread and wine, isolating it from the whole of the Eucharistic prayer.[160] As a result, the ecclesial dimension of Christ's Eucharistic presence was eclipsed by the notion of substantial presence.[161] At the time of Aquinas, consecration was understood as effected *ex* *opere operato* by virtue of the power of ordination at the recitation of the words of institution over the bread and wine.[162] Eventually, the moment of the pronouncement of the words of institution by the priest *in persona Christi* became the "moment of consecration" and the words of institution itself came to be regarded as consecratory.[163] The thinking of this period is reflect- ed in the words of Aquinas:

> Whence it must be said that if the priest utters only the aforementioned words ['Hoc est corpus meum'] with the intention of confecting this sacrament, this sacrament will be effected; because the intention causes these words to be un-

159. Jozef Lamberts, "May Your Spirit, Lord, Come…," *Ephrem's Theological Journal* 2 (1998): 109. As some of the early sources such as Didache, Apostoic Tradition of Hippolytus, Apology of Justin the Martyr, etc. Testify, the early Christian communities identified the presence of Christ in the celebration of the Eucharist or within the ecclesial assembly. See Jones, *Eucharistic Presence;* Powers, *Eucharistic Theology*, 13-22.

160. The idea of the moment of consecration originally goes back to the first half of the fourteenth century. Congar, *I Believe in the Holy Spirit*, 3:228; Lamberts, "May Your Spirit, Lord, Come…," 109; John H. McKenna, *Eucharist and Holy Spirit: The Eucharistic Epiclesis in Twentieth Century Theology (1900-1966)*, Alcuin Club Collections, 57 (Great Wakering: Mayhew-McCrimmon, 1975), 48-90. Dix adds that the concept of the "moment of consecration" finds its expression between 300 and 350 A.D. He says that first it appeared in the writings of the Eastern Fathers (Cyril, Sarapion, Athansius) and later spread to the West (Ambrose). Gregory Dix, *The Shape of the Liturgy* (New York: Seabury Press, 1982), 240.

161. Jones, *Eucharistic Presence*, 25-63.

162. Kilmartin, *Eucharist in the West*, 251. See also Lamberts, "May Your Spirit, Lord, Come…," 110-111.

163. Lamberts, "May Your Spirit, Lord, Come…," 110.

derstood as though they were offered in Christ's person, even if the words preceding this are not said.[164]

This way of understanding sacramental efficacy was the result of a mini-mised notion of priestly action, solely based on a Christology which is divorced from ecclesiology and Pneumatology. This was also the product of the metaphysical way of thinking of that time. The approach that has been developed for understanding presence in terms of givenness has also implications in reinterpreting the role of the priest in the liturgical event. In what follows, we argue that extending the iconic-symbolic understanding to the action of the priest *in persona Christi* will enhance the role of the priest in the liturgical event.

3.3.2. In persona Christi

The role of the priest in the liturgy has been interpreted in a narrow sense without duly considering the role and person of Christ within the larger context of the Church and in relation to the community.[165] Eventually, it led to a divided understanding of the assembly by distinguishing the "sacramental sacrifice" offered by the priest and the "spiritual sacrifice" offered by the people. As such, this minimizes the sacramental nature and actions of the

---

164. Richard Albertine, "The Post Vatican Consilium's (Coetus X) Treatment of the Epiclesis Question in the Context of Select Historical Data (Alexandrian Family of Anaphoras) and the Fragment of *Der Balyseh*," *Ephemerides Liturgicae* 102 (1988): 388. However, we have to bear in mind that Aquinas was aware of the role of the Holy Spirit in consecration. Aquinas, *Summa Theologiae*, 3a.75:1,1; Thomas Aquinas, *Summa Theologiae*, trans. Thomas Gilby, vol. 59 (London: Blackfriars, 1975), 3a.78:5,6. Nevertheless, Aquinas never understood the role of the Holy Spirit within the context of an epiclesis.

165. Sara Butler, "*Quaestio Disputata: In Persona Christi*: A Response to Dennis M. Ferrara," *Theological Studies* 56 (1995): 61-80; David Coffey, "Priestly Representation and Women's Ordination," in *Priesthood: The Hard Questions*, ed. Gerald P. Gleeson (New Town, NSW, Australia: E. J. Dwyer, 1993), 77-99; Dennis Michael Ferrara, "The Ordination of Women: Tradition and Meaning," *Theological Studies* 55 (1994): 706-719; Dennis Michael Ferrara, "Representation or Self-Effacement? The Axiom *in Persona Christi* in St. Thomas and the Magisterium," *Theological Studies* 55 (1994): 195-224; Dennis Michael Ferrara, "*In Persona Christi*: A Reply to Sara Butler," *Theological Studies* 56 (1995): 81-91; Dennis Michael Ferrara, "*In Persona Christi*: Towards a Second Naivete," *Theological Studies* 57 (1996): 65-88; David N. Power, "Representing Christ in Community and Sacrament," in *Being a Priest Today*, ed. Donald J. Georgen (Collegeville, MN: Liturgical Press, 1992), 97-123. See also *Worship*, vols. 63 (Mar, Sept 1989), 65 (Jan, May 1991), 66 (Nov 1992), 67 (May 1993).

Eucharistic assembly.[166] It is true that the traditional understanding of the term *in persona Christi* ascribes the efficacy of the sacraments to the power of Christ, and not to the power of the priest.[167] Therefore, it can be argued that this view does not imply a radical distinction between the "head" and the "body," but emphasizes their unity, while retaining distinctiveness. In this sense, as Gerard Austin observes, when it is said that the priest acts *in persona ecclesiae*, it does not imply that he is the one ordained by the community, but rather by Christ himself.[168] The diverse views can be understood as at- tempts for reconciling the apparent tension in explaining the role of the priest in relation to that of the *ecclesiae*, preserving the notion *in persona Christi* intact. In this connection, the iconic-symbolic approach, supported by Pneumatology, is capable of broadening one's understanding, situating the role of the priest *first* within the larger context of the Church[169]

The Eucharistic hermeneutics provides important insights to explain the role of the priest who breaks the bread and shares the cup, in terms of the icon. It can be said that, in the Eucharist, the priest, in breaking the bread and sharing the cup, acts *in persona Christi*, as the icon of Christ. The iconic-symbolic perspective must be applied, in the first place, in defining the role of the bishop as the head of the assembly. In the second place, it applies to the priests who exercise their ministry in association with his bishop. According to Marion, the bishop [also the priest] is not presiding in his own

---

166. David N. Power, "A Prophetic Eucharist in a Prophetic Church," in *Eucharist toward the Third Millennium*, ed. Marin F. Connell (Chicago, IL: Liturgy Training Publications, 1997), 42. Power shows that this is an adapted version of the Tridentine treatment of the Eucharist in which only the priest receives communion. See David N. Power, *The Sacrifice We Offer: The Tridentine Dogma and Its Reinterpretation* (New York: Crossroad, 1987), 25.

167. The medieval notion of *in persona Christi* is an outgrowth of the patristic notion of the priest as the type of Christ (*typus Christi*). Both these notions imply the theological understanding that identifies the words of the priest with the proper words of Christ upon which the efficacy rests. Mazza, *The Celebration of the Eucharist*, 290.

168. Gerard Austin, "In Persona Christi at the Eucharist," in *Eucharist Toward the Third Millennium*, ed. Marin F. Connell (Chicago, IL: Liturgy Training Publications, 1997), 84. Here, Austin observes that *Inter Insigniores* is reluctant to allow a primary status to *in persona ecclesiae*.

169. The disputed question is not whether or not the role of priest is understood within the context of the Church, but rather, it is understood as prior to the representing Christ. The Vatican Declaration on Women in the Ministerial Priesthood (1976) explicitly states: "It is true that the priest represents the Church, which is the Body of Christ. But if he does so, it is precisely because he first represents Christ himself, who is the head and shepherd of the church." "The Vatican Declaration on Women in the Ministerial Priesthood," *Origins* 6 (1977): 523.

person, but *in persona Christi capitis*.[170] Presiding and acting in his own person would be idolatry, because it prevents the vision and veneration of God. On the contrary, the priest who acts *in persona Christi* functions as an icon provoking a vision beyond him, which leads the community to the veneration of God.[171] On his own account, he is only a member of the community. It is only as a member of the congregation that the priest/bishop can truly be the icon of Christ. It is actually Christ who preaches the word and breaks the bread.[172]

Interpreting the role of the priest, without due regard for his relationship to the assembly, emerges from a totalitarian or idolatrous understanding of priestly ministry. In fact, the mystery of priesthood should not be relegated to instrumental or functional terms. It is important to allow the icon of the priest to manifest itself, without being governed by the metaphysical notions that has framed theological thinking for centuries. Only then, the theological significance of the priest can be re-imagined in relation to Christ, the Church and in terms of his affinity to the assembly. Perhaps, an iconic-symbolic approach may even encourage a resistance to the temptation of identifying the priesthood of Christ to a historical male-figure. Thus, the iconic approach encourages elucidating the role and the identity of both the priest and the community as emerging from a sharing in the same priesthood of Christ which is rooted in the originary call received in the Spirit at baptism.[173] The iconic-symbolic perspective will direct one to go further in understanding the action of the priest as liturgical action, which is actually the action of the whole Christ (*totus Christus*), both the head and body.[174] According to Pow-

---

170. *Catechism of the Catholic Church*, 1348.

171. Smit, "Marion's Eucharistic Hermeneutic," 35.

172. *Ibid.*, Marion's Eucharistic hermeneutic has been criticized as the idolisation of *episcopus* at the expense of the *ecclesia*. The priest acting *in persona Christi* has to be understood in connection with the second part *in persona Chrsti capitis*. However, it seems that such charges are exaggerated as Marion doesn't explicitly undermine the *ecclesia*, although he places much stress on the role of the *episcopus*.

173. However, we maintain the traditional distinction made between the "royal priesthood" and the "ministerial priesthood;" what we emphasise is to see the priestly authority as radically founded and united in one priesthood of Christ enjoyed by every Christian.

174. Gerard Austin sees this more or less the same way. However, he understands the liturgical action on the level of sign. See Austin, "In Persona Christi at the Eucharist," 83. As Chauvet explains, the liturgy is considered as a single sacramental whole. "The Eucharistic presence appears as the *crystalisation* of Christ's presence in the *assembly* (ecclesia) gathered in his name and presided over by himself and in the *Scriptures* proclaimed as his living word." The presence of Christ in the Eucharist can also be understood as the *Christus totus*, the head

er, understanding the action of Christ in union with the action of the whole body will justify explaining the action of the priest in union with that of the assembly.[175] Therefore, in exercising the priesthood in the liturgical action, both the community and the priest act in union with Christ who is the head of the Church.

Moreover, ascertaining the role of the Holy Spirit in the Eucharist has implications in re-interpreting the action of the priest *in persona Christi*. First of all, in uttering the words of Christ, the priest acts in the person of Christ who is the head of the Church. The epiclesis accentuates the originary activity of the Holy Spirit that capacitates and empowers the liturgical action of the assembly by which the celebration becomes Eucharist. Therefore, everything done in the liturgy is initiated and sustained by God alone, especially by the Holy Spirit. Therefore, the gift of the Eucharist cannot be understood without acknowledging the gift of the Holy Spirit originarily given to the Church which is at work prior to the assembly's work in the liturgy. In this sense, the priest can be understood as the icon of Christ. The iconicity of the priest consists of realizing the action of Christ in the Church here and now, retaining the distance. The iconicity of the priest depends on the Spirit, the principle of unity (mediation) and distance (differentiation) in the icon. In the whole Eucharistic action, the priest functions as the icon of Christ. Thus, the liturgical gesture of breaking the bread, symbolically actualizes the gesture of Jesus in the upper room. Therefore, it is Christ himself who breaks the bread for the Church in the Eucharist. When one allows the symbolic gesture to speak to the worshipping community, as in the icon, the worshipping community will be able to recognize (in contrast to cognizing) that the reality that is being represented is truly the act of Christ, although it surpasses the limits of understanding. In the same way, when the Eucharist is distributed, Jesus' gesture of giving at the last supper is actualized for the Church here and now. The whole liturgy is the activity of the Church, but the work of the Holy Spirit precedes and surpasses all human activity, making it really the work of Christ. Thus, liturgy becomes the work of God, God's gift of God's-self in the Word and the Spirit. The Eucharist is actually what God does for the worshipping community. Considering the epiclesis, as an integral unit within the narrative structure of the Eucharistic prayer, sheds more light into the inner dynamics of the originary activity of God in the sacramental event.

---

and the body. The grace of the Eucharist is, actually, Christ, head and body. Chauvet, *Symbol and Sacrament*, 388, 390.

175. Power, "Representing Christ," 114.

3.3.3. Epiclesis

The iconic-symbolic understanding of the liturgy deflates any minimised notion of presence, either confined to the moment of consecration, or to the epiclesis, but as exceeding the limits of human imagination and explanation. The approach regarding the givenness of Christ and the Spirit as constitutive to the givenness of God in excess, offers insights to overcome the tensions between Christology and Pneumatology in the sacraments. As far as the Eucharistic celebration is concerned, conceiving the epiclesis as constitutive to the structure of the Eucharistic prayer has necessary implications in the understanding of the discussion of the moment of consecration. The Western tradition regarded that, if one were to specify "when" and "how" the transformation of the bread and wine takes place, it was held that it was when the priest who acts *in persona Christi* pronounced the words of Christ. The Western emphasis on the words of Jesus as the central words in the Roman canon and its importance as consecratory can only be understood against the background of the fact that it contains no epicletic prayer. A theologically significant step in the post-Vatican II revision of the liturgy is the inclusion of explicit prayers in the Eucharistic prayers that invoke the power and action of the Holy Spirit, which is called "epiclesis." It is theologically important, because these prayers "contain and reflect a rich theology about how God acts in the liturgy and, in particular, what role the Holy Spirit plays in the enactment of the Eucharist."[176] A study of the Roman rite in its present form would shed more light on the power and the activity of the Holy Spirit at work in the Eucharist. When the liturgical symbolic actions are considered as a whole, it can be said that it is the symbolic actions as a whole that constitute and fulfill the sacrament, even though a number of "core words and actions," such as the words of institution, epiclesis, etc. are designated. The studies of the liturgical sources of both the East and the West show that the explicit invocation of the Holy Spirit (epiclesis) is a constitutive element of most of the Eucharistic prayers.[177] The new Eucharistic prayers of the Roman

---

176. Irwin, *Models of the Eucharist*, 264.

177. *Ibid.*, 265. For a study of the Eucharistic prayers, see R.C.D.Jasper and G.J. Cuming, *Prayers of the Eucharist: Early and Reformed. Texts Translated and Edited with Commentary*, 3rd ed. (New York: Pueblo, 1975); Enrico Mazza, *The Origins of the Eucharistic Prayer*, trans. Ronald E. Lane (Collegeville, MN: Liturgical Press, 1995); Mazza, *The Celebration of the Eucharist*.

rite have incorporated the epiclesis without any hesitation.[178] The inclusion of the epicletic prayer into the three Eucharistic prayers newly added to the Roman rite attests to the acknowledgement of the rich tradition of the Eucharistic prayers of both the East and the West.[179] The addition of the epiclesis in the Eucharistic prayers attests to what the Spirit *is* and *does*, as far as the efficacy of the sacrament is concerned. This reveals the renewed understanding of God's initiative in the realization of the sacrament, especially through the power and action of the Holy Spirit.

In the Roman tradition, the first Eucharistic Prayer contains only an implicit invocation of the Holy Spirit immediately before the institution narrative. The prayer is as follows: "Bless and approve our offering; make it acceptable to you, an offering in spirit and in truth. Let it become for us the body and blood of Jesus Christ, your only Son our Lord."[180] Then, there is a less explicit epiclesis for the assembly: "Then, as we receive from this altar the sacred body and blood of your Son, let us be filled with every grace and blessing."[181] The Missal of 1969/1971 of Paul VI makes this epiclesis more obvious.[182] For instance, in the second Eucharistic Prayer, it follows: "Let your Spirit come upon these gifts to make them holy, so that they may become for us the body and blood of our Lord, Jesus Christ."[183] This is followed by an appeal made to the Holy Spirit (after the institution narrative) as a conclusion to the memorial prayer: "May all of us who share in the body and blood of Christ be brought together in unity by the Holy Spirit."[184] The renewed Roman Eucharistic prayers invariably contain an explicit epiclesis such as these, before the words of institution, and also after the institution

---

178. Congar, *I Believe in the Holy Spirit*, 3: 241; Lamberts, "May Your Spirit, Lord, Come...," 99. The revision of the liturgical texts was an aftermath of the Vatican Council's call for pervasive reform by re-discovering the rich heritage preserved in patristic sources. *Sacrosanctum concilium*, no. 21.

179. However, it has to be noted that originally the Roman canon contained no explicit invocation of the Holy Spirit in its structure and content. Some argue that the prayer "may [it] become to us the body and blood of your dearly beloved Son Jesus Christ our Lord" is actually an indirect epiclesis. See for instance, Cipriano Vagaggini, *The Canon of the Mass and Liturgical Reform*, trans. Peter Coughlan (Staten Island, NY: Alba House, 1967).

180. *The Roman Missal*, 544.

181. *Ibid.*, 549.

182. See Aidan Kavanagh, "Thoughts on the New Eucharistic Prayers," *Worship* 43 (1969): 3-5. Here Kavanagh presents a general structure of the New Eucharistic prayers of the Roman rite.

183. *The Roman Missal*, 549.

184. *Ibid.*, 550.

narrative for the assembly. The revision of the Roman canon and the addition of the new Eucharistic prayers signify that the transformation of the bread and wine can no longer be located solely in the words of institution. In spite of the renewed understanding of the role and activity of the Holy Spirit in the liturgy, the West is still reluctant to consider the epiclesis as the high point, such as the Eucharistic prayers of the East, but instead consider the words of institution pronounced by the priest as the high point, although the role of the Holy Spirit is not undermined.[185]

The *General Instruction of the Roman Missal (2002) on the Holy Spirit* clarifies further the Spirit theology that undergirds the revised liturgy.[186] It lays emphasis on the initiative of God, particularly of the Holy Spirit, in the liturgical action of the Church (no. 53). The General Instruction specifically points out the role of the Holy Spirit in grasping the word of God (no. 56). Significantly, the instruction regards the epiclesis as constitutive to the structure of the Eucharistic prayer (no. 79). We read:

> Epiclesis: In which by means of particular invocations, the Church implores the power of the Holy Spirit that the gifts offered by human hands be consecrated, that is, become Christ's body and blood, and that the victim to be received in communion be the source of salvation of those who will partake of it (no. 79).[187]

---

185. See Lukas Vischer, "The Epiclesis: Sign of Unity and Renewal," *Studia Liturgica* 6 (1969): 31. In spite of the call for a pervasive reform of the liturgy, it seems that sufficient action was not taken as far as Pneumatology is concerned. Lamberts has the same view as he says, "the Roman canon can only be reproached for not calling explicitly the Holy Spirit, neither in prayer for the transformation of the gifts, nor in the prayer for the transformation of the communicating congregation." Lamberts, "May Your Spirit, Lord, Come...," 112.

186. Congregation for Divine Worship and the Discipline of the Sacraments, *General Instruction of the Roman Missal*, available from http://www.vatican.va/roman_curia/congregations/ccdds/documents/rc_con_ccdds_doc_20030317_ordinamento-messale_en.html.   (2002, accessed 30 January 2010). As compared to the previous instructions, which appeared from 1970, the instruction of 2002 is characterised by an increased focus of the role and activity of the Holy Spirit. For instance, the instruction of 2002 states that "the Church [is assembled] in the Holy Spirit" (no. 53). The phrase "in the Holy Spirit" does not appear in the former text of 1975.

187. The expression, "the power of the Holy Spirit" does appear only in the revised version of *General Instruction* 2002, but not in the former editions of 1969, or in the first printed versions of 2002. Irwin, *Models of the Eucharist*, 279. Like the *General Instruction of the Roman Missal (2002) on the Holy Spirit* the *Catechism of the Catholic Church* also accentuates the role of the Holy Spirit in the Eucharist as it says about the transformation, "bread and wine which, by the power of the Holy Spirit and by the words of Christ, have become the

Thus, the document affirms the activity of Holy Spirit in the Eucharist with no ambiguity. Regrettably, both the *General Instruction*, as well as the epicletic prayers of the Roman rite in its present form, present the role of the Holy Spirit in "power categories." The expression, "by the power of your Holy Spirit" (Eucharistic Prayer III) and even weaker expressions of other Eucharistic prayers do not adequately represent the personhood and mediatory role of the Holy Spirit in the sacramental event. Eucharistic Prayers II and IV may be an exception to this charge as they use more or less an explicit language that accounts for the personhood and the activity of the Holy Spirit ("Let your Spirit come upon these gifts..." and "may this Spirit sanctify these offerings..." respectively). Eliminating "the power of" (i.e., by your Spirit) would better signify what the Holy Spirit *is* and *does* in the sacramental event. It is important to notice that the memorial-offering prayers use expressions such as "by the Holy Spirit" (Eucharistic Prayer II), "filled with his Holy Spirit" (Eucharistic Prayer III) and "by your Holy Spirit" (Eucharistic Prayer III) that make clearer the personhood and activity of the Holy Spirit in the realization of the unity of the assembly/Church.[188] We purport to argue that the Eucharistic prayers should be revised so as to express the personhood and the mediatory role of the Holy Spirit in the liturgical celebration.

Moreover, the activity of the Holy Spirit must be understood, not only in terms of the realization of the Eucharist and the unity of the Church, but also the very "condition" of that which makes the event possible. As Irwin argues, the inclusion of the epiclesis in the Roman tradition, "(re)establishes the Spirit as the person of the Trinity who initiates and sustains our being able to take part in the paschal victory of Christ through the doing of the Eucharist itself."[189] Employing Marion's insights, it can be said that the participation in the liturgy is not of one's own accord, something that one makes or generates, but rather, it is the originary givenness of the Spirit that initiates and acts in and through the language and symbols, enabling the believer to participate in the mystery of Christ in the Eucharist. Thus, the privileged position ascribed to the epiclesis in the Eucharistic prayer attests to the role of the Spirit in initiating and capacitating us to celebrate the Eucharist.

---

body and blood of Christ" (no. 1357). Therefore, the transformation of the Eucharistic gifts can be understood both from Christological and Pneumatological perspectives.

188. A comparative table of the texts of the Eucharistic Prayers I-IV is available from http://catholic-resources.org/ChurchDocs/EP1-4.htm (accessed 30 January 2010).

189. Irwin, *Models of the Eucharist*, 281.

3.3.3.1. The Iconicity of Epiclesis

The idea that the realization of the sacraments is brought about by the Holy Spirit is not foreign to the Western Church. This is true, especially with regard to the Eucharist. Even though the structure of the Eucharistic prayers of the East and the West slightly differ from each other, they have the same coherence and meaning. The chief difference is that the pre-reformed liturgies of the West do not contain an epiclesis that has an explicitly consecratory function, as in the East, and that the order of the epiclesis is different from that of the Eastern liturgies. Eastern liturgies, in general, place the epiclesis after the memorial-offering prayer, whereas the Western liturgies place it before the institution narrative.[190] In the Eastern Eucharistic prayers, there is a single epiclesis over the gifts and the assembly, after the words of institution and the memorial-offering prayer. For example, in *the Anaphora of the Twelve Apostles*, used in the Syro-Malankara Church, the priest prays: "Have mercy on us, O Lord, have mercy upon us and send down your life-giving Spirit from your holy abode. May he descend over this Offering and make this the life-giving Body; and may he pardon and sanctify us."[191] *The Anaphora of Addai and Mari*, which is used in the Syro-Malabar Church, also contains a similar epiclesis after the institution narrative and the memorial-offering prayer.[192]

The variations in the order of the epiclesis, although important to a certain degree, are not contradictory, especially when one considers the Anaphora in its integrity. Whether or not all the rubrics are found in the same order does not concern the content and character of the Eucharistic prayer as a whole. Congar rightly points out, that if a prayer falls after the institution narrative, it does not mean that consecration is taking place only after it.[193] The entire structure of the Anaphora reveals that "what has to be accomplished in the believers through the action of the Holy Spirit comes from the sacrament-sacrifice, which is the commemoration of the actions and gifts of salvation, for which thanks are given."[194] Despite the differences, the whole liturgical

---

190. Vischer, "Epiclesis," 30-31.

191. *The Order of the Holy Qurbano of the Syro-Malankara Church*, trans. C.A. Abraham (Trivandrum: Malankara Academy, 1986), 54.

192. Syro-Malabar Bishops' Conference, *Syro-Malabar Sabhayude Qurbana*, 74.

193. Congar, *I Believe in the Holy Spirit*, 3: 238.

194. *Ibid.*, 3: 230.

action manifests the Christological and Pneumatological dimensions in realising the sacrament. As Vischer writes,

> [t]he content and character of a Liturgy is not decided by whether a certain rubric appears in a certain place. The whole liturgical event is invocation of the Spirit, the whole liturgical process represents Christ's original action, and the Eucharistic celebration can be understood in this way apart from the position of any individual rubric. In this connection we also ought not to forget that both forms stood alongside one another in the ancient Church without for this reason occasioning tensions or even divisions.[195]

The divergences are significant to the degree that they point to the diverse views regarding the role of Christ and the Holy Spirit in Eastern and Western theology. These divergences can be seen in their mutuality and complementariness, provided that the words of institution and the epiclesis are understood iconically within the whole of the Eucharistic prayer. What is important, however, is to note that both in the Eastern and Western liturgies, in the solemn words pronounced by the priest, it is the whole assembly who prays so that the Holy Spirit may come upon the gift to sanctify them and to sanctify the assembly who partake of them so that the participants may become the true Body of Christ united with the offering of Christ to the Father.[196] The epiclesis, be it in the liturgies of the East and the West, is the *icon* of the abiding presence and work of the Holy Spirit in the Church, which is attested to by the biblical witness, and developed by the ancient liturgies of the East in various directions.[197] Furthermore, the role of the Holy Spirit must be understood in the light of what the Spirit realizes in the individual and collective life of the community.

3.3.3.2. The Spirit and the 'Fecundity' of the Sacrament

The epiclesis of the Eastern liturgies makes clear that the Holy Spirit not only brings about the Eucharistic presence of Christ in the offerings, but also transforms the faithful. Actualising Christ's presence, the Holy Spirit makes the Eucharist the sacrament of the sanctification of the faithful.[198] As it becomes evident from the epiclesis of different liturgies, a two-fold appeal has

195. Vischer, "Epiclesis," 31.
196. Robert J. Daly, "Sacrifice Unveiled or Sacrifice Revisited: Trinitarian and Liturgical Perspectives," *Theological Studies* 64 (2003): 35.
197. Vischer, "Epiclesis," 34. We prefer to replace Vischer's term "sign" with "icon."
198. Hall, *We Have the Mind of Christ*, 117.

been made, namely, for the transformation of the bread and wine and the transformation of the liturgical assembly.[199] The community makes this appeal so that, through this celebration the unity between Christ and his faithful and the unity of the faithful with one another and with the Father in Christ may be deepened and manifested. The Holy Spirit sanctifies the Eucharistic community and enables it to offer acceptable worship to the Father in union with the crucified and the risen Lord.[200] The community firmly believes that its appeal will be heard and that God will be pleased to act according to his promise; it partakes of the gifts in true faith that God has answered its petition.[201] The function of the epicletic prayer, which is traditionally located after the anamnesis and offering, asks for the fruit of unity in the life of the participants. In other words, the effects or the fruits of the epiclesis (through the participation in the Eucharistic elements) are for the benefit of the community: unity and oneness of the body, the liturgical assembly.[202] Epiclesis, in general, places emphasis on the threefold actions of the Holy Spirit, namely, on the participants, on the elements, and in giving the full effect of the Eucharist in the life of the participants.[203] The epiclesis before communion (communion epiclesis) is in view of the transformation of the assembly. There is hardly any liturgy where one cannot find a reference to the Holy Spirit in one form or other.[204] As Congar rightly points out, in the Western liturgies there are prayers having the place of an epiclesis, though they are not indisputably consecratory and Pneumatological in the strict sense.[205] For instance, in the Latin canon, there are texts, which allude to invocation, which contain the value of an epiclesis. For example, the prayer, *Supplices te rogamus* has an epicletic character, in that it contains a supplication that the

199. Of the twofold sanctification that is taking place in the Eucharist, the sanctification of the participating assembly is subordinate to the sanctification of the gifts, though not unimportant. It is subordinate in the sense that the transformation of the gifts is the basis for the transformation of the assembly. Daly, "Sacrifice Unveiled," 39.

200. Kilmartin, "The Catholic Tradition of the Eucharist," 343.

201. Vischer, "Epiclesis," 30-31.

202. Patrick McGoldrick, "The Holy Spirit and the Eucharist," *The Irish Theological Quarterly* 50 (1983/84). In this article, McGoldrick makes a study highlighting the efficacy and fruitfulness of the Eucharist with special emphasis on Pneumatology.

203. *Ibid.*, 54 ff.

204. Vischer, "Epiclesis," 30.

205. Congar also says that though the Latin Church is convinced of the consecratory function of the words of institution, there are enough evidences to testify to the fact that the role of the Holy Spirit was admitted in the realization of the sacraments, especially in the Eucharist. See Congar, *I Believe in the Holy Spirit*, 3: 250-256.

offerings may be accepted by God and accounts for the obtainment of spiritual fruits.[206] The effects of the Eucharist, which the Spirit brings to fullness, are practically the same as what Western theology understands as the *res sacramenti*.[207] Therefore, in general, the transformation of the gifts alone does not explain the whole mystery of the Eucharistic celebration. The transformation of the gift should lead to the greater end, namely the transformation of the assembly, and thereby, the building up of the mystical body of Christ.[208] The real meaning of the transformation is realized only when the faithful are transformed into the body of Christ in the real sense of the term. The ultimate goal of the sacraments, specifically the transformation of the bread and wine, cannot be for the reason that they might simply be there. The final purpose of the gifts becoming the body and blood of Christ is not an end in itself, but it happens so that the worshipping community may become completely and really the ecclesial body of Christ.[209] The Eucharistic gift is given, not only to be consumed and passive, assimilating Christ into the human person, as consuming ordinary food, that find its end in the human person, but rather, the human person is assimilated into the ecclesial body of Christ. As Marion puts it, "[i]n consuming this food [the Eucharist], we do not assimilate the Christ – to our person or to our "social" body…, [o]n the contrary, we become assimilated through the sacramental body of the Christ to his ecclesial body."[210] "The bread and the wine must be consumed, to be sure, but so that our definitive union with the Father may be consummated in them, through communion with the ecclesiastical body of his Son."[211] Therefore, the Eucharistic presence is not for its own sake, but is a presence for the faithful. It is significant to note that the expression "for you" is invariably present with the words over the bread and the words over the cup. Thus, the transformation of the bread and wine is for the partaking of the faithful. Through the partaking of the consecrated bread and wine, the assembly becomes "one body and one spirit in Christ."[212] As Marion points out, the Eucharistic present is a mutuality of "sacramental commitment and ecclesiastic-

---

206. Congar, *I Believe in the Holy Spirit*, 3: 250.
207. See McGoldrick, "The Holy Spirit," 55.
208. McKenna, *Eucharist and the Holy Spirit*, 130.
209. Daly, "Sacrifice Unveiled," 37; Jozef Lamberts, "Eucharist and the Holy Spirit," *Theology Digest* 34 (1987): 55.
210. Here, Marion is referring to Bonaventure, and indicates that the same notion is found in St. Augustine. Marion, *God Without Being*, 179.
211. *Ibid.*, 179.
212. *The Roman Missal*, 554.

al edification."[213] The name of the Holy Spirit was attributed to the fruit of the Eucharist, i.e., the oneness of the assembly as one body, the ecclesia (1Cor 10:17; 11:17). The basis of this oneness is rooted in the givenness of the call at baptism: "In the one Spirit we were all baptized into one body" (1Cor 12:13). Thus, by the sharing of one body, the Eucharistic body, the assembly becomes one body (ecclesia) by the work of the Holy Spirit.

Moreover, the sacrament of the Eucharist cannot be understood merely as the presence of Christ in the consecrated bread and wine, but rather, the Eucharistic presence has to be understood as the liturgical presence of the whole mystery of Christ, because the mystery of Christ is essentially the mystery of salvation. The Second Vatican Council affirms that "the work of our redemption is accomplished" in and through the celebration of the liturgy (SC 7). Through the sacramental event, God gifts Godself to the creatures (us) a share in the divine mystery. The gift that is given in the sacramental event is the event of Jesus Christ, the mystery of our salvation. Therefore, the Eucharistic presence must be explained in terms of the givenness of God as love in the iconic figure of Christ (death), resurrection, the gift of the Spirit, as well as the *parousia*. The ultimate phase of the transformation of the participants is the realization of salvation. The transformation of the participants cannot be viewed as an accomplished reality in this life. However, the faithful, through their participation in the liturgy, try to imbibe the dispositions of Christ in their daily lives, whose complete realization is believed to be an eschatological event.[214] Liturgical anamnesis, not only realizes the past in the present, but the present enactment is oriented towards the future. The celebration of the reality-event (Christ event) becomes meaningful only to the extent that it is valuable and meaningful for the future.[215] In this sense, the eschatological dimension of the Eucharist comes to the forefront. Significant-

---

213. Marion, *God Without Being*, 179.

214. Daly, "Sacrifice Unveiled," 40. According to the Eastern understanding, the Spirit divinizes the community as well. Accordingly, "[t]he Christian community and its members become divinized. This might be a partial explanation of the centrality of the Feast of the Transfiguration in the East. Christ is the prototype; what happens to him is happening to the believing, worshipping Christian in the context of Eucharistic celebration." Albertine, "The Epiclesis Question," 389. In his doctoral dissertation, defended quite recently, John Cherian makes a rather extensive study of the notion of *theosis* in regard to the sacraments from an Eastern perspective. John Cherian, "Being Human Becoming Divine: A Sacramentological Re-interpretation of *Theosis* as a Mirco- and Macrocosmic Metamorphosis" (Unpublished doctoral dissertation, K.U. Leuven, 2008).

215. Worgul, *Magic to Metaphor*, 216.

ly, the account of the Passover that Jesus celebrated with his disciples ends
with an eschatological note (1Cor 11:26; Mk 14:25; Lk 22:16). In this sense,
the Eucharistic presence is the presence of the mystery of Christ for the
community in the present, between the times, "already" and "not-yet." The
Church's liturgical faith, which has been celebrated since the resurrection, is
expressed in the acclamation after the words of institution: "Christ has died,
Christ is risen, Christ will come again."[216] Only the icon permits one to consent to such a presence, the presence between the "already" and "not-yet,"
characterised by "disappearance," "absence," and "distance" that traverses
the limits of the metaphysical concept of presence. The Spirit's operation
consists, not only in making the Eucharist and effecting the fruits of the Eucharist in the participating assembly, but also in the fact that in and through
the Eucharist, the Spirit is given. In other words, the absence of the presence
of God in the present (here and now), is filled by the Spirit, whom Jesus bestows, in accordance with his promise, on the disciples when he goes away
(John 16:17).

Briefly speaking, the whole interplay of language and symbolic actions,
especially the core words and actions of the narrative of institution and the
epiclesis, iconically symbolise the gift of God in Christ and the Spirit, which
the liturgical assembly can, in its own competence, neither realise nor conceptually explain, but only receive as given. The fact that various liturgical
traditions accentuate, in greater or lesser degree, one or the other aspect of
the celebration only exposes the limits of human conceptuality in exhausting
and demonstrating the excess of God's self-giving in the sacraments which
God in his infinite love realizes for the worshipping community. Sacraments
realize the overwhelming presence in the Holy Spirit, in absence (Luke
24:34), which can be received solely as "given" in such a way that we can
never "cognise," but only "recognise" as in the icon. However, understanding
the sacrament as given and viewing the sacrament as the work of the Holy
Spirit, especially the sanctification of the faithful, does not underestimate the
conscious involvement of the subject in the sacramental event. Here lies the
question of ethical engagement and the notion of return.

---

216. These and other forms of acclamations after the words of institution are the addition
of the post-Vatican liturgical renewal.

3.4. 'Re-turn' in the Liturgy

As has been observed already, Chauvet's treatment of the question of return suffers from the notion of "obligatory return" although he tries to purge it by raising the whole scheme to the realm of symbolic exchange.[217] Agreeably, Chauvet's scheme easily incorporates the Christian concept of return. However, its weakness emerges from his fundamental assumption that every gift obligates a return-gift. Thus, his attempt to reconcile "gratuitousness" and "graciousness" fall short of achieving its goal, because the notion of an *obligatory* return counteracts the "gift character" of the gift as gift. On the contrary, Marion has been challenged for watering down the aspect of return, retaining the notion of pure gift. For instance, O'Leary charges that "the ethical purism of his [Marion's] conception of giving might undercut the give-and-take of the Eucharist as a sacrifice and as communal sharing…, [because] [t]he offering of a ritual gift, or a sacrifice, is a risk and a challenge that certainly seeks a response, consisting basically in the recognition of the other party."[218] O'Leary's criticism of Marion, in general, is that his phenomenology fails to take seriously the empirical experiences of giving and receiving as human relational activities which are guided by principles other than that of economy.[219] He implies that the highest form of ethical dynamics of giving of the Eucharist cannot be reduced to mere economic exchange, although it implies the concepts of exchange and return gift. This being the case, rejection of return *as such*, obliterates the whole scheme of return in sacramental economy. Therefore, an understanding of sacramental gift accommodating the notion of return is proposed, examining the liturgical dynamics, as exemplified in the Eucharist, and the involvement of the human subject in the sacramental event.

The notion of return does not favour an explanation of the sacraments as giving and receiving "some-thing" in terms of the giver, the givee, and the gift, on the basis of a subject-object relationship. God's giving is to someone, the human subject, and giving involves a relationship (covenant). However, what is called into question is; first, understanding sacraments as some-thing (a canned substance) which is given "measured," and received passively by

217. "Every gift received obligates … [I]t obligates the recipient to the return-gift of an expression of gratitude." Chauvet, *Symbol and Sacrament*, 267.

218. O'Leary, "The Gift," 147-148.

219. For O'Leary's criticism on "the Reason of the Gift," see O'Leary, "The Gift," 149-166.

the human subject; secondly, the involvement of the subject in terms of an "obligatory" return.

3.4.1. Gift-Exchange

A Pneumatological and phenomenological approach to the sacraments encourages one to re-interpret the gift-exchange in the sacraments in terms of givenness. The term "economy," originally borrowed from the world of commerce, is commonly used in the liturgical vocabulary in order to designate the mystery of redemption enacted in the sacrament. The exchange that takes place in the sacrament is specifically designated by the term *commercium*.[220] However, the sacramental exchange cannot be understood in terms of economic exchange, because, as Power explains, the exchange that takes place in the sacrament is the divine-human exchange in the mystery of redemption which begins in the incarnation. God's giving in the sacraments is not a return for what human beings offer to God from what is given to them, but God's giving itself. Therefore, what constitutes the exchange is not the offering of gifts by the community, but rather, the gift that comes from God as in the incarnation. As he puts it,

> [i]t is God's gift and giving which makes the sacrament, not the people's. The gift given by God is not a return for what the people have brought or offered, but a reversal of the order of giving, placing it totally, like the incarnation, in the gratuitous initiative of God. The *commercium* initiated by the taking on of flesh by the Word is celebrated in thanksgiving, and communicated in sacramental reception.[221]

The exchange that takes place in the sacrament is not concerned with the human person's giving of something back to God. Therefore, the sacramental gift has to be thought of as beginning from the originary gift of God. The worshipping community bring and offer the gifts to God so that they may be taken up into the celebration of God's giving in the Word made flesh so that the gifts may be incorporated in the Spirit in the communion of the body and blood of Christ.[222] Just as the Word assumed flesh in the incarnation, mediated by the Spirit, the gifts are transformed into the gift of God, the body and blood of Christ.

---

220. Power, "Sacrament: An Economy of Gift," 147; Power, *Sacrament*, 277
221. Power, "Sacrament: An Economy of Gift," 147.
222. Power, *Sacrament*, 277.

The liturgical celebration is characterised by the interplay of two elements, namely "reception" and "oblation." According to Power, paradoxically, the sacramental gift is received by thanksgiving: "the *reception*" effected
by means of *oblation … [the] appropriation is through disappropriation.*"[223]
In the Eucharist, this is symbolised in the ritual oblation of the anamnesis.
Oblation is not considered to be a return gift for the gift received in the sacrament. Instead, the gift aspect must be placed before that of the oblation.
Power charges that Catholic theology tends to emphasize the "ecclesial action of offering sacrifice more than the receiving the gift of Christ's body and
blood with thanksgiving."[224] He argues that according to the early Eucharistic
tradition, the blessing and thanksgiving prayer over the gifts itself was called
sacrifice. Therefore, he suggests for retrieving the "table" placing the "gift"
at the center of our understanding of the Eucharist, because

> [t]he gift – of God's love, of Christ, of Spirit, of one to the other, enfleshed
> and bestowed with promise – is the central image, not the sacrificial action of
> the church. It is in the giving of the gift, indeed with blessing, that the sacri-
> fice of Christ is in the first place sacramentally renewed. We must learn anew
> that what counts is not what is *done* but what God gives and humans re-
> ceive.[225]

In the Eucharistic prayer, God's gift is praised and given thanks. A gift is
given to someone, the gifted. In the liturgy, it is to the Church that the gift is
given. A gift given establishes a relationship, which is gratuitous and gracious, not of obligation, but evokes a gratitude and response which manifests
itself in praise and thanksgiving. This thanksgiving is clearly manifested in
the preface, a thanksgiving addressed to God as a response to the divine gift.
However, thanksgiving is not, in the strict sense, an equal return to the divine
gift, which human beings, in their capacity, are unable to make, but a response and thanksgiving in appreciation and acceptance. Thus, the gratitude
and praise become the mode in which the gift of God is actually accepted,
but it is not a return gift to the gift of God. In this sense, the obligatory return, as in the gift-exchange scheme of Mauss, cannot be retained in explaining the Eucharist gift.[226] Moreover, can there be the gift at the point of rejec-

223. *Ibid.*, 277.
224. *Ibid.*, 277.
225. Power, "A Prophetic Eucharist," 43.
226. Even though Mazza attempts to explain the Eucharist from the perspective of the gift
employing the gift-exchange scheme of Mauss, he acknowledges the notion of Eucharistic gift
traverses the anthropological notion of the gift. See Enrico Mazza, *The Eucharistic Prayers of*

tion? Marion's view retains the gift, even at the point of rejection, either rejected or misunderstood. The gift becomes true gift at the point of rejection
and abandonment, whereas for Chauvet, rejection breaks the circuit of exchange. In that case, one cannot receive the gift as gift. However, in line with
the thought of Marion, the gift remains as gift irrespective of the response of
the givee. The graciousness and gratuitousness of the gift can be fully retained only by thinking of the gift in terms of an *apriori* givenness which
makes gift a gift. The return gift is not a return as such, but it is entering the
course of gift in reception by thanksgiving. Even if the givee fails to enter
this flow, the circuit is unbroken, as opposed to Chauvet. Those who do not
silence voice of the Spirit, or hinder the augmentation of the Spirit will surely
enter into the circuit, and the reception in praise and thanksgiving will out-
burst as charity in a living in grace with others, which can be designated as
sacramental ethics.

3.4.2. Doxology

A sacramental theology in terms of givenness encourages us to illustrate the
connection between "doxology/praise" and "presence/gift." According to
Marion, God's presence is received by a blessing as witnessed by the Emmaus event and ascension. The risen Christ "took bread, blessed and broke it,
and gave it to them. Then their eyes were opened and they recognized him"
(Lk 24:30-31). According to Luke's first account of the ascension (Lk 24:50-
53), Jesus blesses (εὐλόγησεν) the disciples while he was being taken up to
heaven, and the disciples return to Jerusalem blessing (εὐλογοῦντες) God.
As Marion puts it, "[t]he presence of Christ ... discloses itself by a gift; it can
therefore be recognized only by a blessing ... [and] received only in being
blessed."[227] According to him, "the blessing, at the heart of which the Ascension is accomplished, cannot be separated from the Eucharistic blessing."[228]
Even though, as testified in both instances, the departure and disappearance
coincides with blessing, paradoxically, the gift of presence is realised in departure, distance, disappearance and absence; the very moment of pres-
ence/recognition is paradoxically the moment of departure/ disappearance
(Lk 24:31,51). Therefore, in this sense, it is possible to say that what the

the Roman Rite, trans. Mathew J. O'Connel (New York: Pueblo, 1986), 44-47; Enrico Mazza,
The Celebration of the Eucharist, 283-284.
    227. Marion, *Prolegomena to Charity*, 129.
    228. *Ibid.*, 55.

Church does in the liturgy is to fulfill the *only* function and mission of welcoming and acknowledging "the gift of the presence of God in and as Christ."[229] Therefore, the function of the liturgical assembly is not to "summon" Christ's presence "here and now," but rather, recognize God's gift-giving in Christ.

The interrelationship between presence and praise does not mean that the latter constitutes the condition of the former, but rather the condition for recognizing presence. Thus, in the community's blessing God, the language of liturgical praise, and thanksgiving (*eucharistia*), is for recognizing God's gift of presence, without being mis-recognized and disfigured.[230] In this sense, our Eucharistic praise and thanksgiving, first and foremost, manifests the community's grateful reception of the gift of presence. As Marion states,

> [n]ot that the blessing of men functions as the condition for the possibility of the presence of Christ, but of Christ's being recognized by them. Christ can give the present of his presence without any condition; but as long as men do not bless God, this presence offered remains … rejected and disfigured.[231]

The liturgical evidence of the early Church also attests to this inseparable relationship between praise and presence/gift. Mazza explains the dual aspects that constituted the "eucharist" in the early Church as it is evident from *Didache* 9 and 10.[232] In the first place, the bread and wine, the gift of the Eucharist that God gives, and the Eucharistic prayer in which the human being give thanks to God, represent the human person's gift in response to the gift of the Eucharist. The gift given in thanksgiving is nothing other than the gift the human person receives from God, because God's giving exceeds one's ability to make an adequate return on the human person's own accord. Therefore, it goes beyond the scheme of gift-exchange, but human persons can only give an appropriate response of praise and thanksgiving which is actually a simple way of acknowledging and accepting the gift.

---

229. *Ibid.*, 130.

230. The term comes from the verb *eucharistein* (to give thanks) which designates "thanksgiving" which belongs to the Eucharist from the beginning (1Cor 1:23-25). The oldest reference to the name "Eucharist" is found in *Didache* where *eucharistia* is translated as "thanksgiving" (9:1) and as "Eucharist." See Paul F. Bradshaw, *Eucharistic Origins* (New York: Oxford University Press, 2004), 25; Eugene LaVerdiere, *The Eucharist in the New Testament and Early Church* (Collegeville, MN: Liturgical Press, 1996), 1-2.

231. Marion, *Prolegomena to Charity*, 129.

232. Mazza, *Eucharistic Prayers*, 45.

In the Eucharistic celebration, the community reaches the high point of the order of gifts, and the believers even pass beyond that order, since their gratitude, the gift they offer to God in exchange, does not represent an exchange in the true and proper sense. In fact, gratitude is simply the way of receiving and accepting a gift. The members of the assembly even pass beyond the order of giving, because here there is no return of an authentic gift on their part; such a return is simply impossible for them, since all what they have has been freely received from God.[233]

3.4.2.1. The Spirit and Praise

As has already been explained, the basic symbolic reality of the Church as a worshipping community is based on our identity as *l'adonné* which is realized by the Spirit. The basic symbolic reality of the Church is manifested in the praise and thanksgiving of the liturgical community that shares the same Spirit who makes them call God, "Abba," "Father" (Gal 4:6, Rom 8:15-16) and establishes a relation of filiation between the members. Thus, the role of the Holy Spirit in the liturgy, especially as manifested by epiclesis, is very important. Human persons are not the authors of their thanksgiving; it is God who produces thanksgiving in human persons, even the desire for giving thanks. As the fourth preface for weekdays states, "our desire to thank you is itself your gift." The prefaces commemorate and describe the gift God has given to the entire humanity, particularly the gift of grace and salvation.[234] As LaVerdiere points out, "remembering an act of memory is the spark of thanksgiving."[235] Therefore, in the Eucharist, thanksgiving is through the act of memory. There is a close connection between the liturgical acts of praise and thanksgiving (*blessing*), anamnesis (*memorial*), and presence. The narrative of institution finds its place in relation to the realisation of the salvation in Jesus, and as its fulfilment in the future of the Church. The epiclesis occupies a central place in the narrative, because the story is narrated as a living memorial in the Spirit. The Spirit brings into historical presence the past, relating it to the future. "In order for the past of what is commemorated in the narrative of the institution (of the Eucharist) to be sacramentally given us in the present and to open a future for us, the Spirit must bring it to the memory

---

233. *Ibid.*, 46.
234. *Ibid.*, 44.
235. LaVerdiere, *The Eucharist*, 17.

of the Church."[236] It is in this sense that Marion says, "the highest presence of Christ lies in the Spirit's action of making us, with him and in him, *bless* the Father."[237] This way of understanding liturgy is in line with the patristic understanding of the liturgical dynamics as a movement from the Father through Christ in the Spirit and back to the Father. Accordingly, every liturgical movement was understood to be a movement "from the Father, through Christ His Son, in the Spirit, to the Father, blessed Trinity, one God."[238] The liturgical dynamics consists of a double movement: God's gift of himself, and humankind going back to the Father. It is a Trinitarian movement. God comes to human persons through the Son in the Spirit, and humankind goes back to the Father through the Son in the Spirit. A moderate way of expressing this would be by regarding epiclesis as an integral part of the narrative of the memorial event. Chauvet makes this connection quite obvious in his presentation of the narrative analysis of the Eucharistic prayer, placing epiclesis in the narrative movement of the whole Eucharistic prayer.[239] He explains how the narrative programme of the Eucharistic prayer brings into focus the integral relationship between the past, present, and future in the liturgical dynamics. Accordingly, the sacramental "presence" (the coming-to-presence) of Christ can only be understood in relation to the twofold memorial, namely, the memorial of the past in thanksgiving, and a memorial of the future in supplication.

Strictly speaking, Chauvet never regards the *oblation* as a return gift for the gift of God, but it is for receiving or appropriating grace, which is beyond "object" and "value." However, Chauvet points out that the return-gift, symbolically represented in the ritual, needs to be "verified" elsewhere, in an

236. Chauvet, *Symbol and Sacrament*, 510.

237. Marion, *Prolegomena to Charity*, 144.

238. Cipriano Vagaggini, *Theological Dimensions of the Liturgy* (Collegeville, MN: The Liturgical Press, 1976), 116. McDonnell points out that this liturgical dynamic, as understood by the Fathers, is based on their understanding of the Father as the source from which the double mission goes out and to which they return: a *Patre ad Patrem*. The patristic way of understanding the liturgy is based on the biblical witness which juxtaposes the mission of Christ and the Spirit (Rom 8:15; Gal 4:6; Eph 2:18; 1Cor 15:24). See McDonnel, "A Trinitarian Theology of the Holy Spirit," 211.

239. Chauvet, *Symbol and Sacrament*, 268-272. Considering the Eucharistic prayer as a single unit will help us to understand the account of institution and epiclesis as mutually complementary. As Kilmartin says, the integration of the liturgical account of institution into the literary-theological movement consists of showing how the narrative institution and anamnesis-offering prayer form a unit and how the unit of epiclesis-intercessions is linked to the former unit. Kilmartin, *Eucharist in the West*, 354.

ethical engagement. According to Chauvet, the return-gift is indispensable, so much so that lacking this obligatory return breaks the circuit of exchange and prevents the individual from receiving the gift as gift, although the return-gift cannot be regarded as a *pay off* towards God, which is humanly impossible. Nevertheless, the ritual-offering symbolises a return-gift that pertains to the realm of our ethical relationship with others.[240] Although Chauvet tries to overcome the vestiges of economic exchange in his symbolic scheme, it continues to be tainted by the insistence on the *obligatory* return. Therefore, the notion of obligatory return, in some way diminishes the freedom of the individual and the gratuitousness of God's gift of grace. In contrast to Chauvet, what must be upheld is a way of looking at the question of return in the sacramental economy, beginning from the *apriori* givenness of God.[241]

In this regard, can one think of a return-gift as a response augmented by the Spirit, who mediates the sacramental gift to the community? Instead, the return-gift is more a *re-turn*, which is, in fact, to consent to the givenness of the Spirit, who is working in the Church who makes the community the body of Christ, by augmenting the liturgy of the neighbour. The individual freedom, the free response to the grace would mean allowing, or not hindering, the work of the gift of the Spirit. It is not an "obligatory" response, but rather it allows room for the Spirit to work in the believing subjects. The notion of "obligatory" return seems to obliterate the graciousness and gratuitousness of God's giving and the free human response. The augmentation of the Spirit in the sacraments has another dimension. As shall be expatiated below, just like the augmentation of the Spirit is manifested in the liturgical praise, the activity of the Spirit must be evident in one's ethical commitment as well.

3.4.3. Sacramental Praxis

The inseparable relationship between the sacraments and ethics has been emphasised in sacramental theology with diverse emphases. Theological manuals laid much stress on the moral disposition of the recipient in the reception of the sacraments, particularly of the Eucharist. Moreover, moral theology was even considered, to a great extent, as a part of sacramental the-

240. Chauvet, *Symbol and Sacrament*, 282.
241. It must be noted that the Eucharistic ethics that we develop in the following pages is in tune with what Chauvet's "ethics," one of the tripod. However, as was mentioned earlier, we differ from Chauvet in viewing ethics in terms of "return" and in characterizing the return as mediated (augmented) by the Holy Spirit.

ology. However, in contemporary discussions in sacramental theology, the relationship between the sacraments and ethics pertains mainly to the question of the nature of the relationship between the sacrament and certain disciplines of life.[242] As Van Eijk further explains, this does not consist in a "consequent ethics," but rather, "constitutive ethics." It does not mean that the sacraments constitute a specific way of living, but ethical living precedes the sacraments; in other words, ethics is not the result of being the Church, but ethics is the very being (ontological category) of the Church. There is a mutual coherence and interdependence between ethics and the sacraments. The classical axiom, "the law of prayer establishes the law of belief" (*legem credendi lex statuat supplicandi*) denotes the intrinsic relationship that exists between what community prays and what the community believes.[243] In the same way, there must be an integral relation between what the community says in liturgy (*orandi*), what the community believes through liturgy (*credendi*), and how the community views and live their lives (*vivendi*).[244] In this connection, it is remarkable to note that Christians were named after the peculiar way in which the first Christians lived their lives. Balthasar emphatically points this out as he says, "[t]he sacraments are dispensed in daily life, not in the church; in conversation, not during a sermon."[245] Thus, sacramental praxis belongs integrally to the life of the Christians as individuals, and to the community as a whole.

A sacramental hermeneutics founded on the phenomenology of givenness does not reduce human subjects to passive recipients. Instead, it encourages one to consider the individual as an active participant in the whole "sacramental process," which is a process of giving initiated and moved by the Spirit. For, as Daly observes,

---

242. A. H. C. van Eijk, "Ethics and the Eucharist," *Bijdragen, Tijdschrift voor filosofie en theologie* 55 (1994): 351. A major course in the post-Vatican II period is the influence of praxis methodologies of liberation theology on sacraments and liturgy. See Power, Duffy, and Irwin, "Sacramental Theology: A Review," 675-684. For instance, Feminist theologians have broadened the sphere extending ethical concerns to gender issues. Susan Roll, "Language and Justice in the Liturgy," in *A Tribute to Silveer De Smet*, ed. Lambert Leijssen, Textes et études liturgiques/Studies in Liturgy (Leuven: Abdij Keizersberg/Faculteit der Godgeleerdheid, 1992); Susan A. Ross, *Extravagant Affections: A Feminist Sacramental Theology* (New York: Continuum, 1998).

243. Irwin, *Context and Text*, 3-43. See also Kevin W. Irwin, "Origins of the Notion of 'Liturgical Theology'," in *Liturgical Theology: A Primer* (Collegeville, MN: Liturgical Press, 1990), 11-17.

244. Irwin, "Sacramentality and the Theology of Creation," 169.

245. See Balthasar, *Glory of the Lord*, 371-378.

... if the transformation of the Eucharistic elements is not having its effect in the virtuous dispositions of the participants, if the participants are not at least beginning to be transformed, at least beginning to appropriate the self-offering virtuous dispositions of Christ, then there is no Eucharistic presence.[246]

Therefore, the mystery celebrated in the sacraments must find concrete expression in the life of the participants. In agreement with Daly, it can be affirmed that the real meaning of the Eucharist is accomplished by the reception of the liturgical assembly. However, one must be cautious not to deny the teaching of an objective real presence of the Eucharist. In the strict sense, the real presence of the Eucharist cannot be dependent on the reception and the belief of the individual, but rather, it can be said that Christ's sacramental offer assumes full meaning when this offer is accepted by the faithful.[247] Nevertheless, the offer, the gift, even if not received, does not cease to be an offer. In fact, the sacramental offer of the Eucharist becomes "real" for the faithful as far as it is accepted in true faith. In this sense, Eucharistic presence cannot be confined to the somatic real presence divorced from the liturgical context and independent of the faithful. The somatic presence of Christ in the Eucharist is meant to result in a fuller presence in the faithful, and thereby, actualise their sanctification.[248] Therefore, the response of the faithful is important to the meaningful sacramental life of Christians who partake of them. This pertains to the responsibility of responding positively to the gift given in the sacrament by contributing to the building up of the ecclesial body of Christ. As Leijssen rightly points out, even our response to God's love must be understood as the work of the "Spirit active and moving within us" who is given to us in and through the sacraments.[249]

The relationship between the sacraments and ethics is based on the relationship between the Eucharistic body and the ecclesial body. The Eucharistic presence was integrally related to "the liturgical context in which it arises, and from the ecclesial context for which it arises."[250] This relationship be-

---

246. Daly, "Sacrifice Unveiled," 37.

247. McKenna, *Eucharist and the Holy Spirit*, 191; Schillebeeckx, *The Eucharist*, 140-141.

248. John H. McKenna, "Eucharistic Epiclesis: Myopia or Microcosm," *Theological Studies* 36 (1975): 266.

249. Leijssen, *The Silent Glimmer*, 35.

250. Chauvet, *Sacraments*, 140. The inseparable relationship between the Eucharistic body and the ecclesial body is very well explained by St. Paul in 1Cor 11:17-34; See also 1Cor 10:17. As Chauvet explains, in the tradition of the Church, we identify the threefold body of

tween the Eucharistic body and the ecclesial body is expressed in the communion epiclesis of the third Eucharistic prayer. The *return-gift* implied in
the *reception* of the *gift* of the Eucharist (Eucharistic body) implies the task
of building up the body of Christ. The "embodiment" of the sacraments is
through the mediation of the Holy Spirit. This is clear from the Eucharistic
prayer. The Spirit embodies the historical body of Christ (the Spirit in the
incarnation), the Eucharistic body, and the ecclesial body (first and second
epiclesis). So, the Spirit's action is linked, not only to the liturgical memorial, but also in "embodying" the "body of the Church," the ecclesia. Both
koinonia and *diakonia* inform each other, and they jointly constitute the center of being the Church. The liturgical celebrations bring to the fore the essential identity of the Church as a community, whose being is for others.

The mutual relationship between the Eucharistic body and the ecclesial
body expresses itself in living the mystery we celebrate, and celebrating the
mystery we live. Saturated with the divine love, the sacramental Church becomes the real icon of God's love which is celebrated in the mystery of the
Cross.[251] Thus, the Eucharistic memory perpetuates a memory in the life of
Christians effecting *metanoia* in themselves, and in the world in which they
live. As Power expresses it, "Eucharistic ritual is with a story and logic of
action that moves "out of" the story. The logic of the actions is inspired by
the story, but must move into another story, the story of the people gathered."[252] He goes on saying that "[i]n times of social and cultural crisis and
oppression, the Body of Christ is called to portray the life of an alternative
humanity in which God's Spirit works overcoming the death-dealing forces
aboard in the world."[253] The sacramental gift of love, the gift of himself and
of the Spirit should enable one to give oneself in love as a response to the
voice of the vulnerable in society. As Power puts it, "[d]rawing life from
within its liturgical gathering, the Church in its membership can speak with a
prophetic voice in the shaping of society, in the assurance of a divine love
and a divine generosity that is beyond measure, and of a divine justice

Christ, namely, the historical and glorified body of Christ, the Eucharistic (sacramental) body
of Christ and the ecclesial body of Christ. Up to the ninth century, the faith in the sacramental
body or in the presence of Christ in the Eucharist was professed, apparently without problem.
The emphasis was laid more on the relationship between the Eucharistic body and the ecclesial
body. Chauvet illustrates this in the light of the Pauline texts mentioned above, where Paul
speaks about the Eucharist in Corinthian community. See *idem*, 140-141.

251. Worgul, "Sacraments: Iconic Interruptions," 167.
252. Power, "A Prophetic Eucharist," 35.
253. *Ibid.*, 28.

beyond all justice."[254] This is the way that the liturgical assembly, as a community, is called to the excess of givenness that they receive in the gift of the
sacraments.

Marianne Sawicki observes that the early Christians "re-designed" the
figure of Christ after his death and disappearance. Jesus gave himself away at
three tables, namely, at the table of the word, at the table of the bread, and at
the table of the poor (where hunger and thirst becomes concrete venues of
experiencing the Risen One).[255] This parallels the three dimensions of the
liturgy, namely, the liturgy of the Word, the liturgy of the Eucharist and the
liturgy of the neighbor. According to Chauvet's triple structure of sacramentality, these are the three Christian tables, namely, the word, sacrament, and
ethics, exemplified in the Eucharist. The word preached, the word celebrated,
and the word practiced, constitute the sacramentality. Sacramental ethics, i.e.,
the word practiced, is integrally linked to the notion of sacramentality. In
fact, Christian life is the verification of the first two, namely, the word
preached and the sacrament celebrated. According to Chauvet, the word,
sacrament, and ethics symbolically constitute the Church, the body of Christ.
The word and the sacrament are authenticated or verified, not only by the
grace that they give, but also by the life they promote. In this sense, Chauvet
speaks about a unique sacramental ethics.[256] The ethical dimension of the
Eucharist that Chauvet develops is not merely moral, but rather, it is theological, because of being integral to sacramentality as such. The ethics in Chauvet's scheme is a counter-gift (human response) to the divine gift, which
makes it really Christian ethics.[257] Everyday life becomes the privileged
place of the liturgy of the neighbor wherein the real *euhcharistein* and *eucharistia* are taking place.

4. Conclusion

To sum up, in this chapter, we have proposed a sacramental thinking in terms
of the gift from a phenomenological and Pneumatological point of view. In
doing so, we have addressed the question of sacramental efficacy from a non-
metaphysical perspective, taking into account the developments in philoso-

---

254. *Ibid.*, 31.
255. Marianne Sawicki, *Seeing the Lord* (Minneapolis, MN: Fortress Press, 1994), 296-
297.
256. Chauvet, *Symbol and Sacrament*, 268.
257. Van Eijk, "Ethics and the Eucharist," 366.

phy and theology, especially in phenomenology and Pneumatology. Employing the notion of the icon, we have proposed a new understanding of sacraments as "iconic-symbols," in order to explain the excess of givenness in Christ and the Spirit, realized in and through the sacraments. This has been done with special reference to the Eucharist. From an iconic-symbolic perspective, we have also addressed a number of significant issues in sacramental theology in general, particularly of sacramental presence and grace with its corollary notions such as *in persona Christi*, the words of institution, epiclesis, etc. from a liturgical-theological point of view. Moreover, bearing in mind the question of the gift in contemporary postmodern theology, it has been argued that the "gift-reception-return" scheme is retainable in the understanding of sacramental and liturgical celebration and sacramental praxis (ethics), disengaging "return" from "obligation." Furthermore, any kind of automatic or self-contained efficacy to language and symbols, and interpreted symbolic efficacy was disclaimed in terms of "pneumatic augmentation" positing the work of the Holy Spirit as originary to the understanding of efficacy. Consequently, we keep a balance between the understanding of sacramental efficacy as symbolic efficacy and the efficacy, as by the Holy Spirit while weaving them together.

309 ~ 319

In conclusion, we will recapitulate the main points that form a postmodern understanding of the sacraments discussed at length in preceding pages of this work. Admittedly, any mode of expression, even those outlined in this project, fall short of the excess and superabundance of the gift of God. Therefore, the current theological enquiry, above all, ought to give way to the acts of praise and wonder in the face of the ineffable gift of love being given in the sacraments. The sacramental symbols can never wholly symbolize the God who gifts himself as love in Christ and the Spirit. For this reason, having ruled out any claim of comprehensiveness and rigidity, the results of this study are proposed for enhanced understanding and further reflection.

The historico-theological survey undertaken in the first chapter introduces different shifts in the understanding of the sacraments in the early Church to the present. Even though the treatment of the subject is short and concise, it draws attention to the Pneumatological shortfall that marks sacramental thinking throughout history, especially in the Medieval era when sacramental thinking was developed based on Medieval philosophy and theology. This chapter observed that in patristic period there was fluidity in the understanding of the sacraments. In this period, particular ritual celebrations which came to be known by the Church as "sacraments" were unquestionably believed to have possessed a mysterious, divine reality beyond and behind what is visible and tangible to the senses, although they were interpreted differently. It is only with the surge of metaphysics into sacramental thinking that the efficacy was explained under the rubric of causality, which in turn moved sacramental thinking away from the manner it was done in the first millennium.

The call of Vatican II for a renewed and deeper understanding of the liturgy encouraged sacramental and liturgical theologians to integrate the insights provided by developments within systematic theology, biblical, and patristic studies. As a result, a reflection of the sacraments was made possible in its proper liturgical and theological context. Moreover, the critique of the modern subject and phenomenology's turn to religion reduces the gap between theology and philosophy and encourages sacramental theology to base itself on a non-metaphysical foundation with due regard for the Trinitarian structure of God's self-communication.

In the second chapter, we emphasized the need for re-discovering the role of the Holy Spirit for a better hermeneutic of sacramental efficacy. In this regard, we explained and affirmed the importance of Pneumatology as an essential component for understanding the sacraments. This is done by proposing a Pneumatological theology, a Pneumatological approach to theology *as such*, in order to show how sacramental theology should be viewed. This systematic construction was made by investigating the creedal formulation, showing its weakness in adequately affirming what the Spirit *is* and *does* in the economy, in the light of the presence and the activity of the Holy Spirit in Jesus' life as revealed in the Scriptures. It was learned that the creedal formulae are weak in duly representing the personhood of the Holy Spirit and the mutual dependence of the Son and the Spirit. Therefore, it becomes necessary to re-construct the intra-Trinitarian relationship so as to manifest the mutual dependence of the Son and the Spirit on each other for their personhood and mission in the light of the economy. Then, we attempted to retrieve the personhood and role of the Holy Spirit by conceiving the processions of the Word and the Spirit as the dual aspects of God's self-communication in the entire salvation history as attested by the New Testament. Thus, the personhood and the role of the Holy Spirit are located equal to the mission of the Word.

Furthermore, we argued that a composite theology of Christ and the Holy Spirit in this manner within the scheme of God's self-communication has necessary implications for understanding of the sacraments. It was also remarked that the Christological overemphasis at the expense of Pneumatology in the West and the ascendance of Pneumatology over and against Christology in the East were characterised by their respective ways of explaining the processional relationship of the Spirit in the Trinity. Therefore, by reconstructing the inner Trinitarian relationship to reflect the biblical revelation of the Son and the Spirit brings out the relevance of the missions of the Word and the Spirit in the economy. Thus, we argue that both these missions are interconnected and complementary, and not exclusive to each other. Accordingly, the mutuality of persons and missions of the Son and the Spirit revealed in the economy of salvation can effectively be represented by the mode of intra-Trinitarian relationship proposed in this chapter. Such an approach to the mission of the Son and the Spirit is necessary for understanding sacraments from a Pneumatological perspective.

The Pneumatological theology that we propose is, in fact, a robust Trinitarian theology. This is because of two reasons: first, Pneumatological theology is done within the framework of a sound Trinitarian theology, and second, it understands Pneumatology as the key to the theology of the Trinity and Christology. The arguments in support of Pneumatological theology are based on the theological reflection of God's engagement in history, with specific focus on the role of the Spirit in relation to the Son and the Father. Pneumatological theology affirms the Christian doctrine of God as triune, and therefore bridges the gap between the treatise on the One God (unity/oneness of God) and the Triune God (multiplicity/threeness of God), which patterned Western theology. This centers God-talk around the diversity of persons, as manifested in history, with the biblical, creedal and liturgical confessions of the Church. Moreover, it also helps us see that the missions of the Son and the Spirit constitute a single self-communication of God. This helps to understand God's continued gift of himself in and through the Church and the sacraments as a continuation of this double mission through the Word and the Spirit. Therefore, neither Pneumatology nor Christology can be subjugated or denied in sacramental thinking. In the second chapter we pointed out the inadequacy of the one-sided emphasis on Christology which gained dominance in sacramental theology can be overcome by acknowledging the determinative role of Pneumatology in shaping Christology, ecclesiology, and sacramental theology.

In the second chapter, we have also pointed out that the advantage of the Pneumatological approach, especially within sacramental theology, is that it counteracts a static or frozen notion of sacramentality and broadens it, highlighting the universal presence and activity of God in and through the Spirit in creation, the incarnation, and in the unfolding of the destiny of human beings and the entire cosmos. The New Testament revelation of the Holy Spirit as the third person of the Trinity must be understood against the background of the Old Testament revelation where the Spirit is understood as the creative and sustaining power of the universe. Such an understanding helps to incorporate the patristic understanding of salvation as the work of the Trinity and to expand the horizon of salvation to the entire universe. Therefore, sacramentality, understood in a broader sense, incorporates soteriological concerns – not only of human beings but of the entire cosmos.

This all-embracing activity of the Spirit should not be understood in isolation but as the unified activity of the whole Trinity.

Moreover, acknowledging the Spirit as the innermost reality of beings (creatures) not only affirms their relation to God who is the source of their origin and self-transcendence, but also affirms the fellowship all creatures have in that God, the source of their common origin, process of unfolding and finality. This understanding serves as the basis of human beings' respect for creation which opens theology toward an ecological awareness and poses new ethical commitment toward the universe. A Pneumatological worldview and sacramentality takes into account human beings' relatedness to the entire universe and helps to get rid of an excessively anthropocentric worldview. In this understanding, salvation is not considered solely as human salvation, but as the recapitulation or restoration of the whole universe toward its final end. Therefore, creation theology is incomplete if it remains truncated from the question of the finality of universe. Hence, in the second chapter we proposed that sacramental theology will be incomplete unless it takes into account the sacramentality of the universe and creation. The sacramentality of creation must be the preliminary step in the reflection of the sacraments. Sacramentality cannot be compacted either into the seven sacraments, or into the sacramentality of the Church but must be extended to the entire cosmos; although the sacraments are, in themselves, unique phenomena of sacramental presence. This allows for a broader understanding of sacramentality in the light of the overwhelming presence and activity of the Spirit in creation, the unfolding of the universe, and the entire history of grace that culminates in the person of Jesus Christ. More importantly, the key to understanding the sacraments of the Church in this way is to understand them Pneumatologically.

This study ascribes to the Spirit a personal "status," and defines the role of the Spirit as "mediated immediacy" which lies behind the sacramental understanding of the Church and the efficacy of the sacraments. Thus, in brief, this study claims that Pneumatological theology discovers, or defines, the role of the Spirit in the sacramental event. Today, the presence and activity of Christ that the Church realizes and mediates becomes tangible in the sacramental mediation of the Spirit. Thus, we conclude that the fundamental basis of the sacramentality of creation, the mystery of Christ and the Church, and of the sacraments is one and the same Holy Spirit. There is an unbroken lineage of the experience of the Spirit in the unfolding of God's engagement with the world, beginning with creation and culminating in the mystery of Christ, the reception of God's gift of himself made available in Christ, mediated by the Spirit in the Church, particularly in the celebration of the sacraments.

As was noted at the outset of this book, the way we conceive God-human relationship is fundamentally connected with our understanding of God and how this relationship is interpreted (among other disciplines) in sacramental theology. Therefore, the third chapter demonstrates how Marion's phenomenology opens the way to reflect on revelation from a phenomenological perspective and provides a unique way of God-talk outside the category of Being. As we have explored, the non-metaphysical understanding of God developed through contrasting notions of the icon and the idol encourages us to develop a concept of God in terms of givenness. The notion of givenness radically and paradigmatically shifts our concept of God which is conformed to the representation of the human subject to the one that is revealed in the Bible as Love. Moreover, the notion of a God in terms of givenness not only shatters the image of God formed according to the representation of the human subject, but also re-interprets the subject as *l'adonné* (the gifted one). Thus givenness ensures the possibility for God to reveal himself without being confined to the limits of human experience and reason. It is only in the icon that God can reveal fully as he is, as excess of givenness; as saturated phenomenon. In such an understanding, the constituting subject loses its identity and becomes the one who is "gifted." The 'constituting subject' becomes 'constituted' and becomes mere recipient and the gifted.

Marion's notion of saturated phenomenon and the theological status of the icon help us to overcome the metaphysical idolatry in reflecting on God. We argue that "saturation" is a more appropriate way of understanding the human person's relationship with God outside of onto-theology. Thus, as the third chapter argues, theology is able to overcome the metaphysical impasse in reflecting upon the Christian God who is revealed as Charity within phenomenology. This chapter also develops a phenomenological understanding of the Spirit within the New Testament by following Marion's argument of Christ as the saturated phenomenon (saturation of saturation), the iconic figure of Christ on the Cross, where God's givenness is realized in maximum phenomenality. The excess of the Spirit that Christ experienced throughout his life and ministry, and especially the gift of the Spirit which was given to the Church in excess at Pentecost, actually complements the mystery of the revelation of God. Thus, God's givenness, which is God's self-communication, is understood as a Trinitarian event, a givenness through Christ and the Spirit. It is in such a phenomenological scheme that God's givenness in the Word and the Spirit can be thought of non-onto-theologically. Furthermore, it becomes clear that in a phenomenological framework, the Trinitarian dimension of God's self-communication can also be retained intact.

The third chapter also demonstrates how the metaphor of the gift actually designates the relationship between God and human beings. Understanding God in terms of the gift, other than Being, has implications for understanding the divine-human relationship and the sacraments. Therefore, a theology of givenness within the phenomenology of givenness was developed so that the gift of God in divine economy, which finds expression in the sacraments, could be explained. Since the constituting subject becomes the gifted one, in the scheme of the gift, sacraments are no longer regarded as produced, either by human capacity or by the power of language and symbols, but solely received as given. Moreover, the theology of giving that was constructed accommodates the Christian concept of return without falling into the scheme of economic exchange. Only the notion of pure gift as held by Marion can uphold the notion of God's free and gratuitous gift. Thus, the notion of gratuity and the notion of return/response to God's giving can be upheld while subscribing to a unilateral gift outside economic exchange. The notion of pure gift in the strict sense disallows the notion of return, but it incorporates the Christian understanding of response without falling into the vicious circle of economic exchange as exemplified in the Law of Love as manifested in the love of God revealed in Jesus. This is done by placing givenness as originary to the Being of God as modelled on the Trinity, where the giving of divine persons is actually pure and untarnished by reciprocity. What is rejected in the theology of giving is an equal return, return of the same, and not an appropriate response which is fairly intelligible.

Marion's notion of the gift transcends the requirements of reciprocity by bringing in the notion of *agape*. The true gift is the gift of love (*agape*), which incurs no reciprocity or return, but only a response in love. For him, the gift operates according to the norm of *agape*, which is found in the love of God manifested in the "disfigured-figure" of Christ. A Christian theology of the gift operates according to the notions of "excess" and "asymmetry." Accordingly, we maintain the view that the initial gift-giving does not call for a counter-gift, but rather, a response extended toward ethical engagement, which is qualified as *re-turn* rather than *return*. The "fatherhood image" represents such a unilateral gift. Thus, the language of the gift ought to consume one's thinking about God. It must also be used to explain the reception of divine gift, especially God's giving in the sacraments. The Christian response to God's giving does not negate giving, but only affirms excess and extravagance of giving which assumes the forms of mutuality and sharing, a living in and for/with each other and liturgical praise.

In this regard, we call into question the application of the gift-reception-return paradigm to the understanding of sacramental gift. Even though the sacramental exchange is elevated to symbolic exchange in such a scheme, it is marred by obligatory generosity. We purport to argue that the idea of "obligatory return" that it entails reduces the symbolic exchange to the level of economic exchange. The theology of the gift that is outlined in this study rules out the "obligatory nature" of return, and to interpret the return as a response of the gifted which consists in "living out the grace" given in the sacraments. The response is not understood as a giving back on the same scale in the face of an infinite demand or under obligation, but rather, further giving out of pure appreciation for the gift *as such*. Conceiving the response to the gift in this manner ensures the freedom of the recipient in living out the gift given for its own sake.

In the fourth chapter, we take up the question of sacramental efficacy in the light of the theological and philosophical thinking pursued in the second and third chapters. We present a sacramental hermeneutics which focuses on the sacramental presence and grace along with considering other interrelated questions. Remaining on the track of postmodern thinking, we reject, on the whole, the notion of the metaphysics of presence and develop an iconic mode of presence which is neither ruled by a negative theology, nor by an affirmative theology, but instead, by the notion of excess and the saturated phenomenon. The iconic mode of presence is governed by the notion of distance, absence and withdrawal. However, these do not imply an emptiness but an excess, whereby the divine gives itself in the icon in maximum phenomenality as saturation of saturation, without being limited to subject and language. It is only in the iconic mode that God can give himself without the interference of the subject. Thus, the sacraments are understood as iconic-symbols (saturated phenomena) in which God's givenness expresses itself in maximum phenomenality.

The iconic-symbolic approach applies to the sacraments in general and in particular to the Eucharist. A sacramental hermeneutic of the Eucharist must begin by locating the originary givenness of God antecedent to the

Eucharistic gift and presence. The iconic-symbolic approach allows the Eucharistic presence of Christ to determine itself without reducing Christ's presence to our own horizons, to the visible alone. Paradoxically, God's gracious gift of the Eucharist discloses itself as the excess of God's givennesss in the body and blood of Christ, and while concealing it and retaining the radical difference and otherness of God. The notion of presence as given and excess helps us to overcome the twofold idolatries generated by metaphysics of presence, namely, either reducing presence to a manipulable thing or to the consciousness of the community, as Marion has observed.

The presence is, first and foremost, received as gift, as given. However, God's gift in the Eucharist cannot be viewed as isolated from God's gift of himself which is progressively manifested in creation, in the history of Israel, culminating in the incarnation. Moreover, the Eucharist is God's gift of love (the icon of love) which actually overflows in the *kenosis*, in giving himself in the form of lowly food. The Eucharistic gift in the species of consecrated bread and wine encompasses the whole mystery of salvation. What is actually given exceeds that which is given in the present (bread and wine). The "reality" of the body and blood of Christ which is given sacramentally is invisible to the ordinary gaze (idolatrous), but the iconic gaze sees Christ through the species and it is Christ who appears "behind" them. Only an iconic gaze that remains in contemplation and consents itself to distance can "'see" the "reality" of the Eucharistic gift under the "corporeality" of the species. Furthermore, the phenomenology of givenness helps us to consider the Eucharistic gift in its past, future, and temporal dimensions on the basis of a non-metaphysical concept of time as a given. Accordingly, the Eucharistic gift, the gift of (real) presence is a presence realized in the present, the past, and the future.

The notion of presence in terms of givenness surpasses the notion of metaphysics of presence. However, the question as to how presence is given, or realized, is tenable. The West traditionally ascribes Christ's agency and power for the efficacy of the sacrament. However, the gift of presence can be explained only with reference to the givenness of the Spirit, highlighting the role of the Spirit in realizing presence in terms of the past and the future. Therefore, we emphasize the agency and power of the Holy Spirit in the sacramental event, in realizing the memory of Christ, which we prefer to designate as "mediation" which has its basis in the mission of the Word and the Spirit. Thus we explain the sacramental gift, the gift of presence and grace in terms of the originary givenness of the Spirit who mediates Christ's presence in the celebration of the Church. There is an array of rituals, symbols and language that interplay in the sacramental celebration. But beyond and behind all symbolic and ritual interplay, the originary givenness and activity of the Holy Spirit ought to be emphasized.

Accordingly, we interpret the sacraments as iconic symbols on the basis of the phenomenology of givenness, duly integrating both Pneumatological and Christological dimensions. Our approach to the sacraments is informed or governed by the icon, the power of the icon to conceal and reveal the invisible in the visible other than the way of language and causality. The power of the icon consists in the power to construct the reality, not by resemblance or imaging, but by non-resemblance, by revealing the like in the unlike. In the liturgy, when the symbols are used as iconic, they function as giving truth, meaning, and life of the mystery being celebrated. The reality that is iconically represented and actualized is something that surpasses human imagination and comprehension. However, the ritual symbolic enactment becomes really effective and becomes sacramental, augmented by the power and orginary activity of the Holy Spirit. Thus, the sacraments become saturated phenomena, or the icons of God's gift of himself through Christ and the Spirit. The Paschal event is not mediated by the inherent power of language and symbols, or by the intervention of the human subject. Above all, this study upholds the power and agency of the Spirit in realizing the sacramental gift, as in God's gift of himself in the economy.

In this regard, we propose that the phenomenological and symbolic turn in sacramental theology must be complemented by a solid Pneumatological content. This is what is achieved in the current study, by situating the Spirit at the centre of the whole understanding of sacramentality. Thus, the notions of automatic efficacy in terms of causality, or any sort of self-contained efficacy based on the inherent power of language and symbols or symbolic efficacy are overcome by shifting the efficacy to the mediatory role of the Holy Spirit, by which the language and symbols are augmented in such a way that they contain and effect the sacrament. Thus, efficacy is transposed from the power of language and symbols to the Holy Spirit who is at work in the sacramental event. Sacramental mediation cannot be reduced solely to symbolic mediation. Even the metaphor of the gift remains inadequate, unless interpreted in terms of God's gift of God's-self in the Word and the Spirit. Thus, the sacramental hermeneutics of givenness that has been proposed places the mediatory role of the Spirit at the center of conceiving God's gift-giving in the sacraments. Accordingly, sacramental presence and grace are viewed in the light of an *a priori* givenness based on the phenomenology of givenness. Thus, grace is received as pure gift from God; a gift of God himself, as excess, in Christ and the Spirit in the mode of the icon.

The response to the gift of grace is not considered as "obligatory," although it allows a response. The givenness of the call and the gift of identity as *l'adonné* enables one to be graced by God, an experience of "being given." God's gracious gift is nothing less than himself; he bestows himself graciously and gratuitously and draws the human person to a communion with him. God's giving is by retaining distance, because in giving, God does not give himself away. It is the human person's participation in God's life; it is a dynamic relationship with God established and nurtured in Christ and the Spirit. Sacraments, as iconic symbols, mediate the gift of grace; as iconic-symbols they confer and symbolize grace (conceal and reveal). In mediating grace, the Spirit remains as the "mediated immediacy," as the gift and the giver.

Even though the gift received engages a task, it evokes a free human response. It cannot be considered as obligatory return, but rather, the grace given is viewed in terms of love, which allows the "gifted" the freedom to receive and respond to this love in love. Therefore, being graced, the grace ensures the freedom to go forth, living in grace, living in love. The giving of grace and the response of the *l'adonné* are sacramentally enacted and iconically symbolized paradigmatically in the Eucharistic celebration. However, liturgical dynamics do not automatically construct meaning and efficacy, but rather, the liturgical event (language event) becomes a Spirit event by the originary activity of the Holy Spirit which lies even behind the gathering of the assembly. Thus, the Spirit makes the celebration fecund so as to mediate presence and grace.

We explain how the Pneumatological and symbolic dimensions function in the liturgy of the word and the liturgy of the Eucharist from an iconic-symbolic perspective. Furthermore, we purport to argue that the iconic-symbolic perspective is helpful to ease the tension between Christology and Pneumatology, the tendency to minimize the notion of presence to an imaginary space represented, either by pronouncement of the words of institution, or the epiclesis. The epiclesis and the words of Christ pronounced by the president (*in persona Christi*) constitute jointly the structure of the Eucharistic prayer. Thus, the interplay of language and symbols in the liturgy, especially the key words and actions, iconically symbolize the gift of

God in Christ and the Spirit. The sacramental gift is received in praise and thanksgiving, which is, in fact, entering into the circuit of the gift, augmented by the Spirit. The iconic-symbolic dynamics of the liturgy also consists in symbolising the return dimension of the sacramental event. The sacramental event evokes a response which expresses itself in praise and thanksgiving, and ultimately, in the liturgy of the neighbour, a living in grace by a co-existence and pro-existence.

BIBLIOGRAPHY

The bibliography is divided in two sections: (1) primary sources and (2) secondary sources. Primary sources are arranged alphabetically within subsections. Secondary sources are classified according to genre (books and articles), and within these genres, first alphabetically, then chronologically, starting with the most recent one.

1. Primary Sources

1.1. Church Documents and Liturgical Texts

Catechism of the Catholic Church. London: Geoffrey Chapman, 2000.

Congregation for Divine Worship and the Discipline of the Sacraments. *General Instruction of the Roman Missal*. 2002. Available from http://www.vatican.va/roman_curia/congregations/ccdds/documents/rc_con_ccdd s_doc_20030317_ordinamento-messale_en.html (accessed March 11, 2008).

Eucharistic Prayers I-IV. http://catholic-resources.org/ChurchDocs/EP1-4.htm (accessed January 30, 2010).

John Paul II. *Encyclical Letter Ecclesia de Eucharistia: On the Eucharist in Its Relationship to the Church*. Boston, MA: Pauline Books and Media, 2003.

National Conference of Catholic Bishops of America. *The Roman Missal*. Translated by The International Commission on English in the Liturgy. New York: Catholic Book Publishing Co., 1985.

"The Nicene Creed." *The Nicene and Post-Nicene Fathers*, 2nd Series, ed. Philip Schaff and Henry Wace, 14, 3-7. Edinburgh: T & T Clark, 1991.

"The Order of the Holy Qurbana of the Syro-Malankara Church." Trivandrum: Malankara Academy, 1986.

Syro-Malabar Bishop's Conference. *Syro-malabar Sabhayude Qurbana*. Trivandrum, Kerala: San Jos Press, 1989.

Tanner, Norman P., ed. *Decrees of the Ecumenical Councils*. 3 vols. London: Sheed & Ward, 1990.

Theological-Historical Commission. *The Holy Spirit, Lord and Giver of Life*. New York: Crossroad, 1997.

"The Vatican Declaration on Women in the Ministerial Priesthood." *Origins* 6 (1977): 517-524.

1.2. Patristics

"Amphilochi Episcopi Iconii Epistola Synodica." *Patrologia Graeca*, ed. J.P. Migne, 39, 93-98. Paris: Seu Petit-Montrouge, 1858.

Charlesworth, James H., ed. *The Odes of Solomon*. Oxford: Clarendon, 1973.

Dressler, Hermigild, Robert Sider, Thomas P. Halton, Rowan Williams, and others, eds. *Marius Victorinus: Theological Treatises on the Trinity*. The Fathers of the Church, 69. Washington, DC: The Catholic University of America Press, 1981.

Ephraim the Syrian. "Hymns and Homilies." *The Nicene and Post-Nicene Fathers*, 2nd Series, ed. John Gwynn, 13, 112-340. Edinburgh: T & T Clark, 1979.

Aphrahat the Persian Sage. "Demonstrations." *The Nicene and Post-Nicene Fathers*, ed. John Gwynn, 13, 342-412. Grand Rapids, MI: Eerdmans, 1979.

Athanasius. "Expositio in Psalmum." *Patrologia Graeca*, ed. J.P. Migne, 32, 59-546. Paris: Seu Petit-Montrouge, 1857.

Athanasius. "Letter to Serapion." *The Letters of Saint Athanasius Concerning the Holy Spirit*, ed. C.R.B. Shapland, 210-213. London: The Epworth Press, 1951.

Augustine. "Homilies on the Gospel of John." *The Nicene and Post-Nicene Fathers*, 1st Series, ed. Philip Schaff, 7, 7-452. Edinburgh: T & T Clark, 1991.

Augustine. "Christian Doctrine." *The Nicene and Post-Nicene Fathers*, 1st Series, ed. Philip Schaff, 2, 519-597. Grand Rapids, MI: Eerdmans, 1979.

Augustine. "De Trinitate." *The Nicene and Post-Nicene Fathers*, 1st Series, ed. Philip Schaff, 3, 17-228. Grand Rapids, MI: Eerdmans, 1978.

Augustine. *The Trinity*. Translated by Stephen McKenna. The Fathers of the Church, 45. Washington, DC: Catholic University of America Press, 1963.

Basil. "De Spiritu Sancto." *The Nicene and Post-Nicene Fathers*, 2nd Series, ed. Philip Schaff and Henry Wace, 8, 1-50. Edinburgh: T & T Clark, 1996.

Basil. "Homily on the Hexaemeron." *The Nicene and Post-Necene Fathers*, 2nd Series, ed. Philip Schaff and Henry Wace, 8, 510-107. Edinburgh: T & T Clark, 1996.

Chrysostom, John. "Homilies on the Gospel of St. John." *Nicene and Post-Nicene Fathers*, 1 Series, ed. Philip Schaff, 14, 1-334. Edinburgh: T & T Clark, 1996.

Chrysostom, John. "Homilies on the Gospel of Saint Matthew." *The Nicene and Post-Nicene Fathers*, 1st Series, ed. Philip Schaff, 10, 1-534. Grand Rapids, MI: Eerdmans, 1978.

Cyprian of Carthage. "Epistles of Cyprian." *Ante-Nicene Fathers*, ed. James Donaldson, 5, 275-409. Grand Rapids, MI: Eerdmans, 1978.

Cyril of Jerusalem. "On the Mysteries." *Nicene and Post-Nicene Fathers*, 2nd Series, ed. Philip Schaff, 7, 149-150. Edinburgh: T & T Clark, 1996.

Gregory of Nyssa. "Against the Macedonians." *The Nicene and Post-Nicene Fathers*, 2nd Series, ed. Philip Schaff and Henry Wace, 5, 315-325. Edinburgh: T & T Clark, 1994.

Gregory of Nyssa. "Oration on the Son." *The Nicene and Post-Nicene Fathers*, 2nd Series, ed. Philip Schaff and Henry Wace, 7, 518-524. Edinburgh: T & T Clark, 1996.

Hilary of Poitiers. "On Matthew." *The Nicene and Post-Nicene Fathers*, 2nd Series ed. Philip Schaff and Henry Wace, 9, 52-61. Edinburgh: T & T Clark, 1979.

Hilary of Poitiers. "Tract on the Psalms." *The Nicene and Post-Nicene Fathers*, ed. Philip Schaff and Henry Wace, 9, 236-248. Edinburgh: T & T Clark, 1979.

Irenaeus. "Against Heresies." *The Ante-Nicene Fathers*, ed. Alexander Roberts and James Donaldson, 1, 309-567. Edinburgh: T & T Clark, 1996.

Irenaeus. "The Demonstration of the Apostolic Preaching." *Translations of Christian Literature*, ed. W.J. Sparrow Simpson and W.K. Lowther Clarke, 69-151. New York: Macmillan, 1920.

John of Damascus. *On the Divine Images: Three Apologies against those Who Attack the Divine Images*. Translated by David Anderson. Crestwood, NY: Vladimir's Seminary Press, 1980.

Justin Martyr. "The First Apology." *The Ante-Nicene Fathers*, ed. Alexander Roberts and James Donaldson, 1, 159-187. Edinburgh: T & T Clark, 1966.

Origen. "De Principiis." *The Ante-Nicene Fathers*, ed. James Donaldson and A. Cleveland Coxe, 4, 239-382. Edinburgh: T & T Clark, 1979.

Socrates and Sozomen. "The Ecclesiastical History." *The Nicene and Post-Nicene Fathers*, ed. Philip Schaff and Henry Wace, 2, 239-427. Grand Rapids, MI: Eerdmans, 1979.

Tertullian. "Against Praxeas." *Ante-Nicene Fathers*, ed. Alexander Roberts and James Donaldson, 3, 597-632. Grand Rapids, MI: Eerdmans, 1993.

1.3. Scholastic Sources

Aquinas, Thomas. *Summa Theologiae*. Translated by David Bourke. Vol. 56. London, New York: Blackfriars, 1975.

Aquinas, Thomas. *Summa Theologiae*. Translated by James J. Cunningham. Vol. 57. London, New York: Blackfriars, 1975.

Aquinas, Thomas. *Summa Theologiae*. Translated by Thomas Gilby. Vol. 59. London, New York: Blackfriars, 1975.

Aquinas, Thomas. *Summa Theologiae*. Translated by Cornelius Ernst. Vol. 30. London, New York: Blackfriars, 1972.

Aquinas, Thomas. *Summa Theologiae*. Translated by Ceslaus Velecky. Vol. 6. London, New York: Blackfriars, 1965.

Aquinas, Thomas. *Summa Theologiae*. Translated by William Barden. Vol. 58. London, New York: Blackfriars, 1965.

Aquinas, Thomas. *Summa Theologiae*. Translated by Timothy McDermott. Vol. 2. London, New York: Blackfriars, 1964.

Bonaventura.   *Sentences*.   Available   from   http://www.franciscan-
   archive.org/bonaventura/opera/bon04019.html (accessed August 12, 2008).
Lombard,   Peter.   *Sentences: On   the   Doctrine   of   Signs*.   Available   from
   http://www.franciscan-archive.org/lombardus/opera/ls4-01.html   (accessed
   September 2, 2008).

1.4. Works of Karl Rahner

Rahner, Karl. *The Trinity*. Translated by Joseph Donceel. New York: Crossroad,
   1997.
Rahner, Karl. "Oneness and Threefoldness of God in Discussion with Islam."
   Theological Investigations, 18, 105-121. London: Darton, Longman & Todd,
   1984.
Rahner, Karl. *Schriften zur Theologie*, 16 vols., Einsiedeln: Benziger, 1954-1984.
Rahner, Karl. *Foundations of Christian Faith: An Introduction to the Idea of
   Christianity*. Translated by William V. Dych. New York: Crossroad, 1978.
Rahner, Karl. "Introductory Observations on Thomas Aquinas' Theology of the
   Sacraments in General." *Theological Investigations*, 14, 149-160. London:
   Darton, Longman & Todd, 1976.
Rahner,   Karl.   "Reflections   on   Methodology   in   Theology."   *Theological
   Investigations*, 11, 68-114. New York: Crossroad, 1974.
Rahner, Karl. "Some Implications of the Scholastic Concept of Uncreated Grace."
   Theological Investigations, 1, 318-346. London: Darton, Longman & Todd,
   1974.
Rahner, Karl. *Opportunities for Faith: Elements of a Modern Spirituality*. Translated
   by E. Quinn. New York: Seabury, 1970.
Rahner, Karl. "Evolution." *Sacramentum Mundi*, ed. Henri Crouzel, 2, 289-297.
   New York: Herder and Herder, 1968.
Rahner, Karl. "Nature and Grace." *Theological Investigations*, 4, 165-188. London:
   Darton, Longman & Todd, 1966.
Rahner, Karl. "Dogmatic Questions on Easter." *Theological Investigations*, 4, 121-
   133. London: Darton, Longman & Todd, 1966.
Rahner, Karl. "On the Theology of Incarnation." *Theological Investigations*, 4, 105-
   120. London: Darton, Longman & Todd, 1966.
Rahner, Karl. "Remarks on the Dogmatic Treatise 'De Trinitate'." *Theological
   Investigations*, 4, 77-102. London: Darton, Longman & Todd, 1966.
Rahner, Karl. "The Concept of Mystery in Catholic Theology." *Theological
   Investigations*, 4, 36-73. London: Darton, Longman & Todd, 1966.
Rahner, Karl. "The Theology of the Symbol." *Theological Investigations*, 4, 221-
   311. London: Darton, Longman and Todd, 1966.
Rahner, Karl. *The Church and the Sacraments*. Translated by W.J. O'Hara. New
   York: Herder and Herder, 1963.

1.5. Works of Jean-Luc Marion

Marion, Jean-Luc. *The Visible and the Revealed*. Translated by Christina M. Gschwandtner. Bronx, New York: Fordham University Press, 2008.

Marion, Jean-Luc. *The Erotic Phenomenon: Six Meditations*. Translated by Stephen Lewis. Chicago, IL: University of Chicago Press, 2007.

Marion, Jean-Luc. "The Reason of the Gift." *Givenness and God: Questions of Jean-Luc Marion*, ed. Ian Leask and Eoin Cassidy, 101-134. New York: Fordham University Press, 2005.

Marion, Jean-Luc. *The Crossing of the Visible*. Translated by James K.A. Smith. Stanford, CA: Stanford University Press, 2004.

Marion, Jean-Luc. *Le phénomène érotique: Six méditations*. Paris: Grasset, 2003.

Marion, Jean-Luc. *Being Given: Toward a Phenomenology of Givenness*. Translated by Jeffrey L. Kosky. Stanford, CA: Stanford University Press, 2002.

Marion, Jean-Luc. "They Recognised Him; and He Became Invisible to Them." *Modern Theology* 18 (2002): 145-152.

Marion, Jean-Luc. *In Excess: Studies of Saturated Phenomena*. Translated by Robyn Horner and Vincent Berraud, Perspectives in Continental Philosophy, ed. John D. Caputo. New York: Fordham University Press, 2002.

Marion, Jean-Luc. *Prolegomena to Charity*. Translated by Stephen Lewis. New York: Fordham University Press, 2002.

Marion, Jean-Luc. "La phénoménalité du sacrement: être et donation." *Communio* 40 (2001): 59-75.

Marion, Jean-Luc. "Réaliser la présence réelle." *La Maison-Dieu* 225 (2001): 19-28.

Marion, Jean-Luc. *The Idol and Distance*. Translated by Thomas A. Carlson. New York: Fordham University Press, 2001.

Marion, Jean-Luc. "'Christian Philosophy': Hermeneutic or Heuristic?" *The Question of Christian Philosophy*, ed. Francis J. Ambrosio, 247-264. New York: Fordham University Press, 1999.

Marion, Jean-Luc. "In the Name: How to Avoid Speaking of 'Negative Theology'." *God, the Gift, and Postmodernism*, ed. John D. Caputo and Michael J. Scanlon, 784-800. Bloomington, IN: Indiana University Press, 1999.

Marion, Jean-Luc. "Sketch of a Phenomenological Concept of Gift." *Postmodern Philosophy and Christian Thought*, ed. Merold Westphal, 122-143. Bloomington, IN: Indian University Press, 1999.

Marion, Jean-Luc. *Reduction and Givenness: Investigations of Husserl, Heidegger, and Phenomenology*. Translated by Thomas A. Carlson. Evanston, IL: Northwestern University Press, 1998.

Marion, Jean-Luc. "Metaphysics and Phenomenology: A Summary for Theologians." *The Postmodern God: A Theological Reader*, ed. Graham Ward, 279-296. Oxford: Blackwell, 1997.

Marion, Jean-Luc. "Metaphysics and Phenomenology: A Relief for Theology." *Critical Inquiry* 20 (1994): 572-591.

Marion, Jean-Luc. *God Without Being*. Translated by Thomas A. Carlson. Chicago, IL, London: University of Chicago Press, 1991.

Marion, Jean-Luc. "Distance et béatitude: sur le mot capacitas chez Saint Augustin." *Réssurection* 29 (1968): 58-80.

2. Secondary Sources

2.1. Books

Aristotle. *Aristotle: Selected Works*. Translated by H.G. Apostle and Lloyd P. Gerson. Grinnell, IA: Peripatetic Press, 1982.

Badcock, Gary D. *Light of Truth & Fire of Love: A Theology of the Holy Spirit*. Grand Rapids, MI, Cambridge, U.K.: Eerdmans, 1997.

Barrett, Charles Kingsley. *The Holy Spirit and the Gospel Tradition*. London: SPCK, 1966.

Barth, Karl. *Schleiermacher-Auswahl mit einem Nachwort von Karl Barth*, ed. Heinz Bolli. Munich: Siebenstern-Taschenbuch, 1968.

Barth, Karl. *Church Dogmatics*. Translated by G.T. Thomson. Vol. 1/1. Edinburgh: T & T Clark, 1963.

Beasley-Murray, G.R. *Baptism in the New Testament*. New York: Macmillian, 1962.

Betz, Johannes. *Die Eucharistie in der Zeit der Griechischen Väter: Die Aktualpräsenz der Person und des Heilswerkes Jesu im Abendmahl nach der Vorephesinisschen Griechishen Patristik*. 1/1. Freiburg: Herder, 1955.

Bilaniuk, Petro B. T. *Theology and Economy of the Holy Spirit*. Bangalore: Dharmaram Publications, 1980.

Boeve, Lieven and John C. Ries, eds. *The Presence of Transcendence*. Leuven, Paris, Sterling, VA: Peeters, 2001.

Boff, Leonardo. *Trinity and Society*. Maryknoll, NY: Orbis Books, 1988.

Bogaert, P.-M., J.-M. Auwers and A. Wénin. *The Ruah of Gen. 1, 2 and Its Reception History in the Syriac Tradition*. Bibliotheca Ephemeridum Theologicarum Lovaniensium, 144. Leuven: Leuven University Press, 1999.

Bourdieu, Pierre. *Language and Symbolic Power*. Translated by Gino Raymond and Matthew Adamson, ed. John B. Thompson. Cambridge, U.K.: Polity Press, 1991.

Bourdieu, Pierre. *The Logic of Practice*. Translated by Richard Nice. Stanford, CA: Polity Press, 1990.

Bradshaw, Paul F. *Eucharistic Origins*. New York: Oxford University Press, 2004.

Bremmer, Jan N., ed. *The Apocryphal Acts of Thomas*, Studies in Early Christian Apocrypha, 6. Leuven: Peeters, 2001.

Brinkman, Martien E. *Sacraments of Freedom: Ecumenical Essays on Creation and Sacrament – Justification and Freedom*. Zoetermeer: Meinema – IIMO Research Publications, 1999.

Brock, Sebastian, ed. *Fire from Heaven: Studies in Syriac Theology and Liturgy*, Variorum Collected Studies Series. Hampshire, U.K.: Ashgate, 2006.

Brown, Raymond E. *An Introduction to the New Testament.* New York: Doubleday, 1997.

Brown, Raymond E. *The Birth of the Messiah.* London: Chapman, 1977.

Brown, Raymond E. *The Gospel according to John (I–XII).* Vol. 2 The Anchor Bible Commentary. Garden City, NY: Doubleday, 1966.

Bultmann, Rudolf. *The Gospel of John.* Translated by G.R. Beasley-Murray. Oxford: Blackwell, 1971.

Burge, Gary M. *The Anointed Community: The Holy Spirit in the Johannine Tradition.* Grand Rapids, MI: Eerdmans, 1987.

Burgess, Stanley M. *The Holy Spirit: Eastern Christian Traditions.* Peabody, MA: Hendrickson, 1989.

Burgess, Stanley M. *The Holy Spirit: Ancient Christian Traditions.* Peabody, MA: Hendrickson, 1984.

Cabasilas, Nicholas. *A Commentary on the Divine Liturgy.* Translated by J.M. Hussey and P.A. McNulty. London: SPCK, 1966.

Caputo, John D. and Michael J. Scanlon, eds. *God, the Gift and Postmodernism.* Bloomington, IN: Indiana University Press, 1999.

Carlson, Thomas A. *Indiscretion: Finitude and the Naming of God.* Chicago, IL: University of Chicago Press, 1999.

Casel, Odo. *The Mystery of Christian Worship.* Translated by Darton, Longman and Todd, Milestones in Catholic Theology, ed. Burkhard Neunheuser. New York: Crossroad, 1962.

Chauvet, Louis-Marie. *The Sacraments: The Word of God at the Mercy of the Body.* Collegeville, MN: Liturgical Press, 2001.

Chauvet, Louis-Marie. *Symbol and Sacrament: A Sacramental Reinterpretation of Christian Existence.* Translated by Patrick Medigan and Madeleine Beaumont. Collegeville, MN: Liturgical Press, 1995.

Cherian, John. "Being Human Becoming Divine: A Sacramentological Re-interpretation of *Theosis* as a Mirco- and Macrocosmic Metamorphosis." Unpublished doctoral dissertation, K.U. Leuven, 2008.

Chupungco, Anscar J., ed. *Liturgical Time and Space.* Handbook for Liturgical Studies, 5. Collegeville, MN: Liturgical Press, 2000.

Clarke, W. Noris. *The Philosophical Approach to God: A Neo-Thomist Perspective,* ed. William E. Ray. Winston-Salem: Wake Forest University, 1979.

Coffey, David. *Deus Trinitas: The Doctrine of the Triune God.* New York: Oxford University Press, 1999.

Colle, Ralph Del. *Christ and the Spirit: Spirit Christology in Trinitarian Perspective.* New York: Oxford University Press, 1994.

Colwell, John E. *Promise and Presence: An Exploration of Sacramental Theology.* Waynesboro, U.K.: Paternoster, 2005.

Congar, Yves. *I Believe in the Holy Spirit.* 3 vols. Translated by David Smith, Milestones in Catholic Theology. New York: Crossroad, 2006.

Congar, Yves. *Tradition and Traditions: A Historical and Theological Essay*. Translated by Thomas Rainsborough. London: Burns and Oates, 1966.

Congar, Yves. *Sainte Église: Études et approches ecclésiologiques*. Unam Sanctam, 41. Paris: Cerf, 1963.

Conley, Verena Andermatt. *Hélène Cixous: Writing the Feminine*. Lincoln, NE: University of Nebraska Press, 1984.

De Lubac, Henri. *Catholicism: A Study of Dogma on Relation to the Corporate Destiny of Mankind*. London: Burns, Oates & Washbourne, 1950.

Derrida, Jacques. *The Gift of Death*. Translated by David Wills. Chicago, IL, London: University of Chicago Press, 1995.

Derrida, Jacques. *Given Time: 1. Counterfeit Money*. Translated by Peggy Kamuf. Chicago, IL: University of Chicago, 1992.

Dix, Gregory. *The Shape of the Liturgy*. New York: Seabury Press, 1982.

Dulles, Avery. *Models of Revelation*. Maryknoll, NY: Orbis Books, 1992.

Dunn, James D.G. *Christology in the Making: A New Testament Inquiry into the Origins of the Doctrine of the Incarnation*. London: SCM Press, 1980.

Dunn, James D.G. *Jesus and the Spirit: A Study of the Religious and Charismatic Experience of Jesus and the First Christians as Reflected in the New Testament*. London: SCM Press, 1975.

Edwards, Denis. *Jesus the Wisdom of God: An Ecological Theology*. Maryknoll, NY: Orbis Books, 1995.

Falque, Emmanuel, ed. *Larvatus pro Deo: Jean-Luc Marion's Phenomenology and Theology*. Edited by Kevin Hart. Notre Dame, IN: University of Notre Dame Press, 2007.

Farrell, Walter. *A Companion to Summa*. Vol. 1. New York: Sheed & Ward, 1945.

Fields, Stephen M. *Being as Symbol: On the Origins and Development of Karl Rahner's Metaphysics*. Washington, DC: Georgetown University Press, 2000.

Fitzmyer, Joseph. *Romans: A New Translation with Introduction and Commentary*. The Anchor Bible, 33. New York: Doubleday, 1993.

Fitzmyer, Joseph. *The Gospel According to Luke I–IX*. The Anchor Bible, 28. Garden City, NY: Doubleday, 1981.

Garland, Peter B. *The Definition of Sacrament According to St. Thomas*. Ottawa: University of Ottawa Press, 1959.

Garrigan, Siobhán. *Beyond Ritual: Sacramental Theology after Habermas*. Hampshire: Ashgate, 2004.

Gauchet, Marcel. *The Disenchantment of the World: A Political History of Religion*. Translated by Oscar Burge. Princeton, NJ: Princeton University Press, 1999.

Godbout, Jacques and Caillé Alain. *The World of the Gift*. Translated by Winkler Donald. Montreal, Quebec: McGill-Queens University Press, 2000.

Groppe, Elizabeth Teresa. *Yves Congar's Theology of the Holy Spirit*. New York: Oxford University Press, 2004.

Gunton, Colin E. *Father, Son & Holy Spirit: Toward a Fully Trinitarian Theology.* London, New York: T & T Clark, 2003.

Gunton, Colin. E. *The Promise of Trinitarian Theology.* Edinburgh: T & T Clark, 1997.

Haenchen, Ernst. *The Acts of the Apostles: A Commentary.* Philadelphia, PA: Westminster Press, 1971.

Haight, Roger. *Jesus Symbol of God.* Maryknoll, NY: Orbis Books, 1999.

Hall, Jerome M. *We Have the Mind of Christ: The Holy Spirit and Liturgical Memory in the Thought of Edward J. Kilmartin.* Collegeville, MN: Liturgical Press, 2001.

Hanson, Richard Patrick Crosland. *The Search for the Christian Doctrine of God: The Arian Controversy 318-381.* Edinburgh: T & T Clark, 1988.

Heidegger, Martin. *Being and Time.* Translated by John Macquarrie and Edward Robinson. Oxford: Blackwell, 2004.

Heidegger, Martin. *Identity and Difference.* Translated by Joan Stambaugh. Chicago, IL: Chicago University Press, 2002.

Heidegger, Martin. *Sein Und Zeit.* Tübingen: Niemeyer, 1986.

Heidegger, Martin. *L' être et le temps.* Paris: Gallimard, 1964.

Hill, William J. *Search for the Absent God: Tradition and Modernity in Religious Understanding,* ed. Mary Catherine Hilkert. New York: Crossroad, 1992.

Hill, William J. *The Three-Personed God.* Washington, DC: Catholic University of America Press, 1988.

Horner, Robyn. *Jean-Luc Marion: A Theological Introduction.* Aldershot, U.K., Burlington, VT: Ashgate, 2005.

Horner, Robyn. *Rethinking God as Gift: Marion, Derrida, and the Limits of Phenomenology.* New York: Fordham University Press, 2001.

Hughes, Graham. *Worship as Meaning: A Liturgical Theology for Late Modernity.* Cambridge, U.K.: Cambridge University Press, 2003.

Husserl, Edmund. *Ideas Pertaining to a Pure Phenomenology and to a Phenomenological Philosophy.* Translated by Fred Kersten. Dordrecht: Kluwer, 1982.

Husserl, Edmund. *The Crisis of European Sciences and Transcendental Phenomenology: An Introduction to Philosophical Phenomenology.* Translated by David Carr. Evanston, IL: Northwestern University Press, 1970.

Husserl, Edmund. *Phenomenology and the Crisis of Philosophy: Philosophy as Rigorous Science and the Crisis of European Man.* Translated by Lauer Quentin. New York: Harper Torch Books, 1965.

Irwin, Kevin W. *Models of the Eucharist.* New York, Mahwah, NJ: Paulist Press, 2005.

Irwin, Kevin W. *Context and Text: Method in Liturgical Theology.* Collegeville, MN: Liturgical Press, 1994.

Janicaud, Dominique, Jean-Francois Courtine, Jean-Louis Chrétien, Jean-Luc Marion, Michael Henry and Paul Ricœur. *Phenomenology and the "Theological*

Turn:" The French Debate. Perspectives in Continental Philosophy, ed. John D. Caputo. New York: Fordham University Press, 2000.

Janicaud, Dominique, Jean-Francois Courtine, Jean-Louis Chrétien, Jean-Luc Marion, Michael Henry and Paul Ricœur, eds. *Le tournant théologique de la phénoménologie française.* Paris: Éditions de l'Éclat, 1991.

Jasper, R.C.D. and G.J. Cuming. *Prayers of the Eucharist: Early and Reformed. Texts Translated and Edited with Commentary.* New York: Pueblo, 1975.

Jenson, Robert W. *The Triune God.* Systematic Theology, 1. New York: Oxford University Press, 1997.

Johnson, Luke Timothy. *The Acts of the Apostles.* Collegeville, MN: Liturgical Press, 1992.

Jones, Paul H. *Christ's Eucharistic Presence: A History of the Doctrine.* New York: Peter Lang, 1994.

Kärkkäinen, Veli-Matti. *Pneumatology. The Holy Spirit in Ecumenical, International and Contextual Perspective.* Grand Rapids, MI: Baker Academic, 2002.

Kärkkäinen, Veli-Matti. *Towards a Pneumatological Theology: Pentecostal and Ecumenical Perspectives on Ecclesiology, Soteriology, and Theology of Mission*, ed. Amos Yong. Lanham, MD: University Press of America, 2002.

Käsemann, Ernst. *Commentary on Romans.* Grand Rapids, MI: Eerdmans, 1980.

Kaniyamparampil, Emmanuel. *The Spirit of Life: A Study of the Holy Spirit in the Early Syriac Tradition.* Kottayam, Kerala: Oriental Institute of Religious Studies India, 2003.

Kant, Immanuel. *Critique of Pure Reason.* London: Macmillian, 1933.

Karotemprel, Sebastian. *The Glorification of Jesus and the Outpouring of the Spirit*, The Promise of Living Water. Bombay: Asian Trading Corporation, 1977.

Kasper, Walter. *The God of Jesus Christ.* Translated by Matthew J. O'Connell. New York: Crossroad, 1986.

Kasper, Walter. *Jesus the Christ.* New York: Paulist Press, 1976.

Kasper, Walter. *Jesus der Christus.* Mainz: Matthias-Grünewald, 1974.

Kavanagh, Aidan. *The Shape of Baptism: The Rite of Christian Initiation.* Collegeville, MN: Liturgical Press, 1991.

Kelley, J.N.D. *Early Christian Creeds.* London: Longman, 1950.

Kilmartin, Edward J. *The Eucharist in the West: History and Theology*, ed. Robert J. Daly. Collegeville, MN: Liturgical Press, 1998.

Kilmartin, Edward J. *Christian Liturgy: Theology and Practice.* Kansas City, MO: Sheed & Ward, 1988.

Kloppenburg, Bonaventure. *The Ecclesiology of Vatican II.* Translated by Matthew J. O'Connell. Chicago, IL: Franciscan Herald Press, 1974.

Kösters, Oliver. *Die Trinitätslehre des Epiphanius von Salamis: Ein Kommentar zum „Ancoratus"*. Forschungen zur Kirchen und Dogmengeschichte, 86. Göttingen: Vandenhoeck & Ruprecht, 2003.

Kretzmann, Norman and Eleonore Stump, eds. *The Cambridge Companion to Aquinas*. Cambridge: Cambridge University Press, 1993.

Küng, Hans. *On Being a Christian*. London: Collins, 1977.

Kuss, Otto. *Der Römerbrief*. Vol. 2. Regensburg: Friedrich Pustet, 1959.

LaCugna, Catherine Mowry. *God For Us: The Trinity and Christian Life*. San Francisco, CA: Harper, 1991.

Lafont, Ghislain. *God, Time, and Being*. Translated by Leonard Maluf. Petersham, MA: Saint Bede, 1992.

Lampe, Geoffrey. *God as Spirit*. Oxford: Clarendon, 1977.

Lash, Nicholas. *Believing Three Ways in One God: A Reading of the Apostle's Creed*. London: SCM Press, 1992.

Lathrop, Gordon W. *Holy People: A Liturgical Ecclesiology*. Minneapolis, MN: Fortress Press, 1999.

Lathrop, Gordon W. *Holy Things: A Liturgical Theology*. Minneapolis, MN: Fortress Press, 1993.

LaVerdiere, Eugene. *The Eucharist in the New Testament and Early Church*. Collegeville, MN: Liturgical Press, 1996.

Leeming, Bernard. *Principles of Sacramental Theology*. London, New York, Toronto: Longmans, Green & Co., 1955.

Leijssen, Lambert J. *With the Silent Glimmer of God's Spirit: A Postmodern Look at the Sacraments*. Translated by Marie Baird. New York, Mahwah, NJ: Paulist Press, 2006.

Lévinas, Emmanuel. *Totality and Infinity*. Duquesne Studies. Philosophical Series, 24. Pittsburgh, PA: Duquesne University Press, 1979.

Lévi-Strauss, Claude. *Introduction to the Work of Marcel Mauss*. Translated by F. Baker. London: Routledge and Kegan Paul, 1987.

Lévi-Strauss, Claude. *The Elementary Structures of Kinship*. Translated by James Harle Bell and John Richard von Sturmer, ed. Rodney Needham. London: Eyre, 1969.

Lies, Lothar. *Sakramententheologie: Eine Personale Sicht*. Graz: Styria, 1990.

Lintner, Martin M. *Eine Ethik des Schenkens: Von einer Anthropologischen zu einer Theologisch-Ethischen Deutung der Gabe und ihrer Aporien*. Studien der Moraltheologie, 35. Wien, Berlin: LIT Verlag, 2006.

Lonergan, Anne and Carolyn Richards. *Thomas Berry and the New Cosmology*. Mystic, CT: Twenty-third Publications, 1991.

Lossky, Vladimir. *The Mystical Theology of the Eastern Church*. London: James Clarke & Co., 1957.

Lotz, Johannes B. *Vom Sein zum Heiligen: Metaphysisches Denken nach Heidegger*. Frankfurt am Main: Joseph Knecht, 1990.

Lotz, Johannes B. *Martin Heidegger und Thomas von Aquin: Mensch-Zeit-Sein*. Pfullingen: Günther Neske, 1975.

Loughlin, Gerard. *Telling God's Story: Bible, Church and Narrative Theology*. Cambridge, New York: Cambridge University Press, 1996.

Lukken, Gerard. *Per Visibilia ad Invisibilia: Anthropological, Theological and Semiotic Studies on the Liturgy and the Sacraments.* Liturgia Condenda, 2, ed. Louis Van Tongeren and Charles Caspers. Kampen: Kok Pharos, 1994.

Lyotard, Jean François. *The Postmodern Explained.* Translated by Don Barry et al. Minneapolis, MN: University of Minnesota Press, 1993.

Malinowski, Bonislaw. *Argonatus of Western Pacific.* New York: E.P. Dutton, 1961.

Martos, Joseph. *Doors to the Sacred: A Historical Introduction to Sacraments in the Catholic Church.* Liguori, MS: Liguori Publications, 2001.

Mauss, Marcel. *The Gift: The Form and Reason for Exchange in Archaic Societies.* Translated by W.D. Halls. London: Routledge, 2002.

Mauss, Marcel and Claude Lévi-Strauss. *Sociologie et anthropologie.* Paris: Presses Universitaires de France, 1950.

Mazza, Enrico. *The Celebration of the Eucharist: The Origin of the Rite and the Development of Its Interpretation.* Collegeville, MN: Liturgical Press, 1999.

Mazza, Enrico. *The Origins of the Eucharistic Prayer.* Translated by Ronald E. Lane. Collegeville, MN: Liturgical Press, 1995.

Mazza, Enrico. *The Eucharistic Prayers of the Roman Rite.* Translated by Mathe J. O'Connel. New York: Pueblo, 1986.

McDonnell, Kilian. *The Other Hand of God: The Holy Spirit as the Universal Touch and Goal.* Collegeville, MN: Liturgical Press, 2003.

McDonnell, Kilian. *The Baptism of Jesus in the Jordan: The Trinitarian and Cosmic Order of Salvation.* Collegeville, MN: Liturgical Press, 1996.

McDonnell, Kilian and George T. Montague. *Christian Initiation and Baptism in the Holy Spirit: Evidence from the First Eight Centuries.* Collegeville, MN: Liturgical Press, 1994.

McKenna, John H. *Eucharist and Holy Spirit: The Eucharistic Epiclesis in Twentieth Century Theology (1900-1966)* Alcuin Club Collections, 57. Great Wakering: Mayhew-McCrimmon, 1975.

McVey, Kathleen. *Ephrem the Syrian.* Mahwah, NJ: Paulist Press, 1989.

Meeks, M. Douglas. *God the Economist: The Doctrine of God and Political Economy.* Minneapolis, MN: Fortress, 1989.

Milbank, John. *Being Reconciled: Ontology and Pardon.* Radical Orthodoxy Series, ed. John Milbank, Catherine Pickstock and Graham Ward. London, New York: Routledge, 2003.

Mitchell, Nathan D. *Meeting Mystery.* New York: Orbis Books, 2006.

Moltmann, Jürgen. *The Spirit of Life: A Universal Affirmation.* Translated by Margaret Kohl. London: SCM Press, 1992.

Moltmann, Jürgen. *The Church in the Power of the Spirit.* London: SCM Press, 1977.

Moltmann, Jürgen. *The Trinity and the Kingdom of God: The Doctrine of God.* Translated by Margaret Kohl. London: SCM Press, 1981.

Montague, George T. *The Holy Spirit: Growth of a Biblical Tradition*. New York, Paramus, Toronto: Paulist Press, 1976.

Mühlen, Heribert. *Una mystica Persona: Die Kirche als das Mysterium der heilsgeschichtlichen Identität des Heiligen Geistes in Christus und den Christen: Eine Person in vielen Personen*. Paderborn: Ferdinand Schöningh, 1967.

Mühlen, Heribert. *Der Heilige Geist als Person: Beitrag zur Frage nach der dem Heiligen Geiste Eigentümlichen Funktion in der Trinität, bei der Inkarnation und im Gnadenbund* Münsterische Beiträge zur Theologie, 26. Münster: Aschendorffsche Verlagsbuchhandlung, 1963.

Osborne, Kenan B. *Christian Sacraments in a Postmodern World: A Theology for the Third Millennium*. New York, Mahwah, NJ: Paulist Press, 1999.

Osborne, Kenan B. *Sacramental Theology: A General Introduction*. New York, Mahwah, NJ: Paulist Press, 1988.

Osborne, Kenan B. *The Christian Sacraments of Initiation: Baptism Confirmation Eucharist*. New York, Mahwah, NJ: Paulist Press, 1987.

Palmer, Paul F. *Sacraments and Worship: Liturgy and Doctrinal Development of Baptism Confirmation and the Eucharist*. Sources of Christian Theology, 1, ed. Paul F. Palmer. Westminster, MD: Newman Press, 1957.

Pannenberg, Wolfhart. *Systematic Theology*. Vol. 2. Grand Rapids, MI: Eerdmans, 1994.

Pickstock, Catherine. *After Writing: On the Liturgical Consummation of Philosophy*. Oxford: Blackwell, 1998.

Power, David N. *Sacrament: The Language of God's Giving*. New York: Crossroad, 1999.

Power, David N. *The Sacrifice We Offer: The Tridentine Dogma and Its Reinterpretation*. New York: Crossroad, 1987.

Power, David N. *Unsearchable Riches: The Symbolic Nature of Liturgy*. New York: Pueblo, 1984.

Powers, Joseph M. *Eucharistic Theology*. London: Burns & Oates, Herder & Herder, 1968.

Reid, Duncan. *Energies of the Spirit: Trinitarian Models in Eastern Orthodox and Western Theology*. Atlanta, GA: Scholars Press, 1997.

Ricœur, Paul. *Freud and Philosophy: An Essay on Interpretation*. Translated by D. Savage. New Haven, CT: Yale University Press, 1970.

Ricœur, Paul. *Time and Narrative*. 3 vols. Chicago, IL: Chicago University Press, 1984-1988.

Rosato, Philip J. *The Spirit as Lord: The Pneumatology of Karl Barth*. Edinburgh: T & T Clark, 1981.

Ruether, Rosemary Radford. *Gaia and God: An Ecofeminist Theology of Earth Healing*. San Francisco, CA: Harper San Francisco, 1992.

Saarinen, Risto. *God and the Gift: An Ecumenical Theology of Giving*. Collegeville, MN: Liturgical Press, 2005.

Sanders, Fred. *The Image of the Immanent Trinity*, Issues in Systematic Theology, ed. Paul D. Molnar. New York: Peter Lang, 2005.

Sawicki, Marianne. *Seeing the Lord*. Minneapolis, MN: Fortress Press, 1994.

Schanz, John P. *Introduction to the Sacraments*. New York: Pueblo, 1983.

Schillebeeckx, Edward. *Jesus: An Experiment in Christology*. London: Collins, 1978.

Schillebeeckx, Edward. *The Eucharist*. Translated by N.D. Smith. London, Sydney: Sheed & Ward, 1968.

Schillebeeckx, Edward. *Christ the Sacrament of the Encounter with God*. Translated by N.D. Smith. London: Sheed & Ward, 1963.

Schneider, Theodor. *Zeichen der Nähe Gottes: Grundriss der Sakramententheologie*. Mainz: Matthias-Grünewald, 1987.

Schrag, Calvin O. *God as Otherwise Than Being: Toward a Semantics of the Gift*, Northwestern University Studies in Phenomenology & Existential Philosophy. Evanston, IL: Northwestern University Press, 2002.

Schrift, Allan D., ed. *The Logic of the Gift: Toward an Ethic of Generosity*. New York, London: Routledge, 1997.

Schrijvers, Joeri. "Ontotheological Turnings? The Decentering of the Modern Subject in Recent French Phenomenology." Unpublished doctoral dissertation, Faculty of Theology, K.U. Leuven, 2006.

Schürmann, Reiner. *Heidegger on Being and Acting: From Principles to Anarchy*. Bloomington, IN: Indiana University Press, 1987.

Seasoltz, R. Kevin. *God's Gift Giving: In Christ and through the Spirit*. New York: Continuum, 2007.

Semmelroth, Otto. *Die Kirche als Ursakrament*. Frankfurt: Josef Knecht, 1955.

Smail, Thomas A. *The Giving Gift: The Holy Spirit in Person*. London: Hodder & Soughton, 1988.

Studer, Basil. *Trinity and Incarnation: The Faith of the Early Church*. Translated by Matthias Westerhoff, ed. Andrew Louth. Edinburgh: T & T Clark, 1993.

Taft, R.F. and G. Winkler. *Invocations to/for the Holy Spirit in Syriac Liturgical Texts*. Comparative Liturgy Fifty Years after Anton Baumstark (1872-1948), Orientalia Christiana Analecta, 265. Rome: Pontificio Instituto Orientale, 2001.

Torrance, Thomas F. *Trinitarian Perspectives: Toward Doctrinal Agreement*. Edinburgh: T & T Clark, 1994.

Torrance, Thomas F. *The Ground and Grammar of Theology*. Charlottesville, VA: University Press of Virginia, 1980.

Tracy, David. *The Analogical Imagination*. New York: Crossroad, 1989.

Vagaggini, Cipriano. *Theological Dimensions of the Liturgy*. Collegeville, MN: Liturgical Press, 1976.

Vagaggini, Cipriano. *The Canon of the Mass and Liturgical Reform*. Translated by Peter Coughlan. Staten Island, NY: Alba House, 1967.

Vischer, Lukas, ed. *Spirit of God, Spirit of Christ: Ecumenical Reflections on the Filioque Controversy*, Faith and Order Paper, 103. London: SPCK, 1981.

Von Balthasar, Hans Urs. *Explorations in Theology*. Translated by Brian McNeil. 4 vols. San Francisco, CA: Ignatius Press, 1993.

Von Balthasar, Hans Urs. *The Glory of the Lord: A Theological Aesthetics*. Translated by Brian McNeil. Vol. 7, ed. John Riches. T & T Clark: Edinburgh, 1989.

Von Balthasar, Hans Urs. *The Glory of the Lord: A Theological Aesthetics*. Translated by Erasmo Leiva-Merikakis. Vol. 1. San Francisco, CA: Ignatius Press, 1982.

Von Balthasar, Hans Urs. *On Prayer*. London: SPCK, 1973.

Vorgrimler, Herbert. *Sacramental Theology*. Translated by Linda M. Maloney. Collegeville, MN: Liturgical Press, 1992.

Webb, Stephen H. *The Gifting God: A Trinitarian Ethic of Excess*. New York: Oxford University Press, 1996.

Weber, Max. *Economy and Society: An Outline of Interpretative Sociology*. Berkeley, CA: University of California Press, 1978.

Westphal, Merold. *Overcoming Onto-theology: Toward a Postmodern Christian Faith*. New York: Fordham University Press, 2001.

Westphal, Merold. *God, Guilt, and Death: An Existential Phenomenology of Religion*. Bloomington, IN: Indiana University Press, 1997.

Williams, Rowan. *On Christian Theology*. Oxford: Blackwell, 2000.

Wolfson, Harry Austryn. *The Philosophy of the Church Fathers*. Cambridge, MA: Harvard University Press, 1964.

Wong, Joseph H. P. *Logos-Symbol in the Christology of Karl Rahner*. Rome: Las, 1984.

Worgul, George S. *From Magic to Metaphor*. New York, Ramsey, NJ: Paulist Press, 1980.

Yong, Amos. *Beyond the Impasse: Toward a Pneumatological Theology of Religions*. Grand Rapids, MI: Baker Academic, 2003.

Yong, Amos. *Discerning the Spirit(s): A Pentecostal-Charismatic Contribution to Christian Theology of Religions*. Sheffield: Sheffield Academic Press, 2000.

Zehnle, Richard F. *Peter's Pentecost Discourse*. Nashville, TN: Abingdon, 1971.

Zizioulas, John D. *Being as Communion: Studies in Personhood and the Church*. London: Darton, Longman & Todd, 1985.

2.2. Articles

Albertine, Richard. "The Post Vatican Consilium's (Coetus X) Treatment of the Epiclesis Question in the Context of Select Historical Data (Alexandrian Family of Anaphoras) and the Fragment of *Der Balyseh*." *Ephemerides Liturgicae* 102 (1988): 385-405.

Albertine, Richard. "Problem of the (Double) Epiclesis in the New Roman Eucharistic Prayers." *Ephemerides Liturgicae* 91 (1977): 193-202.

Albertson, James S. "Instrumental Causality in St. Thomas." *New Scholasticism* 28 (1954): 409-435.

Ambrose, Glenn P. "Chauvet and Pickstock: Two Compatible Visions?" *Questions Liturgiques* 82 (2001): 74-84.

Augé, Matias. "A Theology of the Liturgical Year." *Liturgical Time and Space*, ed. Anscar J. Chupungco, Handbook for Liturgical Studies, 5, 317-330. Collegeville, MN: Liturgical Press, 2000.

Austin, Gerard. "*In Persona Christi* at the Eucharist." *Eucharist Toward the Third Millennium*, ed. Marin F. Connell, 81-86. Chicago, IL: Liturgy Training Publications, 1997.

Badcock, Gary D. "The Anointing of Christ and the Filioque Doctrine." *Irish Theological Quarterly* 60 (1994): 241-258.

Barrett, Charles Kingsley. "The Place of Eschatology in the Fourth Gospel." *The Expository Times* 59 (1947-1948): 302-305.

Berry, Donald L. "*Filioque* and the Church." *Journal of Ecumenical Studies* 5 (1968): 535-554.

Blond, Philip. "The Primacy of Theology and the Question of Perception." *Religion, Modernity, Postmodernity*, ed. Paul Heelas, 285-313. Oxford: Blackwell, 1998.

Boniface, Hieromonk. "The Filioque Question." *Ecumenical Trends* 13 (1984): 68-72.

Boulding, Mary Cecily. "The Doctrine of the Holy Spirit in the Documents of Vatican II." *Irish Theological Quarterly* 51 (1985): 253-267.

Bourke, David. "Introduction." *Summa Theologiae*, 56, xiii-xxiii. New York and London: Blackfriars, McGraw-Hill and Eyre and Spottiswoode, 1975.

Bray, Gerald. "The *Filioque* Clause in History and Theology." *Tyndale Bulletin* 34 (1983): 91-144.

Breck, John. "The Lord is the Spirit." *The Ecumenical Review* 42 (1990): 114-121.

Brinkman, Martien E. "Towards a Common Understanding of the Sacraments." *Louvain Studies* 23 (1998): 38-59.

Brinkman, Martien E. "A Creation Theology for Canberra?" *The Ecumenical Review* 42 (1990): 150-156.

Burrel, David B. "Reflections on 'Negative Theology' in the Light of a Recent Venture to Speak of 'God Without Being'." *Postmodernism and Christian Philosophy*, ed. Roman T. Ciapalo, 58-67. Mishawaka, IN: The American Maritain Association, 1997.

Butler, Sara. "*Quaestio Disputata: In Persona Christi*: A Response to Dennis M. Ferrara." *Theological Studies* 56 (1995): 61-80.

Cahoone, Lawrence. "Introduction." *From Modernism to Postmodernism: An Anthology*, ed. Cahoone Lawrence, 1-13. Malden, MA: Blackwell, 1996.

Callahan, Annice C. "Karl Rahner's Theology of Symbol: Basis for his Theology of the Church and the Sacraments." *Irish Theological Quarterly* 49 (1982): 195-205.

Caputo, John D. "Apostles of the Impossible: On God and the Gift in Derrida and Marion." *God, the Gift and Postmodernism*, ed. John D. Caputo and Michael J. Scanlon, 185-222. Bloomington, IN: Indiana University Press, 1999.

Carlson, Thomas A. "Blindness and the Decision to See: On Revelation and Reception in Jean-Luc Marion." *Counter-Experiences: Reading Jean-Luc Marion*, ed. Kevin Hart, 153-179. Notre Dame, IN: Indiana University Press, 2007.

Carlson, Thomas A. "Postmetaphysical Theology." *The Cambridge Companion to Postmodern Theology*, ed. Kevin J. Vanhoozer, 58-75. Cambridge, U.K.: Cambridge University Press, 2003.

Carmody, John. "The Realism of Christian Life." *A World of Grace: An Introduction to the Themes and Foundations of Karl Rahner's Theology*, ed. Leo J. O'Donovan, 138-152. Washington, DC: Georgetown University Press, 1995.

Carr, Anne D. "Starting with the Human." *A World of Grace: An Introduction to the Themes and Foundations of Karl Rahner's Theology*, ed. Leo J. O'Donovan, 17-30. Washington, DC: Georgetown University Press, 1995.

Chauvet, Louis-Marie. "The Broken Bread as Theological Figure of Eucharistic Presence." *Sacramental Presence in a Postmodern Context*, ed. Lieven Boeve and Leijssen Lambert, 236-262. Leuven: Leuven University Press, 2001.

Cixous, Hélène. "Sorties: Out and Out: Attacks/Ways Out/Forays." *The Logic of the Gift: Toward and Ethic of Generosity*, ed. Alan D. Schrift, 148-173. New York, London: Routledge, 1997.

Clapsis, Emmanuel. "The Filioque Question." *Patristic and Byzantine Review* 1 (1982): 127-136.

Coffey, David. "Spirit Christology and the Trinity." *Advents of the Spirit: An Introduction to the Current Study of Pneumatology*, ed. Bradford E. Hinze and D. Lyle Dabney, 315-338. Milwaukee, WI: Marquette University Press, 2001.

Coffey, David. "Priestly Representation and Women's Ordination." *Priesthood: The Hard Questions*, ed. Gerald P. Gleeson, 77-99. New Town, NSW, Australia: E.J. Dwyer, 1993.

Coffey, David. "The Holy Spirit as the Mutual Love of the Father and the Son." *Theological Studies* 51 (1990): 193-229.

Coffey, David. "The 'Incarnation4 of the Holy Spirit." *Theological Studies* 45 (1984): 466-480.

Colle, Ralph Del. "The Holy Spirit: Presence, Power, Person." *Theological Studies* 62 (2001): 322-340.

Dabney, D. Lyle. "Why Should the Last be First? The Priority of Pneumatology in Recent Theological Discussion." *Advents of the Spirit: An Introduction to the Current Study of Pneumatology*, ed. Bradford E. Hinze and D. Lyle Dabney, 240-261. Milwaukee, WI: Marquette University Press, 2001.

Daly, Robert J. "Sacrifice Unveiled or Sacrifice Revisited: Trinitarian and Liturgical Perspectives." *Theological Studies* 64 (2003): 24-42.

Danneels, Godfried. "Liturgy Forty Years after the Second Vatican Council: High Point or Recession." *The Mystery of Faith: Reflections on the Encyclical Ecclesia de Eucharistia*, ed. James McEvoy and Maurice Hogan, 22-42. Dublin: Columba Press, 2005.

Depoortere, Kristiaan. "From Sacramentality to Sacraments and Vice-Versa." *Questions Liturgiques* 82 (2001): 46-57.

Derrida, Jacques and Jean-Luc Marion. "On the Gift: A Discussion between Jacques Derrida and Jean-Luc Marion, Moderated by Richard Kearney." *God, the Gift, and Postmodernism*, ed. John D. Caputo and Michael J. Scanlon, 54-78. Bloomington, IN: Indiana University Press, 1999.

Dilschneider, Otto. "Geistvergessenheit der Theologie." *Theologische Literaturzeitung* 86 (1961): 255-266.

Dugmore, C.W. "Sacrament and Sacrifice in the Early Fathers." *The Journal of Ecclesiastical History* 2 (1951): 24-37.

Dulles, Avery. "The Symbolic Structure of Revelation." *Theological Studies* 41 (1980): 51-73.

Dunn, James D.G. "Spirit, Holy Spirit." *The New International Dictionary of New Testament Theology*, ed. Colin Brown, 689-709. Exeter, U.K.: Paternoster Press, 1978.

Dunn, James. D.G. "The Birth of a Metaphor – Baptised in the Spirit." *Expository Times* 89 (1978): 135-136.

Dych, William V. "Theology in a New Key." *A World of Grace: An Introduction to the Themes and Foundations of Karl Rahner's Theology*, ed. Leo J. O'Donovan, 1-16. Washington, DC: Georgetown University Press, 1995.

Edwards, Denis. "Ecology and the Holy Spirit: The 'Already' and the 'Not Yet' of the Spirit in Creation." *Pacifica* 13 (2000): 142-159.

Elliott, Brian. "Reduced Phenomenon and Unreserved Debts in Marion's Reading of Heidegger." *Givenness and God: Questions of Jean-Luc Marion*, ed. Ian Leask and Eoin Cassidy, 87-97. New York: Fordham University Press, 2005.

Fahey, Michael A. "On Being Christian-Together." *A World of Grace: An Introduction to the Themes and Foundations of Karl Rahner's Theology*, ed. Leo J. O'Donovan, 1-6. Washington, DC: Georgetown University Press, 1995.

Falque, Emmanuel. "*Larvatus pro Deo*: Jean-Luc Marion's Phenomenology and Theology." *Counter-Experiences: Reading Jean-Luc Marion*, ed. Kevin Hart, 182-199. Notre Dame, IN: University of Notre Dame Press, 2007.

Ferrara, Dennis Michael. "*In Persona Christi*: Towards a Second Naivete." *Theological Studies* 57 (1996): 65-88.

Ferrara, Dennis Michael. "*In Persona Christi*: A Reply to Sara Butler." *Theological Studies* 56 (1995): 81-91.

Ferrara, Dennis Michael. "Representation or Self-Effacement? The Axiom *in Persona Christi* in St. Thomas and the Magisterium." *Theological Studies* 55 (1994): 195-224.

Ferrara, Dennis Michael. "The Ordination of Women: Tradition and Meaning." *Theological Studies* 55 (1994): 706-719.

Fields, Stephen M. "The Metaphysics of Symbol in Thomism: *Aeterni Patris* to Rahner." *International Philosophical Quarterly* 37 (1997): 277-290.

Fields, Stephen M. "Blondel's l'Action (1893) and Neo-Thomism's Metaphysics of Symbol." *Philosophy & Theology* 8 (1993): 25-40.

Fiorenza, Francis Schüssler. "Systematic Theology: Tasks and Methods." *Systematic Theology: Roman Catholic Perspectives*, ed. John P. Galvin, 1-88. Dublin: Gill and Macmillan, 1992.

Fransen, Piet F. "Sacraments as Celebrations." *Irish Theological Quarterly* 43 (1976): 151-170.

Fransen, Piet F. "Sacraments, Signs of Faith." *Worship* 37 (1962): 31-50.

Friedrich, Gerhard. "πνεῦμα." *Theological Dictionary of the New Testament*, 6, 396-451. Grand Rapids, MI: Eerdmans, 1968.

Fuchs, Lorelei F. "Louis-Marie Chauvet's Theology of Sacrament and Ecumenical Theology: Connections in Terms of an Ecumenical Hermeneutics of Unity Based on a Koinonia Ecclesiology." *Questions Liturgiques* 82 (2001): 58-68.

Godzieba, Anthony J. "Ontotheology to Excess: Imagining God Without Being." *Theological Studies* 56 (1995): 3-20.

Grisez, Germain. "An Alternative Theology of Jesus' Substantial Presence in the Eucharist." *Irish Theological Quarterly* 65 (65): 111-131.

Groppe, Elizabeth Teresa. "The Contribution of Yves Congar's Theology of the Holy Spirit." *Theological Studies* 62 (2001): 451-478.

Guillet, Jacques. "The Spirit of God." *Dictionary of Biblical Theology*, ed. Xavier Léon-Dufour, 571-576. London: Cassel Publishers, 1988.

Hankey, Wayne J. "*Theoria Versus Poesis*: Neoplatonism and Trinitarian Difference in Aquinas, John Milbank, Jean-Luc Marion and John Zizioulas." *Modern Theology* 15 (1999): 387-415.

Hart, Trevor. "Person & Prerogative in Perichoretic Perspective: An Ongoing Dispute in Trinitarian Theology Observed." *Irish Theological Quarterly* 58 (1992): 46-57.

Heidegger, Martin. "The End of Philosophy and the Task of Thinking." *On Time and Being*, 55-73. New York: Harper and Row, 1972.

Hemming, Laurence. "Reading Heidegger: Is God Without Being? Jean Luc-Marion's Reading of Martin Heidegger in *God Without Being*." *New Blackfriars* 76 (1995): 343-350.

Henry, Paul. "The *Adversus Arium* of Marius Victorinus, the First Systematic Exposition of the Doctrine of the Trinity." *Journal of Theological Studies* 1 (1950): 42-55.

Hilberath, Bernd Jochen. "Identity Through Self-Transcendence: The Holy Spirit and the Fellowship of Free Persons." *Advents of the Spirit: An Introduction to the Current Study of Pneumatology*, ed. Bradford E. Hinze and D. Lyle Dabney, 264-294. Milwaukee, WI: Marquette University Press, 2001.

Horn, Friedrich Wilhelm. "Holy Spirit." *The Anchor Bible Dictionary.* Vol. 3, ed. David Noel Freedman, 260-280. New York: Doubleday, 1992.

Hurd, Robert. "A More Organic Opening: Ritual Music and the New Gathering Rite." *Worship* 72 (1998): 290-315.

Irwin, Kevin W. "Sacramentality and the Theology of Creation: A Recovered Paradigm for Sacramental Theology." *Louvain Studies* 23 (1998): 159-179.

Irwin, Kevin W. "Origins of the Notion of 'Liturgical Theology'." *Liturgical Theology: A Primer*, Edward Foley, 11-14. Collegeville, MN: Liturgical Press, 1990.

Irwin, Kevin W. "Sacrament." *The New Dictionary of Theology*, ed. Joseph A. Komonchak, Mary Collins and Dermot A. Lane, 910-922. Dublin: Gill and Macmillan, 1987.

Janicaud, Dominique. "The Theological Turn of French Phenomenology." *Phenomenology and the "Theological Turn": The French Debate*, ed. Dominique Janicaud, Jean-Francois Courtine, Jean-Louis Chrétien, Jean-Luc Marion, Michael Henry and Paul Ricœur, 30-103. New York: Fordham University Press, 2000.

Jordan, Mark D. "Theology and Philosophy." *The Cambridge Companion to Aquinas*, ed. Norman Kretzmann and Eleonore Stump, 232-251. Cambridge: Cambridge University Press, 1993.

Kavanagh, Aidan. "Thoughts on the New Eucharistic Prayers." *Worship* 43 (1969): 2-12.

Kelleher, Margaret Mary. "Sacraments and Ecclesial Mediation of Grace." *Louvain Studies* 23 (1998): 180-197.

Kelley, Gerard. "Eucharistic Sacrifice in the Council of Trent." *Irish Theological Quarterly* 51 (1985): 268-288.

Kerr, Fergus. "Aquinas after Marion." *The Heythrop Journal* 76 (1995): 354-364.

Kilmartin, Edward J. "The Catholic Tradition of the Eucharist: Towards the Third Millennium." *Theological Studies* 55 (1994): 405-457.

Kilmartin, Edward J. "The Active Role of Christ and the Holy Spirit in the Sanctification of the Eucharistic Elements." *Theological Studies* 45 (1984): 225-253.

Kilmartin, Edward J. "The Active Role of Christ and the Holy Spirit in the Divine Liturgy." *Diakonia* 17 (1982): 95-108.

Kilmartin, Edward J. "Christ's Presence in the Liturgy." *Bread from Heaven: Essays on the Eucharist*, ed. Paul Bernier, 102-113. New York: Paulist Press, 1977.

Kilmartin, Edward J. "Sacrificium Laudis: Content and Function of Early Eucharistic Prayers." *Theological Studies* 35 (1974): 268-287.

La Caze, Marguerite. "Seeing Oneself through the Eyes of the Other: Asymmetrical Reciprocity and Self-respect." *Hyptia: A Journal of Feminist Philosophy* 23 (2008): 118-135.

Lamberts, Jozef. "May Your Spirit, Lord, Come...," *Ephrem's Theological Journal* 2 (1998): 99-115.

Lamberts, Jozef. "Eucharist and the Holy Spirit." *Theology Digest* 34 (1987): 51-55.

Leask, Ian. "The Dative Subject (and the "Principle of Principles")." *Givenness and God: Questions of Jean-Luc Marion*, ed. Ian Leask and Eoin Cassidy, 182-189. New York: Fordham University Press, 2005.

Leijssen, Lambert J. "Grace as God's Self-communication: The Starting Point and Development in Rahner's Thought." *Louvain Studies* 20 (1995): 73-78.

Leijssen, Lambert J. "Rahner's Contribution to the Renewal of Sacramentology." *Philosophy & Theology* 9 (1995): 201-222.

Leithart, Peter J. "'Framing' Sacramental Theology: Trinity and Symbol." *Westminster Theological Journal* 62 (2000): 1-16.

Leo XIII. *"Divinum illud munus." Acta Apostolica Sedis* 29 (1896/1897): 644-658.

Levesque, Paul J. "A Symbolic Sacramental Methodology: An Application of the Thought of Louis Dupré." *Questions Liturgiques* 76 (1995): 161-181.

Lock, Charles. "Against Being: An Introduction to the Thought of Jean-Luc Marion." *St. Vladimir's Theological Quarterly* 37 (1993): 370-380.

Loughlin, Gerard. "Transubstantiation: Eucharist as Pure Gift." *Christ: The Sacramental World*, ed. David Brown and Ann Loades, 123-141. London: SPCK, 1996.

Lukacs, Laszlo. "Communication – Symbols – Sacraments." *Questions Liturgiques/Studies in Liturgy* 81 (2000): 198-214.

Lynch, Patrick J. "Servant Ecclesiologies: A Challenge to Rahner's Understanding of Church and World." *Irish Theological Quarterly* 57 (1991): 277-298.

Mackinlay, Shane. "Eyes Wide Shut: A Response to Jean-Luc Marion's Account of the Journey to Emmaus." *Modern Theology* 20 (2004): 447-456.

Maldonado, Louis and David Power. "Symbol and Art in Worship." *Concilium* (1980): 112-119.

Martis, John. "Postmodernism and God as Giver." *The Way* 36 (1996): 236-244.

Martis, John. "Thomistic *Esse* – Idol or Icon? Jean-Luc Marion's God Without Being." *Pacifica* 9 (1996): 55-67.

Martos, Joseph. "The Copernican Revolution in Sacramental Theology." *The Church in the Nineties: Its Legacy, Its Future*, ed. Pierre M. Hegy, 104-116. Collegeville, MN: Liturgical Press, 1993.

Martos, Joseph. "Sacraments and the Human Sciences." *The Dictionary of Sacramental Worship*, ed. Peter E. Fink, 576-586. Dublin: Gill and Macmillan, 1990.

McDonnell, Kilian. "A Response to D. Lyle Dabney." *Advents of the Spirit: An Introduction to the Current Study of Pneumatology*, ed. Bradford E. Hinze and D. Lyle Dabney, 262-264. Milwaukee, WI: Marquette University Press, 2001.

McDonnel, Kilian. "A Trinitarian Theology of the Holy Spirit?" *Theological Studies* 46 (1985): 191-227.

McDonnel, Kilian. "The Determinative Doctrine of the Holy Spirit." *Theology Today* 39 (1982): 142-264.

McDougall, Dorothy. "Towards a Sacramental Theology for an Ecological Age." *Toronto Journal of Theology* 19 (2003): 41-51.

McDougall, Dorothy. "The Cosmos as Primary Sacrament: An Ecological Perspective for Sacramental Theology." *Questions Liturgiques* 81 (2000): 293-301.

McGoldrick, Patrick. "The Holy Spirit and the Eucharist." *Irish Theological Quarterly* 50 (1983/84): 48-66.

McIntyre, John. "The Holy Spirit in Greek Patristic Thought." *Scottish Journal of Theology* 7 (1954): 353-375.

McKenna, John H. "Eucharistic Epiclesis: Myopia or Microcosm." *Theological Studies* 36 (1975): 265-284.

McNeil, Brian. "The Spirit and the Church in Syriac Theology." *Irish Theological Quarterly* 49 (1982): 91-97.

Meynell, Hugo. "Two Directions of Pneumatology." *Irish Theological Quarterly* (1982): 172-183.

Milbank, John. "The Soul of Reciprocity Part One: Reciprocity Refused." *Modern Theology* 17 (2001): 335-391.

Milbank, John. "The Soul of Reciprocity Part Two: Reciprocity Granted." *Modern Theology* 17 (2001): 485-507.

Milbank, John. "Can a Gift be Given? Prolegomena to a Future Trinitarian Metaphysics." *Modern Theology* 11 (1995): 119-122.

Militello, Cettina. "A Theology of Liturgical Space." *Liturgical Time and Space*, ed. Anscar J. Chupungco, Handbook for Liturgical Studies, 5, 397-415. Collegeville, MN: Liturgical Press, 2000.

Miller, Mark. "The Sacramental Theology of Hans Urs von Balthasar." *Worship* 64 (1990): 48-66.

Miller, Vincent J. "An Abyss at the Heart of Mediation: Louis-Marie Chauvet's Fundamental Theology of Sacramentality." *Horizons* 24 (1997): 230-247.

Mitchell, Nathan D. "Liturgy's Language of Presence: Light from the Bible." *Worship* 80 (2006): 162-176.

Mitchell, Nathan D. "Christ's Presence in the Assembly." *Worship* 80 (2006): 252-265.

Mitchell, Nathan D. "But Only Say the Word." *Worship* 80 (2006): 453-466.

Mitchell, Nathan D. "Real Presence." *Worship* 80 (2006): 551-556.

Mitchell, Nathan D. "Mystery and Manners: Eucharist in Post-Modern Theology." *Worship* 79 (2005): 130-151.

Mitchell, Nathan D. "Symbols are Actions, Not Objects." *Living Worship* 13 (1977): 1.

Molnar, Paul D. "*Deus Trinitas*: Some Dogmatic Implications of David Coffey's Biblical Approach to the Trinity." *Irish Theological Quarterly* 67 (2002): 33-54.

Molnar, Paul D. "God's Self-communication in Christ: A Comparison of Thomas F. Torrance and Karl Rahner." *Scottish Journal of Theology* 50 (1997): 288-320.

Moltmann, Jürgen. "Heiliger Geist in der Geschichte." *Orientierung* 47 (1983): 128-145.

Montague, George T. "The Fire in the Word: The Holy Spirit in Scripture." *Advents of the Spirit: An Introduction to the Current Study of Pneumatology*, ed. Bradford E. Hinze and D. Lyle Dabney, 35-65. Milwaukee, WI: Marquette University Press, 2001.

Moorhead, John. "The Spirit and the World." *The Greek Orthodox Theological Review* 26 (1981): 113-117.

Moss, David. "Costly Giving: On Jean-Luc Marion's Theology of the Gift." *New Blackfriars* 74 (1993): 392-399.

Motzko, Maria Elizabeth. "Karl Rahner's Theology: A Theology of the Symbol." Unpublished doctoral dissertation, Department of Theology, Fordham University, New York, 1976.

Mühlen, Heribert. "Das Christusereignins als Tat des Heiligen Geistes." *Mysterium Salutis: Grundriss Heilsgeschichtlicher Dogmatik*, 3/2, 513-545. Einsiedeln: Benziger, 1969.

Murchadha, Felix O. "Glory, Idolatry, Kairos: Revelation and the Ontological Difference in Marion." *Givenness and God: Questions of Jean-Luc Marion*, ed. Ian Leask and Eoin Cassidy, 69-86. New York: Fordham University Press, 2005.

Nissiotis, Nikos. "Pneumatological Christology as a Presupposition for Ecclesiology." *Oecumenica: Jahrbuch für ökumenische Forschung* (1967): 235-252.

O'Connor, Terrence R. "Homoousios and Filioque: An Ecumenical Analogy." *Downside Review* 83 (1965): 1-19.

O'Donohue, John. "The Absent Threshold: An Eckhartian Afterword." *Givenness and God: Questions of Jean-Luc Marion*, ed. Ian Leask and Eoin Cassidy, 258-283. New York: Fordham University Press, 2005.

O'Leary, Joseph S. "The Gift: A Trojan Horse in the Citadel of Phenomenology?" *Givenness and God: Questions of Jean-Luc Marion*, ed. Ian Leask and Eoin Cassidy, 135-166. New York: Fordham University Press, 2005.

O'Meara, Thomas F. "A History of Grace." *A World of Grace: An Introduction to the Themes and Foundations of Karl Rahner's Theology*, ed. Leo J. O'Donovan, 76-91. Washington, DC: Georgetown University Press, 1995.

Outler, Albert. "Veni, Creator Spiritus: The Doctrine of the Holy Spirit." *New Theology* 4 (1967): 195-196.

Pilario, Daniel Franklin. "'Gift-Exchange' in Sacramentology: A Critical Assessment from the Perspective of Pierre Bourdieu." *Contemporary Sacramental Contours of a God Incarnate*, ed. Lieven Boeve and Lambert Leijssen, 85-101. Leuven: Peeters, 2001.

Power, David N. "Sacrament: An Economy of Gift." *Louvain Studies* 23 (1998): 143-158.

Power, David N. "A Prophetic Eucharist in a Prophetic Church." *Eucharist Toward the Third Millennium*, ed. Marin F. Connell, 27-50. Chicago, IL: Liturgy Training Publications, 1997.

Power, David N. "Representing Christ in Community and Sacrament." *Being a Priest Today*, ed. Donald J. Georgen, 97-123. Collegeville, MN: Liturgical Press, 1992.

Power, David N., Regis A. Duffy and Kevin W. Irwin. "Sacramental Theology: A Review of Literature." *Theological Studies* 55 (1994): 657-705.

Ratzinger, Joseph Cardinal. "Eucharist and Mission." *Irish Theological Quarterly* 65 (2000): 245-264.

Ricœur, Paul. "Time and Narrative." *Critical Inquiry* (1980): 169-190.

Robinette, Brian. "A Gift to Theology? Jean-Luc Marion's 'Saturated Phenomenon' in Christological Perspective." *The Heythrop Journal* 48 (2007): 86-108.

Roll, Susan. "Language and Justice in the Liturgy." *A Tribute to Silveer De Smet*, ed. Lambert Leijssen, 12, 66-81. Leuven: Abdij Keizersberg/Faculteit der Godgeleerdheid, 1992.

Rosemann, Philipp Wolfram. "Postmodern Philosophy and J.-L. Marion's Eucharistic Realism." *The Mystery of Faith: Reflections on the Encyclical Ecclesia de Eucharistia*, ed. James McEvoy and Maurice Hogan, 224-244. Dublin: Columba Press, 2005.

Runyon, Theodore. "The World as the Original Sacrament." *Worship* 54 (1980): 495-511.

Schwarz, Hans. "Reflections on the Work of the Spirit outside the Church." *Neue Zeitschrift für Systematische Theologie und Religionsphilosophie* 23 (1981): 197-211.

Silos, L. "A Note on the Notion of 'Selbstvollzug' in Karl Rahner." *Philippine Studies* 13 (1965): 461-470.

Skira, Jaroslav Z. "The Ecological Bishop: John Zizioulas' Theology of Creation." *Toronto Journal of Theology* 19 (2003): 199-213.

Smail, Thomas. "The Holy Spirit in the Holy Trinity." *Nicene Christianity: The Future for a New Ecumenism*, ed. Christopher R. Seitz, 149-165. Grand Rapids, MI: Brazos Press, 2001.

Smit, Peter-Ben. "The Bishop and His/Her Eucharistic Community: A Critique of Jean-Luc Marion's Eucharistic Hermeneutic." *Modern Theology* 19 (2003): 29-40.

Sneller, Rico. "Incarnation as a Prerequisite: Marion and Derrida." *Bijdragen: International Journal in Philosophy and Theology* 65 (2004): 38-54.

Tanner, Kathryn. "Theology at the Limits of Phenomenology." *Counter-Experiences: Reading Jean-Luc Marion*, ed. Kevin Hart, 201-231. Notre Dame, IN: University of Notre Dame Press, 2007.

Tillard, Jean-Marie. "Blessing, Sacramentality and Epiclesis." *Blessing and Power*, ed. David Power and Mary Collins, Concilium, 178, 96-110. Edinburgh: T & T Clark Ltd., 1985.

Tillich, Paul. "The Meaning and Justification of Religious Symbols." *Religious Experience and Truth: A Symposium*, ed. Sydney Hook, 301-321. New York: New York University Press, 1961.

Tillich, Paul. "Die Idee der Offenbarung." *Zeitschrift für Theologie und Kirche* 8 (1927): 403-412.

Valenziano, Crispino. "Liturgical Architecture." *Liturgical Time and Space*, ed. Anscar J. Chupungco, Handbook for Liturgical Studies, 5, 381-396. Collegeville, MN: Liturgical Press, 2000.

Van den Bossche, Stijn. "From the Other's Point of View: The Challenge of Jean-Luc Marion's Phenomenology to Theology." *Religious Experience and Contemporary Theological Epistemology*, ed. L. Boeve, Y. de Maeseneer and S. Van den Bossche, 61-82. Leuven: Leuven University Press, 2005.

Van den Bossche, Stijn. "A Possible Present for Theology: Theological Implications of Jean-Luc Marion's Phenomenology of Givenness." *Bijdragen: International Journal in Philosophy and Theology* 65 (2003): 55-78.

Van den Bossche, Stijn. "God Does Appear in Immanence Afterall: Jean-Luc Marion's Phenomenology as a New First Philosophy for Theology." *Sacramental Presence in a Postmodern Context*, ed. Lieven Boeve and Leijssen Lambert, 325-346. Leuven: Leuven University Press, 2001.

Van Eijk, A.H.C. "Ethics and the Eucharist." *Bijdragen: Tijdschrift voor filosofie en theologie* 55 (1994): 350-375.

Vincie, Catherine. "The Liturgical Assembly: Review and Assessment." *Worship* 67 (1993): 123-144.

Vischer, Lukas. "The Epiclesis: Sign of Unity and Renewal." *Studia Liturgica* 6 (1969): 30-39.

Voulgaris, Christos S. "The Holy Trinity in Creation and Incarnation." *The Greek Orthodox Theological Review* 42 (1997): 245-258.

Ward, Graham. "The Theological Project of Jean-Luc Marion." *Post-Secular Philosophy*, ed. Philip Blond, 229-239. New York: Routledge, 1998.

Ward, Graham. "Introduction." *The Postmodern God*, ed. Graham Ward, xi-xlvii. Oxford: Blackwell, 1997.

Ward, Graham. "Introducing Jean-Luc Marion." *New Black Friars* 76 (1995): 317-324.

Weber, Max. "Religious Rejections of the World and their Directions." *From Max Weber: Essays in Sociology*, ed. H.H. Gerth and C.W. Mills, 323-359. London: Routledge and Kegan Paul, 1974.

Welten, Ruud. "Saturation and Disappointment: Marion according to Husserl." *Bijdragen: International Journal in Philosophy and Theology* 65 (2004): 79-96.

Westphal, Merold. "Vision and Voice: Phenomenology and Theology in the Work of Jean-Luc Marion." *International Journal of Philosophy of Religion* 60 (2006): 117-137.

Worgul, George S. "Sacraments: Iconic Interruptions of the Loving God." *Gods sacramentele aanwezigheid in de wereld van vandaag. Hulde aan professor dr. Lambert Leijssen bij zijn emeritaat*, ed. Thomas Knieps-Port le Roi and Lieven Boeve, 157-167. Leuven,Voorburg: Acco, 2008.

Young, Iris Marion. "Asymmetrical Reciprocity: On Moral Respect, Wonder, and Enlarged Thought." *Constellations: An International Journal of Critical Democratic Theory* 3 (1997): 340-363.

2.3. Electronic Sources

Emerson, Ralph Waldo. *Essays: XIII. Gifts*. 1844. Available from http://www.bartleby.com/5/113.html (accessed August 16, 2008).

Hölderlin, Friedrich. *Patmos*. Gemeinfreie Gedichte, Available from http://hor.de/gedichte/friedrich_hoelderlin/patmos.htm (aaccessed September 2, 2008).

Johann Christian Friedrich Hölderlin. 2003. Available from http://www.kirjasto.sci.fi/holderli.htm. (accessed April 12, 2008).

The Oxford English Dictionary [CD-ROM]. version 3.0., 2 ed. New York: Oxford University Press, 2002.

PRINTED ON PERMANENT PAPER • IMPRIME SUR PAPIER PERMANENT • GEDRUKT OP DUURZAAM PAPIER - ISO 9706

N.V. PEETERS S.A., WAROTSTRAAT 50, B-3020 HERENT